A Century of Women's Basketball

From Frailty to Final Four

Joan S. Hult
Marianna Trekell
Editors

National Association for Girls and Women in Sport
An association of the
American Alliance for Health, Physical Education,
Recreation and Dance

ISBN 0-88314-490-5

Purposes of the American Alliance for Health, Physical Education, Recreation and Dance

The American Alliance is an educational organization, structured for the purposes of supporting, encouraging, and providing assistance to member groups and their personnel throughout the nation as they seek to initiate, develop, and conduct programs in health, leisure, and movement-related activities for the enrichment of human life.

Alliance objectives include:

1. Professional growth and development—to support, encourage, and provide guidance in the development and conduct of programs in health, leisure, and movement-related activities which are based on the needs, interests, and inherent capacities of the individual in today's society.

2. Communication—to facilitate public and professional understanding and appreciation of the importance and value of health, leisure, and movement-related activities as they contribute toward human well-being.

3. Research—to encourage and facilitate research which will enrich the depth and scope of health, leisure, and movement-related activities, and to disseminate the findings to the profession and other interested and concerned publics.

4. Standards and guidelines—to further the continuous development and evaluation of standards within the profession for personnel and programs in health, leisure, and movement-related activities.

5. Public affairs—to coordinate and administer a planned program of professional, public, and governmental relations that will improve education in areas of health, leisure, and movement-related activities.

6. To conduct such other activities as shall be approved by the Board of Governors and the Alliance Assembly, provided that the Alliance shall not engage in any activity which would be inconsistent with the status of an educational and charitable organization as defined in Section 501 (c)(3) of the Internal Revenue Code of 1954 or any successor provision thereto, and none of the said purposes shall at any time be deemed or construed to be purposes other than the public benefit purposes and objectives consistent with such educational and charitable status.

Bylaws, Article III

iii

National Association for Girls & Women in Sport

For nearly a century, NAGWS has been committed to the professional development of women in sports, the advancement of female sports knowledge, and the development of sport programs and increased leadership roles for women in sport. The seeds of NAGWS were sowed in 1899 when a committee was assembled to study basketball rules for girls. In the early years, NAGWS concentrated on the development of appropriate rules for girls' and women's sports. The focus later changed to the introduction of games specifically geared to women as well as the development and promotion of standards different from those associated with men's sports. Throughout its development, NAGWS has continued to influence programs and organizations that sponsor and/or promote healthy female sport participation.

NAGWS today ...

- is a nonprofit educational association located in Reston, Virginia.
- serves a membership of over 10,000 administrators, teachers, coaches, officials, and sport leaders throughout the United States.
- is the only national professional organization devoted exclusively to providing opportunities for girls and women in sport-related careers.
- is one of six associations within the American Alliance for Health, Physical Education, Recreation, and Dance (AAHPERD), an organization with over 33,000 educators and professional members.

NAGWS has grown from a small group of women interested in basketball to a stronghold of 10,000 men and women interested in addressing current concerns and taking action on several different levels and projects.

NAGWS's current focus is on increasing the number of qualified women in coaching and sport administrative positions in educational institutions and Olympic programs, from the developmental to the elite levels.

Contents

The Changing Woman Basketball Player

Top left: players in the first decade of women's basketball; center, Helen Manley, 1918, basketball coach at Kirksville (Mo.) High School, and later a president of the American Association for Health, Physical Education, and Recreation; right, Gypsy Butcher, one of the Dallas, Texas, Cyclones, champions in the early 1930s; bottom, Cheryl Miller, University of Southern California, an NCAA star player of the 1980s.

Foreword

DARLENE A. KLUKA
NAGWS President, 1990–91

During the decade of the 1990s, the National Association for Girls and Women in Sport (NAGWS) and the sport of women's basketball will celebrate their one hundredth anniversaries. The histories of NAGWS and of the sport of basketball for girls and women are intertwined. Rules and rule guides were first prepared in 1899 and published in 1901 by those professionals committed to basketball for girls and women.

In addition to establishing women's basketball rules, NAGWS and its antecedents discussed issues that concerned those who taught and coached females through basketball. These issues were also published annually in the *Guides* and other association publications.

NAGWS is dedicated to the promotion of research relative to women in sport and sport leadership, and this book will serve as an important resource and stimulus for future research. It recognizes the contributions of the association in the development of basketball for girls and women in the United States in the last 100 years.

NAGWS is proud to sponsor this publication celebrating the centennial year of women's basketball and will continue into the next century to be committed to advocacy and enhancement of participation for girls and women in all sport.

JODY CONRADT
Head Coach, Women's Basketball, University of Texas
1991 NAGWS Guiding Woman in Sport Award Recipient

In the past two decades the growth of women's sports—and women's basketball in particular—has been unprecedented. For years, women athletes were seldom taken seriously, a fact that reflected our society's perception of women in general. Fortunately, pioneer sportswomen endured and persevered, so that today millions of aspiring talents have the opportunity to excel. This book tells the story—much of it unknown to us all—of the many girls and women devoted to teaching and playing the game of basketball from the year of its invention until the present day.

Women's basketball has become the model for women's athletics in this country. Since the implementation of Title IX in 1972, the number of women and girls participating in sports has increased dramatically and a great proportion of these athletes participate in basketball. Perhaps more importantly, basketball has moved to the forefront of sports media coverage and has created an intense interest that has swept the entire nation. Without question, basketball has set the stage for ever greater success in other sports.

Women's basketball experienced tremendous public support in the 1980s and is now one of the most visible sports in the country. The first live broadcast of a regular season women's basketball game was a definite turning point for women in all sports. The recent publicity afforded women's basketball shows that society acknowledges and appreciates the excellence demonstrated by girls and women in sport. The most critical element in this success, however, is the female athlete's new self-acceptance as a valuable member of our society.

As we reflect on the past 100 years of women in sport, we must remember that the progress we have made is the direct result of tireless effort and commitment from women and girls of diverse ethnic, socio-economic, and cultural backgrounds. This book, for the first time, gives a glimpse of their devotion over a century of play.

During 1991, we therefore not only celebrate NAGWS's contribution to the growth of women's basketball over the past 100 years. We also salute the women and girls all over America—past, present, and future—who exemplify power, pride, and dignity through their participation in sports.

Preface

This book celebrates the hundred-year heritage of girls and women's basketball. It honors the sport of basketball and the foremothers and prime movers who served on the Women's Basketball Committees and as officers and members of the National Association for Girls and Women in Sport (NAGWS) and its antecedents, as well as the many participants in recreational and competitive basketball. *A Century of Women's Basketball: From Frailty to Final Four* was sponsored by the American Alliance for Health, Physical Education, Recreation and Dance (AAHPERD) Archives and the NAGWS.

Since all women's basketball really began in the educational domain, the writings herein focus on the role of physical educators in the growth and development of the sport and the evolution of competitive basketball. The sport is and has been since its early years the most popular competitive and recreational sport for women.

Throughout its history, the NAGWS and its antecedents sought to govern girls and women's athletics. The organization assumed responsibility for the original women's rules and modifications, officiating, and control of basketball. A significant number of essays herein are devoted to the role of women leaders and the story of NAGWS/AIAW (Association for Intercollegiate Athletics for Women, founded in 1971). The Introductions to Part I and Part II describe the social and cultural context and illuminate the writings found in this volume; these chapters enable the reader to unravel the baffling rule modifications, philosophical tenets, and governance structures in women's athletics. Two essays examine the cultural and medical influences on basketball and the remaining chapters give an account of the sport, providing glimpses of early competition and modern coaches' personal experiences. *A Century of Women's Basketball* dramatically documents the evolution of the women's game.

This work provides undergraduate and graduate students in physical education, sport history, and women's history with an evidential base for understanding the unique world of women's basketball, sports, and athletics. With one exception, the collection consists of original manuscripts written especially for this volume, and thus it provides new rich primary sources. Enthusiasts of the game (both of the three-court and two-court variety) will find enjoyable reading, especially among the personal reflections and descriptions of early competition. Further, the book will be of special interest to college and secondary school women physical educators and basketball players and coaches who are part of the story.

The women's basketball *Guides* contain the rules of the sport, and served as major primary sources for the articles on rule modifications and officiating. The *Guides* also supplemented the research data for a majority of the other articles. The *Guides* were published as part of the Spalding Library by the American Sports Publishing Co. from 1901 to 1938; by A.S. Barnes and Company from 1938 to 1949; and by AAHPERD from 1949 until the last publication in 1985. The AAHPERD Archives houses the only complete collection of these publications so vital to an understanding of the rules and rationale for changes, officiating techniques, medical viewpoints, cultural and social attitudes, and the changes in teaching and coaching strategies. Early articles in the *Guides* reflect the concern for proper basketball behavior and issues of the appropriateness of competition. Officiating became progressively more important as reflected in the later *Guides*, which concentrate on rule clarifications, officiating strategies, and techniques and advanced skills.

Between 1901 and 1920, the *Guides* published photographs of high school, college, and some industrial league basketball teams. Unfortunately, they lack detailed information about games, the teams, or the athletes, but some photos are reproduced here to provide a flavor of the changing times.

Acknowledgements

We are grateful to the AAHPERD Archives for supplying the authors with necessary research materials for the project and making available their exceptionally fine women's collection, especially the NAGWS papers and the *Guides*.

We are indebted both to AAHPERD and to NAGWS for sponsoring this centennial book and bearing the costs of extensive research and photocopying of materials. We especially appreciate the efforts of Mike Everman, past archivist, Nancy Dosch, and the NAGWS Board of Governors for planting the seed and helping to design this project. Dosch, administrative assistant in the AAHPERD Archives and the project coordinator, spent untold hours collecting the research materials essential for the authors, preparing the photographs, writing the contributors' biographies and assisting in the details of the publishing tasks.

We would like to express our heartfelt thanks to each of the authors who contributed to the collection. Our special appreciation goes to Carol

Jackson, special technical editor, for preparing most of the manuscripts, notably the Hult essays. We are also grateful for the willingness of Rosalie Gershon to donate her talents to the final chapter and for her assistance with several other manuscripts. We deem ourselves extraordinarily fortunate to have worked with Nancy Rosenberg, the AAH-PERD book editor, whose commitment to the success of the publication and careful attention to detail have made this book a reality. Our sincere thanks to Carla Cash for secretarial support and to the Department of Kinesiology at the University of Maryland for its backing of the project. Thanks also to Patti Greenwood, librarian of the College of Applied Life Studies, University of Illinois, for her assistance.

Much appreciated also was the work of the Maryland Room's Special Collections staff at the University of Maryland for their untiring efforts to provide access to the AIAW Collection materials that have only received preliminary inventory. We also wish to acknowledge the Special Collections, College Park Libraries, for permission to quote from those materials.

Finally, we would like to thank our friends and families who have been so understanding and who gave constant encouragement, especially during the final difficult months of the project. We both have fond memories of our friends, colleagues, and mentors in our years of work in DGWS/NAGWS/AIAW and wish this commemorative collection to serve as a special tribute to all of them.

JOAN S. HULT
MARIANNA TREKELL

Contributors

Joan S. Hult is associate professor of kinesiology at the University of Maryland, College Park. She played for the YWCA Daughters of Bethlehem and several industrial leagues and coached for 25 years in five sports. She was a national official, on the Executive Board of NAGWS, and chair of the AIAW Ethics and Eligibility Committee. She received the Educationalist Award from the United States Olympic Academy. She is an Honor Fellow of the National Association for Girls and Women in Sport, a Hoover Scholar, and first woman inductee of the Concordia College Athletic Hall of Fame. She has written extensively on women Olympians, sport governance, and women's athletics.

Marianna Trekell is associate professor of kinesiology at the University of Illinois-Urbana. She has received the AAHPERD Honor Award. She played varsity basketball in high school and at the University of Northern Iowa. She coached at Ohio State, was a national official for 20 years, and served as the NAGWS secretary. Her writings focus on education and the history of physical education and sport.

Roxanne M. Albertson is associate professor of kinesiology at the University of North Texas, Denton. She played basketball at Ursinus College. She coached field hockey, basketball, and tennis and officiated basketball, field hockey, and softball. She continues to write about Southern women in sport.

Mildred Barnes is professor at Central Missouri State University, Warrensburg. A player at the national level in lacrosse and field hockey as well as basketball, she coached the University of Iowa to the Final Four and the U.S. team in Jones Cup competition. She chaired the U.S. Women's Olympic Basketball Committee and acted as manager for the U.S. Women's Basketball Team at the Pan American Games. Author of *Women's Basketball*, she has written extensively on basketball and other sports for women. She served as trustee of the Basketball Hall of fame and as president of NAGWS. She is a member of the Boston University Hall of Fame and an NAGWS Honor Fellow.

Janice A. Beran is professor of physical education at Iowa State University, Ames. She also taught at Stillman University in the Philippines. Her writing, covering international sport and physical education, focuses on Iowa women's sport with a special interest in basketball. Through her inspiration and hard work, a team from Iowa State is demonstrating games in period uniforms using the early women's basketball rules.

Steveda Chepko is assistant professor and associate chair of physical education at Salisbury State University, Maryland. She played basketball at West Virginia University, coached at Castleton State College, Vermont, and was a national official. Her writing concentrates on women, sport, and culture.

Joanna Davenport is associate professor at Auburn University, Alabama, where she served as women's athletic director from 1976 until 1985. A former collegiate basketball and tennis player at Skidmore College, New York, she coached at the high school and college level. Davenport was a nationally rated official who served as chair for the DGWS sports guides. She was president of NAGWS and is an Honor Fellow. Her writing is on sportswomen and on the Olympic movement.

Nancy Cole Dosch is assistant archivist at AAHPERD and coordinator for the Women's Basketball Centennial Project. She played at the University of Maryland and coached at Mary Washington College, Fredericksburg, Virginia, and at Trinity College, Washington, D.C. She is currently finishing work on her doctoral dissertation at the University of Maryland.

Lynne Fauley Emery is professor of physical education, California State Polytechnic University, Pomona. She has written a book about black dance in the United States. Her more recent work focuses on the sporting experience of women and blacks in California and the West.

Rosalie M. Gershon owns Oral History and Memoirs, a desktop publishing company, and is a freelance writer. She played high school basketball intramurals in California. She is also a former administrative assistant for the AIAW Committee on Ethics and Eligibility.

Brad Hedrick is assistant professor of rehabilitation and supervisor of recreation and athletics at the University of Illinois-Urbana. He is the head coach of the University of Illinois men's and women's wheelchair basketball teams. In 1981 he was a member of the U.S. World Champion wheelchair basketball team and in 1988 he coached the U.S. Women's Wheelchair Basketball Team to the Paralympic World Championship in Seoul, Korea.

Sharon Rahn Hedrick was a four-year letter winner on the University of Illinois women's wheelchair basketball team and won a gold medal as a member of the 1988 U.S. Paralympic World Champion women's wheelchair basketball team. In 1977 she was the first wheelchair woman to compete in the Boston Marathon.

Phyllis Holmes is a professor at Greenville College, Illinois. She played basketball at Greenville College and has over 20 years of coaching and officiating experience. As an administrative assistant for the U.S. team, she has toured all over the world. She served as chair of the NAIA Women's Basketball Committee. In 1989 she was recipient of the First Lady Award for contributions to basketball by the Iowa Girls High School Athletic Union. She was elected to the NAIA Hall of Fame as a coach in 1987, and in 1988 she became the first woman president of NAIA.

Jill Hutchison is head women's basketball coach in her twentieth year at Illinois State University, Normal. She led her team to eight AIAW regional play-offs. Her record ranks twelfth in career wins among active NCAA Division I women's coaches. She has coached for ABAUSA, the Junior Pan American team on a tour of Central and South America, and guided the World University Games team to a gold medal in Edmonton, Alberta. She served as editor of the NAGWS basketball guides, on the basketball committee of AIAW, and two terms as president of the Women's Basketball Coaches Association. She writes extensively on coaching women's basketball; her most recent book is *Coaching Girls' Basketball Successfully*.

Betty Jaynes is executive director for the Women's Basketball Coaches Association, Atlanta. She coached basketball at James Madison University. She was a member of the AIAW Basketball Committee and served as chair of the Kodak All-America Basketball Selection Committee and the U.S. Girls and Women's Basketball Rules Committee. She is currently a trustee and vice president of the Women's Sports Foundation, a trustee and member of the Executive Committee of the Naismith Memorial Basketball Hall of Fame, and a member of the advisory committee for the Center of the Study of Sport in Society.

Fran Koenig recently retired as associate athletic director and director of women's athletics at Central Michigan University, Mt. Pleasant. She played basketball at Brown University and coached basketball at Concordia College and Central Michigan University. She has contributed more than 25 years of leadership in basketball officiating, as a national official and as chair of the DGWS Officiating Services Area and the AIAW National Championship Officials Committee. Koenig was the first woman to serve as an AAU basketball official. She was president of NAGWS and is an Honor Fellow.

Lucille Kyvallos teaches at Queens College, New York, and coached the women's basketball team. She played on a variety of New York City athletic league basketball teams in high school and played semi-pro basketball during and after college. She coached at West Chester State College, Pennsylvania before going to Queen's College, where her team was the first women's team to play at Madison Square Garden. She served as chair for the AIAW basketball committee, and as tournament director for the AIAW national championship in 1973. She coached the U.S. team at the World University Games in Bulgaria. Kyvallos received the Founders Award from Kodak and the U.S. Basketball Writers Association for her contributions to the development of women's basketball.

Patsy Neal is wellness coordinator at the Mission Hospital, Asheville, North Carolina. She played for the Wayland Baptist "Flying Queens" while in college, was selected as an AAU All-American three times, and participated in the Pan-American Games and world tours to the Soviet Union, Germany, and France. She has coached, officiated, and written extensively about women's basketball, including *Basketball Techniques for Women* and *Coaching Methods for Women.*

Joan Paul is professor and chair of the Department of Human Performance and Sport Studies at the University of Tennessee, Knoxville. She played AAU basketball for Epps Jewelry during her years at Samford University in Birmingham, Alabama, and once scored 63 points in a game. She coached and officiated girls club, church, and recreation league basketball. She has received the Outstanding Contribution Award from SAPECW and the Louisiana AHPER Honor Award. The Joan Paul Award was established at Hewitt-Trussville High School to honor an outstanding scholar-athlete. She has written on sport, physical education, and American culture.

Betty Spears is professor emerita, Department of Sport Studies, University of Massachusetts, Amherst, and former director of physical education, Wellesley College. She has written extensively on the history of sport, including *History of Sport and Physical Education in the United States* with Richard A. Swanson and *Leading the Way*, a biography of Amy Morris Homans, chapters in books, and numerous articles in professional journals. Spears is also a member emerita of the American Academy of Physical Education.

Peggy Stanaland is professor of physical education at Eastern Kentucky University, Richmond. When she coached at Punta Gorda High School in Florida in the 1940s, her team used the unlimited dribble. She also coached at the University of Kentucky and at the University of Louisville. She was a nationally rated official and chaired the Kentucky Officials Rating Board. She writes on Kentucky sportswomen and Southern women in sport.

Margaret Toohey-Costa is professor and director of special major programs at the California State University, Long Beach. She refereed and coached in Australia. Since coming to the United States, she has written extensively on politics and the history of women in sport.

Nancy Weltzheimer Wardwell is coordinator of sport and leisure studies at The Ohio State University, Columbus. She has a pervasive interest in the history and promotion of women's athletics. Her doctoral dissertation was on Rachel Bryant.

Marcy Weston is associate director for women's athletics, Central Michigan University, Mt. Pleasant. She played basketball at the University of Dayton and coached at the University of Wisconsin-Whitewater and at Central Michigan University. She has officiated at the NCAA Division I Finals. She currently serves as the NCAA secretary/rules editor and as a member of the NCAA Committee on Officiating and the NCAA Women's Basketball Rules Committee.

PART I
THE EARLY YEARS OF BASKETBALL
1890s–1930s

Meadville (Pa.) High School Team (1908 *Basket Ball Guide*)

M Street High School Basket Ball Team, Washington, D.C. (1911 *Official Handbook*, Inter-Scholastic Athletic Association of Middle Atlantic States)

Dwight Indian Training School Team, Marble City (Okla.)
(1917–18 *Basket Ball Guide*)

1

Introduction to Part I

Joan S. Hult

The sport of women's basketball is not a phenomenon apart from American life and mores. Sport history, as Roberta Park notes, must have more sufficient "immersion in the general literature of the period being studied . . ." and no longer remain ". . . isolated from other important social, cultural or intellectual issues."[1]

Several articles in Part I place basketball in its historical and cultural framework. They investigate the writings and actions of women basketball leaders and recurring themes affecting the development and control of basketball. A majority of the writings, however, are descriptive or narrative and specific to basketball. This Introduction discusses the recurring themes in American society with the greatest impact on women's basketball not discussed by our authors. The reader will also note some ways in which basketball has, in a reciprocal way, influenced the culture.

In their articles, Steveda Chepko and Nancy Dosch discuss five important cultural themes influencing the attitudes and beliefs of female physical educators: (1) femininity vs. masculinity, (2) biology is destiny (i.e., female differences from male), (3) separate gender spheres of influence, (4) fear of unwomanly behavior, and (5) medical views. Betty Spears describes the roots of femininity and masculinity and suggests the changes in role expectations embodied in the "New Woman" of the 1890s.

Several other themes affecting sport that are not discussed by our authors include: (1) physical appearance and beauty, (2) the implications of gender differences and boundaries, (3) labor movements, (4) gender relations, and (5) ideologies. Many of these themes overlap and are interwoven in the very fabric of social and cultural interrelationships. They all affect women's lives in the culture, sport, and basketball participation.

3

This Introduction also gives a brief overview of the complex inter-action of biology, economics, politics, and ideology in two loosely de-fined eras within the first fifty years of women's basketball. The two eras are 1890–1920, the Progressive Era of the "New Woman," and the 1920s and 1930s, the "Roaring Twenties" and the Great Depression.

An overview of the social and cultural values enables us to see how the New Woman physical educators of the 1890s emerged with their ideals and values having been cradled in middle class experiences and educational ideologies. Within their "separate sphere" of physical ed-ucation, these women had both the responsibility and the power to direct its course. Thus, they were significant change agents in what were per-ceived as proper sporting behaviors throughout the 1890s–1930s. This ideology of women controlling women and mandating the "right spirit" or kind of cooperative competition impelled the women physical edu-cators to establish the play day model.

The Beginnings

By 1870, when women entered higher education in noticeable num-bers, gender roles had already been well defined. The center of the American economy and productivity had moved to the marketplace. Men went out to their jobs and women stayed at home. Thus, women and men no longer shared work in the same way. The normative per-sonality traits, social responsibilities, and behavior patterns for middle and upper class women had changed and become more narrowly defined compared to those of the former agrarian society.

This polarization formed the roots of masculinity and femininity in American life. The increasing number of men who worked beyond the immediate surroundings of home and community demanded that moth-ers fill the breach. Women became the obvious parent responsible for child-rearing. By the post-Civil War era women were professional home-makers; the domestic world was theirs to rule. All other arenas were male-dominated.

Coupled with the Victorian concept of "cult of true womanhood" was Theodore Roosevelt's philosophy that sport could be used to define manliness. He declared that aggressive sport could re-create "the brawn, the spirit, the self-confidence and the quickness of men."[2] Thus mas-culine sport was to provide a "rite of passage" to manhood and become the antithesis of what defined the ideal women. The athletic "rite of passage" vs. the "cult of true womanhood" was a central theme affecting woman's freedom to participate in sport. Culture as manifested in social institutions was masculine; sport as well was clearly masculine.

Medical. The male medical profession attempted to gain and maintain control of women. Nowhere were power relations and gender relations so apparent as in physicians' demanding authority over women's bodies. Under a pseudo-scientific pretext male medical "experts" in the last three decades of the nineteenth century set themselves up as arbiters in matters of female health and physical behavior. Their best wisdom insisted it would be harmful to reproduction and to women's frail nervous constitution if they attended college. As women nonetheless did so, and without dire consequences, the medical profession shifted its view to accommodate their educational presence while retaining control and authority over women's bodies.[3] The medical influences in relationship to women in physical education, sport, and most especially basketball, are presented in Dosch's chapter.

1890–1920—The "New Woman"

The end of the first wave of American industrialization and urbanization increased the number of men who worked in factories. The appropriate profession for women remained homemaking. By the 1890s lower paid and more tractable immigrant women largely replaced those women who had been factory workers, so that "respectable" (i.e., middle class) women would not work at unwomanly factory jobs or as servants. Working class women did not want these unwomanly factory positions but they worked out of need as they awaited their opportunity for marriage and family. At the same time the number of middle class families increased, creating in turn greater numbers of "ladies of leisure" since it was not respectable to work in low paid jobs. Middle class women attempted to improve the social value of a new white collar labor market that would provide permissible paid employment for women. Thus the clerical and secretarial work force experienced an enormous shift to women occupying those roles. Men moved to other types of employment and the white collar jobs became acceptable, respectable positions for women who wanted to work. These expanding employment opportunities opened new vistas for women.[4]

Many middle class women remained in the culturally approved domestic role. Leisure activities relieved their boredom at home and many women were drawn to the volunteer reform movements of the era, providing the bedrock of the progressive reform movements. Volunteerism fit nicely into the category of service orientation as an extension of the home and also brought women into the community where they could interact with other women and experience challenging, rewarding options outside the home. These volunteer reformers fought for legislation to improve working conditions and institute child labor laws, educational reforms, sanitation improvements, and prevention of the physical abuse of women.[5]

In addition to the white collar job market and volunteerism, steady growth was apparent in higher educational opportunities by the turn of the century. This opened professional occupations and new nontraditional jobs for women.

The New Woman had for the first time the choice to become a wage-earner or a household caretaker. This posed new social dilemmas, resolved to a large extent by many professional women and most physical education leaders by their remaining single. Female physical educators characterized their profession as service-oriented and nurturing work. As typical single women they wanted economic independence and intrinsically satisfying work. While theirs was admittedly an alternative route in life, they nevertheless maintained "respectable" cultural trappings and ideals as they set their goals for programs of physical education and sport. They were intense about the responsibility to oversee the health and welfare of "their" female students and unlike many other single career women they demonstrated little disillusionment with their decision. Biographies and articles on women physical educators suggest they remained happily dedicated to their profession.[6]

American women used the political arena to make a better society. Many activists joined organizations for suffrage and many others joined the Women's Christian Temperance Union (WCTU). Both political issues were central to a better life for women. One would allow them to speak for themselves, thereby gaining power denied them in the past. The other addressed the problem of abuse by alcoholic husbands. Women knew they needed to gain access to the power positions essential for reform and self-preservation. The WCTU, for example, organized a department of physical culture hoping, in part, to lure men away from taverns and into the sports arena. The WCTU also worked toward passage of required physical education in the schools to provide alternatives in leisure activity and new viable nondrinking avenues.[7]

Tensions in gender relations, as women flexed their political muscles, rose steadily from 1890 to 1920. Women seeking social reforms, broader freedoms, and independence ultimately accepted the narrower victory at the ballot box. The women's movement subsided as an activist force in society. However, since women's gender boundaries had widened, their role expectations expanded in the next two decades even without a strong feminist advocacy group.

Widespread changes occurred in many behavior patterns. Single "bachelor" women could live alone in large cities, share an apartment with other women, or live at home. This new freedom in their lifestyles easily carried over to the "Roaring Twenties."

Bloomers provided new freedom of movement for the "new woman"
members of the 1898 basketball team from North Dakota Agricultural
College, Fargo (now North Dakota State University).

1890–1920 leisure activity.   The famous *Godey's Lady's Book* definitely encouraged affluent New Women of the 1890s to pursue recreational activity. This popular magazine for women described the etiquette of sport and set boundaries for sporting endeavors. It supported
recreational pastimes, education, and nonvigorous sporting activities.[8]
   There is little question that college women and middle class women
took to outdoor activites in the 1890s, especially bicycling. Health concerns fueled a new allegiance to physical activity. Bicycling had a profound effect on the women's sports movement, and on the bachelor girl
of the 1890s. It was a recreational activity that male medical authorities
pronounced beneficial, pleasurable, and healthful if indulged in mod-
eration. (The physicians, however, denounced new racing and record-
breaking efforts as "physiological crimes.") Women bicyclers enjoyed
great liberation of spirit and talked about the sport as freeing their mind,
giving them courage, and offering an unchaperoned outdoor experience.
Many feminists saw this cycling craze as a public display and public
statement in favor of women's independence.[9]

Dress reform of the 1890s.   The dress reform occurred quite apart from
sports fashions, although it was opportune in terms of bicycling and
basketball. Women were seeking freedom from the bondage of long

skirts, petticoats, and the tightly laced corsets that threatened their vigor and stamina. Early in sporting experiences, women wore their tight clothing including corsets for tennis, croquet, and archery. But in the era of the 1890s they moved to the bloomer attire and wore modified versions of male attire—shirt and skirt. Dress reform surely made sports activity more viable, enjoyable, and potentially more vigorous. If bloomers could appear outside on cycling paths, they could also be acceptable on outdoor basketball courts. The uncorseted, loose, shorter dress supplemented by bloomers rather than petticoats also improved the exercise potential for women. It gave the cycling girl and ultimately the basketball player a greater freedom of movement. The interest in fitness and the happy happenstance of the safety bike, clothes reforms, and basketball's popularity contributed to one another and permitted all three to grow in popularity.[10]

The sporting tradition of the 1890s expanded steadily in kind and number, as Spears describes. Colleges provided the entre for the middle class women to gain experiences in sports. In addition, country clubs, athletic clubs, and local and national championships in "elite" sports became acceptable activity for the ladies of leisure. A growing concern for health and well-being and recognition that physical activity contributed to that healthy state encouraged sports participation. Physical fitness became important: The old Dio Lewis and Catherine Beecher exercises were "out" and the Delsarte and Sargent movement was "in." Vigorous exercise and healthy living through sport was the motto of the era.[11]

Cathy Peiss claims in *Cheap Amusements* that dances, movies, and amusement parks were the primary leisure activities of single low-paid working class women.[12] By contrast, the New Woman selected elite sporting activities.

Roaring Twenties and the Great Depression

Congress and the necessary 37 states passed the Equal Suffrage Amendment and by 1920 women began to attend large state universities in numbers comparable to men. Working class women in factories and in white collar jobs outnumbered those in domestic service amid growing economic prosperity, political power, and optimism. American affluence, the reduction of sexual restrictions, the mobility of society, and the number of women who worked changed the cultural fabric considerably.

The tens of thousands of American women employed in industry, including some who had served overseas in the First World War, had by 1920 brought together some necessary ingredients for women's emancipation. Women's experiences in roles associated with World War I had made them realize their strength, power, and ability to withstand the rigors of war.

There was an elaborate reappraisal of the free-spirited, now middle-class office girl-cum-flapper. While many single women expressed their confidence and self-image in the flapper dress and demeanor as they achieved greater freedom of movement and a wider range of behavioral patterns, little changed for married women. Their culture still discouraged married women from working, although they did slowly move into the marketplace in newly established white collar positions. It was the new group of single white collar workers who sought leisure activity beyond the elite sports of their married sisters.[13]

The actress and athletic woman were the new role models. The chorus line brand of beauty and a new athleticism flourished side by side in the decades of the twenties and thirties. The Gibson Girl appearance yielded to the boyish-looking flappers of the 1920s. As the trim athletic model evolved, patterned after the 1930s athletic heroes, a Golden Age of Sport for Women emerged. The sportswoman was a popular role model, surpassed only by the film star. While the real heroes were the sportswomen in individual sports, athletes in team sports and competitive athletics received some praise—if they were beautiful. The dances of the 1920s, whereby the athletic Charleston replaced the sensual tango, and women enjoyed more freedom of movement, may well be another manifestation of the same independence expressed in the sports domain.[14]

Female physical educators continued to be comfortable in their "nurturing" profession. By the 1920s and 1930s society embraced as acceptable several professions that met the nurturing, service-oriented criteria for married as well as single women. These professions included teaching, nursing, social work, and library work, among others. For the women in physical education, this broader social redefinition of appropriate women's roles enhanced their power base to control girls and women's sporting behaviors and experiences.[15]

Also, white collar jobs for women included hospital workers, secretaries, and clerical and sales workers. These jobs, which had previously been exclusively male, were redefined as female. The pay level was reduced accordingly. The status of the jobs themselves improved. Women in these middle class jobs had access to middle class leisure activities but previously working class women entering these now white collar jobs also retained some of their working class leisure attitudes and behaviors.[16]

Blue collar working women's pay was lower still, partly because they were so often barred from union positions, and traditionally female occupations were not unionized. The basic differences between men's and women's pay were built into the labor market movements. African-American women workers, mostly domestics, held even lower-paid jobs with lower status as well.[17]

In summary, not all Victorian constraints had succumbed to women's desires by the 1920s, but the affluence and lifestyle freedom of the 1920s resulted in extraordinary athletic freedom through the 1930s. A popular health movement and a new athleticism nourished a greater emphasis on the health and fitness concept throughout these decades. The Great Depression changed the wage earning capabilities of women, but it did little to rescind their new freedoms.

1920–1930 leisure activity.   The ladies' magazines of the 1920s and 1930s and even the newspapers honored sporting women, freeing them for a wider selection of sporting activities. Women physical educators capitalized on the new athleticism and interest in athletic heroes but at the same time they cautioned about the extent and the kind of competition being suggested. The fit and healthy woman was certainly a priority in both the culture and in education, but the means to that end were not mutually agreed upon. The culture saw, in part, that high level competition could be used to achieve fitness and health objectives, whereas the educators spoke against it as the wrong kind of competition.[18]

The middle class and college women of the era still had role restrictions mandating only sporting experiences that had historically been acceptable for the New Woman—the men's elite sports with no physical contact. Basketball, however, fit into the category of acceptable recreational sport because rule modifications restricted physical contact. Further, in the author's view, women's basketball was different enough from the men's game to not be a threat in any way to the male sport establishment. Even so, college women were expected to avoid "unwomanly" behavior during play.

The working girls could participate in sporting experiences with wider gender boundaries in both decorum and types of sports than middle class women. So too, in the 1920s the development of industrial leagues in sport drew working women. Recreational centers in cities, the YWCA and YMCA, as well as church leagues, AAU leagues, and schools all supported competitive athletics. Working women, primarily those who were single, competed on teams without expressing concern at being outside of gender role expectations. As long as they maintained the physical attractiveness or used heavy make-up they were considered feminine.[19]

The government supported sport facilities and sponsored programs in recreational and competitive sports including those for girls and women. While poverty during the Depression reduced the spectator activities of the culture, Franklin D. Roosevelt's New Deal, with its Works Project Administration (WPA) and Civilian Conservation Corps (CCC), increased the recreational activities open to working women.[20]

African-Americans, too, found recreational outlets in the black YWCA and YMCA, settlement houses, and recreation centers in their communities. Photographs throughout this book illustrate the presence even before 1920 of black basketball competition, but to date details of programs have not been uncovered. Throughout this era, most of the black women's basketball experiences appear to be in exclusively black settings.

Physical education programs.   The physical education programs during the 1920s and 1930s supported the sports of middle class women, with team sports taking an important place. Educators saw a need for cooperative and recreational competition for the masses. Their new knowledge about physiology began to replace myth, especially regarding the relationship to athletic participation of the menstrual cycle. Scientific inquiry became the basis for physical education programs as progress and achievement were increasingly measured by knowledge and skill tests. Women researchers designed ability and achievement tests for ability grouping, which the basketball committee applied to basketball and rules modification. The female physical educators also began offering higher levels of skills in each sport, instead of constantly repeating beginning levels. The basketball *Guides* reflected this shift in emphasis.

Janet Owen, writing for the *New York Herald* in 1932, commented on physical education at colleges in the East as "growing out of its wand-and-dumbbell infancy into maturity as a science. . . ."[21] More and more schools had a genuine department of physical education for women, recognized in an increasing number of institutions. The goals became improvement of physical condition, establishment of health habits, and the development of a permanent interest in sports and recreation as primary aims.

Physical Appearance and Beauty

Lois Banner, in *American Beauty*, argues that the New Woman was embodied by the Gibson Girl (named for fashion artist Charles Dana Gibson, who created the "Gibson look" in *Life* magazine in 1890). The physical attributes of the Gibson Girl were a tall and commanding appearance, "thick dark hair swept upward in the prevailing pompadour style".[22] She had a thinner rather than a more voluptuous figure but roundness of bosom and hips. Her casual attire and frequent appearance in a sport setting, according to Charlotte Perkins Gilman, bespoke a woman "braver, stronger, more healthful and skillful and able and free, more human in all ways."[23]

There were really, however, two Gibson Girls, one for the middle class/college woman's role model and the other, the working girl's role model. Each group held its own attitudes toward behavior and achieving the ideal look. Chepko's work focuses on middle class and college women and their role expectations.

The working class Gibson Girl model has not been as well researched. While both Gibson Girl models were similar in physical appearance, there were differences in a natural vs. made-up standard of beauty and in restricted vs. relaxed gender defined behaviors. The middle class Gibson Girl had restrictions on her role expectations; the working class Gibson Girl was a more sensual embodiment.[24]

The working girls' Gibson Girl achieved beauty through make-up and artificial curls and had sensual traits, freer sexual behavior, and more latitude to engage in all sports than her middle class/college sister. The latter saw natural beauty as central, and sexual behavior restricted. These two different models of the same ideal broadened the cultural role expectations for women and their activities from the 1890s through World War I. In the 1920s and 1930s the Gibson Girl gave way to the flapper and the athletic boyish ideal of the sporting woman of the next two decades.

The inauguration of the Miss America contest is an example of the importance of physical appearance and role requirements for women. As Banner speculates, the message is clear: "Beauty is all a woman needs for success, and as a corollary, that beauty ought to be a major pursuit of all women."[25] The emergence of the fashion model (a result of beauty contests), the film queen, and the cosmetic industry all suggest the importance of women being beautiful. Still, middle class women favored the natural look, trim but with muscle tone. Another emphasis was their demand for comfortable and healthy lives.

Every sport had its women champions and the beautiful ones were as popular as a film star. The media-glorified portrayal of women's role models in the 1920s sport domain led to public acceptance of skilled athletes such as Gertrude Ederle, Helen Wells, Suzanne Lenglen, Eleanor Holm, Glenna Collett (Vare), Sonja Henie, and Annette Kellermann, the athlete-actress from Australia. The greatest favorite of them all was Amelia Earhart.[26]

Grace, form, and beauty were essential attributes in these role models for the sporting women. If a sport for women was graceful then its participant posed no challenge to the norm, masculinity derived from sport, or to the fixed meaning of sport for males (strength, power, and might). Similarly, women avoided a great athletic performance if it did

BEAUTY QUEEN OF CAGE MEET

Beauty contests for players were conducted at the AAU national championship tournament in the 1930s, when the role model for the sporting woman combined athletic ability with grace and made-up feminine beauty.

not embrace the feminine sport behaviors. While many would consider Babe Didrikson the epitome of the modern sportswoman, her success in basketball and the Olympics did not make her a role model. In fact, it was not until she achieved success in golf that she was accorded the heroic status of other women mentioned above. (Babe was not a beautiful woman, although she attempted to use heavy make-up once she was a successful athlete.)[27]

Working class women and many members of the new white collar class lacked entirely the financial means to participate in middle class elite sports and had limited opportunity for individual sports. However, industrial athletics and high level competition were well within the accepted gender norms so long as women made sure their physical appearance included made-up feminine beauty and a sensuous look. The outside trappings, not the behavior, mattered during the contest. There was no incongruence, therefore, with playing AAU tournament basketball, for example, and being a part of a beauty contest to select a tournament queen.

One of the best examples of this combined attractive physical appearance and aggressive behavior is the Redheads, a women's professional basketball team originating in 1936. The Redheads, with their dyed red hair or red wigs, defied role expectations and barnstormed the country competing against men's teams. Yet the team members were held to a standard of femininity in their physical appearance, uniforms, and made-up beauty consistent with the behavior expectations of the 1930s.[28]

Biology Is Destiny (Women's Autonomy)

A part of women's struggle for autonomy involved seeking new freedom for birth control. As early as the turn of the century birth control methods were successful in reducing family size. This represents an early attempt to prevent biology from being destiny. The 1930s brought birth control devices, the use of which had important implications for women's role in society. Fewer children per family drastically reduced the child-rearing years and offered new opportunities for self-realization. Mothers had more leisure time and more hours for volunteer work or paid employment. However, the greatest contribution to sport was in a woman's beginning awareness of her right to own her body, for this awakening leads to the freedom of a woman to play sport for herself (even developing muscles), and not only to watch or be watched by men.[29]

Gender relations, or power relations between men and women in the culture and in the sporting traditions, are important throughout basketball's 100 year history. In any discussion of gender relations a basic reality is that males have the dominant power in the culture, as well as in sport. Women have attempted to take some of that power away from men in order to empower women.

Women did not doubt the authority of men to control men's athletics, but determined that women should retain the power to control the separate sphere of women's athletics. They called upon men to uphold that right to control. Gender relations, then, became a central issue only when men decided to dominate the women's sphere.

In the sports arena from the 1890s through the 1930s the major gender relations issues and power struggle occurred between the AAU and the women's organizations. The details of that struggle are discussed in "The Governance of Athletics for Girls and Women." The governance structure of the antecedents of the National Association for Girls and Women in Sport (NAGWS) are described, and the attempt of the Amateur Athletic Union (AAU) to control women athletes and women's basketball rules is discussed. Gender issues and gender equality became more directly influential in the second half of the twentieth century when the liberation movement revived in the 1960s. Therefore, the more detailed contextual examination of gender relations and their influence on basketball in the age of liberation, revolution, and reforms is discussed in Part II of this collection. It is when the liberation movement revived in the 1960s that sportswomen's goals included gender equality.

Play Day Movement

By the early 1920s a vast number of colleges, high school recreation programs, industrial leagues, and the AAU offered high level competition for females. This activated the anti-varsity, anti-Olympic and anti-male leadership campaign of the leaders of the female physical education establishment.

High level competition, in which the male model of athletics was used for women, conflicted with the female physical educators' philosophical commitment to recreational sport. This led them to design a more acceptable form of women's sporting experiences. They believed their design had all the attributes of men's varsity programs and would satisfy feminine cultural expectations for middle class women. Their new design was an alternative model of athletics called the "play day."

Basketball was the most popular play day sport and as such was included in over three-quarters of collegiate and high school play days. The play day had three or more colleges (leagues or clubs) meet for competition, but instead of being organized under the school colors, teams were comprised of athletes intermixed from all of the schools. The physical educators manipulated the male model of varsity athletics to this alternative version of competitive athletics and based the play day on the underlying principles of universal participation, recreational competition, and democratic ideals.[30]

The "right spirit of play" (play day) really needs no introduction to most readers. The play day of the 1920s and 1930s is well documented in the physical education literature. Because it is generally known and researched, its story does not appear herein. Evidence abounds of the thousands of play day events in high schools and colleges each year from the early 1920s to the mid-1930s. Millions of young women experienced this brand of sport. However, the physical education literature leads one to believe this form of competition, along with the telegraphic meets, prevailed for at least two decades. The literature also asserts that the play day overshadowed all other forms of competition and influences on programs in education and the public sector. It now appears more accurate to shorten the time span in which the play day prevailed and to challenge the extensiveness and exclusiveness of the movement's influence on colleges after the mid-1930s.

Evidence that highly competitive sporting experiences were culturally acceptable during the same period is constantly being uncovered. The writings in Section 3 dispel the myth of the exclusiveness of play days.

Comments on Part I

The writings in Part I present the origin and prime movers in modifying women's basketball in its developmental years. Authors describe the women's governance structure and organization patterns and analyze rule modifications throughout basketball's 100 year history. The writings also address the influence of women physical educators who expressed in the basketball *Guides* their beliefs, social and medical attitudes, and behaviors in conducting basketball programs.

The remainder of Part I consists of selected articles that reveal glimpses of competitive basketball throughout the country in basketball's first fifty years. These readings dispel the myth that competitive athletics were buried upon the birth of the play day and illustrate widespread interest in women's basketball throughout the first fifty years.

Several missing links from the book need to be researched in order for us to understand fully the role, function, and meaning of basketball to the participant, to the culture, and within the sport milieu. These include: (1) the history of the growth and development of high school basketball, (2) competitive and intramural programs of basketball through the YWCA and the YMCA, (3) basketball in the international and Olympic movement, and (4) public recreation programs. While brief glimpses of AAU basketball programs are found herein, the entire AAU basketball program for women needs to be researched since the AAU provided the means for the female athlete to express herself at the pinnacle of competitive programs until the second half of the twentieth century. In fact, all these missing links obscure the complete understanding of basketball's role in the lives of females.

All of these stories should be told and their function and meaning for the female basketball player explored. Until that happens, this collection represents some of the best current thought about the opportunities and experiences for girls or women in the expanding role of basketball in its first fifty years.

Notes

1. Roberta J. Park, "Special Essay Research and Scholarship in the History of Physical Education and Sport: The Current State of Affairs," *Research Quarterly for Exercise and Sport* 54 (1983): 100.

2. As quoted in Joe L. Dubbert, *A Man's Place: Masculinity in Transition* (Englewood Cliffs, N.J.: Prentice-Hall, 1979), 116–117. See also D. Cavallo, *Muscles and Morals: Organized Playgrounds and Urban Reform, 1880–1920* (Philadelphia: University of Pennsylvania Press, 1981), 32–48, 55–65.

3. Patrica Vertinsky, "Body Shapes: The Role of the Medical Establishment in Informing Female Exercise and Physical Education in Nineteenth-century North America," in *From Fair Sex to Feminism, Sport and the Socialization of Women in the Industrial and Post-Industrial Eras*, eds. J. A. Mangan and Roberta J. Park (London: Frank Cass and Company, 1987), 256–281.

4. Alice Kessler-Harris, "Independence and Virtue in the Lives of Wage-Earning Women: The United States, 1870–1930," in *Women in Culture and Politics: A Century of Change*, eds. Judith Friedlander et al. (Bloomington: Indiana University Press, 1986), 3–17; Alice Kessler-Harris, *Out to Work: A History of*

Wage-Earning Women in the United States (Oxford: Oxford University Press, 1982); Julie A. Matthaei, *An Economic History of Women in America: Women's Work, the Sexual Division of Labor, and the Development of Capitalism* (New York: Schocken Books, 1982), 187–231.

5. Ann Firor Scott, *Making the Invisible Woman Visible* (Chicago: University of Illinois Press, 1984), 279–284; Linda K. Kerber and Jane DeHart Mathews, *Women's America: Refocusing the Past* (New York: Oxford University Press, 1982), 3–22, 209–213.

6. Matthaei, *Economic History*, 203–205, 209–213, 256–277. See also Thomas Woody, *A History of Women's Education in the United States Vol. II* (New York: Science Press, 1929), 639–649; Barbara Miller Solomon, *In the Company of Educated Women: A History of Women and Higher Education in America* (New Haven: Yale University Press, 1985); Betty Spears, *Leading the Way: Amy Morris Homans and the Beginnings of Professional Education for Women* (New York: Greenwood Press, 1986); Betty Spears, "Success, Women, and Physical Education," in M. Gladys Scott and Mary J. Hoferek, eds., *Women as Leaders in Physical Education and Sport* (Iowa City: University of Iowa, 1979), 5–19.

7. Scott, *Making the Invisible Woman Visible*, 204–208, 215–216; Deobold B. Van Dalen and Bruce L. Bennett, *A World History of Physical Education: Cultural, Philosophical, Comparative* (Englewood Cliffs, N.J.: Prentice Hall, 1971), 404.

8. B. Benough, "The New Woman Athletically Considered," *Godey's Lady's Book* (January 1896): 23–29. See also W. Ayres, "Smith College," *Godey's Lady's Book* (July 1895): 25.

9. W. H. Fenton, "Cycling for Ladies" (*19th Century* 39:796–801, 1896) as quoted in Mary Lou Remley, "The American Sportswoman in Transition, 1880–1910," in *Proceedings of the Jyvaskyla Congress on Movement and Sport in Women's Life* (Jyvaskyla, Finland: The Press of the University of Jyvaskyla, 1989), 147; Lois W. Banner, *American Beauty* (Chicago: University of Chicago Press, 1983), 145–146; Frances E. Willard, *A Wheel Within a Wheel* (Chicago: Woman's Temperance Publishing Association, 1895); M. Merington, "Women and the Bicycle, *Athletics: The Out-of-Door Library* (Vol. 5), 209–230.

10. R. L. Dickinson, "Bicycling for Women: The Puzzling Question of Costume," *Outlook* (April 25, 1896); Willard, *A Wheel Within a Wheel*; Banner, *American Beauty*, 145–146; James Laver, *Costume and Fashion: A Concise History* (New York: Thames and Hudson, 1982), 204–209; Richard Harmond, "Progress and Flight: An Interpretation of the American Cycle Craze of the 1890's," in *The American Sporting Experience: A Historical Anthology of Sport in America*, ed. Steven A. Riess (New York: Leisure Press, 1984), 190–208.

11. Banner, *American Beauty*, 203; Harvey Green, *Fit for America: Health, Fitness, Sport and American Society* (New York: Pantheon, 1986), 217–316; Roberta Park, "Healthy, Moral, and Strong: Educational Views of Exercise and Athletics in Nineteenth-Century America," in Kathryn Grover, *Fitness in American Culture: Images of Health, Sport, and the Body, 1830–1940* (Rochester, N.Y.: Margaret Woodbury Strong Museum, 1989), 123–168.

12. Cathy Peiss, *Cheap Amusements: Working Women and Leisure in Turn-of-the-Century New York* (Philadelphia: Temple University Press, 1986).

13. Matthaei, *An Economic History*, 250–255; Banner, *American Beauty*, 280–283; Deckard, *The Women's Movement*, 291–294; Kessler-Harris, *Out to Work*, 217–249. See also Martha Verbrugge, *Able-Bodied Womanhood: Personal Health*

and Social Change in 19th Century Boston (Oxford: Oxford University Press, 1988), 97–192.

14. Joan S. Hult, "American Female Olympians as Role Model, Mentors, and Leaders," *Proceedings of the Jyvaskyla Congress on Movement and Sport in Women's Life*, 107–119; idem, "The Female American Runner: A Modern Quest for Visibility," in *Female Endurance Athletes*, ed. Barbara L. Drinkwater (Champaign, Ill.: Human Kinetics, 1986), 12–15; Judith A. Davidson, "The 1930s: A Pivotal Decade for Women's Sport" (unpublished qualifying manuscript, University of Massachusetts, 1978).

15. Solomon, *In the Company of Educated Women*, 157–185; Matthaei, *An Economic History*, 256–300.

16. Ibid.

17. Kessler-Harris, *Out to Work*, 250–272.

18. Davidson, "A Pivotal Decade for Sport"; Agnes Wayman, "All Uses—No Abuses," *American Physical Education Review* (November 1924): 517.

19. Joan S. Hult, "Have the Reports of the Death of Competitive Women's Athletics 1920–35 Been Exaggerated?" Unpublished paper presented at the Seventh Annual Convention of the North American Society for Sport History, Banff, Canada, May 1980. See also Harry Stewart, "A Survey of Track Athletics for Women," *American Physical Education Review* (January 1916): 13–21; Banner, *American Beauty*.

20. A. F. Wileden, "Recreational Trends in the Rural Community," *Recreation* (December 1948): 413; E.C. Worman, "Trends in Public Recreation," *Recreation* (August 1938): 267–269; C.W. Hackensmith, *History of Physical Education* (New York: Harper & Row, Publishers, 1966), 435–36.

21. Janet Owens, "Sports in Women's Colleges," reprinted from the sports pages of the *New York Herald Tribune*, 1932.

22. Banner, *American Beauty*, 154.

23. Ibid., 156.

24. Banner, *American Beauty*, 154–174; Peiss, *Cheap Amusements*, 56–87.

25. Banner, *American Beauty*, 249.

26. Hult, "American Female Olympians"; idem, "The Female American Runner," 14.

27. William Oscar Johnson and Nancy P. Willamson, *Whatta-Gal: The Babe Didrikson Story* (Boston: Little, Brown and Company, 1977).

28. "All American Red Heads" Program, 1969.

29. Carl N. Degler, *At Odds: Women and the Family in America from the Revolution to the Present* (New York: Oxford University Press, 1980); Margaret Sanger, "My Fight for Birth Control," in Kerber and Mathews, *Women's America*, 310–318; Linda Gordon, "Birth Control and Social Revolution," in Nancy F. Cott and Elizabeth H. Pleck, *A Heritage of Her Own* (New York: Simon and Schuster, 1979), 445–475.

30. Women's Division of the National Amateur Athletic Federation (NAAF), *News Letter*, 1929–1935. These *News Letters* reported activities in state high schools, colleges, industrial, and recreational programs. Much of the reporting was about play days and some sports days. AAHPERD Archives, Reston, Va. (News Letters, NAAF files); Women's Division NAAF "News Letters" 1923–1934 (random number after 1928), Lou Henry Hoover files, Red Cross and Other Organizations, NAAF-WD "Folder News Letters," West Branch, Iowa.

Section 1
In the Beginning . . .

2

Senda Berenson Abbott
New Woman: New Sport

Betty Spears

Senda Berenson was not the typical New Woman of the 1890s. The idea of the New Woman evolved from decades of slowly changing perceptions of desirable traits in women. Mid-century women cultivated "true womanhood" characterized by piety, purity, domesticity, and submissiveness. Some women challenged these tenets, especially submissiveness, and initiated the women's rights movement at Seneca Falls, New York, in 1848. Other women, in response to the demands of the Civil War, proved themselves to be excellent administrators, nurses, fund raisers, and able to undertake a wide variety of responsibilities. By the 1880s women had become college and university graduates. More and more women widened their accepted sphere of home and family to include activities outside the home in new occupations or volunteer associations. The New Woman had arrived.

Usually upper class or middle class and from an established American family, the New Woman represented only a small number of women in the United States. However, they caused much public discussion from the effect of a college education on their health to the outrageous suggestion that they be permitted to vote. Vigorous and better educated than most, they perceived themselves as reformers of society. They agreed with the common belief that women were morally superior to men. To prove themselves, they engaged in many reforms from bettering the health of school children to raising the standards for patients in asylums. Women's "special mission in public life was to purify, uplift, control, and reform; to improve men, children, and society to extend the values of the home."[1] Senda Berenson's childhood and background were unlike those of most New Women.

19

From Frail Immigrant to New Woman

Senda Berenson's family was neither an established American family nor upper class. Senda, then Senda Valvrojenski, was born on March 19, 1868 in a *shtetl* near Vilnius, Russia. Her father emigrated to America in 1874 where he settled in Boston's crowded West End. He changed his name from Albert Valvrojenski to Albert Berenson and became a peddler in and around Boston. A year later, Senda, then seven, arrived with her mother, her adored brother Bernard, two years older than Senda, and a younger brother, Abie. Mr. Berenson demanded that the family become Americanized as quickly as possible. He insisted that the family speak only English and that they sever all connections with the Jewish religion. Senda's two sisters were born in Boston, Elizabeth in 1878 and Rachel in 1880. Also, in 1880, Mr. Berenson became a citizen, making the entire family American citizens. Throughout her childhood and youth Mr. Berenson's short temper caused a problem for he often scolded Senda and Bernard.

Senda and Bernard formed a close lifelong relationship. Although Mr. Berenson remained a peddler throughout his working years, he was well read, a liberal thinker, and he prized education. Before they immigrated Senda and Bernard could speak several languages. Whether or not Mr. Berenson had upper-class aspirations is not known, but Bernard did. He became the model for the other children, especially Senda. In 1884 Bernard left home to enter Harvard College in Cambridge, Massachusetts, and never again lived with his family. Although Bernard had a scholarship, Mr. Berenson grumbled about the expense of his son's education, but later spoke proudly of his achievements. Bernard invited Senda, then in her middle teens, to attend functions at Harvard where she saw a life very different from that she experienced in the West End.

Senda, frail throughout her childhood, never graduated from grammar school, but under Bernard's and possibly her father's direction, read widely and studied languages. She attended Girl's Latin School, but did not finish. After his graduation from Harvard in 1887, Bernard went to Europe under the sponsorship of several Boston philanthropists. He finally settled in Italy and became a renowned art critic. Senda's aim was to follow in her brother's footsteps. In her notes and writing in later years, Senda made many comments about "aiming high" and the importance of having a noble attitude toward life as a whole.[2] There is no evidence of such thoughts in her early years, but it is clear that, like Bernard, she wanted to leave the West End.

At twenty-one Senda was petite and attractive, with dark curly hair and clear green eyes. Possibly with the idea of preparing to become a piano teacher, she entered the Boston Conservatory of Music, but was unable to continue because of her health. At the suggestion of a friend she enrolled in the Boston Normal School of Gymnastics (BNSG) to improve her strength and vigor so that she could return to the conservatory.

When she entered BNSG in the fall of 1890 Senda Berenson's life changed dramatically. Founded just a year earlier and directed by Amy Morris Homans, the school was planned to prepare teachers of exercise (called gymnastics at that time). Homans demanded the best from her students and imbued them with a missionary zeal to go forth and improve the health of American women. She had assisted the wealthy Boston philanthropist, Mary Hemenway, in many of her endeavors, and chose to instill upper-class standards and behavior in her students. At first Berenson hated BNSG, but gradually, as her health improved, she became a believer in gymnastics and an ardent follower of Homans. At BNSG Berenson studied anatomy, physiology, hygiene, and pathology as well as Swedish gymnastics. Senda learned to feel at ease in the strange clothing required for gymnastics—long, dark woolen bloomers, long-sleeved blouse to match the bloomers, dark stockings, and flat-heeled soft shoes. When she returned for her second year, she found a greatly improved curriculum with courses taught by Harvard University and Harvard Medical School faculty.

Berenson's success at BNSG was apparent in January 1892 when Homans selected her to fill a vacancy at Smith College in Northampton, Massachusetts, created when their gymnastics teacher left due to illness. At Smith Berenson found herself in an atmosphere for which she had longed. Her colleagues were well educated and engaged in the pioneering effort of educating women. She could do her part in assisting the students to have optimum health. *And* she was away from Boston's West End and her father's tirades. Not only could she send money home to assist the family, but also she could live the life of an independent, professional woman. Senda Berenson had become a New Woman.

When Berenson arrived at Smith College in 1892 the college had just opened Alumnae Gymnasium, a wonder of the times, housing administrative offices, the latest Swedish gymnastic equipment in the gymnasium, dressing rooms, and a swimming pool. There was a tennis court for the students and many paths for walking on the college grounds.

Thoroughly grounded in Swedish gymnastics from BNSG, Berenson was well prepared to teach gymnastics. She determined to develop the best possible program in physical education based on her courses at BNSG and Homans' philosophy. Later, Berenson wrote, "when I went to Smith I had fixed ideals in my mind wh. [which] I prayed I cd. [could] be able to realize. . . . To make the aim of it the attainment of phys.

Senda Berenson, in 1891, just before her arrival at Smith College as gymnastics instructor. (Photo by Epler & Arnold, Saratoga, N.Y., used with permission of the Smith College Archives)

[physical] health and efficiency for the indiv. [individual] and to never lose sight of this fact."[3] Berenson became immediately popular and was described as looking "cute" in her gymnastics costume. Berenson had much to learn. She decided that it would be insulting to college women to take roll, but soon discovered that, while the enthusiastic students came to class, many of the less enthusiastic did not. She learned to take roll. From the beginning, Berenson made special efforts to interest the students who were weaker or had a history of ill health.

Beginnings of Basketball

Within a few weeks after her arrival at Smith, Berenson, the enthusiastic young instructor, accidentally transformed the world of women's sport. There is no evidence that she understood the magnitude of her "experiment" with the new game of basket ball (basketball was two words at that time). In 1892, some women, especially the New Woman with her zest for life, enjoyed a number of sports, but not "team sports" such as basket ball. They rode horses, hiked, rowed boats, swam, bicycled, bowled, fenced, shot archery, roller skated, ice skated, played golf, tennis, a form of baseball, and enjoyed informal games.

These sports, with the exception of tennis and baseball, tended to be largely individual sports in which the woman performed alone. While competitive events were possible in many of these sports, only tennis and baseball required opponents. In tennis singles one woman played against another and, in doubles, two players challenged two others. The players occupied separate, clearly defined spaces which largely controlled the play. In baseball one team was assigned positions on the field of play and the opposing team took turns at bat. At the most, four members of the batting team might be on the field at one time. Even on the field each woman ran between the bases in a prescribed pattern— to first, second, third, and then home.

Women did not play games with five or more players on a team and with both teams occupying the same space at the same time. The new game, basket ball, required just such a situation. In her notes Berenson writes that "Group games of any kind were unheard of—. . . I read in small mag [magazine] on phys. ed.[physical education] that the Spring[field] training school was publishing monthly an indoor game that was invented, as a class exercise by one of the men—called Basket Ball. . . . We no sooner tried it [in class] than we liked it. . . ."[4]

Men's Basket Ball

During the winter of 1891, James Naismith, a young instructor at the YMCA Training School at Springfield, Massachusetts, was assigned a task of finding an indoor sport for men. The result was basket ball. Naismith explained the principles on which he based his game: (1) the ball should be large and light; (2) there should be no running with the ball; (3) no man on either team should be restricted from getting the ball at any time that it is in play; (4) both teams were to occupy the same area, yet there was to be no personal contact; and (5) the goal should be horizontal and elevated.[5] Once he had established these principles, Naismith developed basket ball.

The new game was played by two teams of several men in a gymnasium free of apparatus. The first game had nine men on each team. The object was to score points by throwing the ball into the opponents' basket suspended some ten feet above the floor. Naismith's rules included throwing the ball in any direction with one or both hands; batting the ball in any direction with one or both hands, never with the fist; not running with the ball; and holding the ball in or between the hands and not using the arms for holding the ball. The game did not permit shouldering, holding, pushing, tripping, or hitting an opponent. The rules defined fouls, detailed officials' duties, and described the scoring. In the January 1892 issue of *The Triangle* Naismith described the game and listed the rules. There was an illustration with one man throwing a ball at a basket.[6]

Women's Basket Ball

After reading Naismith's article, Berenson wondered whether or not the new game would be a good activity for women. Could women play a game designed for men? Would such a game be too strenuous and too physically demanding for women? Would women be tainted if they played a man's game? Would she, Berenson, be accused of fostering traits that were unwomanly?

Firmly imbued with Homans' ideas of womanliness and not wishing to offend the Smith College administration or parents, Berenson faced the problem of creating a game that would be both womanly and vigorous. She had to prove that games like basket ball would not make women masculine. Berenson immediately disassociated the women's game from the men's game. She designed women's basket ball to avoid physical roughness, often associated with men's games such as football, lacrosse, and soccer. She solved the question of overtaxing the women physically by dividing the court into three equal sections and requiring players to stay in their assigned section. Thus, the players could not run all over the court and become exhausted. Later she justified the three-section court because it encouraged team play. To assure womanly play Berenson prohibited players from snatching or batting the ball from the hands of another player. To increase the pace of the game, players were not permitted to hold the ball for longer than three seconds and they could not bounce or dribble the ball more than three times. Berenson felt these changes prevented the women's game from being likened to the men's game. Within a short time after her arrival at Smith in January 1892, Berenson had created basket ball for women and introduced the game to the Smith students who liked the game immediately.

Naismith's account of the beginnings of basket ball for women differs. He recalled that, after the men at the YMCA Training School had been playing for about a month, women teachers from the Buckingham Grade School happened to be passing the gymnasium and stepped in to see why there was so much shouting. They saw men were playing basket ball. Later, with Naismith's permission, they tried the game and enjoyed it. Soon other women organized a second team, and then more women wanted to play. Naismith suggests that Berenson became interested in basket ball following a physical education meeting at Yale in 1893.[7] Berenson's notes show that she introduced basket ball for women in early 1892.

Berenson seemed undaunted in solving the problems she faced in introducing basket ball. She had to find an Association football or soccer ball and locate two peach baskets. She must have coaxed the building custodian to fasten the baskets in the proper place. The students had to learn to throw or pass the ball to their own teammates, try to prevent their opponents from catching the ball, and to throw the ball into the peach basket. First, Berenson taught the students tag and a game called "hanging cats" to develop speed and running.[8]

The new game spread quickly to other colleges, schools, YWCAs, and civic groups. One can imagine letters to students in other colleges and families and visits from nearby Mount Holyoke College students. Perhaps weekend guests from Wellesley College and Radcliffe near Boston saw the game and returned to their schools to start playing basket ball. Normal or teacher training institutions took up the game. Faculty members may have traveled to Smith to observe basket ball for women or written to Berenson to inquire about the game. By 1894 Berenson had begun to publish articles about basket ball for women.[9]

Just eleven months after Berenson introduced the game to Smith students, the first interinstitutional contest among women took place on November 18, 1892 between the University of California-Berkeley and Miss Head's School.[10] Mt. Holyoke College in Massachusetts and Sophie Newcomb College in Louisiana both played in 1893. Hundreds of women's teams all across the country played the new game by 1895.[11]

Writing in 1894 Berenson claimed that basket ball "combined both the physical development of gymnastics and the abandon and delight of true play" and that the game "requires the action of every part of the body, that develops physical courage, self-reliance, quickness, alertness; and no one who has ever seen it played can question the enthusiasm it arouses."[12] In the same year Edward Hitchcock, a leading physical educator from Amherst College, supported basket ball for women. "Basket Ball seems to be . . . a kind of complementary foot ball game for woman development. It requires hardihood, alertness, quick perception, and volition, without the excessive energies required for the men's game."[13]

Berenson saw basket ball as a game for the woman of the 1890s—a new game for the New Woman. She pointed out that basketball "came on at the right moment in the history of the development of games for women. One of the strong arguments in the economic world against giving women as high salaries as men for similar work is that women are more prone to illness than men. They need, therefore, all the more to develop health and endurance if they desire to become candidates for equal wages. . . . And how valuable a training it is which enables a woman to meet an unexpected situation, perhaps of danger, with alacrity and success."[14] Berenson also believed that women should have a thorough medical examination before being permitted to play basket ball.

Alice Bertha Foster, writing in 1895, agreed with Berenson that basket ball provided important lessons for the modern woman. She felt that girls should learn to compete. She theorized that boys were pushed forward, but girls were held back and denied the opportunities to learn

FRESHMAN-SOPHOMORE GAME AT SMITH COLLEGE, 1909 VS. 1908. PLAYED IN 1906.

qualities that they would need in the modern world. Basket ball taught women to make rapid decisions and to cooperate. Foster stressed that vigorous physical activity did not make women masculine.[15]

Intramural Competition

Based on other sports such as football and soccer, men's basket ball teams at YMCAs, colleges, and high schools regularly played teams from other Ys, colleges, and schools. Interinstitutional competition and intercollegiate athletics were integral to men's sport. Berenson, as well as other physical educators, scorned such play as unnecessary and hinting of professionalism. Berenson saw basket ball as a game which should foster the highest development of each woman. "The aim in athletics for women should above all things be health—physical health and moral health."[16] Sports should foster womanhood, which in the 1890s, even for the New Woman, included neither the rough and tumble activities of the football field nor intercollegiate athletics. What form of competition was appropriate for women?

Intramural competition was the answer. Despite the 1892 game in California and occasional contests throughout the country, games between classes in college or intramurals became the accepted form of competition for women. At Smith, the annual freshman-sophomore match became one of the most popular events of the college year and was reported in newspapers in Northampton and Springfield, Massachusetts. For the game on March 17, 1893 the students decorated the gymnasium in violet and yellow, the class colors, wore their class colors, and lustily sang their class songs.[17]

Lydia W. Kendall, class of 1895, described a game with the following enthusiastic words in her journal. "The balconies were filled with spectators and the cheering and shouting was something tremendous. The Freshman held one side, decorated with lavender in every shade and shape, while the opposite side was radiant in the brilliant green of '95. . . . when Miss Martin [student captain] received the white silk flag with the golden S the girls raised her on their shoulders and marched with her about the hall."[18]

Class members sang songs to familiar tunes to encourage their team and to intimidate the opponents. The following basket ball song used the familiar tune, "Way down upon the Swanee River."

Way down upon the College Campus,
Not far away;
There's where we play our Basket-Ball game
On an April day.

Chorus

Up and down the Freshmen hurry,
Doing nought at all:
While ninety-niners cheer their captain
Putting in the ball.

Sad will the Freshmen be at sunset,
As they homeward go;
Leaving the dear old green triumphant
Waving o'er every foe.

Chorus

Homes and centers, guards and captain,
See them winning all!
Cheer, class-mates, cheer our team forever
Champions at Basket-Ball.[19]

Governance of Basket Ball for Women

Most women modified the men's basket ball rules, but not necessarily in the same way. Berenson did not publish a list of the rules used at Smith, but in 1894 explained how she changed Naismith's rules to benefit women.[20] Clara Baer, who taught in Louisiana, named the game "Basquette" and patented her rules in 1895. These rules varied considerably from Berenson's.[21] Other women created their own rules as they saw fit.

By 1899 the problems generated by a lack of common rules became a concern at a conference held at the YMCA Training School in Springfield, Massachusetts. Bertha Alice Foster read a paper on women's basket ball which created much discussion after which a committee was appointed to study the problems of women's basket ball. Foster of Oberlin College was appointed chair of the committee. Other members were Ethel Perrin, Boston Normal School of Gymnastics; Elizabeth Wright, Radcliffe College; and Senda Berenson. During the conference the committee met and agreed on rules for women's basket ball. The new rules were read before the conference, discussed, and approved. The rules, together with articles dealing with the women's game, were to be published by Spalding's Athletic Library with Senda Berenson suggested as editor.[22]

Spalding's Athletic Library was an accepted source of rules for men's sports, including basket ball, and now became the publisher of rules for a woman's sport, basket ball. That a woman was chosen editor of such a project was a first in sport organizations. At that time seven national sport associations existed, at least six of which had women members in 1899, but no woman held an office or a position of power.[23] However, not only had women belonged to the American Association for the

Advancement of Physical Education (AAAPE) from its beginning in 1885 but also a woman, Helen C. Putnam, held the office of vice president. Berenson was a member of the AAAPE and in 1895 presided at the opening session of the annual meeting. By 1899 articles by women had appeared in several professional journals.

The 1899 conference at Springfield was held under the auspices of the YMCA Training School and the supervision of Luther Gulick. The conference focused on the physiology of exercise and the psychology of play. Gulick was an authority in physical education and a member of AAAPE. Because of his experience with women taking leadership roles in AAAPE, he may have believed that a committee of women was appropriate.

Berenson had published at least one article on basket ball and attended professional meetings such as the one held in Springfield. She appeared to assume her new leadership role with ease. She was re-

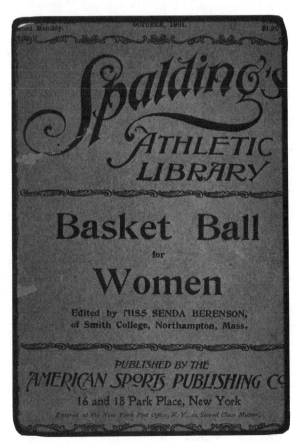

sponsible not only for editing the rules but also for obtaining articles on the subject of women's basket ball. From the beginning she sought well-qualified authors to write on a variety of subjects.

The first guide included an editorial by Berenson that reviewed the circumstances under which the committee was formed and the rules were determined, an article by Gulick on "Psychological Effects of Basket Ball for Women," and one by Theodore Hough on "Physiological Effects of Basket Ball for Women." Berenson also wrote an article, "Significance of Basket Ball for Women."[24] The guide concluded with the new "standard" rules of basket ball for women. From the beginning, each guide contained pictures of teams from many parts of the country, demonstrating the popularity of the game.

In his article, Gulick stresses the importance of teamwork, which he suggests is more difficult for girls to learn than boys. He theorizes that because women are entering a greater variety of occupations, they should learn teamwork and that basket ball teaches teamwork. "Loyalty to the team and the playing of team-work appears to me to be no mean factor in the development and expression of this quality upon which our civilization rests—the capacity for co-operation, the capacity for being willing to set aside a part even of one's own rights in order to win the larger benefits of co-operative endeavor." Hough justifies Berenson's modifications of the men's game for women on physiological bases. He believes that gymnastics is good for corrective work, but that basket ball is better training for the heart and respiratory apparatus. Berenson's article criticizes the undesirable elements of men's athletics and stresses the need for women to cultivate fair play and good sportsmanship in athletics. She emphasizes the need for the modern woman to cultivate physical and moral courage, and she also justifies the modifications of women's basket ball that protect women from the evils of men's athletics.

Published yearly, the Spalding guides became the standard source of basket ball rules and pertinent articles for women physical educators. During the years three issues emerged: (1) the necessity for playing the "official" rules for women; (2) the importance of women coaches for women's and girls' teams; and (3) the extent, if any, to which basket ball and athletics made women masculine. Berenson and her authors stressed that only the "official" rules should be used; that women should coach women's and girls' teams; and that basket ball, properly played, did not make women masculine, but rather contributed to the development of traits important to the New Woman. In the 1908–1909 guide Agnes Wayman wrote, "The athletic girl has come to stay. Athletics for women are no longer a fad but a well-recognized factor in the better development of women and, incidentally, of the race."[25] While Spalding's rules became widely used in schools and colleges, a variety of rules, including men's, continued to be played in many places.

In spite of the general enthusiasm for women's basket ball, there was an occasional objection. At a meeting of the Boston Physical Education Society Lucille Eaton Hill of Wellesley College spoke out against the dangers of unsupervised basket ball for younger girls. As evidence, she cited the injuries with which some Wellesley freshmen arrived. Women from Bryn Mawr College, Swarthmore College, the Philadelphia High School for Girls, and Drexel Institute spoke in favor of basket ball, but agreed that the game should be well supervised and not played at too young an age.[26]

Basket ball changed little during Berenson's years with the sport. For sixteen years she provided leadership in basket ball through editing the Spalding Athletic Library, writing articles, and, perhaps, speaking engagements. The rules committee established at the YMCA conference in 1899 continued as an entity until 1905. At that time an Executive Committee on Basket Ball Rules was formed under the auspices of the American Physical Education Association with Berenson as editor of the rule book.

Life at Smith

Basket ball was not Berenson's only interest at Smith. She took great pride in the development of the physical education program. She remained an enthusiastic follower of Amy Morris Homans and, as she added to her faculty, hired only BNSG graduates. When she arrived in 1892, Berenson was the sole member of her department. By 1899–1900 she had three assistants, including her sister, Bessie, who completed the work at BNSG in 1899. Berenson's goals included health, vitality, and efficiency for each student. She saw physical education as ethical, mental, and moral forces in her students' lives. Remembering her own childhood as a frail child, she made special efforts to assist weak students. In spite of her growing interest in sports, she considered Swedish gymnastics the most important part of her program because she believed that it was essential for the health and well-being of the students. Berenson added sports to her program and invited field hockey enthusiast Constance M.K. Applebee to visit Smith and introduce the game to the students. A new outdoor facility, Allen Field, opened in 1906. At the field day held that year, all classes competed in basket ball, field hockey, tennis, cricket, volleyball, archery, clock golf, and croquet.[27]

Berenson's salary of $1,000 in 1892 was better than the salaries of ministers and high school teachers of the period. Smith raised her periodically and in 1897 she made $1,200 which permitted her to assist her family, to buy pretty clothes, and to make frequent trips to Italy to see

Bernard and travel to other countries in Europe. She first visited Bernard in the summer of 1892 on a two-month tour with Mary Jordan of the Smith faculty. In 1894 Bernard made one of his rare trips to the United States and visited Senda in Northampton. Senda and Bernard maintained their close relationship through a constant exchange of letters.

In 1897, after a summer of study at the Royal Central Institute of Gymnastics in Stockholm, Berenson was awarded a certificate for the completion of her work at BNSG. Interestingly, she is listed with the class of 1892, with which she entered. In 1910 Berenson was among the small group of women whom Homans invited to Wellesley College to explore the possibility of forming a professional association of women in physical education. She seemed to like life as a single, professional woman in a community of other single, professional women. Berenson also enjoyed the company of men and turned down at least one proposal of marriage. She became increasingly sophisticated, which pleased Bernard.

Together with others from the Smith College faculty, Berenson belonged to the Frivol Club devoted to frivolity. Club members met to cook their supper in a nearby cabin, sing, and enjoy the evening. Among the members was Herbert Abbott, witty and soft spoken, a member of the English language and literature department, who had come to Smith in 1905. Berenson and Abbott developed a close relationship and were married on January 15, 1911. Berenson resigned from Smith College after nineteen years and set up housekeeping in Northampton. She taught a few hours each week at the Burnham school in Northampton and continued her responsibilities as editor of the basket ball rule book.

In 1916 the National Council of the American Physical Education Association found sufficient interest in women's athletics to appoint committees to oversee not only basket ball, but also field hockey, track and field, and swimming. Berenson Abbott resigned as editor of the basket ball guide, asking that others assume the responsibilities. Recognizing Berenson Abbott's many important contributions to basket ball from the time of the first guide in 1901, the new committee persuaded her to continue as chair of the basket ball committee for one year. The responsibility of editing the rules and the guide was assigned to a sub-committee chaired by Helen M. McKinstry.[28] After 1917, Berenson Abbott accepted no further responsibilities with basket ball.

The Abbotts frequently traveled to Italy to visit Bernard and enjoyed life in Northampton. Herbert Abbott's health failed and eventually he resigned his position at Smith due to ill health. After her husband died in 1929, Berenson Abbott lived in Northampton for a few years. In 1934 she moved to California to be with her sister, Bessie. That same year the Alumnae Association of Smith College made Senda Berenson Abbott an honorary member. The sisters enjoyed the California sunshine, traveled to Italy to be with Bernard, and also visited in Northampton. Berenson Abbott was among fourteen outstanding alumna of BNSG recognized at the 1952 Wellesley College symposium on "Physical Education for Women in Modern Times."[29]

In 1985 Senda Berenson Abbott became the first woman to be inducted into the Basketball Hall of Fame in Springfield, Massachusetts. Dorothy Ainsworth, former director of physical education of Smith College, first nominated Berenson Abbott on February 2, 1972. Several faculty members sent supporting letters. At that time there were no women in the Hall of Fame and basketball was not yet an Olympic sport. In the early 1980s, as women's basketball became increasingly popular, several persons nominated Senda Berenson Abbott to be the first woman inducted into the Hall of Fame. The Enshrinement Program called her "A petite, five-foot pioneer who organized the first women's game in March, 1893, . . . the "Mother of Women's Basketball."[30]

New Woman: New Sport

Basket ball appeared to open the door for other team sports. During the period from 1892 to 1917 when Berenson was closely associated with basket ball, women across the country participated in an increasing variety of sports in colleges, schools, private clubs, public parks, and other rural and urban settings. Women's athletic clubs flourished in a number of cities such as New York, Chicago, New Orleans, Los Angeles, and Brooklyn. Colleges and schools built gymnasiums, athletic fields, tennis courts, and other sport facilities. Although Goucher College played field hockey in 1897, Applebee is credited with the development of field hockey in the United States, beginning in 1901. Students enjoyed cricket, baseball, volleyball, and lacrosse. They also participated in golf, rowing, bowling, swimming, archery, and other sports. Although a few colleges held intercollegiate contests, most conducted intramural competition, shunning intercollegiate athletics as suggesting professionalism, being too much like men's athletics, and focusing attention on a few women rather than many women. In high schools, however, basket ball could be found in private schools and, frequently, in small rural towns.

Senda Berenson Abbott would not recognize basketball for women today. The three-section court gave way to two sections in 1938 and, in 1971, women officially played the full court with teams of five. The ball, at first an Association football or soccer ball, then a larger women's ball, in 1982 was made smaller, similar to the size of the ball in Berenson's day. Today, women move more quickly and with more speed

The three court game players are ready for action, starting with a center jump.

than young Senda Berenson could ever imagine. They dribble and dart over the floor with amazing speed and shoot baskets with astonishing accuracy. Basketball is the fastest growing sport for girls and women. Interscholastic and intercollegiate basketball are considered essential for good sport programs. College women now play for a national championship. International play increased until women's basketball became an Olympic sport in 1976.

People who knew Berenson Abbott in her later years say that one would never know that she ever had any interest in sport or basketball. But, at 23 years of age the attractive, petite young Senda Berenson who had been Senda Valvrojenski from Russia, transformed women's sport when she modified Naismith's basket ball game for men to basket ball for women. At a time when women ordinarily did not hold leadership positions in sport she edited and published the rules of basket ball. She also published articles on her new sport. For twenty-five years she held leadership positions in women's sport.

Berenson knew she was a pioneer in sport and physical education. She wrote that "a great deal of what we did was pioneer work. . . . [We] had to feel our way and introduce our theory."[31] She had definite theories. Gymnastics led to better health and efficiency. Basket ball for women should be different from basket ball for men. Basket ball, a new sport, provided women with the physical and moral qualities demanded for the New Woman. In the 1890s Senda Berenson, a New Woman, established a new sport for women.

Notes

1. Nancy Woloch, *Women and the American Experience* (New York: Alfred A. Knopf, 1984), 270.

2. "Speeches—Notes," Berenson Papers, Smith College Archives, Northampton, Mass.

3. Ibid.

4. Ibid.

5. James Naismith, *Basketball: Its Origins and Development* (New York: Association Press, 1941), 62.

6. James Naismith, "Basket Ball," *The Triangle* 10 (January 1892): 145–147.

7. Naismith, *Basketball*, 161–163.

8. Senda Berenson, "Basket Ball for Women," *Physical Education* 3 (September 1894): 107.

9. Ibid., 106–109.

10. Roberta J. Park, "History and Structure of the Department of Physical Education at the University of California with Special Reference to Women's Sports," (unpublished paper, 1976), 5.

11. Virginia L. Evans, "The Formative Years of Women's College Basketball in Five Selected Colleges 1880–1917" (Master's thesis, University of Maryland, 1971), 59.

12. Berenson, "Basket Ball for Women," 106.

13. Edward Hitchcock, "Basket Ball for Women," *Physical Education* 3 (August 1894): 100.

14. "Speeches—Notes," Berenson Papers.

15. Alice Bertha Foster, "Basket Ball for Women," *Physical Education* 4 (August 1895): 75–77.

16. "Speeches—Notes," Berenson Papers.

17. Florence Smith, "Basket-Ball Game," *Smith College Monthly* 1 (November 1893): 36–37.

18. Lydia W. Kendall, "Journal," Class of 1895 Records, Smith College Archives, Northampton, Mass.

19. "Class Song," Basketball File, Smith College Archives, Northampton, Mass.

20. Berenson, "Basket Ball for Women."

21. Joan Paul, "Clara Gregory Baer: Harbinger of Southern Physical Education," *Research Quarterly for Exercise and Sport* (Centennial Issue, 1985): 48. See also chapter on Baer in this volume.

22. Senda Berenson, ed., *Basket Ball for Women* (New York: American Sports Publishing Co., 1901), 6, 7.

23. Ellen W. Gerber et al., *The American Woman in Sport* (Reading, Mass.: Addison-Wesley, 1974), 44; Virginia L. Evans, "The Status of the American Woman in Sport, 1912–1932" (Ph.D. diss., University of Massachusetts, 1982), 201.

24. Berenson, ed., *Basket Ball for Women*, 1901, 6, 19, 21–29, 31–45.

25. Agnes R. Wayman, "Hints Along General Lines," in *Spalding's Official Basket Ball Guide*, ed. Senda Berenson (New York: American Sports Publishing Co., 1908), 59.

26. History: Newspaper Clippings 1893–1977, 3L Department of Hygiene and Physical Education, Wellesley College Archives, Wellesley College, Mass.

27. Berenson, "Speeches—Notes."

28. "Editorial Comment," in *Spalding's Official Basket Ball Guide*, ed. Helen M. McKinstry (New York: American Sports Publishing Co., 1917–18), 6.

29. Alumnae Association: "Physical Education for Women in Modern Times: Report of a Symposium held at Wellesley College June 26, 27, 28, 1952," 3L, Wellesley College Archives. In 1909 the Boston Normal School of Gymnastics affiliated with Wellesley College.

30. "18th Annual Enshrinement Dinner," Archives, Basketball Hall of Fame, Springfield, Mass.

31. Berenson, "Speeches—Notes."

3

Clara Gregory Baer
Catalyst for Women's Basketball

Joan Paul

On the evening of March 13, 1895, 560 of the most fashionable women of the city gathered at the Southern Athletic Club in New Orleans to witness the first publicly played basketball game in the South. Sixty young women belonging to the ladies' physical culture classes, initiated and taught by Clara Gregory Baer of Sophie Newcomb College, marched out before their audience dressed in blue bloomers and blue with white trimmed blouses, the colors of the Southern Athletic Club. Baer had them perform synchronized Swedish gymnastic routines to begin the evening's festivities. Then, two teams of eleven players each took positions on a floor divided into a court of eleven squares, with a player from each team occupying one of the spaces. This was the main event of the evening, a demonstration of the new game, "basket ball." Each player had a white or blue sash "artistically draped" around the waist of her gymnasium costume for team identity.

This strange game probably appeared even stranger to the all-female audience, which had no prior knowledge of the game of basketball or its rules and was seeing its first team sport played between women contestants. When the game ended, hair pins and handkerchiefs littered the floor. Because the rules disallowed a player leaving her "base," one viewer later described the game as "something like baseball." With 560 out of 600 invited women attending the performance and the reception which followed, the newspapers reported the occasion as representative of the most fashionable social element in New Orleans, and the night was termed a huge success.[1]

For basketball to first be played and viewed by women rather than men in a geographic area as conservative as the South is surprising. The woman who was responsible for this notable event was diminutive in stature, but gargantuan in her accomplishments for women in sport and physical education. Many of her pioneer achievements have been overlooked by sport and physical education historians, including the facts that she wrote and published the first rules of basketball for women, was responsible for the game's introduction to the South, and for continuing to promote the sport for decades. Clara Gregory Baer was educated primarily in the upper-south and the northeast, and perhaps because of this she was less inculturated to the smothering domesticity that permeated the lives of most middle- and upper-class Southern women, keeping them away from the playing fields. She was the quintessential champion of the Southern woman in sport and exercise from the early 1890s until her death in 1938.[2]

Baer's Early Life

Clara Baer was born on August 27, 1863 in Algiers, Louisiana to Hamilton John Baer, a broker/flour merchant, and his wife, Ellen Douglas Riley, daughter of a well known ante bellum steam boat captain.[3] There were a number of factors that probably influenced John Baer's decision to send his daughter, Clara, to Louisville, Kentucky to attend high school. Algiers was an isolated island in the nineteenth century, lying just across the Mississippi River from New Orleans, where access to the city could only be gained by boat as there were no bridges. When Clara was born, the city of New Orleans lay under Union siege and had since April 28, 1862.[4] Baer's mother died when Clara was only four years old, so her maternal grandmother, Margaret Riley, moved from Woodville, Mississippi to Algiers to live with John Baer and his family to care for Clara, her sister, and two brothers.[5]

The era from 1865 to 1877, generally referred to as the Period of Reconstruction, was a difficult time for the South politically, economically, and educationally. Reconstruction was not a very accurate title for this time as little rebuilding was occurring; it simply notes when there was military occupation of the South by federal troops. The state and local governments were unstable, most crops in this agricultural land could not be sold nor did banks have money to lend, and educational opportunities were limited as well as poor. Only 21 percent of the New Orleans children attended school in 1870, and as late as 1877 only 20 percent of the children in the entire state of Louisiana were enrolled in schools. Although the state legislature passed a compulsory school attendance law that year, it was never enforced, and there were no public high schools in Louisiana until the 1880s.[6]

Education

Because of these circumstances Clara Baer was sent to live with relatives and attend high school in Louisville, Kentucky.[7] After high school Baer went to Boston in the late 1880s to further her education. She studied under S. S. Curry at the Boston School of Expression, under Charles Emerson of the Emerson School of Oratory, and then in 1890 she became a student of Nils Posse.[8] Posse had directed the Boston Normal School of Gymnastics the year before beginning his own school, and it was with Posse that she specifically found her life's calling. Baer had planned to be a teacher of expression, but after reading an advertisement about the Posse School, the new subject of "physical education" became her total focus for the next 38 years.[9]

Physical Education Career

Turning down a regular faculty appointment to teach Swedish gymnastics at the Boston School of Oratory where she had taught in the summer of 1891, Baer opted to return to New Orleans and the challenge of creating a department of physical culture at the newly established H. Sophie Newcomb Memorial College.[10] Sophie Newcomb College, opened in 1887, was an affiliate of Tulane University and the first degree-granting coordinate college in the country.[11]

On October 1, 1891 Clara Baer became instructor of physical culture at Sophie Newcomb at a yearly salary of $1,600. By her second year she was given the title of director of physical education and her salary was increased to $2,400.[12] Baer began the first certification programs in physical education in Louisiana and the South in 1893-94 and instituted the first four-year program in physical education leading to a bachelor's degree in 1907.[13] This program was fourteen years prior to the physical education major created by Alfred D. Browne at Peabody College in Nashville, Tennessee, that is often credited with being the first major program in the South.[14]

Physical education was not only a novelty in the South in the 1890s, but controversial, as many students and their parents felt that strenuous exercise for women was not socially appropriate nor healthy. Clara Baer had to have great tact and courage to develop a department of physical education for women in a community such as the New Orleans of 1891.[15] The young women who attended Newcomb College in the 1890s were often driven to the college in carriages, accompanied by their "mammy nurses" who waited outside while they attended classes.[16]

When Baer introduced the bloomer suit as required gymnastic class attire in 1894, the young women who came to class in long dresses, bustles, hats, gloves, and heels balked at this perceived immodesty. For three years Baer had led her students in gymnastic drills and had them play games in their long voluminous skirts and shirt waists with tight, form-fitting corsets worn beneath. It was only after the students were exercised more strenuously in the warm and humid climate of New Orleans that Baer was able to "sweat off" the corsets from beneath the bloomers.[17]

Baer was an energetic crusader for physical education. Besides teaching at Newcomb College, she spent her winter evenings and her summer vacations during the 1890s in the promotion of physical education. She taught gymnastics to the more elite women of New Orleans at the exclusive, all-male Southern Athletic Club, which allowed the wives, sisters, and daughters of its members to attend Baer's classes there one evening a week.[18] Two other nights a week Baer taught her gymnastics and games at the Sophie Newcomb gymnasium to the city's working women, primarily stenographers, store clerks, and public school teachers.[19] Baer taught three summers in the Louisiana Chautauqua at Ruston,[20] one summer at the Summer School of Methods in Waynesville, North Carolina,[21] and for several week during seven summers she taught in educational institutes in small towns throughout the state.[22] From 1898 through 1910 Baer taught in and directed the Monteagle Summer School for Higher Physical Culture in the Cumberland Mountains of Tennessee. Teachers throughout the South as well as from other geographic regions attended this school in the summers, and this extended Baer's sphere of influence.[23]

Professional Contributions

Clara Baer was active in professional physical education organizations, served as officer and filled responsible committee roles, gave lectures at state and national conventions, published in professional journals, and was a force in shaping physical education at the local, state, regional, and national levels. She was instrumental in getting a compulsory physical education law passed in 1894, making Louisiana the second state in the nation behind Ohio (1892) to have such a law.[24] Baer was the first Southern physical educator known to apply the science of anthropometry to physical education, the first to gain the rank of full professor (1899), the first to teach adapted or remedial exercises,[25] the first to write a physical education text,[26] the first and perhaps only one to invent a popular game and revolutionize another to make it appropriate for women, and the first to develop certification and a major's degree program in physical education. These accomplishments are of the magnitude to give her permanent stature as a truly outstanding leader in the early development of physical education.[27]

Basketball at Newcomb College

Basketball, the only major sport to develop from a physical education need, was invented by James Naismith at Springfield College in December 1891. By the fall of 1892 the women at Smith College had begun playing the game under the leadership of Senda Berenson.[28] In 1893 baseketball was introduced to Sophie Newcomb College and to the South by Clara Gregory Baer.[29] The Newcomb version of basketball quickly spread throughout the state of Louisiana.

Baer published the first basketball rules for women in 1895,[30] the same year she publicly introduced the game of basketball to the city of New Orleans. Before publishing her rules Baer contacted Naismith, inventor of the original game, to solicit his approval and permission for the many changes she had made. Naismith thought her modifications were so numerous that he suggested she consider having them printed with a different title. Baer did publish her game under the name "Basquette,"[31] appropriate because of southern Louisiana's French culture and the feminine connotation of the name.

For almost a decade Baer's students in the outdoor classes at Newcomb College played basketball in their long skirts. Baer favored the out-of-doors for her "girls," but it was considered daring to wear the bloomer suit indoors, much less out in public. It was around 1902 before classes were taken outside for games or exercises in their bloomers.[32] Basketball and Newcomb Ball were probably most responsible for the Sophie Newcomb women accepting bloomers as soon as they did. These games could be played and enjoyed so much more freely and comfortably in the bloomers rather than in their long, voluminous skirts, high-necked and long-sleeved shirtwaists, with corsets worn underneath.

Baer's strong advocacy for physical education focused on hygienic objectives, but she saw health in the broadest sense as including mental, spiritual, and emotional aspects as well as physical. She believed exercise was important for women as well as men, and that it was necessary in achieving total well-being. Baer also believed that exercise was much more effective when it was experienced in an enjoyable manner.

Nineteenth century physical education was primarily composed of formal Swedish and German gymnastics; synchronized wand, dumbbell, and Indian club drills; marching; calisthenics; and the taking of anthropometric measurements. Sports and games, although played by school boys and college men since early in the century, were looked upon more as extracurricular activities than as academic endeavors. The women physical educators were the first to make sport a regular part of their education curriculum. More of the male physical educators emphasized varsity sports, but they were slower to merge them with class work.

Perhaps Baer saw basketball as a sport that would help entice the young upper-class women students of Newcomb College, who generally showed an aversion to exercise, into becoming more willing participants of physical education activities. When she first introduced the game to her students in 1893, she found that the rules were too strenuous and allowed for entirely too much roughness for women. After a few trials with the men's rules and objections from parents and physicians became numerous, she decided the game would have to be modified or abandoned. Most of her students were delicate, unaccustomed to exercise, and found any type of strenuous activity distasteful.[33] In spite of its early failure, Baer saw possibilities in the game of basketball if it could be modified to more readily meet the needs of women. She decided this could and should be done, and in January 1894, she modified the game.[34]

"Victorianizing" the Game

The first elements that Baer removed from the game were features that caused overexertion or led to what she called "nervous fatigue".[35] To prevent too much running, Baer divided the court into many sections. Although Naismith, John Betts, and others credit Baer with the three-division court, she never used less than seven divisions in her regulation games.[36] She did suggest in 1911 that practice games could be played on a court with five divisions if there were no more than ten players involved. In Baer's first modification of basketball, she divided the court into eight and eleven squares, and the floor divisions used depended upon whether sixteen or twenty-two girls played at once.[37] One player per team occupied each square, and this limited running to no more than a few steps. Jay Seaver, when president of the New York Chautauqua School of Physical Education, wrote Baer to express his approval of her rules for women's basketball. He stated that her use of the multiple sectioned court was "rational and helpful in developing the game for girls." He went on to mention that allowing girls to move only when the ball was in the air cultivated rapid thinking and made passing more important than continual running.[38]

To further ensure that the young women were not overactive within their limited playing area, which at the largest in 1895 was no more than a 23' × 25' space and could be as small as 8' × 12', Baer disallowed any running except when the ball was in the air. When she went to the seven division court in 1908, the centers area was expanded to 16' × 46', the forward and backward guard spaces to 30' × 23', and the goal area 12' × 12'. She also instituted a rule that gave a player six seconds, later reduced to four, to aim at the goal without interference from anywhere on the court before shooting.[39]

Clara Baer, whose rules for *Basquette* were first published in 1895, popularized basketball for women in the South during the game's first decades. (From a newspaper drawing)

The second objective in Baer's modification of basketball was to change all rules that resulted in rough play. To do this she eliminated dribbling, disallowed all guarding or attempts to interfere with an opponent's pass or shot for the goal, and made falling down a foul. By limiting the floor space and allowing no more than two players to occupy an area, collisions were practically eliminated.

Next Baer felt she should introduce features into the game that were uniquely suitable for women and would reinforce values held dear by women and men. When Baer had gone to Newcomb in 1891 to create the department of physical education, the college president, Brandt V. B. Dixon, received many letters of protest from parents supported by physicians that claimed young ladies would be made coarse and unfeminine or their health could be harmed by unladylike exercises.[40] Baer was well aware of the potential upheaval the game could cause if it did not comform to the Victorian concepts revered by Southerners. Women were expected to be nonaggressive, gentle, poised, quiet rather than boisterous, and always mannerly and ladylike. They were never expected to be too competitive, act proud or haughty, or glory in physical prowess to the demise of more gentile qualities.

For these special needs, Baer put in rules that called for goals to be changed after every score, which reversed the offensive and defensive duties of the players, countering the possibility that one player could become a "star." Baer used "running" centers rather than "jumping" centers so height would not be a factor in the game.[41] She disallowed any yelling or talking by players during a game, and even made audible signals a foul. If a player aimed for the goal and then did not shoot, this also constituted a foul. One wonders if Baer was trying to cultivate decisiveness on the part of the players with this rule since women had the reputation of being fickle and changeable and were thought to find it difficult if not impossible to make up their minds.

Two decades after Baer published the first basketball rules for women, she stated that her rules developed along original lines because Newcomb College was so far from other women's colleges.[42] Certainly her rules published in 1895 under the name "Basquette" were distinctive, and many of the more unusual aspects of her game were intact through their final revision in 1914.

Invention of Newcomb

The introduction of basketball to the Newcomb College students provided the stimulus for Baer to invent a game of her own. While waiting for goals to be delivered so basketball could be played with standard equipment, Clara Baer devised a lead-up or practice game for basketball which she called "Newcomb." It was a game that could be played in a smaller area than basketball, could accommodate almost any number of students, and required only a rope, a ball, and three division lines marked on the floor.[43] The purpose of the game was to teach throwing and catching, which were the most basic skills used in Baer's game of basketball. Points were scored by throwing the ball in the opponent's court where it could not be caught by a player. The game of Newcomb provided for a change of routine, was recreational, was lively enough to provide exercise, and was pleasurable to the students.

Newcomb ball was so simple and fun that it quickly spread to schools and playgrounds. It even became a varsity sport for males and females in the public schools and colleges of Louisiana, and then spread to all parts of the country by the end of the first decade of the twentieth century. Some of the states fielding varsity teams between 1900 and 1914 besides Louisiana were Oklahoma, Ohio, Michigan, Texas, Massachusetts, Tennessee, New York, Mississippi, and Missouri.[44] When Baer published her first set of basketball rules in 1895, she patented and published rules for Newcomb at the same time. This game continues to be described in modern elementary physical education texts and game books and is still played by children in America's parks and playgrounds.

Values of Basketball: 1895-1922

Basketball was being played by women in almost every part of the country by 1895. The rules used were dependent upon the school or college where it was played, and the games ranged from using men's regulation rules to extreme modification.[45] Wherever the game was introduced, it seems to have quickly gained popularity with the students. The women's colleges were the leaders in the promotion of the game, and most of the schools in the South and East appeared to hold similar philosophical views regarding the game's purpose and significance. Where Western colleges were more inclined to accept intercollegiate play, the Eastern and Southern women's schools were opposed to highly competitive contests.[46] The schools in these more conservative areas saw basketball as a means to an end rather than as an end in itself. The leading women's colleges playing basketball in the 1890s were Smith, Vassar, Wellesley, Bryn Mawr, and Sophie Newcomb.

Some of the major views of the game as seen by the early physical education directors in these elitist schools were that (1) basketball was a worthwhile game because it combined pleasure with exercise,[47] (2) basketball was important to women's symmetrical development rather than for training athletes,[48] (3) it helped to develop better physiques and greater strength and endurance,[49] (4) the game promoted cooperation among players, (5) the game had educational and health related benefits, and (6) it was thought to teach personal esthetics to the players.[50] Women who played basketball were said to develop "quick perception and judgment" and "physical and moral courage, self-reliance and self-control, that ability to meet success and defeat with dignity."[51] Baer thought the game caused women to think while helping them develop gracefulness.[52]

There was also some concern about possible negative outcomes to women who played basketball. Berenson warned that women should always be on guard to not allow the excitement of the game coupled with the desire to win make them "do sadly unwomanly things."[53] Baer was attentive to these things, but another of her worries was for a player to appear concerned with "star" status. To prevent such undesirable attitudes, Baer made her rules to counteract this problem and specifically had this thought in mind as she formulated her rules.[54]

Newcomb College Basket Ball's Distinctiveness

Clara Baer published revisions of her rules in 1908, 1911, and 1914 under the title *Newcomb College Basket Ball Rules*, dropping the title "Basquette" with the second publishing. The rules now advocated only seven court divisions rather than the eight to eleven used in 1895. Her court divisions always matched the number of players per team. From 1908 until 1922 when Newcomb College moved to Spalding rules, Baer advocated seven players per team. Other than a change in court divisions, her rules remained fairly consistent throughout the quarter of a century of their use.

The distinctive features of Baer's rules contrasted with other rules used for women around the country were (1) the running centers, (2) changing baskets after each goal, (3) not stopping the game for fouls, (4) the elimination of "guarding" and "dribbling," (5) using no backboards on the baskets, (6) allowing only one-handed shooting and passing,[55] (7) the manner of scoring,[56] (8) allowing no movement on the court except when the ball was in the air, (9) declaring falling down a foul, (10) allowing no talking or audible signals during the game, and (11) the many divisions of the court.[57]

Baer believed that her rules calling for a seven-division court provided near equal opportunities for both strong and weak players. The strongest players were centers and the weakest were put at "goal." Since the game was not stopped for fouls, the scorers marked all fouls as they occurred. At the end of each half, the fouls were canceled out with the team having the fewer fouls receiving one point for each of the opponent's excessive fouls.

The one-handed push shot required by Baer's rules introduced this major shooting technique years before it became popular and was recognized as the most scientifically accepted method.[58] The mandatory

BASQUETTE.
Diagram of the Floor for Twenty-two Players.
11.

{ B } Forward Goal		
Left Forward	Forward Center	Right Forward
Left Center	Center	Right Center
Left Back	Back Center	Right Back
	Backward Goal { B }	

Left, one of the floor diagrams from *Basquette*, published in 1895. Baer's multiple sectioned court was designed to avoid overexertion and what she called "nervous fatigue." Right, illustration of a double throw for basket, which compressed the chest and was therefore labeled a foul. Far right, a jump for basket, illustrating "perfect poise." (Both photos from the 1911 edition of *Newcomb College Basket Ball Guide*) one-hand push shot, except from center, was to secure "a more upright and graceful position, put the ball in line of vision," and secure freer respiration.[59] The two-handed pass or throw was made a foul because it was said to cause the shoulders to be forwardly inclined, with "consequent flattening of the chest."[60]

Women's basketball grew rapidly in the South, but it followed a pattern consistent with the social and cultural mores of the region. Sport for women in the South was looked upon more favorably when it was viewed as contributing to good health or as reinforcing social expectations. Clara Baer, as well as most other Southern leaders prior to the mid-1920s, never advocated interscholastic or intercollegiate sport for women. The major basketball contests for the year at Newcomb College were games between the freshmen and the sophomore classes and the alumnae game each spring between the graduates and the "varsity" basketball team. The "varsity" team was composed of the best players in the college, or what later was called the "all-star" team.

These special basketball games were turned into gala affairs at Sophie Newcomb College and became classic events. The alumnae game was considered the height of the athletic season. Hundreds of the alumnae, who were now society matrons, debutantes, teachers, and young business women, returned to either play or spectate and cheer. It was claimed that the Louisiana State University-Tulane football squads had nothing on the Newcomb cheers, as the society matrons dropped their dignity in the heat of the struggle to join in the boisterous rooting.[61] Although the women students and graduates of Newcomb College loudly and

enthusiastically cheered their teams, Baer's rules always disallowed verbal signals or talking by players during the game. J. E. Lombard, who became Louisiana's first state director of physical education in 1918,[62] wrote in 1910 that he believed, too, there should be no talking during a game between members of a team unless it was a quiet conversation during time out. He also felt that clapping by players made the game less scientific than when silent signals were used.[63]

By the second decade of the twentieth century, most of the Southern schools, both secondary schools and colleges even in Baer's state of Louisiana, had adopted the "official" Spalding rules for basketball. However, Baer was still recognized and credited with blazing the path for the spread of basketball among women in the South and Southwest.[64]

Conclusion

In the spring of 1929, Clara Gregory Baer retired from Sophie Newcomb College with the title of professor emeritus, after spending 38 years as head of the Department of Physical Education, which she had created.[65] Clara Baer had made a significant impact on the growth of physical education and women's basketball in the South that also had repercussions across the country.

Only recently has Baer received the historical credit for publishing the first rules on women's basketball.[66] By introducing the game of basketball to every little hamlet across Louisiana in the state's Chautauqua and institute programs, teaching the game to all of the teachers attending the Monteagle, Tennessee Summer School of Physical Culture for twelve years, spreading the game through her major students and gymnastic clubs, and by publishing rules for women several years before any others were in print, Baer was a prime catalyst, perhaps second to none, in the sport's early growth and development. Certainly Clara Gregory Baer deserves much recognition and belated accolades for the important pioneer role she played in the promotion and acceptance of basketball for girls and women.

Notes

1. "Fair Women Make Fair Athletes," *The Daily Picayune* (New Orleans), 14 March 1895, 3.

2. As a child Baer was thought to be tubercular, so she was encouraged to play "tomboyish" games in the outdoors. See Charles L. Richards, "Likes Short Skirts and Bobbed Hair," unidentified newspaper clipping (1929), in Sophie Newcomb Physical Education Department Scrapbook. On January 19, 1938, in

the middle of her seventy-fifth year, Clara Baer died of an apparent heart attack. For accounts of her death, see "Pay Tribute to Gym Founder," *The New Orleans Item*, 20 January 1938, in Louisiana Collection, Special Collections Division, Tulane University Library; "Retired Newcomb College Teacher Fatally Stricken: Miss Clara G. Baer, Physical Education Pioneer Succumbs," *The Times-Picayune*, nd, supplied by New Orleans Public Library; "Retired Newcomb College Teacher Fatally Stricken," *The Times-Picayune*, 20 January 1938, 2.

3. Jane Hemenway (Bolingbrook, Illinois), letter to author, 4 November 1983; "Interesting Career of Late Mrs. Margaret A. Riley," *The Times Democrat* (New Orleans), 11 August 1904.

4. Edwin Adams Davis, *Louisiana: The Pelican State*, 4th ed. (Baton Rouge: Louisiana State University Press, 1975). In the Hemenway letter, it was stated that H.J. Baer nicknamed his daughter "Dixie." This may have been in defiance of the situation into which she had been born. Baer's nieces and nephews called her "Aunt Dixie" all of their lives.

5. "Interesting Career of Late Mrs. Margaret A. Riley." Two children, a boy and a girl had died in childhood; see Hemenway, 1983.

6. Even in the 1890s most often it was only the well-to-do children in Louisiana who received a secondary education. Davis, *Louisiana: The Pelican State*; "Biennial Report of the State Superintendent of Public Education to the General Assembly, 1892–1893," *The Advocate, Official Journal of the State of Louisiana* (Baton Rouge, 1894), 41–45; C.A. Ives, "As I Remember," in *Bureau of Educational Materials and Research* (Baton Route, 1964), 105–108, Louisiana Department of Educational Research Library.

7. Clara G. Baer, letter to Robert Sharp, president of Tulane University (New Orleans), 5 February 1916; "Retired Newcomb College Teacher Fatally Stricken."

8. Ruth Marshall, reference librarian, Boston Public Library, letter to author, 29 October 1983.

9. For a more definitive review of Baer's work in physical education, see Joan Paul, "Clara Gregory Baer: Harbinger of Southern Physical Education," *Research Quarterly for Exercise & Sport* (Centennial Issue, April 1985): 46–55.

10. Baer, letter to Sharp.

11. Radcliffe was founded in 1879, eight years prior to Newcomb, but was not chartered and empowered to grant degrees until 1894. See John P. Dyer, *Tulane: The Biography of a University, 1834–1965* (New York: Harper and Row, 1966). See also *Tulane University Catalogue: 1888–89* for complete history of Newcomb's founding.

12. "Information Card," Baer File, Tulane Archives.

13. This was the first such program in physical education in the South until after World War I.

14. Anna Ley Ingraham, professor, Department of Teaching and Learning, George Peabody College/Vanderbilt University, letter to author, 9 September 1983.

15. Dean Pierce Butler, letter to the Carnegie Foundations, 27 January 1938, Baer File, Tulane University Archives.

16. Marie Louise Tobin, "Newcomb Reviews Half a Century," *The Times Picayune* (New Orleans), 11 October 1936, Louisiana State University Archives, Baton Rouge.

17. "Newcomb Athletics," unidentified newspaper clipping, 1922, in *Sophie Newcomb Scrapbook, II: 1916–1929*, 92.

18. The New Orleans Southern Athletic Club purchased a complete Swedish gymnastics outfit consisting of ladders, oblique ropes, vaulting boxes, stall bars, benches, and vertical ladders so that Baer could instruct the members' wives, sisters, mothers, and daughters in gymnastics. See "Ladies' Gymnasium," *The Daily Picayune*, 28 October 1891, 3.

19. "The Stenographers Class in Physical Culture," *The Daily Picayune*, 4 February 1895, 3; "A 'Women Workers' Physical Culture Class," *The Daily Picayune*, 21 March 1895, 3; "Woman's World and Work-Ladies Evening Gymnastic Club," *The Daily Picayune*, 31 May 1895, 3.

20. "The Louisiana Chautauqua—Faculty and Lecturers," *The Daily Picayune*, 12 April 1895, 21.

21. Baer, letter to Sharp, 5 February 1916.

22. By 1896 only a small percentage of Louisiana teachers had attended college; it was suggested that no more than one high school teacher per parish had a bachelor's degree. See Ives, "As I Remember."

23. At its peak, Monteagle had 19 schools in which teachers could receive credit toward degrees and certification. Physical education became a part of the Summer School in 1890. In 1895 Vanderbilt University accredited graduates of the Monteagle Summer School of Higher Physical Culture. See Katherine Strobel, "The Monteagle Summer School," *Journal of Physical Education and Recreation* 50 (April 1979): 80–84; *Monteagle Summer School Programs*, 1899–1910, Monteagle Archives, Tennessee.

24. The law approved on 7 July 1894 stated that the laws of health and physical education should be taught in every district of the state. Act #78, 1894 Legislature, Archives and Records Service, State of Louisiana, 90; "A Talk with Miss Clara G. Baer," *The Daily Picayune*, 4 October 1895, 8.

25. Clara Gregory Baer, "The Health of College Women," *National Education Association* (1916), 690–693; Clara Gregory Baer, "Therapeutic Gymnastics as an Aid in College Work," *American Physical Education Review* 21 (December 1916), 513–521.

26. See Clara G. Baer, *Progressive Lessons in Physical Education* (New Orleans: School Board of New Orleans, 1896).

27. It appears remarkable that Baer's accomplishments would have been so obscure as to continue to escape the notice of physical education and sport historians. The only references to Baer in history texts are to briefly mention her in connection with basketball, and most often refer to her as the one responsible for the three-division court, which is absolutely in error.

28. See Senda Berenson, "Basket Ball for Women," *Physical Education* 3 (September 1894), 106–109.

29. Clara Gregory Baer, "History of the Development of Physical Education at Newcomb College," *National Education Association* (1914), 701–704; Clara Gregory Baer, *Newcomb College Basket Ball Rules for Girls and Women* (New Orleans: Tulane Press, 1908).

30. The history books always give credit to Senda Berenson because she chaired the committee that wrote the first "official" rules for women in 1901. Baer published her rules six years prior to Berenson's; note should be made of this.

31. Clara Gregory Baer, *Basquette* (New Orleans: L. Graham and Sons, 1895); Baer, *Newcomb College Basket Ball Rules*.

32. "Dancing and Athletics Making N.O. College Girls Into Athletes Who Rival

Best Country Can Produce," unidentified newspaper clipping (probably 1920s), Newcomb Scrapbook. Although most references designate 1903 as the first year Newcomb women played outdoors in bloomer suits, a picture in the 22 February 1902 *Harpers Weekly* shows the Newcomb women outdoors in their bloomers.

33. Baer, *Basquette.*

34. Clara Gregory Baer, *Newcomb College Basket Ball Guide for Women* (New Orleans: Tulane Press, 1914), in Tulane Archives.

35. Baer, *Basquette.*

36. See John Rickards Betts, *America's Sporting Heritage: 1850–1950* (Reading, Mass. Addison-Wesley Publishing Company, 1974). There are two possible explanations for Baer being credited with the three-division basketball court. James Naismith claimed in his 1941 book, *Basketball: Its Origins and Development* (New York: Associated Press), that Baer mistakenly thought he had intended for the court to be marked into three divisions because she had misread his directions. Since the book was written 50 years after the fact, Naismith may have inadvertently remembered the wrong person who first used the three divisions, and other writers simply repeated what he had said. The other possible solution to the mystery is that writers, as well as Naismith himself, confused "Newcomb Ball" with "Newcomb Basket Ball." The Newcomb Ball rules called for the three-division court and were first published the same year as Baer's basketball rules (*Basquette*); her revisions to Newcomb were also made in the same years as her basketball revisions.

37. Baer, *Basquette.*

38. Parts of Seaver's letter are quoted in Baer's 1911 *Basket Ball Rules.* This gives credence to the probability that the use of Baer's rules went beyond Southern boundaries.

39. A shot from center would be 30 feet or more and thus it was given a value of four points.

40. Dale A. Somers, *The Rise of Sport in New Orleans, 1850–1900* (Baton Rouge: Louisiana State University Press, 1972).

41. The ball was put in play by an out-of-bounds official who threw the ball chest-high between the two centers, who tried to capture the ball. The centers also had the largest division on the court to cover and had the greatest distance to shoot at the goal.

42. Baer, "History of the Development of Physical Education."

43. Clara Gregory Baer, *Newcomb Ball: A Game for the Gymnasium and Playground* (New Orleans: L. Graham & Sons, Ltd., 1895).

44. Baer's Newcomb Ball rule books contain pictures of playground and school teams of all ages from across the country. They also show Newcomb Ball varsity college teams for men as well as women. See Baer, *Newcomb Ball.*

45. Senda Berenson, "Editorial," *Basketball for Women* (New York: American Sports Publishing Co., 1903).

46. Sophia Foster Richardson, "Tendencies in Athletics for Women in Colleges and Universities," *Popular Science Monthly* 50 (February 1897), 517–526.

47. "College Girls and Basket-Ball," *Harper's Weekly* 46 (22 February 1902), 234–235.

48. Richardson, "Tendencies in Athletics."

49. Senda Berenson, "The Significance of Basket Ball for Women," *Basket Ball for Women* (New York: American Sports Publishing Co., 1901), 20–27.

50. Baer suggested that her rules demanded esthetics such as how women stand, walk, run, and throw plus their neat appearance. See Baer, *Newcomb College Basket Ball Guide.*

51. Berenson, "The Significance of Basket Ball for Women."

52. Baer, *Newcomb College Basket Ball Guide.*

53. Berenson is primarily warning against rough play. See Berenson, "The Significance of Basketball for Women."

54. The reason Baer had the team change goals after each basket was to ensure that players spent equal time on offense and on defense. She believed that the glory would go to those who made the most points, and by changing goals players would have a more equal opportunity to score.

55. Baer appeared to be influenced by Nils Posse, her teacher, who believed that no exercises should be taught that "compressed the chest," and Baer felt two-handed passes or shots would do this. See Baron Nils Posse, *Swedish System of Education Gymnastics*, 2nd ed. (Boston: Lee and Shepard, 1896.)

56. A basket from center counted four points, from guard three, and from goal two.

57. In Baer's 1895 rules she included a choice of two courts depending on the number of players per team. One court was divided into eight sections with goals at diagonal corners of the gymnasium, and the other had 11 divisions with the goals at the middle ends of the court. Her 1908, 1911, and 1914 rules all called for the seven division court, although she suggested that practice games with only ten players might be played on a five division court.

58. Hank Lusetti from Stanford is credited with initiating the one-handed push shot in the 1930s, but Baer's "girls" were using it three decades earlier.

59. Baer, *Newcomb College Basket Ball Rules*, 1911.

60. Ibid.; Paul, "Clara Gregory Baer," *Research Quarterly*, 1985.

61. "Frantic Yells Help Varsity to Big Victory Over Alumnae," unidentified newspaper clipping (10 April 1920), in *Newcomb Scrapbook*, Physical Education Department.

62. Joan Paul, "Fifty Years of LAHPERD," presentation at the Louisiana Association for Health, Physical Education, Recreation and Dance Convention, 9 March 1984.

63. J.E. Lombard, "Basket Ball for Women in the South," *Spalding's Official Women's Basket Ball Guide, 1910–1911* (New York: American Sports Publishing Co.), 59–61.

64. Ibid.

65. A.B. Dinwiddie, "President's Statement: Commencement," *The Tulane News Bulletin* 9 (June 1929); "Information Card," Baer File, Tulane Archives.

66. As early as 1914 Clara Baer realized that she was not being given credit for her pioneer work in the development of women's basketball or for the publication of the first rules. In the 1914 edition of her rules she pointed out this fact and said it was not meant to reflect on the work of others, just to be historically correct. For other works on Baer, see Joan Paul, "Clara Gregory Baer: An Early Role Model for Southern Women in Physical Education," unpublished paper presented at the NASPE History Academy, AAHPERD Convention, 8 April 1983; Paul, "Clara G. Baer: Pioneer in Sport for Southern Women," paper presented at the NASSH Convention, 19 May 1984; Paul, "Clara Gregory Baer," *Research Quarterly*, 1985.

4

The Governance of Athletics for Girls and Women

Leadership by Women Physical Educators, 1899–1949

Joan S. Hult

The year 1899 marked the first time women physical educators organized athletics for girls and women. The result was the Women's Basketball Committee. During the next fifty years various organizations led by women physical educators succeeded this initial enterprise: National Women's Basketball Committee (1899–1917); Committee on Women's Athletics (1917–1927); Section on Women's Athletics (1927–1931); Rules and Editorial Committee (a standing committee of American Physical Education Association) (1931–1932); and National Section on Women's Athletics (1932–1949).[1] Though distinct in name, these organizations were the antecedents of the present National Association for Girls and Women in Sport.

Over this fifty year period, women physical educators who sought to govern athletics for girls and women altered both their perceptions of athletics and the structures within which they would obtain their goals. They began wanting to order the entire "world" of female athletics. They attempted to accomplish this on a piecemeal basis, sport by sport. By 1949, however, they governed only women's athletics in educational institutions. What had affected this change primarily was the women's own unwillingness to compromise with men who had a different set of political guidelines and who had a different philosophical commitment to and for athletics.

Between 1920 and 1935 especially, these philosophical differences came to light. While women physical educators tried to impose upon all women's programs an "anti-varsity, anti-elite" athlete framework for competition, men in local and national amateur athletic organizations, primarily the Amateur Athletic Union (AAU), encouraged and fostered the expansion of competition. Thereafter, women physical educators began to readjust their conception of competition and their services to amateur athletics, and they began to cooperate with their male counterparts in amateur athletics. By 1949, however, the process of change was far from complete. Varsity competition remained an issue, and women's governance of athletics for girls and women remained incomplete.

Background

By the time the Association for the Advancement of Physical Education was founded in 1885, women were already participating in sport. The nature of this participation was recreational, not competitive—at least as competitive sport has come to be known in the twentieth century. Physical education programs existed in all eastern women's colleges and many midwestern colleges and universities had some type of sports for women in 1885. The sports in which these young women were involved were nature-related (e.g., hiking, mountain climbing, skating) or had a strong Victorian social aspect (e.g., croquet, archery). Outside of the colleges, upper class women participated as members of private athletic clubs in such sports as tennis, sailing, and equestrianism.[2]

In the 1870s and 1880s several colleges appointed female physical education instructors to teach gymnastics and calisthenics to the increasing numbers of young women who had begun to enter institutions of higher learning.[3] This was stimulated by nineteenth century concerns that women's physical frailties would prevent their successful adaptation to college life and that they would begin to break down physically under the strains of the demands of intellectual studies.[4] The medical as well as the laymen's view of women's frailties ultimately conflicted with the vision of the "new woman" of the 1890s, but the belief that the pressures of academic life could damage women's health prevailed well into the twentieth century.[5]

Throughout the nineteenth century marriage and motherhood had been the prevailing feminine "occupations." The two generations born between 1860 and 1900 included the first appreciable sized cohort of women who would assume public vocations. Many women who entered some type of public occupation chose not to marry and thus escaped the exclusive domestic experience which late-Victorian values had assigned to females.[6] As many as 10 percent of all women in the first generation of the group born between 1860 and 1890 remained single.

Statistics indicate that nearly half of the women teachers, and 90 percent of the women physical educators who ultimately assumed leadership positions in women's athletics were not married during their years of service. Most successful female physical educators in the late nineteenth and early twentieth centuries were celibate, relatively unburdened by domestic chores, and able to channel their energies into teaching and dealing with women's athletics.[7]

Teaching physical education to girls and young women, however, was a career that, while not in the mainstream of the domestic ideal, shared a number of features with it. There was a strong tendency among women physical educators in the period from 1899 to 1949 to attempt to exercise the same types of control over their charges that mothers might be expected to exert over their daughters.

Several studies have documented that after 1885 more forms of sports began to become attractive to women in colleges and in the broader society, including various forms of "competitive" sports. One of the most popular was cycling, where sport and various efforts at dress reform seemed to reinforce each other.[8] Golf, tennis, crew, and swimming were well-established sports for college women by 1900.[9] In 1892 women students at Smith College participated in the first collegiate game of basketball. By 1896 co-eds at the University of California and Stanford University had engaged each other in the first officially recognized varsity game.[10] In the 1890s basketball was the fastest growing sport for women in the country, and it remained so well into the middle of the twentieth century.

Organizational History

In 1895 one of those who helped to establish the game of basketball in colleges, Clara Baer, presented the rules developed at Sophie Newcomb College (Newcomb: a substitute for basket ball) at the AAAPE national convention.[11] Four years later, at the now famous 1899 Conference of Physical Training held at Springfield College, a committee headed by Alice Foster was appointed to draw up rules for basket ball. At the time "scarcely two institutions of education played with precisely the same rules."[12] A major concern underlying the evolution of women's basketball rules was the question of roughness. Senda Berenson, who introduced the game at Smith College stated, "Rough and vicious play seems worse in women than in men," describing a contest she had witnessed in which the first half, which was played by men's rules, disintegrated into mayhem, while the second half, played by women's rules, showed skill, alertness, and coolness.[13]

In October 1901 the first official women's basket ball rules were published in the *Spalding Athletic Library Series* ("Little Red Book"). Senda
Berenson was the editor.[14] The next eighty-three years would be spent
in discussion and debate over the rules of the women's game. A permanent National Women's Basketball Committee was appointed by the
APEA in 1905, chaired by Senda Berenson, and expanded to eight
members including three men. The committee was charged "to carefully
and impartially make such revisions in the rules as seemed wise and
best." The second of Spalding's "Little Red Book" series, *Official Wom-
en's Basketball*, appeared in 1906.[15]

The bottom was removed from the basket in 1918 to speed up the
game, and more changes in the women's rules were made to reduce, if
not eliminate, physical contact and promote "fair play." The three court
game played by women precluded the running that characterized the
men's game, as running was thought to be physiologically too demanding
for women and too apt to promote individual rather than team play.[16]

The structure of the National Women's Basketball Committee remained the same until 1917 when the Committee on Women's Athletics
(CWA) was established. (The editor of the women's rules, Senda Berenson, also retained this position until 1917.) In January 1917 APEA
President William Burdick appointed Elizabeth Burchenal chairman of
the new committee. By the April 1917 National APEA Convention,
Burchenal had made the National Women's Basketball Committee a
subcommittee of CWA.[17] In her capacity as chairman of the CWA,
Burchenal formed four other rules and editorial subcommittees for the
following sports: field hockey, swimming, track and field, and soccer.[18]
Blanche Trilling became chairman of the Committee on Women's Athletics in 1921. She immediately formed an Executive Committee of the
CWA composed of the five chairmen of the sport subcommittees. The
remaining members of the appointed CWA committee became advisory
members. The primary function of each subcommittee was "to make,
revise, and interpret rules." In addition, the committee concerned itself
with publicizing the "standards and content of athletic programs."[19]

For many years prior to its official recognition as a section of the
APEA, the CWA functioned effectively to exercise considerable control
over women's athletics in schools and colleges. Blanche Trilling sat as
a guest on the National Council of APEA, offered resolutions, requested
funding and speaking rights, and acted in many ways like a regular
council member.[20] In 1922 Trilling succeeded in convincing the National
Council to pass a resolution regarding women's athletics, which aimed
at resisting affiliation with the AAU, and vigorously protested the inclusion of women's athletics in the First Women's International Track
and Field Meet to be held in Paris in August 1922.[21] Fearing that wom-

Members of the Committee on Women's Athletics and its subcommittees at the 1923 convention of the American Physical Education Association held in Springfield, Mass. This was the year CWA published its first handbook, setting forth sports standards specifically for women.

en's collegiate athletics would soon incorporate the elitism and exploitation that they—and numerous male critics—felt had infiltrated men's intercollegiates, the AAU, and Olympic athletics, the women physical educators intensified their efforts to become an official section of the APEA. They rushed to complete their first publication concerned with standards in girls and women's sports, the *Official Handbook of the National Committee on Women's Athletics*, which was first published in 1923. In the foreword to the *Handbook*, the CWA explained the situation that had prompted them to undertake this preparation:

> Insistent and increasing demands coming in from all parts of the country for assistance in solving problems in connection with the athletic activities for girls and women, demonstrated the need for a set of standards which should be based on the limitations, abilities, and needs of the sex rather than the continuation of applying a set of rules and standards designed primarily for men.[22]

The members of the Women's Committee were especially devoted to the concept of a varied yet comprehensive program of athletic activities for girls and women, and they gave particular attention to those activities that would provide students with "all round preparation necessary to fit them to meet with power and equanimity the varied emergencies of life."[23]

Related to the AAU's effort to gain jurisdiction over female athletes was the formation of the Women's Division of the National Amateur

Athletic Federation (NAAF-Women's Division) in April 1923.[24] Instrumental in organizing the group was Blanche Trilling, the CWA chairman. According to Mary Lou Remley, Trilling worked with Mrs. Herbert Hoover, its first chairman, and Colonel Breckenridge, president of NAAF, on all the details for the April 6 and 7, 1923 organizational meeting, including who should be invited. In response to questions from CWA members about the new organization, Trilling advised: "It seems to me . . . that unless a very definite stand is taken . . . we will find ourselves fighting the same vicious system that the men are doing, and that our women will be having commercially sponsored athletics."[25]

The NAAF-Women's Division became dominated by women physical educators. While the CWA was primarily a rules-making body concerned with establishing programs in educational institutions, the NAAF-Women's Division's Platform was developed for all women's athletics, but it functioned primarily in sports outside the educational setting. Together these two organizations formed a united front that opposed the AAU, collegiate, and any other efforts to provide elite and varsity athletic competition for women.

The APEA saw no urgency in the CWA request for section status; therefore it was refused until Florence Somers, chairman of the CWA, made an appeal for more careful consideration of its case. At the APEA National Convention in April 1927, the request was granted, thus expanding the potential influence and function of the Section on Women's Athletics.[26] In 1932 it became the National Section on Women's Athletics (NSWA), but not before a protracted struggle had occurred over several issues. This struggle will be discussed in the following section. The NSWA developed a constitution and set about establishing athletic programs that its members deemed appropriate for girls and women. In addition to promulgating standards for players, officials, program leaders, and administrators, the NSWA attended to making, revising, and publishing *Sport Guides*, developing convention programs and special publications, forming officiating boards, and fostering research in the field of women's athletics.[27]

During the 1930s and 1940s NSWA activities were carried on under the general guidance and supervision of its legislative board. The chairman held a position of considerable power. The NSWA served effectively as a clearinghouse for information on girls and women's athletics, and because of its prestige, influence, and authority it shaped the dominant form of intercollegiate and interscholastic sports participation for women and girls throughout the United States. Within the APEA, where its right to control women's athletics was accepted or at least acknowledged by men, the NSWA enjoyed almost uncontested authority.

The NSWA also gained prestige through its large number of informative publications. Because these were held to represent the best thinking on the subject, they contributed to the group's national influence. Some of the widely distributed ones include: *Standards in Athletics for Girls and Women*, first published in 1937 and reissued in 1948; *Desirable Practices for Girls and Women in Sport*, a brief pamphlet about the standards (1941); *The Girls Athletic Association Handbook*, a guide to the formation of girls athletic associations (1942); and *The Doctor Answers Some Practical Questions on Menstruation* (1938). The *Service Bulletin*, primarily for high school teachers, was published six times a year between 1936 and 1942. It was replaced by the *Sports Bulletin* from 1946 to 1948.[28]

The most important publications, however, were the *Sport Guides* prepared by the Rules and Editorial Committees. These were developed for a large number of team and individual sports.[29] The *Guides* included skill development, coaching strategies, techniques of officiating, and direct and implied statements of belief regarding what values should occur from sports, as well as problems to be avoided. Because the *Guides* were so widely used they were powerful educational and proselytizing devices and served as the basis for claimed authority over the various sports. The income from their sales provided the financial support for the Section's many other projects; consequently, any "take-over" by other rules-making bodies could affect the total program of the Women's Section.[30]

Sports participation for women had become more extensive after the First World War. In response to what was seen as a growing need for local control, the position of state basketball chairman was established in 1922. The state system became so effective that in 1936 the NSWA authorized a plan for state representatives to oversee all women's athletics in each state.[31] The number of officiating boards that actively enforced competitive standards across the country increased from eight in 1928 to over 100 in 1949, adding to local autonomy.[32]

In 1937 over 750 women (1,000 women by 1949) were involved in various NSWA committees. A strong and dedicated network of physical educators committed to the organization's goals was developed through a "mentorship ethic" which pervaded the national leadership. According to Eline von Borries:

> Those who now hold the most responsible positions have given their services voluntarily and have gradually climbed up the ladder to the place where they are able to direct and guide the policies of the organization. As their experience grows they are given increased responsibilities which make it possible for continuity and significant growth, both for themselves and through them of the Section. At the same time, younger members are being constantly taken on and trained so that they may be qualified to accept in their turn the torch which was lighted in 1899 and which has ever since been borne proudly and steadily ahead.[33]

This combination of a tightly knit structure and intensely dedicated group persisted for decades and was one of the main reasons why the NSWA was able to retain its almost monopolistic hold over girls and women's sports in educational institutions. Their authority, however, was not as pervasive or secure in nonschool organizations.

In 1939 the Women's Division of NAAF found its grant from the American Children's Fund being liquidated and its membership fees inadequate to support the organization; consequently, it sought to merge with AAHPER.[34] The NSWA and NAAF had worked in harmony for many years, but in the last three years there had been "problems, conflicts, and duplication." Perhaps the chief cause was NSWA's publication of its own *Standards*. The NAAF, which had developed the first set of standards with its 1923 *Platform Statement* on conduct of athletics, saw itself as a standards-setting organization. It defined the NSWA's province as primarily a "service organization and rule-stating group." The NSWA replied that it could not "divorce principles and standards from practice." Moreover, the NAAF was convinced that the 1937 *Standards* were too permissive and ambiguous.[35]

The NAAF proposed a merger with AAHPER in which it would become an integral part of the Association as a "National Committee on Standards," asking for a separate membership for nonschool members and assurance of support for its own programs. This proposal was vigorously opposed by the NSWA, which steadfastly insisted the NAAF should be incorporated into its structure. Subsequent proposals did place the Women's Division-NAAF under NSWA jurisdiction, but as a separate "Community Contacts Committee" or a "Standards Promotion Bureau," with the financial obligations of the structure falling to NSWA; hence, both plans were rejected. After several such abortive attempts at merger, a plan submitted by NAAF was mutually acceptable. The Women's Division-NAAF would merge with AAHPER with the stipulation that there be provisions for nonschool personnel to gain membership rights within the Association.[36] Thus, on 15 June 1940, this pioneer women's organization that had contributed immeasurably to the "controlled development of women's athletics, closed its books and ceased all official activities."[37]

The decade of the 1940s opened with the NSWA vigorously supporting the National Preparedness Program under the direction of a NSWA Emergency Committee.[38] After the declaration of World War II, a permanent War Emergency Committee was established to coordinate all projects with the war effort.[39] The NSWA passed a "Credo in Time of War" to serve as a guide for all leaders in recreational activities.[40] Much of the usual business of the section was suspended as all energies were directed toward civil defense programs. Many members turned their attention to the development of fitness programs and tests for high school girls in behalf of the War Department. Still others served on the federally supported National Sports Boards, worked with the armed services, or developed programs for the USO. In all sport programs sponsored by NSWA or its members, the focus of attention was on fitness.[41] Some competition previously not endorsed was permitted, if it met the fitness objective the country saw as essential in war-time, and adhered to the new standards of the NSWA "Desirable Practices in Girls and Women's Athletics."[42]

The years following World War II were critical ones for NSWA in coping with the expanded programs and complexities of the Section, both in relation to its philosophical stance on competition and its structural and financial difficulties. The years 1945–1949 were spent searching out solutions to these problems. Few of the questions on competition were resolved; however, satisfactory solutions were found for the structural and budgetary problems.

The financial constraints were considerably alleviated by developing a working agreement with the AAHPER. After several years of discussions and negotiations, the AAHPER agreed to hire a full-time professional consultant to guide and direct the organization, and to become the publishers of NSWA *Sport Guides* and special publications. The burden of the cost was to be shared by both organizations. The publication rights were transferred from A. S. Barnes to the AAHPER on 1 August 1949; the new consultant, Rachel Bryant, began work in September 1950.[43]

A revised Code of Operation was near completion by the end of 1949. The new Code reduced the responsibilities of the national officers and increased the delegated authority of the districts and states. The Plan of Reorganization included a NAPECW liaison and a commitment to more cooperative ventures with other sport governing bodies.[44] The philosophical issues were not so easily resolved. Amid confusion and controversy, the revising of the general standards and creating a set of specific standards for each sport was completed.[45] The debates surrounding the new standards and related competition issues will be discussed in the Competitive Restraints section.

In a pageant entitled "Women in Action: The Story of DGWS, 1892–1958," which was presented in March 1958 at the 60th Anniversary Convention of the AAHPER, Eleanor Metheny described the principles that had guided the organization during its first sixty years:

> But always, no matter what we argued about, we were genuinely concerned with "the good of those who play." And we shall go on talking about that, no matter what our structure, our squabbles, our name, because this is really the reason for our existence as an organization.[46]

The Struggles for Control

In the half century between 1899 and 1949, those who sought to guide the development of girls and women's sports for "the good of those who play"—at least as they perceived that good—faced numerous problems. Two conflicts in particular were both intense and extremely important in shaping the contours that dominated high school and collegiate sport for females. These were internal struggles within the APEA and conflicts with the Amateur Athletic Union (AAU).

The crisis created by the struggle with the AAU in 1922–23 over the control of female athletes convinced the leadership of the CWA that it must achieve status as a section within the APEA in order to exert a national influence.[47] Section status, it was believed, would bring; (1) automatic voting rights on the APEA Council; (2) an identifiable presence and right to present sessions at national conventions; (3) a reliable source of funds; and (4) increased prestige. In 1927 a heated debate erupted within the APEA over the special treatment received by the CWA in its election of a chair, the women's desire to become a separate section, and the private treasury the organization had garnered from its sale of *Guides*. The debate reflected the "uniqueness" with which the CWA viewed itself—an attitude that sought to place the CWA beyond the organizational restraints of the APEA while still benefiting from a central affiliation with the national organization.[48] (The CWA was in *some* ways unique. It carried on its activities all year, not just at the annual meetings, and was fervently dedicated to what it considered an almost sacred trust: the "controlled development" for women's sports.[49]) In the end, the APEA agreed to a Women's Athletics Section.

The APEA's decision in 1930 to reorganize its structure caused the NSWA to reconsider the relative merits of becoming a separate organization or remaining within the structure and constraints of the APEA. After much debate, the legislative board of NSWA decided that membership within the APEA offered the best alternative and actively began to prepare a proposal for acceptance in the new organization plan.[50]

Mabel Lee, the president of APEA during the turbulent 1931–32 years, has referred to the matter as a men-versus-women struggle. In her book, *Memories Beyond Bloomers*, and her personal papers, she claims that a large and vocal group of men, inspired by some women outside the leadership positions, were opposed to section status for the NSWA. She suggests the men were afraid of women running things, resented her as a woman president, and saw the leaders of NSWA as a self-perpetuating group.[51] These views are partially corroborated by Helen Hazelton's account of the dispute which ensued. In addition Lee referred to another issue that some (those who did not believe a separate section in women's athletics was necessary) were concerned about, namely, that more women's groups (such as swimmers) would seek to become a section.[52] After various compromises and alterations in the proposed lines of authority the Executive Committee of APEA voted 3–2 in favor of accepting the WAS as a section, and in 1932 the National Section of Women's Athletics (NSWA) became one of the sections of the APEA.[53]

In its endeavors to provide leadership for and control the direction of women's sports in the United States, the CWA found it expedient to ally itself with various other groups that were interested in similar activities. Those with which it most closely worked were the National Association for Physical Education of College Women (NAPECW), the Athletic Federation of College Women (AFCW), and the Women's Division of the NAAF.[54] These were largely, if not entirely, composed of professional women physical educators. The same individual might belong to more than one group—and occasionally all four. The four organizations spoke almost as a single voice in opposing varsity sports for women, as well as in formally protesting the participation of women in the 1928, 1932, and 1936 Olympic games.[55] When the AAU sought to gain jurisdiction over all women's sports in January 1923, the CWA and other supportive groups were galvanized into action.[56] The leaders of the CWA refused the AAU's request for affiliation and repeatedly resisted the AAU's overtures to gain its support in women's basketball and track and field.[57]

The CWA and the AAU differed on a number of issues, two of which seemed almost irreconcilable. The CWA was especially distressed by the absence of women in leadership positions in the AAU's women's sports program. On the other hand, the CWA had gained the authority that the AAU wanted over women's basketball rules. Events came to a head in 1932. The AAU thought that either basketball needed to be modernized or new rules needed to be developed. Consequently, they applied for membership on the Women's Basketball Rules and Editorial Committee. Because the AAU did not have women in charge of its basketball committee, or any other decision-making structure, the request was denied.[58]

In an attempt to appease the CWA between 1933–1934, the AAU formed a sixteen-member women's advisory committee and appointed a woman chair of its women's basketball committee. Women officials were also selected to run a national women's track and field meet in Madison Square Garden.[59] The NSWA finally approved the AAU's membership on the basketball committee in 1934.[60] However, the AAU voted to develop and publish its own women's basketball rules (the first appeared in 1936–37) and proceeded with its own programs. The AAU/NSWA rift had the long-term effect of moving more of women's athletics outside education and into the public sector.

Competitive Restraints

"A sport for every girl" and "Every girl in a sport" were the ideals that guided the CWA and the NSWA. The phrases became almost a creed to those who subscribed to them. Their philosophical orientation resulted in two major approaches: "Competitive restraints and female self-determination in athletic governance."

A CWA/NSWA member during the 1920s and 1930s would be quick to point out that the organization was not "anti-competition," but merely against the "wrong kind" of competition, namely varsity or elite athletics at the expense of opportunities for the majority of girls and women. It was argued that the financial drain upon educational institutions and personnel would be excessive if they were called upon to provide athletics for the masses and for a small number of expert players for varsity or Olympic competition.[61]

While it is true that the CWA and the NSWA policies effectively served to limit the amount and type of athletic competition that was available to American girls and women in the period between 1899 and 1949, it is not correct that these organizations rejected all forms of more advanced levels of competition. The 1937 *Standards*, for example, declared:

> Occasionally it is stimulating to play against a very superior opponent, but it is not wise to play such competition often. Varsity competition by 1937 has become another form of competition neither better nor worse than intramurals, once it is clear that "sport for the masses" is being achieved.[62]

The full impact of the drive for universal participation in recreation activities was experienced during the depression years. The federal government's support to build facilities and to sponsor programs accelerated recreational and competitive sports for girls and women. Judith Davidson argues in her study "The 1930s: A Pivotal Decade for Women's Sport" that society's acceptance of the elite athlete and the increase in participation in competitive sports sparked an interest and a need to extend forms of extramural competition. By the mid-1930s a trend toward extramural competition could be discerned.[63] In 1936 (and again in 1941) Gladys Palmer of Ohio State University urged the formation of a new rules-making body for intercollegiates called "The National Women's Sport Association."[64] In December 1937 the NSWA sponsored a Mid-Winter Sport Conference where a heated panel discussion arose on "Interscholastic Athletics for High School Girls."[65] In 1940 the Eastern District NSWA members requested deletion of the term "play day" from the literature because it did not reflect what competition really was, stating the term "sports day" should be used. The NSWA did not concur.[66] Over the strong objections of the NSWA to conducting a national event, Ohio State University sponsored the First National Women's Golf Championship in June 1941.[67]

A landmark decision of the National Section on Women's Athletics was made in April 1941 to "authorize state representatives to work in the name of the section with other organizations, even though policies of these organizations run counter to those of NSWA to the end that the standards of NSWA be promoted." This established the principle of providing services to amateur athletics regardless of the policies of the sport organization.[68]

This decision was tested throughout the Second World War years as the NSWA was asked to render services to the Armed Services and USO recreation programs in which "fitness through competition" was the objective. Even in the educational sector, one approach of the U.S. Office of Education to acquiring physical fitness was through participation in competitive sports programs carried on in accordance with the recommendations of the National Section. Competition for girls and women took on a new meaning, and the controversy surrounding appropriate competition for women's athletics was stilled for a time.[69]

Just prior to the end of the War, a proposal was made for a governance structure for women's athletics which would provide "a program of sponsorship of women's athletics throughout the nation." This would be financed by solicited funds. "It was to take into account all women's athletics not just in schools and colleges." The proposal was studied and ultimately rejected as too extensive. It would reappear with a collegiate focus in subsequent years.[70]

In the years following World War II attitudes concerning women in general, and their participation in sports, had begun to change. So too had the National Section's attitude toward its role and function in athletics. The leadership wished to extend its involvement in the larger amateur athletic sphere and recognized that this might require surrender of some of the opposition to elite competition for the highly skilled athlete. The issue of endorsement and promotion of competition in athletics caused a split between established leaders of the association and some of the younger members working their way up the mentorship system. The latter favored varsity and elite competition in a controlled environment, while the former were reluctant to sanction any athletics beyond sports days.

These differences led to some inconsistencies in decision making. Examples include: failure to either sanction or censure state golf or tennis tournaments;[71] rejection of the statement "The varsity type of competition is not approved" but an unwillingness to define (in the *Standards*) varsity sports as an appropriate form of extramurals;[72] acceptance of the contradictory statement providing that "a nationally rated official may officiate at an AAU basketball game where AAU rules are used provided she does so as an individual and does not represent a board"; ambivalence toward the 1948 Olympics while urging the United States Olympic Committee to apply the NSWA *Standards* to all Olympic-sponsored sport programs.[73]

Both groups within the NSWA did agree, however, on two significant concepts. The first was to aggressively seek the endorsement of the NSWA *Standards* by all sports governing bodies and interested organizations. The second was to work in a spirit of cooperation with such male-dominated sports governing bodies as the AAU, the National Federation of State High School Athletic Associations (NFSHSAA), and the USOC.[74]

Acting upon this new cooperative attitude, the NSWA invited the AAU and the NFSHSAA to speak as members of a panel to discuss "Cooperative Action Among Groups Sponsoring Athletics for Girls and Women" at the 1947 National AAHPER Convention, followed by a meeting of the groups.[75] Another joint meeting was planned for the three organizations in March 1949 to discuss women's basketball rules. At that time the NSWA authority as a rules-making body for basketball rules was once again in jeopardy. The joint meeting with the NSWA Basketball Committee was designed to ease the tensions and to work toward a common set of women's basketball rules. (Three major rule changes were made for the 1949–50 season, including an experimental rule on the unlimited dribble.[76]) The new friendly relationship with the NFSHSAA prompted the NSWA to vigorously encourage the state representatives to seek an alliance with their state high school athletic associations.

Female Self-Determination in Athletic Governance

The single sex structure of separate men's and women's physical education departments that existed in American colleges and universities well into the 1970s provided the environment in which women physical educators could have substantial freedom to promote their own system of values concerning sport. Female self-determination in athletic governance was a major tenet of the CWA, the NSWA, and the Women's Division. An indication of this may be seen in Agnes Wayman's article "Women's Athletics: All Uses—No Abuses," which appeared in the November 1924 *American Physical Education Review*:

> What is sauce for the gander is *not* sauce for the goose. . . . Men took the tiller—they offered us the tow, and we, forgetting that we

During the first two decades of this century, many girls and women's basketball teams had men coaches. Above are members of the 1917–18 Philander-Smith College (Little Rock, Ark.) women's basketball team with their coach. (Owner of the photograph is Anne Wilson McKindra, seated on left end.) Below is the ladies' team of the Rome (N.Y.) Catholic Association, posing with their coach for a photograph that appeared in the *Official Women's Basket Ball Guide* (1908–09) during the period when the *Guides* featured team pictures.

are a frail craft, so to speak, took it . . . it just happens that we
don't like the route which they have chosen. . . . We are setting
forth under our sail with women at the helm and women manning
the whole craft.[77]

Strong prohibitions were placed on male coaches for girls and women's
teams. There were several reasons for this and one which was frequently
stated was that only women could understand the psychological, moti-
vational, and physiological needs of the female. There was also grave
concern that the exploitation of the participants, commercialism, and
over-emphasis on winning that had come to characterize men's athletics
by the 1920s could creep into the women's programs unless these were
carefully guarded by women.[78]

This is not to suggest that no girls or women's teams had men as
coaches. Male coaches were active in girls and women's basketball from
the beginning, especially in rural high schools and some smaller colleges.
It was the male coaches, such as Harry Stewart, who took the first U.S.
female Olympic team members to Paris in 1922 and led the fight for
competitive athletics for women in the 1920s and 1930s.[79] In the 1940s
it was once more male coaches who initiated a considerable amount of
the varsity and elite competitition. At the same time the increase in
competition brought a dramatic influx of male coaches. For example,
in 1948, at state basketball tournaments in Oklahoma, Texas, and Georgia over 90 percent of all the teams were coached by men.[80] Similarly
30 of 32 of the teams in the 1946 AAU National Basketball Tournament
were coached by men. The NSWA was extremely distressed by the
increasing numbers of men coaches.[81]

Opposition to male referees created a different dilemma. As girls and
women's sport participation grew in the 1930s and 1940s, there were
not enough officials to handle the volume of games in some parts of the
country. Thus, in spite of the fundamental commitment the CWA and
NSWA had to female self-determination, the choice lay between having
either male officials or no officials at all. After much initial resistance,
the executive committee of the NSWA ultimately approved a policy in
the 1940s whereby local officiating boards could issue ratings to men
when this became absolutely necessary. Men could only earn *local* rating,
however; they were prohibited from holding *national* NSWA ratings.[82]

Interestingly, the NSWA was concerned the most about officiating
ratings for the sport of basketball. During the first five decades of the
twentieth century, the majority of required physical education programs
for girls and women placed considerable emphasis on team sports. These
were seen to provide important training in group cohesion, the type of
socialization that conformed to the NSWA's emphasis on cooperation
rather than competition. Such team sports, especially basketball, it was

felt, also were likely to place strenuous demands on the female participant. A woman official (or coach) could better guard against the type of play which might harm the physical health or well-being of the participant.[83]

Another issue exemplifying the NSWA's insistence on the health standards for the participants was the women's football case. A furor arose in opposition to Jack Spaulding's (the originator of the game) publication in 1939 of the rules for *American Football for Women*.[84] Through the intervention of NSWA and AAHPER the sport did subside, only to emerge as an issue again in 1947. The NSWA remained opposed to women's football because the sport was "inappropriate for women" and dangerous to the "health and welfare of the female participants."[85] This preoccupation with the good of the participant—in social and psychological, but mostly in physiological matters—is a recurring theme in the literature of the period.

Varsity and Elite Competition

As has been suggested earlier in this paper, more sports competition for girls and women existed in the years between 1899 and 1949 than is customarily assumed. Sport historians have underestimated the amount. Additionally, it is sometimes claimed that during the period from 1920 to 1950 the play day almost completely replaced competitive athletics.[86] The play day was widely influential only from approximately 1925 to 1935, however, and even then largely in city schools rather than in rural areas. Moreover, various forms of AAU, industrial, and community-based competitions for girls and women continued to grow to such an extent that by the late 1930s the NSWA was forced to concede that in many regions of the nation females could find considerable opportunities for competition.

The period from 1900 to 1920, sometimes referred to as the rise of varsity and elite competition for women, was characterized by a particular growth and development of team sports. Women physical educators in these decades exhibited an almost missionary zeal for providing opportunities for their charges in sports such as basketball and field hockey. Team games frequently began in educational institutions and then expanded outward into the broader society as a highly competitive sport.[87] The enthusiasm for field hockey led the way to various types of international competition in sports. An All-Philadelphia team, coached by Constance M. K. Applebee, visited Great Britain in 1920, "the first to represent the United States in any international team game competition for girls."[88]

In a typical New York City girls outdoor game, at Jamaica High School, the teacher starts the "toss up," wearing "proper" dress while the players are in more practical outfits. (*Official Basket Ball Guide for Women, 1912–13*)

An examination of such relevant literature as Spalding's *Sport Guides* and the *American Physical Education Review* strongly suggests that there was considerable varsity basketball for girls and women in the first two decades of the twentieth century. The earlier *Guides* often show pictures of female varsity players with their male coaches, although such photographs disappear around 1920.[89] Articles in the *Guides* before World War I indicate a preference for varsity or elite competition. The most universally accepted evidence that varsity and high level competition had been discontinued on college campuses has been the two surveys by Mabel Lee reported in the *American Physical Education Review* in 1924 and the *Research Quarterly* in 1930.[90] The questionnaires upon which these surveys were based were sent to women physical educators who were members of the NSWA or the Women's Division-NAAF, and consequently, the respondents were likely to be predisposed to a non-varsity model. Additionally, 17 of the institutions that did not return questionnaires in 1930 did, in fact, have varsity programs.

Competitive interscholastic programs for secondary school girls, particularly in varsity basketball and track and field, certainly existed throughout the play day era. The majority of such programs appear to have been conducted in small, often rural, schools. Frequently, they were organized and run by male coaches. Reflecting both the concern of professional women physical educators and the reality of the situation in many parts of the country, Helen Coops reported in the November 1926 *American Physical Education Review*:

> The development of sport for women has reached a most critical state throughout the country. Popular interest is centering around girls' athletic teams everywhere, and the whole matter has grown into an acute problem of national importance. I wonder if you have ever realized how many private schools advertise solely through pictures of their athletic opportunities.[91]

The author indicated that although the NAAF philosophy of "athletics for all" might be on the ascendence in most women's colleges, high school principals were often proving to be formidable opponents.

The extent of such high school competition is also attested to by a report of Women's Athletic Section questionnaires that appeared in the official *Basketball Guide* for 1924–25 and 1925–26. Slightly more than half of the 1,600 schools responding claimed they approved of interscholastic basketball for girls and had such programs. Over half of the schools in Kansas, West Virginia, and Pennsylvania had basketball varsity programs in 1937.[92]

Such interscholastic competition was not confined to basketball. Articles which appeared in the June 1927 *Athletic Journal* also suggested that girls' high school and even junior high school track meets were being conducted in many places.[93] The 1923 *Track and Field Athletics for Girls Guide* reported that girls' track and field meets were conducted in many major cities and that state high school tournaments were held in such geographically separate areas as Chicago, New Jersey, St. Louis, and Southern California by the end of the 1920s.[94] Interscholastic field hockey leagues, clubs, and tournaments are frequently reported in the *Field Hockey Guides* throughout the fifty years.[95] The National Association of Secondary School Principals was concerned about burgeoning high school girls' athletics and in 1925 passed a resolution to eliminate state tournaments and varsity teams.[96] Of the 37 states that had basketball championships, 21 dropped the tournaments, but rural areas often maintained the county or local championships.[97] Nevertheless, by the late 1920s a considerable amount of the high school basketball and track and field competition for girls had been curtailed. At least 33 states reported the initiation of intramural programs and play days between 1929 and 1933. These changes occurred primarily in larger high schools where women physical educators were in charge of the programs.[98]

In the 1940s a shift back to varsity athletics for high school girls occurred at a rapid rate. In addition to the well-known basketball states like Iowa and Oklahoma, which sponsored state tournaments, seven other states formed a girls' basketball committee and adopted a modified set of girl's rules for varsity competition. By 1949 two other states had joined this group. Martha Gable, chairman-elect of NSWA, expressed the concern of the state representatives that the problem of "interscholastic competition for girls is rearing its head all over the country."[99]

Intercollegiate competition for college women was not completely eliminated in the 1920s and 1930s as many textbooks have contended. Collegiate field hockey players had frequent opportunities to compete in varsity athletics (often labeled a club team) throughout the period. A typical illustration was the intercollegiate hockey tournament held at the College of William and Mary, Williamsburg, Va., 31 October 1930, with nine colleges taking active part.[100] There is also evidence of varsity basketball teams, primarily from small colleges, competing against nearby colleges. A sampling of such schools includes Lake Erie College in Ohio, Ursinus College in Pennsylvania, Western Maryland College, Connecticut Agricultural College, Nashville Business College, and Swarthmore College.[101]

As early as 1931 a tri-college sports day featured Goucher College, American University, and George Washington University in abbreviated basketball contests.[102] In 1934 Illinois State Normal University sponsored a college sport day, "beginning a trend which accelerated in the forties."[103] On the East Coast and the West Coast, sport days replaced play days beginning in the mid-thirties.[104] Jessie Godfrey found by the mid-1940s that 80 percent of the AFCW institutions reporting had sports days. Over 22 percent also had varsity teams.[105] In 1940 Dorothy Sumption, the first person to write a chapter that acknowledged the imminence of intercollegiate athletics for women, ended with a warning, "Intercollegiate competition for women is definitely here to stay!"[106]

The NSWA and the Women's Division of the NAAF were also not able to have much influence over the competitive programs for girls and women that church leagues, private clubs, the AAU, industrial leagues, YWCAs, and recreational organizations conducted. Although such organizations might selectively use the platform of the Women's Division to assist them in controlling certain aspects of their programs, during the 1920s and the 1930s all such groups continued to organize and conduct competitive sports for girls and women.[107] A poll of the 65 organizations that held membership in the NAAF in 1930 disclosed that all of these offered some type of competitive team or league play for females.[108] It is patently clear, by the tone of the discussions, bombardment of complaints, concerns registered with NSWA, and the debates that frequently erupted within the National Section during the 1940s, that nonschool competition was prevalent.

In a paper entitled "Policies in Women's Athletics" presented to the Mid-West College Physical Education Society and subsequently published in the *Journal of Physical Education*, Gladys Palmer declared: "The year 1938 finds the physical education profession without a generally accepted policy in regard to sports competition for women and with a great need for one."[109]

Palmer then pointed to a number of paradoxes in the existing situation. Some leaders among college directors approved of women engaging in international field hockey tournaments but not in the Olympic Games; others thought that international competitions as organized by the USLTA might be acceptable for other sports as well. Palmer also declared that since 1923 there had been an increase in state, national, and international women's events, and that the Women's Division of the NAAF would have been in a much stronger position if it had not taken such an adamant stand against such competitions.

If one looks closely at the statements of the Women's Division of the NAAF and NSWA a certain heirarchy of approved sports for elite competition becomes evident. Among team games, field hockey was usually considered quite acceptable. It was, in the United States, a sport organized and conducted almost solely by women. Among the individual sports, tennis, golf, and swimming, generally perceived to be "feminine" sports, were most acceptable. All of these were also considered elite sports. Basketball, softball, and track and field, on the other hand, were usually thought to be rough, plebeian, and tainted with male values and practices. Competitions in elite sports might be approved for college women, while the other sports were increasingly forced underground where they emerged in industrial leagues and in AAU competitions. College sports were to help form "ladies." Community sports were for the masses.

Conclusion

The ideas and practices that framed this dichotomy between college and community sports for women would change gradually in the decades after the 1940s. By the mid-twentieth century, the leadership of the National Section on Women's Athletics lacked the singleness of purpose and direction upon which this distinction had depended. Women physical educators who comprised the organization's leadership had begun to readjust their conception of competition, to reconcile their practices and their rhetoric with the reality of what many girls and women were doing. Particularly in the public sector, at least a generation of female participants had engaged in elite levels of competition. Although still reluctant to accept the worth of such competition, the NSWA had begun to rethink the nature and values of competition for girls and women, the services that the section might provide, and how it might work with all amateur and nonschool sport governing bodies. Unlike its predecessor organizations, the NSWA had become ambivalent about varsity, elite athletic competition by 1949. It would neither endorse and promote nor sanction and condemn such competition. The task of attempting to resolve this ambivalence was left to future generations of women physical educators.

The NSWA can best be understood, perhaps, as a pivotal link between previous organizations and those that formed in the future, like the Division for Girls and Women's Sports and the Commission on Intercollegiate Athletics for Women. On the one hand, the leadership of the NSWA did maintain the fundamental goal of the earlier organizations: the "good" of the participant. It continued to make and enforce playing rules in various sports. It demanded that women serve as coaches and officials (although over time men were increasingly visible in both capacities), and it continued to enforce standards of conduct in sports programs for girls and women. By such means, the NSWA prolonged the tradition of governance of women's athletics by women.

On the other hand, the NSWA's ambivalent posture concerning emerging views of the acceptibility of elite competition for girls and women was not compatible with the social movement for equality for women that arose in the 1960s. In the face of the political pressures of the 1970s and the force of federal legislation concerning athletics for women in educational institutions, the traditional philosophies concerning athletic competition for girls and women were rapidly, if somewhat begrudgingly, swept aside.

Notes

This chapter was originally published, with the same title, in the Special Centennial Issue of the *Research Quarterly of Exercise & Sport* (April 1985), pp. 64–77. The illustrations were added for its publication here.

In conducting the research, extensive use was made of the archives of the National Association for Girls and Women's Sports and the Women's Division of the National Amateur Athletic Federation (AAHPERD, Reston, Va.). Unless otherwise noted, all manuscript material cited is from these archives. They also include the majority of the sports guides—especially *Spalding Athletic Library Series*—used in this study. The archival collection of the Amateur Athletic Union (Indianapolis, Ind.) also proved to be helpful.

1. The National Section on Women's Athletics (1932–1953) became: National Section for Girls and Women's Sports (1953–1956); Division for Girls and Women's Sports (1957–1974); National Association for Girls and Women in Sport (1974–present).

2. Harriet Ballintine, "Out-of-Door Sports for College Women," *American Physical Education Review* 3 (March 1898), 38–43; "A Belle on Rollers," *Harper's Weekly* 21 February 1885, 121–122; W. Benough, "The New Woman Athletically Considered," *Godey's Lady's Book* 132 (January 1896), 23–

29; "Swimming," *Godey's Lady's Book* 57 (August 1858), 123–125.

3. Midwest Association of College Teachers of Physical Education for Women, *A Century of Growth: The Historical Development of Physical Education for Women in Selected Colleges of Six Midwestern States* (Ann Arbor, Mich.: Edwards Brothers, 1951); S. F. Richardson, "Tendencies in Athletics for Women in Colleges and Universities," *Popular Science* 50 (February 1897), 517–526; Albert Shaw, "Physical Culture at Wellesley," *Review of Reviews* 6 (December 1892), 545–547.

4. Caroll Smith-Rosenberg and Charles Rosenberg, "The Female Animal — Medical and Biological Views of Woman and Her Roles in Nineteenth Century America," *Journal of American History* 60 (September 1973), 332–356; Winfred Ayres, "Smith College," *Godey's Lady's Book* 131 (July 1895), 25.

5. Mary L. Remley, "The Steel-Engraving Lady and the Gibson Girl: The American Sportswoman in Transition: 1880–1910" (paper delivered at the Twelfth Annual Convention of the North American Society for Sport History, University of Louisville, May 1984), 3–7.

6. Julie Matthaei, *An Economic History of Women in America: Women's Work, the Sexual Division of Labor and the Development of Capitalism* (New York: Schocken Books, 1982), 203–205, 209–213; Kate Gannett Wells, "The Transitional American Woman," *Atlantic Monthly* (December 1890), 819; Linda K. Kerber and Jane DeHart Mathews, eds., *Women's America: Refocusing the Past* (New York: Oxford University Press, 1982), 3–22.

7. Matthaei, *Economic History of Women*, 209–213, 256–300; Kerber and Mathews, *Women's America*, 3–25, 257–260; Leslie Parker Hume and Karen M. Offen, "Introduction to Part 3, The Adult Woman's Work" in Erna Olafson Hellerstein, Leslie Parker Hume, and Karen M. Offen, eds., *Victorian Women: A Documentary Account of Women's Lives in Nineteenth Century England, France, and the United States* (Stanford, Calif.: Stanford University Press, 1981), 272–290. The figure of 90 percent is from a tabulation of women leaders of the CWA/NSWA.

8. "Crusade Against the Wheel for Women," *The Literary Digest* 13 (July 1896), 361; R. L. Dickinson, "Bicycling for Women: The Puzzling Question of Costume," *Outlook* (April 25, 1896), 751–752; Marguerite Merington, "Woman and the Bicycle," *Athletic Sports — The Out-of-Door Library* 5 (1897), 209–230; "Skating Suits," *Harper's Bazaar* 11 (January 1873), 51.

9. Betty Spears, "The Emergence of Women in Sport" in Barbara J. Hoepner, ed., *Women's Athletics: Coping with Controversy* (Washington, D.C.: American Association for Health, Physical Education and Recreation, 1974), 26–39.

10. Senda Berenson, "Editorial," in *Basket Ball for Women, 1901*, 5–7; Lynne Emery, "The First Intercollegiate Contest For Women: Basketball, April 4, 1896," in Reet Howell, ed., *Her Story in Sport: A Historical Anthology of Women in Sports* (West Point, N.Y.: Leisure Press, 1982), 417–423; Ronald A. Smith, "The Rise of Basketball for Women in Colleges," *Canadian Journal of History of Sport and Physical Education* 2 (December 1970), 18–36.

11. Clara Baer, "Newcomb: A Substitute for Basket Ball," in *Proceedings of the American Association for the Advancement of Physical Education, New York, 1895* (Concord, N.H.: Republican Press Association, 1896), 87–92; idem, *Newcomb and Basquette* (New Orleans: Graham and Son, 1895), 13.

12. Berenson, *Basket Ball, 1901*.

13. Berenson, "The Significance of Basketball for Women," 20–27; Alice Fos-

ter, "Basket Ball for Girls," *American Physical Education Review* 2 (September 1897), 152–154.

14. Berenson, *Basket Ball, 1901.*

15. Berenson, "Preface," in *Official Basket Ball Guide 1906*, 6.

16. Dorothy S. Tapley, "Thirty Years of Girls' Basketball Rules," in *Official Women's Basketball Guide, 1936–1937*, 49–53; Luther Gulick, "The Psychological Effects of Basket Ball for Women," in Berenson, ed., *Basket Ball, 1901*, 11–14; Senda Berenson, "Are Women's Basket Ball Rules Better for Women than Men's Basket Ball Rules?" in *Women's Basket Ball Guide, 1908*, 59–73.

17. "Annual Meeting of the Council," *American Physical Education Review* 22 (January 1917), 32–35; "American Physical Education National Council Executive Committee Meeting," ibid., 47; "Council Meeting, William Penn Hotel, April 7, 1917," *American Physical Education Review* 22 (May 1917), 314. At the 1917 Convention Burdick reported that "the Basket Ball Committee, a subcommittee of the Women's Athletic Committee, had been appointed by Miss Elizabeth Burchenal." (NB: The January *Review* reported that Burdick had appointed Ethel Perrin.)

18. "Report of the Annual Meeting of the Council, December 28, 1918," *American Physical Education Review* 24 (January 1919), 37; "Meeting of the Council at Chicago, Illinois, April 12, 1919," *American Physical Education Review* 24 (May 1919), 290; "News Notes," *American Physical Education Review* 27 (June 1922), 298–299.

19. Eline von Borries, "History of Development of Section: Report of Policy and Finance Committee," 1 March 1937, 15; "The National Section on Women's Athletics Report on Activities, 1935–35," *Journal of Health and Physical Education* 7 (November 1936), 572–573; 592–593. This article contains the wrong date (1898) as the origin.

20. "Report of the Business Meeting, May, 1922," *American Physical Education Review* 27 (September 1922), 332–335; "Report of the National Council Meeting, held on Saturday, April 26, 1924," *American Physical Education Review* 29 (June 1924), 357–358. See also Eline von Borries, *History and Functions of the National Section on Women's Athletics* (Washington, D.C.: AAHPER, 1941).

21. "Report of the Business Meeting, May, 1922," 334.

22. Elizabeth Burchenal, ed., *Official Handbook of the National Committee on Women's Athletics and The Official Rules for Swimming, Track and Field, and Soccer, 1923–24*, 14.

23. Ibid., 14–15.

24. For a history of the organization see Alice Allene Sefton, *The Women's Division National Amateur Athletic Federation* (Stanford, Calif.: Stanford University Press, 1941).

25. Letter from Blanche M. Trilling to Lou Henry Hoover, 2 February 1923; letter from Blanche M. Trilling to Elizabeth Stoner, 21 February 1923; letter from Blanche M. Trilling to Lou Henry Hoover, 27 February 1923 as cited in Mary Lou Remley, "The Contributions of Blanche M. Trilling to the Establishment of the Women's Division, National Amateur Athletic Federation" (paper delivered at the "Research Consortium," Ninety-sixth Annual Convention of the AAHPERD, Boston, April 1981), 5. Also, letter from James McCurdy to Blanche Trilling as cited in Eline von Borries, *History and Function*, 10.

26. "Council Meeting of APEA," *American Physical Education Review* 32 (June 1927), 439.

27. National Section on Women's Athletics, "Constitution," 1932; "Report of the Rules and Editorial Committee of the Women's Athletic Section," December 1932.

28. National Section on Women's Athletics, *Standards in Athletics for Girls and Women* (Washington, D.C.: AAHPER, 1937); idem, *Desirable Practices for Girls and Women in Sport* (New York: A. S. Barnes, 1941); idem, *The Girls Athletic Association Handbook* (Washington, D.C.: AAHPER, 1942); Margaret Bell, *The Doctor Answers Some Practical Questions on Menstruation* (Washington, D.C.: AAHPER, 1938). See also two publications of the National Section on Women's Athletics: *Service Bulletin*, 1936 to 1942 and *Sports Bulletin*, 1946 to 1948.

29. "The Five Little Red Books Have Now Grown to Seven," *The Sportswoman* 8 (September 1931), 14–15; Eline von Borries, *History and Function*, 8; Publications Committee, "Minutes of the Legislative Board Meeting, 28–29 December 1949."

30. "Report of Council Meeting, APEA, April, 1924," *American Physical Education Review* 29 (June 1924), 357–358 (the royalty money from basketball was $125); "Report of Annual Meeting of Executive Committee on Women's Athletics," 31 December 1929 ($1,130 in royalties); "Report of Publications Committee, December 15, 1948" ($3,536 in royalties).

31. National Section on Women's Athletics, "Newsletter to State Representatives," 26 September 1936.

32. "Wanted: Basketball Officials," *American Physical Education Review* 34 (October 1929), 476; Josephine Fiske, "Twenty Years with WNORC," *Journal of Health, Physical Education, Recreation* (March 1949), 170–171; National Section on Women's Athletics, "Report of the WNORC, December 1949, to The Legislative Board," 29 December 1949.

33. Eline von Borries, "Section V Educational Outcomes Derived from Membership in Committees of the Section," Report of Policy and Finance Committee, 1 March 1937, 46; "Minutes of Legislative Board," 28–29 December 1949, 1. See also Betty Spears, "Success, Women, and Physical Education," in M. Gladys Scott and Mary J. Hoferek, eds., *Women as Leaders in Physical Education and Sport* (Iowa City: University of Iowa, 1979), 5–19.

34. Women's Division, National Amateur Athletic Federation, "Meeting March 10, 1939 Re Proposed Merger of the Women's Division of the National Amateur Athletic Federation with the American Association of Health, Physical Education, and Recreation."

35. Jane W. Shurmer, "Unofficial Report Re Proposed Merger of Women's Division, NAAF with AAHPER," 1 May 1939; Elinor M. Schroeder, "Minutes, Legislative Board, 3 April 1939"; Report of Policies and Finance Committee, 4 May and 6 May 1939.

36. Women's Division, National Amateur Athletic Federation, "Meeting March 10, 1939, Re Proposed Merger"; Jane W. Shurmer, "Unofficial Report Re Proposed Merger, May 1, 1939"; Memo to the Council of American Association for Health, Physical Education, and Recreation, "Negotiation Platform," n.d.; "National Section on Women's Athletics," Recommendation to AAHPER, March, 1939; "Minutes of the Executive Meeting of Women's Division, National Amateur Athletic Federation," 22 March 1939; cf. Mabel Lee, "A Pretty Kettle of Fish," in *Memories Beyond Bloomers: 1924–1952* (Washington, D.C.: AAHPER, 1978), 282–303.

37. Letter from Emma Waterman to N. P. Neilson, President, American Association for Health, Physical Education, and Recreation, 15 June 1940.

38. Louise Kjellstrom, "National Section on Women's Athletics," To: Legislative Board Members, State Representatives, and Committees of NSWA, From: NSWA Emergency Committee on the National Preparedness Program," n.d. in "Minutes of Legislative Board Files"; Ruth H. Atwell, "Chairman's Report of Current Happenings and Problems," 28 December 1940.

39. "Minutes of the Legislative Board, December 28–29, 1941"; Ruth H. Atwell, "Chairman's Newsletter," January 1942.

40. Louise Kjellstrom, "Credo in Time of War" in Report of the War Emergency Committee Activities, 17 December 1942.

41. Alice Schriver, "Letter to Members of Legislative Board," December 1942.

42. National Section on Women's Athletics, "Desirable Practices in Girls and Women's Athletics," 1941; "Minutes of the Steering Committee," 23–24 May 1942.

43. Alfreda Mosscrop, National Section on Women's Athletics, Report of Section Chairman, 1947–48, 4; "Minutes of the Legislative Board," 28–29 December 1949.

44. National Section on Women's Athletics, "Code of Operation," (1949 Revision); "Minutes of the Legislative Board," 28–29 December 1949.

45. Alfreda Mosscrop, National Section on Women's Athletics, Report of Section Chairmen, 1947–1948; "Minutes of Standards Committee, Report to Legislative Board," December 1948.

46. Eleanor Metheny, "Women in Action: The Story of DGWS, 1892–1958," in Connotations of Movement in Sport and Dance (Dubuque, Iowa: Wm. C. Brown, 1965), 147.

47. "NSWA Section II History" in "Report of Policy and Finance Committee," 1 March 1937, 13–16.

48. Eline von Borries, History and Function; Marguerite M. Hussey, "Report of Annual Meeting of Executive Committee on Women's Athletics of the APEA, December 30, 1927," American Physical Education Review 33 (May 1928), 361; Eline von Borries, "Report of Policy and Finance Committee," (1 March 1937), 14–17.

49. Helen Hazelton, "Report of Promotions Committee," 1939; Edith Gates, "Report of Executive Committee Meeting Held Wednesday, April 2, 1930"; Eline von Borries, History and Function, 11–13; cf. Mabel Lee, "Foreword to History of Organization of the National Section on Women's Athletics."

50. "Report of Annual Meeting Executive Committee on Women's Athletics," 31 December 1930; Ethel Bowers, "Minutes of Special Meeting of Executive Committee of the Women's Athletic Section," 1 April 1931; Helen Hazelton, "Report of the Women's Editorial and Rules Committee, March 1931–April 1932."

51. Mabel Lee, Memories Beyond Bloomers, (Washington, D.C.: AAHPER, 1978), 181–201; idem, "Foreword to History of NSWA," 7–12.

52. Helen Hazelton, "Report of the Women's Editorial and Rules Committee, March 1, 1931–April, 1932"; idem, "Suggested Plan for the Reorganization," n.d.; "Memorandum of Activities of Women's Athletic Editorial Committee," Forty-seventh National Convention of the American Physical Education Association, 20–23 April 1932.

53. "Memorandum of Women's Athletic Ed. Committee," 20–23 April 1932. The NSWA gave the APEA a "peace offering" of $200.

54. See Phyllis Hill, *The Way We Were: A History of the Purposes of NAPECW 1924–1974* (Washington, D.C.: AAHPER, 1975); Alyce Cheska, *Historical Development and Present Practices of Women's Athletic/Recreation Association* (Washington, D.C., AAHPER, 1966).

55. Joan S. Hult, "The Role of Women Physical Educators and Organizations in American Women's Struggle for the Olympic Gold, 1922–1968" (paper delivered at the Ninety-seventh Annual Convention of the AAHPERD, Houston, April 1982); "News of Girls and Women's Athletics, Section on Women's Athletics of the American Physical Education Association," *American Physical Education Review* 34 (May 1929), 310; "Minutes of the Legislative Board of NSWA," April 1935.

56. Amateur Athletic Union of the United States, "Report of Committee on Women's Athletics," November 1923; "Report of Committee on Women's Athletics, National Convention, New York, 1922"; *Minutes of the AAU, 1923*, 138–142. (These items are in the Archives of the AAU, Indianapolis, Ind.)

57. Letter to Ethel Perrin from John Griffith, 27 May 1931 concerning AAU/National Section on Women's Athletics conflicts; "Memorandum of Activities of Women's Athletic Editorial Committee," 20–23 April 1932; letter to the "Council of the American Physical Education Association" from the AAU, 22 April 1932, concerning the Joint Committee for Women's Basketball.

58. Letter to J. Lyman, Assistant to the President of AAU, from Eline von Borries, 28 April 1932; letter from Mrs. Richard Folsom to Eline von Borries, 6 November 1932.

59. "A Woman's Sports Committee of the AAU (1933)," *The Sportswoman* 9, 21; Olga Becker, "Ex-Champion Now Chairman," *Amateur Athlete* (February 1934), 11–12; "Basketball Committee Report to American Physical Education Association Council, Cleveland, 1934," n.d.

60. Basketball Committee Report to American Physical Education Association Council, "Request to Rescind 1932 Ruling"; "The AAU Problem" Report to the Rules and Editorial Committee Meeting, December 1938.

61. Blanche Trilling, "The Playtime of a Million Girls or an Olympic Victory, Which?" *The Nation's Schools* 6 (August 1929), 52; Women's Division National Amateur Athletic Federation, *Platform* (New York: Women's Division National Amateur Athletic Federation, 1924).

62. National Section on Women's Athletics, *Standards*, 36–37.

63. Judith A. Davidson, "The 1930s: A Pivotal Decade for Women's Sport" (Unpublished Qualifying Manuscript, University of Massachusetts, 1978); Joan S. Hult, "Have the Reports of the Death of Competitive Women's Athletics, 1920–35, Been Greatly Exaggerated?" (paper delivered at the Seventh Annual Convention of the North American Society for Sport History, Banff, Canada, 1979).

64. Gladys Palmer, "Report of Committee on Policy of Women's Athletic Section," 24 March 1936; "Minutes of the Legislative Board, April 24, 1936."

65. Martha Bugbee, "Mid-Winter Sports Conference—Notes on Panel Discussion on 'Interscholastic Competition for High School Girls and College Women,' December 30, 1937," in "Minutes of Legislative Board," 29–31 December 1937.

66. "Report of the Eastern District Representative to the Legislative Board," Move to Drop the Terminology Play Days from Further Use, Minutes of the

Legislative Board; "Minutes of Meeting of the Policy and Finance Committee (April 21, 1940)."

67. "Minutes of the Legislative Board," 29–30 April 1941 and 1–3 May 1941; Report of Gladys Palmer, 29 April 1941; Christine White, "Minutes of Meeting of Policy and Finance Committee," 21 April 1945.

68. "Minutes of the Legislative Board," 29–30 April 1941 and 1–3 May 1941.

69. Federal Security Agency, U.S. Office of Education, *Physical Fitness for Students in Colleges and Universities* (Washington, D.C.: Government Printing Office, 1943), 58–59, 88; idem, *Physical Fitness Through Education for the Victory Corp* (Washington, D.C.: Government Printing Office, 1943); "Minutes of the Legislative Board," April 1942.

70. Anna S. Espenschade, "To the Legislative Board and Committee Chairmen," June 1945.

71. Wilhelmine Meissner, "Minutes of Meeting of Policy and Finance Committee, April 21, 1945"; National Section on Women's Athletics, "Minutes of the Legislative Board Meetings," 15–16 September 1945.

72. Elinor M. Schroeder, "Standards Review Committee," January 1948.

73. "Policy and Finance Committee Meeting," 3 January 1947; "Minutes of the Legislative Board Meeting," 22 April 1947; Martha Gable, "Report of the National Section on Women's Athletics for the Year 1948–49."

74. Alfreda Mosscrop, "Highlights of the NSWA Legislative Board Meetings, January 4–5, 1947," *Sports Bulletin* (January 1947); Claire M. Johnston, "National Section on Women's Athletics," *Journal of Health and Physical Education* 18 (March 1947), 175.

75. Mildred Wohlford, "NSWA National Convention," *Sports Bulletin* (January 1947); "Minutes of the Legislative Board Meeting," January 1947.

76. "Basketball Committee Report to Legislative Board," December 1948; "Basketball Committee Report," 20 March 1949.

77. Agnes Wayman, "Women's Athletics: All Uses—No Abuses," *American Physical Education Review* 29 (November 1924), 517.

78. E. B. DeGroot, "Should Girls' Teams Be Coached or Managed by Men?" in *Women's Basket Ball Guide 1907–1908*, 71–78; "Minutes of the Legislative Board Meeting," 23 April 1940.

79. Harry Stewart, "Track Athletics for Women," *American Physical Education Review 27* (May 1922), 207–211; idem, "Track Athletics for Women," *American Physical Education Review* 27 (June 1922), 280–290.

80. Alfreda Mosscrop, "Report to the Legislative Board, NSWA," April 1948. (This report summarizes information received from all the states.) Christine White, "Policy and Financial Committee Meeting," 24–25 May 1947.

81. Muriel M. Lomax, "Report of the AAU Annual Basketball Tournaments" in "Minutes of the Legislative Board Meetings," 9–11 April 1946.

82. Letter from Carl Webb to Josephine Fiske, December 1941; letter from Josephine Fiske to Carl Webb, 31 December 1941; letter to WNORC (1944) from Margaret Weeks, "Just what rating in basketball officiating may be given to men? Can't find women and can find men," n.d.; "Minutes of the Legislative Board," April 1940; letter from Florence Hupprich to Margaret Weeks, 11 January 1945; "Minutes of the Legislative Board," 15–16 September 1945.

83. Grace E. Jones, "Sportsmanship," in Eline von Borries, *A Handbook of Basketball for Women* (Baltimore, Md.: Sutherland Press, 1929), 10.

84. John Spaulding, *American Football for Women* (New York: Spalding, 1939); "Minutes of the Legislative Board Meeting," 29–30 December 1939; letter to Legislative Board from Jane W. Shurmer on "Resolution, February 6, 1940"; idem, "Chairman's Report of Current Happenings and Problems," 18 April 1940.

85. "Minutes of Legislative Board Meeting," 4–5 January 1947, 11; "Policy and Finance Committee Meeting," 24–25 May 1947; Evelyn Browne, "Touch Football for Girls," *Sports Bulletin* 2 (December 1947), 3–10; Esther French, "Minutes of the Legislative Board Meeting," 2–4 January 1948, 12.

86. Ellen Gerber, "The Controlled Development of Collegiate Sport for Women, 1923–36," *Journal of Sport History* 2 (Spring 1975), 1–28; Mary Lou Remley, "Twentieth Century Concepts of Sports for Women" (Ph.D. diss., University of Southern California, 1970).

87. Dorothy Ainsworth, *History of Physical Education in Women's Colleges* (New York: Columbia University Press, 1927); Gertrude Dudley and Frances A. Kellor, *Athletic Games in the Education of Women* (New York: Henry Holt, 1909).

88. Hilda W. Smith and Helen K. Welsh, "Constance M. K. Applebee, The English Tour, 1920," *Field Hockey Guide 1921*; Krumbhaar and Ann Townsend, "The United States Field Hockey Association Team's British Tournament," *Field Hockey Guide 1924*.

89. Elizabeth Richards, "Everyday Problems in Girls' Basketball," *American Physical Education Review* 25 (December 1920), 407–414; Harry E. Stewart, "A Survey of Track Athletics for Women," *American Physical Education Review* 21 (January 1916), 13–21; Florence Burrell, "Intercollegiate Athletics for Women in Coeducational Institutions," *American Physical Education Review* 22 (January 1917), 17–19. See also the 1932 publication of the New York Herald Tribune entitled *Sports in Women's Colleges*, which is a compilation of articles by Janet Owen, Herald Tribune reporter.

90. Mabel Lee, "The Case for and Against Intercollegiate Athletics for Women and the Situation as It Stands Today," *American Physical Education Review* 29 (January 1924), 13–19; idem, "The Case for and Against Intercollegiate Athletics for Women and the Situation Since 1923," *Research Quarterly* 2 (May 1931), 93–127.

91. Helen Coops, "Sports for Women," *American Physical Education Review* 31 (November 1926), 1086. See also "A Southern California Sports Day," *The Sportswoman* 2 (May 1926), 12.

92. Eline von Borries, "Questionnaire Results," *Official Rules of Women's Basketball 1924–25;* idem, "Questionnaire Results," *Official Rules of Women's Basketball, 1926–27;* Sefton, *Women's Division*, 48–49.

93. Tom Sayers, "Track and Field, *Athletic Journal* 3 (June 1927), 20–24. See also "Minutes of the AAU Annual Meeting," "Track and Field Women's Committee," 1923; ibid., 1924. (AAU Archives)

94. "Introduction," *Official Track and Field Athletics for Girls*, 1923, 8; "Questionnaire Results," *Official Track and Field Athletics for Girls*, 1924; "Questionnaire Results," *Official Track and Field Athletics for Girls*, 1925.

95. Harold Clarke Durrell, "Interscholastic Field Hockey in Greater Boston," in *Field Hockey Guide*, 1923, 97–98; "Hockey Throughout the United States," *Field Hockey Guide, 1931*, 58–59; Hazel J. Cubberly, "Hockey in California," *Field Hockey Guide, 1929*, 60–62.

96. "Resolutions Passed by the Association," *National Association of Secondary School Principals Ninth Year Book* (Washington, D.C.: National Education Association, 1925); Sefton, *Women's Division*, 44–46.

97. Albert C. Kelly, "West Virginia High School Girls' Basketball Tournament," in *Official Basketball Guide for Women, 1921–22*, 69.

98. "Newsletter" No. I of the Women's Division National Amateur Athletic Federation, February 1929; Sefton, *Women's Division*, 44–50; see also Paula Welch, "Interscholastic Basketball: Bane of Collegiate Physical Educators" in *Her Story in Sport*, 424–431; Helen N. Smith and Helen Coops, *Play Days: Their Organization and Correlation with a Program of Physical Education and Health* (New York: A. S. Barnes, 1928). Additionally over 250 programs of individual play days are included in "Dr. Cobaine's Play Day Files" located in AAHPERD Archives.

99. "Annual Report of Chairman-elect" in "Minutes of the Legislative Board, April 1948," 3; "Report of the Basketball Committee to Legislative Board," 2–3 January 1947; "Report of the Basketball Committee to Legislative Board," 28–29 December 1949.

100. Cubberly, "Hockey in California," 60–61; "Hockey Throughout the United States," 54–63; "Field Hockey, Season of 1930," *Field Hockey Guide, 1931*, 6–7.

101. MACTPEW, "A Century of Growth," 46; "Basketball Report to the Executive Committee," 1929; Mabel Lee, "A Case on Intercollegiates 1923, 1930"; "Report of the Basketball Committee to NSWA Legislative Board, April 1938."

102. Women's Division of NAAF, "Newsletter," 3 (March 1931).

103. MACTPEW, "A Century of Growth," 47.

104. "Minutes of the Legislative Board, April 1948"; "Report of the Eastern District Representative to the Legislative Board, 1947–48."

105. Jessie Godfrey, "The Organization and Administration of Women's Athletic and Recreation Associations" (Master's thesis, Wellesley College, 1951), 100–119; see also M. Gladys Scott, "Competition for Women in American Colleges and Universities," *Research Quarterly* 16 (March 1945), 49–71; Mary F. Jackson, "Practices and Opinions in Intercollegiate Athletics for Women" (Master's thesis, University of Southern California, 1953).

106. Dorothy Sumption, *Sports for Women* (New York: Prentice Hall, 1940), 72.

107. Edith M. Gates, "Trends in Athletics for Girls and Women in Employed Groups," *American Physical Education Review* 34 (June 1929), 366.

108. Sefton, *Women's Division*, 32–33.

109. Gladys E. Palmer, "Policies in Women's Athletics," *Journal of Health and Physical Education* 9 (November 1938), 565–567, 586–587.

5

The Tides of Change in Women's Basketball Rules

Joanna Davenport

Basketball, as invented by James Naismith in 1891, was one of the few sports not a mixture of many activities. It was a game designed by Naismith's ingenuity. Undoubtedly, he never dreamed that his creation would become the most popular sport for girls and women all over this country and most of the world. Naismith established his basic rules to be used by all who played basketball, not distinguishing between male or female athletes. (Actually, he designed the game for the young men at the Young Men's Christian Association (YMCA) Springfield College.) And yet, within a few short months his game and his rules would be played by young women and modified by women physical educators. Their changes for girls and women yielded a game quite different from the game originally conceived by Naismith.

This paper summarizes the major rule changes in women's basketball and examines the women's justification for these changes. The analysis is limited to the basketball rules established by the National Women's Basketball Committee (NBC). The Women's Committee was the antecedent of the present National Association for Girls and Women in Sport (NAGWS). While social trends and attitudes most assuredly influence rule changes, there is no attempt to discuss the changes beyond what the committee, the organization, and women physical educators expressed as the rationale for the rule changes.

As a guide in thinking and understanding the women's basketball rules, it is interesting to examine Naismith's five fundamental principles for a nine member basketball team:

1. There must be a ball, it should be large, light and handled with the hands.

2. There shall be no running with the ball.

3. No man on either team shall be restricted from getting the ball at any time it is in play.

4. Both teams are to occupy the same area, yet there is to be no personal contact.

5. The goal shall be horizontal and elevated.[1]

It took women physical educators many years to return to these principles after some major digressions in an effort to adapt the game to the attitudes and behavior patterns expected of young ladies.

Early Rules and the Women Leaders

From the first time girls and women played basketball, it was obvious to some of the women leaders that many students did not have the strength or stamina to participate in the game as Naismith had designed it. Thus, these women modified the game, which prompted the use of different sets of rules for women throughout the country. At Smith College, for example, Senda Berenson changed the basketball rules shortly after the invention of the game. In 1894 she wrote that she modified the rules to control roughness and to encourage teamwork.[2] In her game, the court had three divisions, each player had to stay in the assigned zone, and a person could hold the ball for only three seconds. There could be no snatching of the ball, and a player could use only a three bounce dribble. Many schools copied Smith College's rules while others continued to use men's rules, or made entirely different changes such as those advocated by Clara Baer (see chapter on Baer in this volume).

The three division court caused controversy when games were played against teams using men's rules. The no snatching rule was another controversial rule. Some women's rules allowed snatching while others did not. When teams with different rules about snatching and the dimensions of the court played each other, problems arose and led to an effort to standardize the game. Consequently, at the 1899 Physical Training meeting in Springfield, Massachusetts, the conference leaders appointed a committee to examine the girls basketball situation throughout the country. This original women's basketball committee set out to incorporate all modifications of the women's game into one set of rules that would be suitable for girls and women.[3] The committee made a commitment that the health and welfare of the girls playing was the most important factor in refining the rules.[4]

Among the first "official" girls and women's basketball rules the committee developed were:

1. The court shall be divided into three equal parts.
2. Snatching and batting of the ball is not allowed.
3. Holding the ball longer than three seconds constitutes a foul.
4. There shall only be a three bounce dribble.
5. There may be five–ten players on one team.

The above rules were often referred to as Berenson's Rules, since she was editor of the publication in which they first appeared.[5] Even though these were the official women's rules, different sets of rules continued to be used across the United States. Either they were interpreted differently in various sections of the country, or leaders ignored the revised rules. Furthermore, many men coaches preferred and used the men's rules. Nevertheless, standardizing the rules in women's basketball had been started by this national Women's Basketball Committee.

In 1905 the Basketball Committee became a part of the American Physical Education Association (APEA), known today as the American Alliance for Health, Physical Education, Recreation and Dance (AAHPERD). It became a permanent official Women's Basketball Committee (WBC) within the organization, giving it more status and political clout to control women's basketball.[6]

The Women's Basketball Committee made constant changes in the rules throughout its long history. Two criteria prevailed for each new rule: (1) did it make a better game for girls and women and (2) did it fulfill the initial principle of the health and welfare of the participants?

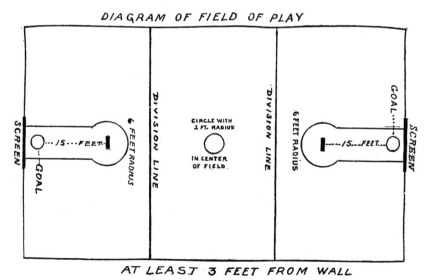

This diagram of the three division court served as frontispiece to the first published official basketball guide in 1901.

The Story of the Rule Changes

1901–1918

In 1901 the American Sports Publishing Company published the 1899 National Women's Basketball Committees Rules in their "Spalding's Athletic Library" series. The first revision in 1903 was interesting, though certainly not major. No longer did the official basketball have to display the signature of the physical education leader, Luther Gulick. The committee also slightly changed the order and wording of rules, which did not have a strong impact on the actual playing of the game.

The first rule book in 1901 used the gender *she* for all rules about the player, and *he* for all actions of the officials. The 1903 rules sometimes interspersed *he* in reference to players, but the rules continued to use *he* throughout for officials until the 1914–15 rule book.[7]

Also, profiting from the new YMCA rules which enhanced the safety and welfare of the players, the women adopted other revisions in 1903:

1. Because the game was considered too long and strenuous for girls, they shortened halves from 20 to 15 minutes.

2. To avoid injury, the rush to retrieve the ball out of bounds, which had been allowed, was replaced by awarding the ball out of bounds to the opponent of the player who caused it to go out. Actually, the women had committed themselves to change their rules in keeping with men's rule changes, if it seemed appropriate.

3. The number of team members changed from five to ten players to six to nine players. The Committee felt five players on a team gave "too much work and too much responsibility to the one centre and . . . ten players proved too many. . . ."[8]

The 1906 *Guide* contained the official rules of the new APEA Women's Basketball Committee. The five seconds out of bounds rule appeared, as did a rule to give one point for a foul (by today's standards), but a free shot for a violation (foul). A description of the backboard followed the design of the present backboards. The number of players returned to five to nine.[9]

In 1908 the WBC added several new fouls to the list of general fouls. Many fouls listed are violations in today's version of basketball. Guarding rules were very strict. For example, boxing up was a foul (two opponents guarding a player in the act of shooting). Also to prevent snatching the ball, placing one hand on the ball already held by an opponent became a foul. A player could hold the ball for three seconds, after which it was a foul to retain possession. Even a line violation was a foul! If a player was fouled three times her team got a point after the third foul instead of one point each time she was fouled. The bounce pass was outlawed. As incidents of fouls were increasing at such an alarming rate, the committee decided the player would be warned after three fouls, and after four would be sent to the bench for the rest of the game.[10]

For the first time the rules recognized that teams were using open bottomed baskets. In such cases, officials needed to be sure the ball had entered and passed through the basket to assure a goal. However, the closed basket, with a chain (or cord) pulled to release the ball, continued to be mentioned in the rules until the 1918–19 *Guide*.[11]

The committee eliminated dribbling in 1910. But in response to constant complaints, they introduced a single dribble in 1913, retaining the requirement that the ball must bounce at least knee high. Berenson had explained the need for the rule in the 1901 *Guide*: "demanding that the ball shall be bounced higher than the knee gives a quick opponent a fair opportunity to bat the ball away when it is between the floor and the player's hands."[12]

The smaller court provision also occurred in 1913. If the playing area was small, the court could be divided in half rather than thirds. This new rule gave many schools the excuse to play the faster two court game. In this situation, if a team had only five players, the center, who wore special markings, could play the entire court but could not shoot for a basket.[13]

In 1916, to speed up the game and prevent constant stopping for free throws, some fouls changed to violations more in keeping with today's violations. The same year, coaching from the sidelines became a foul. This rule certainly was a hardship since there were no time outs and no substitutions. The coach was unable to legally communicate with her players during playing time. Halftime provided the only chance for coaching.[14]

The 1917 season permitted the player five fouls. The player would be warned after four fouls and disqualified when she committed the fifth. In the small two court game, the center player could now shoot for a goal if she played the full court. A shooting foul (by a defensive player) now yielded two free throws.[15]

In 1918 there were some rule modifications beyond rewriting the rules to conform in wording and sequence to the men's rules "without in any way altering the spirit of the women's rules." The Basketball Committee for the 1918 rule changes decided the former women's rules were "verbose . . . overdetailed . . . arrangement was confusing . . . and the men's rules . . . were [written] decidedly better."[16] This was one of several attempts by the women to align their rules with the men's rules.

Some substantial rule changes occurred in 1918:

1. In the punishment for violations, instead of awarding a free throw, an opponent of the offender had a throw in from out of bounds.

2. It was legal to use a bounce pass.

3. Teams could now use substitutes, who could enter the game, but not re-enter the game.

4. The Committee reversed the freedom of a racing center to shoot when playing on the small court. They did so because some women complained that allowing the center to shoot encouraged "a one girl game and . . . bunching under the basket." This was surely not in keeping with the team concept.[17]

1919–1938

Between 1919 and 1937 the revisions of the rules for the most part were minor. Two important exceptions were the 1921 change in the point system and the 1932 guarding change. Since guarding was only allowed on the vertical, there was no way to defend against a two handed overhead throw. Many coaches strategically had their players perfect that shot. Therefore, in 1921, to make the game fairer, a goal using this technique counted only one point instead of the usual two points. By 1925, goals scored by the one hand overhand throw, two hand underhand throw with back to the basket, and the shot put throw also only counted one point. Disqualification followed five technical fouls, four personal fouls, or a combination of personal and technical fouls to equal six. Also, a new substitution rule permitted a player to re-enter the game once.[18] (It would not be until 1939 that a substitute could re-enter the game twice, and another decade before unlimited substitutions were allowed.)[19]

In 1922 an official team changed from five to at least six players. The maximum of nine players remained. As always, guards could not shoot. The Committee decided to let tie games stand. This rule was an effort to "minimize the emphasis upon winning and losing."[20]

By 1923 several technical fouls became violations as they seemed to be minor offenses. In 1924 the official playing time changed from halves to eight minute quarters with two minutes between quarters and a ten minute halftime. No coaching could happen during the two minutes between quarters. Three time-outs of five minutes each had been available to each team since 1918; however, in 1925 these time-outs were also to be used for injuries. By 1926 five minute time-outs seemed unnecessary, so they revised the five minutes to two minutes, and the following year reduced the time-outs from three to two per game. Time-out for injury remained five minutes.[21]

A few years later in 1935–36 the Committee again reduced the time-outs, this time to one minute each, and two per game. By 1939–40 the number of time-outs was increased to three per game. The number per game steadily increased until in the mid-1970s each team had five time-outs in the regular game and one extra time-out during overtime play.[22] (Surely these changes suggest the increasing importance of the coach.)

Returning to the 1930s discussion, in 1932, guarding on any plane was finally made legal. This change had a dramatic effect on the game as it impacted both offensive and defensive play. Consequently, the game became more exciting and skillful, because now the offense had to learn to be more evasive and the defense player could truly play defense. As a result of the new guarding rule, all goals scored two points. The option of a center throw or a jump up could be used to start the game. Perhaps an important change (in 1933) was the demand for two complete passes after a center-throw, thereby preventing a quick move toward the basket immediately after a center throw-in. By 1936, the center throw instead of center jump up was mandatory.[23]

From 1932 until 1942 the WBC made changes in the format of the *Guides*. The *Guide* itself contained only articles and editorials, and the rules were in a small removable pamphlet inserted in a pocket at the back. Here, too, was a large folded basketball technique chart that had teaching tips about the game supplemented by stick figure illustrations.

The year 1938 saw the big rule change. The two court game that had been allowed on small courts since 1914 became the official game for all size courts. Experimental rules, used by a selected number of teams throughout the country, in 1935–37, called for a two court game and a six player team. The experiment was so successful the committee made these rules official. Three guards and three forwards composed a team.[24] A player was either a forward and made points, or a guard and prevented others from scoring; in either case everyone was part of the action.

1939–1949

The two court game brought a decade of stability to the rules. Subsequent changes were minor until the end of the 1940s. In 1947 a happy decision for the officials was that players had to wear numbers both on the front and back of their uniforms. (Starting in 1927, a player had worn a number on her back.)[25]

Starting in 1942, after a goal the team *not* scoring the goal got the ball in the center. Before this time, the teams alternated receiving the ball in the center after a goal. After two years of experimentation, reports indicated that "awarding of the Ball in the center to the team not credited with the score made for a better game." The new rule also applied after a successful free throw. However, teams complained that giving the ball to opponents after a converted free throw might be detrimental to the offensive team. Three years later, the Committee gave the team a choice of taking the free throw, or taking the ball out of bounds at the free throw line.[26]

In the post-war era several rules were considered that would promote a faster-paced game and more actual playing time. The rules were experimental in 1948 and became official for the 1949–50 *Guide*. These included:

1. Time-out was taken for all fouls and free throws.

2. Guarding was redefined. A guard could now use one or both arms, legs, or body in any *plane*. Still, when guarding no physical contact could be made with the opponent.

3. A two bounce limited dribble was legal with no height specification. The experimental rules in 1948 tested both the limited dribble and a continuous dribble. Surprisingly most respondents to a questionnaire preferred the limited dribble, so the Committee retained the two bounce dribble. This may be the only time an experimental rule did not become the official rule the year after experimentation.[27]

1950–1963

Over the next several years some major changes had dramatic effects. For the first time in 1951, players could receive coaching during intermissions and time-outs. The rules surreptitiously stated, "except to consult coaches at or near their benches."[28] The 1952–53 *Guide* revealed a recodification of the rules whereby "the information formally included in 12 rules now appears in 10 rules which are simply stated, logically arranged and organized. . . ."[29] The 1953–54 *Guide* had 17 different minor modifications or wordings of nonessential rules. This was another attempt to change rules which differed from the men's and yet were unimportant to the spirit of the women's rules. However, one new rule reflected a major change in attitude. The Committee permitted tie games to continue for one or more extra periods, with "sudden death" (scoring a total of two points) after the first extra period. They also cautiously reminded the coaches "to use good judgement in permitting overly fatigued players to play in the overtime period." Without any explanation for a new ruling, the team shooting a free throw also would now get the ball out of bounds after the shot.[30]

The rules committee carefully studied and experimented with the three second lane violation (three seconds in the key for the offensive players). In 1955, they enacted the three second violation, not only to make the game fairer (especially if a team had tall players), but also to increase skillful play.[31]

The issue of snatching the ball also arose again in 1956. After much experimentation from 1949 on, the Committee decided a ball could be tied up with "both hands . . . firmly around the ball held by an opponent."[32] Then in 1960, they changed the rule to permit one or two hands held firmly on the ball. The 1960–61 *Guide* stated that this change makes

"it possible to block a shot . . . will encourage faster passing and shooting
. . . [and] allow the guard to better defend against the 'tall' forward."
The guarding rule became more restrictive in that a player could not
face guard an opponent within three feet, nor could two guards extend
their arms to trap an opponent (the horizontal guarding rule).[33]

In 1957, on a trial basis, a missed free throw continued in play, which
brought back the art of rebounding. As usual the experimental rule
stayed and became official in 1959.[34]

Five interesting 1961 changes reflect the new skill level of players and
the influence of liberal basketball proponents.[35]

1. Allowing a three bounce dribble gave players "a greater opportunity to change direction."

2. After a successful free throw, the other team took the ball out of
bounds at the end line, increasing the speed of the game.

3. After a basket, the ball was awarded out of bounds at the end line
to the team that did not score.

4. The old controversial "snatching" rule of years ago returned. On
an experimental basis the Committee would allow a player to take the
ball from an opponent as long as there was no personal contact or
unnecessary roughness. They hoped the new rule would "encourage
players to move the ball faster." At the same time, since the hands were
considered a part of the ball, contact with fingers in tying the ball was
not a foul. This experimental rule appeared officially in the 1962 season.

5. An experimental rule change, almost as revolutionary as the two
court game in 1938, appeared in 1961. Each team was allowed two roving
players who played the entire court. The Committee explained that
controlled experimentation had been conducted the previous year at all
skill levels. This study indicated that the roving player game "provided
more opportunity for team play and that it encouraged all players to
develop the skills of shooting and both defensive and offensive tactics."
The roving player game would not be official until 1962 "so that instructional materials in team play and strategy could be developed. . . ."

1964–1971

Throughout the 1960s the Basketball Committee had done its part to
make the rules as compatible to those of the Amateur Athletic Union
and the National Federation of State High School Athletic Associations
as they could. The National Federation decided against working with
DGWS and published its own girls' rules in 1971. By 1965, however,
the AAU and DGWS rules were nearly exact, so a joint committee of
AAU and DGWS personnel modified the rules. The *Basketball Guide*
for 1964–65 was identical to the "Women's Section" of the *AAU Basketball Rules*. The joint committee worked toward selecting the "best"

from each group of rules thereby arriving at one set. One of Berenson's remaining original rules fell victim to change. The three second limitation on holding the ball changed to a player being free to hold the ball indefinitely if not closely guarded (five seconds if closely guarded). Goal tending returned to the rule book after an absence of over 50 years. Remnants of the vertical guarding rule also returned, as "holding both arms extended horizontally" was prohibited. To "discourage careless or rough play near the end of the game and to make it unprofitable to deliberately foul . . ." the joint committee awarded two free throws the last two minutes of each half. Finally that year the Committee gave officials the right to remove a coach from the playing area for unsportsmanlike conduct.[36]

In 1966 the continuous (unlimited) dribble made its way back to the women's game. This change made the sport much faster, especially combined with the new roving player game. The 30-second clock was another controversial rule under experimentation since 1964. While the continuous dribble was made official, the 30-second clock was made optional because there seemed to be some resistance to it.[37]

For the next few years rule changes were minor until the 1969 experimental rules of a five player, full court game and the 30-second clock.[38] Although a two year trial period was planned for the five player game, due to the lack of resistance only one year was necessary. So the most revolutionary change in women's basketball hardly sent a ripple through the women's basketball world, outside of a few areas such as Iowa. The time had indeed come for most forward-looking physical educators to accept the need for a more skillful and challenging game.

In 1971, the five player game plus the 30-second clock were official. In other words, after approximately 75 years, basketball as played by girls and women had come almost full circle and was nearly back to the game designed by Naismith.[39]

1972–1990

The rules for girls and women's basketball remained fairly constant after adoption of the five player, full court game in 1971, until the experimental rules of 1974–75.[40] The Committee experimented with the 20-minute halves and the bonus rule for free throws. In the bonus rule game no free throws are awarded for common fouls until a team has committed its fifth personal foul in high school games and seventh personal foul in college games. After the fifth or seventh foul, one free throw is awarded; if successful, a bonus free throw follows. Free throws are never taken for offensive fouls and always taken if a foul is committed against a person in the act of shooting, or a flagrant foul. These rules all became official in the next year's 1975–76 *Guide*.[41]

The rule changes from 1976 to 1984 were more rules of refinement and definition. There were some changes in what constituted a foul in offensive and defensive positions and movement patterns, rather than substantial rule changes. These years brought an increase in the number of members and organizations contributing to the basketball rules, including all collegiate governance structures conducting national championships. As of 1983–84, the Women's Basketball Coaches Association (WBCA) had membership on the United States Girls and Women's Basketball Rules Committee, which had been formed in 1979.[42]

A significant controversial change occurred in 1984. After two major research studies, the Basketball Committee legislated a smaller ball. The ball is approximately one inch less in circumference and two ounces lighter than the previous ball—thus the same suggested weight as the women's 1899 basketball. The Committee felt that "the quality of play would be enhanced with the use of the smaller basketball."[43] Many coaches did not want the change. Those who did felt it would make the game faster and enable more young girls to handle the ball and thus "get involved in basketball." At first the rule applied only to the college game, but high school coaches liked the change, so the National Federation also moved to the smaller basketball. Regulations governing the backcourt appeared in the 1984–85 *Guide*, as did the reversal of the 1980 rule against using musical instruments and noisemakers.[44]

The year 1984–85 marked the last year of the publication of the NAGWS *Basketball Guides*. The National Collegiate Athletic Association (NCAA) determined it would publish a women's basketball rule book using the rules of the United States Girls and Women's Basketball Rules Committee. NAGWS still has representation on this large rules committee. Rule changes by this committee complete the tide of change. Three new rules that influence the game only slightly but have implications for coaching are (1) coaches have a specific area called the "coaching box" and the coach may not leave the coaching box without the chance of a technical foul; (2) the time-outs are changed from 60 seconds to 70 seconds, and (3) two free throws are awarded for all technical fouls.[45]

During the academic year 1987–88 a major rule change introduced a three point field goal from a distance of at least 19 feet 9 inches from the center of the basket. Naturally, this rule required additional court markings. The previous year 28 conferences in NCAA had tried it experimentally, and the Committee felt the new rule "added excitement to the game and provided teams an opportunity to come from behind."[46] With the new ball and the provision for the three point goal, the game has become faster, more exciting, and more challenging to the millions of girls and women playing.

The Story Behind the Rules

The evolution of rule changes in women's basketball was a necessary part of self-determination and self-governance for women leaders in basketball. For the many basketball committees the work was exciting but at the same time often caused controversy and confusion. Every facet of the game was subject to modifications. Yet the agreement between rule changes and the objectives and philosophy of NAGWS/WBC is impressive. For example, as players became more skillful, changes were designed to make the game more challenging and exciting. To clearly illustrate the rationale for rule changes a discussion of the actual writings of the physical educators and committee members is essential. Excerpts from various articles in the *Guides* demonstrate the Committee's intent in some rule changes and indicate their concern for the health, safety, and welfare of the female players.

The Dribble

The evolution of the dribble certainly impacted on the game. From Naismith's original unlimited dribble, the rule went to a three bounce dribble at knee height, to no dribble, to one dribble (knee high), to two dribbles, to three dribbles, and then back to the unlimited dribble. The women often criticized the continuous dribble. They felt it made the game too similar to the boys and promoted the development of star players. When the three bounce dribble was reinstated the rule was much the same as in 1901, except the 1961 rendition did not limit the height of the dribble. Thus it took 60 years of study, discussion, and experimentation to return to the initial regulation, and another five years for the unlimited dribble to return to Naismith's original dribbling game. All changes, of course, reflected the central focus, namely, the needs and the best interest of the players!

Guarding

The early vertical guarding rule drastically limited the guards' ability to deny the ball or to prevent a shot at the goal. The limitations this imposed are readily seen in the following descriptions:

> a. Guarding with one or both hands over the ball or touching the ball legally held by an opponent shall be termed overguarding.
> b. Overguarding one's opponent who has the ball consists of (1) guarding with one or both hands or arms or body not in the vertical plane. . . .[47]

It was difficult to officiate legal guarding as, quite naturally, players' arms went from the vertical to the horizontal while trying to guard an opponent. In an article on officiating in the 1930–31 *Guide*, the author emphasized that the official must "recognize any infringement of the guarding rule especially when a tall guard has a short forward for an opponent."[48]

When guarding was finally allowed on any plane, the Committee even liberalized the interpretation of the technique. The following clarification about guarding was in the 1934–35 rules:

> Although basketball is theoretically a "no contact game," it is obvious that personal contact cannot be avoided entirely when players are moving rapidly over a limited space. The personal contact resulting from such movement should not be penalized unless roughness has resulted.

Likewise, the Committee suggested that accidentally touching the ball or hands or arms of a player should not be penalized if accidental and no roughness resulted. In other words, the official used her judgment in this regard.[49]

An important rule change occurred in 1932–33, when guarding was allowed on *any* plane. The illustration at right appeared in the "Basketball Technique" chart dated 1930, which was included as a supplement to the Spalding's *Official Basketball Guide for Women* for several years. It was labeled "Wrong Guarding Not in the Vertical Plane." In the 1932–33 *Guide* it would become a legal guarding technique.

A few years after guarding on any plane was legal these remarks indicated how the new rule had impacted the game:

> The new guarding rule is far reaching in its effect on women's basketball. It has forced changes in the playing, the coaching, and the refereeing of the game. These changes seem to be welcome everywhere, and to players and officials alike. This guarding rule is a natural step forward in the development of girls' basketball, paralleling the development of girls and women in sport.[50]

While there was a new freedom in guarding, zone guarding across the entire lane, or two guards trapping a player, prompted a rule to prevent horizontal guarding. This rule prevented a team from blocking the entire key.

Scoring

When guarding was restrictive, field goals counted as one or two points depending on the type of shot. When fouled, a player received one free throw, except that if in the act of shooting, she received two free throws. One of the more mystifying rulings was the one regarding goal tending that appeared from 1907 until 1918. The 1913–14 *Guide* rules, for example, specified that only one point was allowed "If the basket or ball was touched by opponent when the ball is on the edge of the basket."[51] As the baskets were ten feet high, it seems amazing that the Committee made such provisions against the very tall players. In 1936 Tapley commented, [one] "wonders what kind of players there were in those days."[52] Morrison, in her thesis on basketball, suggested that "the players of that time were either giants or had much more jumping ability. . . if they could reach the basket."[53]

Violations and Fouls

Changes in violations and fouls were constant and increasingly complex to accommodate coaches' increasing skill at devising clever strategies and plays. As mentioned, many of the present day violations were fouls. Since a player received a free throw for being fouled, it is not surprising that the game seemed slow with many interruptions. As Alice Frymir wrote in her classic *Basket Ball for Women*, "many games are ruined because they are too slow, too many fouls are called. . . ."[54] Even stepping on the line was at one time considered a line foul. In 1918, fouls which had been labeled "general" and "specific" were changed to "personal" and "technical."[55] Technical fouls were those transgressions that did not involve personal contact. Today fouls are still classified as "personal" and "technical." There have been many subtle changes through the years in relation to guarding rules and interpretations on exactly what is charging, blocking, and horizontal guarding. The different interpretations seemed ever changing.

Baskets

Early games must have been long and slow as the ball was retrieved from inside a closed-bottom basket opened by a drawstring or chain. An ad in the 1903–1904 *Guide* for the Spalding "Official" Basket Ball Goal indicates that the "nets [are] constructed so that the bottom may be left open in practice games to permit the ball to drop through."[56] The early rules stated that "in case baskets with open bottoms are used, to constitute a goal, the ball must enter and pass through the basket in accordance with the judgement of the referee."[57] The last year of the closed basket rule (1917–18) seems fairly late in the game's evolution to still have closed baskets.

Teams

In the beginning an official team consisted of five players. In 1901 the rules changed to allow five to ten players on a team. Soon after, the numbers changed to six to nine players. There was always an explanation that the size of the floor used for playing determined whether the smaller or larger number of players was used. In 1938, when the two court game became official, a team consisted of six players, three forwards and three guards. This permitted many more plays and better teamwork. As Frymir wrote, "the division of a. . .court into two sections was a step forward. Certainly better team play is possible if the players have room in which to shift positions."[58] In 1962, an official team re-

SPALDING'S BASKET BALL GOODS

Spalding's "Official" Basket Ball Goals.

No. **80.**

Per pair, **$4.00**

EXTRACT FROM THE OFFICIAL RULES.

RULE III—GOALS.

Sec. 3. The Goal made by **A. G. Spalding & Bros.** shall be the official goal.

Official Goal.

mained at six players even when two of the six were rovers who could play the full court. When the game moved to the "men's game," an official team had five players playing anywhere they wished on the court. The changes in women's sport was surely reflected in the revolutionized full court five player women's basketball game.

Playing Court and the Ball

The most dramatic change in the history of women's basketball has been the court division. The game changed from Naismith's full court to three court to make the game less strenuous, to two court to make the game faster and more exciting, and then back again to full court to challenge the players. No doubt there are many former side centers and guards, and even more "stationary guards" from the two court game, who would have loved the option of shooting at the basket and going anywhere on the court. Those lucky enough to have a small court could at least play two court and one player could race the entire court even before the women's right to vote became a reality.

The ball underwent changes as the Basketball Rules Committee tried to perfect women's basketball. The early ball was the men's ball, 18 to 20 ounces. At that time to be official the ball had to be manufactured by A.G. Spalding and bear the written signature of one of the prime movers in physical education, Luther Gulick. A study of the *Guides* in regard to the size and weight of the ball indicates the Committee's attention to detail. The ball's weight remained fairly constant at slightly heavier by an ounce, until 1930 when it was to be "not less than 20 nor more than 23 ounces"[59] (but it returned to 20 to 22 ounces the following year). When the smaller ball became official in 1984, its specified weight was 18 ounces minimum to 20 ounces maximum (a return to the 1901 ball). Likewise, the circumference was fairly constant, but did have many minor changes in dimensions plus some complex specifications, as found in this 1952 ruling:

> When it is dropped to the playing court from a height of six feet, measured from the bottom of the ball, it will bounce between 49 and 54 inches, measured to the top of the ball.[60]

Since 1984–85, specifications for the official ball are succinct and uncomplicated. "The ball shall be spherical and have a leather case. It shall weigh between 18–20 ounces with a circumference of 28 and one half to 29 inches. . . ."[61] A lighter smaller ball had been considered several times before 1984. In the 1922–23 *Guide*, the WBC inserted a questionnaire about possible rule changes. The first question was, "Do you favor standardizing for girls a basketball lighter than the one used for boys and men?" Also, the 1931–32 *Guide* announced: "Anyone interested in trying out a smaller ball for girls than the one now official

Left, a two-point shot. Forward has stepped back with left foot and is shooting with a "chest throw." Right, a one-point shot, a one-hand overhead throw. (From the Basketball Technique chart, a *Guides* supplement)

is asked to write to the Chairman. . . ."[62] Reference to a smaller ball was not made again until the 1960–61 *Guide* when an article appeared entitled "Smaller Ball for Smaller Hands." The author argued convincingly that a smaller ball would "improve skills and control. . . ."[63]

Officials

The early women's basketball games required many officials. As one author wrote, "officials were more in demand. . .than was a team. . . ."[64] It is ironic that even today with all the changes in the game the statement still applies. The game requires more officials than team members. An official game has five players and seven officials: a referee, an umpire, two timers, two scorers, and a 30-second clock operator. There has been speculation for some time that as the game becomes faster, perhaps the number of officials should be increased to eight with an additional referee or umpire.

Length of Game and Time-outs

For many years games consisted of two 15-minute segments with a 10-minute halftime; then the 8-minute quarters arrived. After a series of time-out modifications and amount of time between quarters and halves, the game evolved back to two 20-minute halves with a 15-minute halftime. Similar to other rule changes, game length went full circle. The constant addition of time-outs in the post-War era speaks clearly to the importance of a coach. Coaches felt they needed more time-outs to permit coaching, as well as to permit brief rest periods for players in the faster-paced games.

Coaching from the Sidelines

In light of present-day vocal entreaties from coaches during games, this review of the rules ends appropriately with a description of changes in coaching from the sideline rule. Not only was coaching from the bench prohibited and classified as a foul, the Committee didn't even allow the designated captain to speak to her teammates during a game. They later relented and permitted the captain to speak during play, but it was emphasized that she must speak *quietly*. Finally in 1916, all players were allowed to talk—*quietly*. The rule stipulated "when necessary, but it should be seldom necessary." By 1918, coaching from the sidelines changed from a general foul to a technical foul charged to the captain; nonetheless, a foul. Coaches could not coach during time-outs and between quarters until the 1950s. It took another four generations (17 years) of college students before the Committee saw fit to allow coaching from the sidelines at any time.

Views from the Women's Basketball Committee

The story of women's basketball rules would not be complete without elaborating on the role of the women's basketball committee who guided and controlled the destiny of girls and women's basketball. One point is obvious about the individuals who made up the committee: From its inception in 1899 to the last United States Girls and Women's Basketball Rules Committee in 1984–85, they were a dedicated group of educators. Virtually all women who were prime movers in physical education served at one time or another in some capacity on the committees related to basketball. It was like an apprenticeship as they moved to other significant positions in NAGWS and other organizations. An analysis of all the rule changes illustrates the hard work, deliberation, and vision of these dedicated, courageous women who served without financial compensation. They were willing to give their time and talent for the health, welfare, and enjoyment of the female players.

The basic philosophical tenets "for the good of those who play" were paramount in deliberations. Similarly the women demanded adherence to high standards of sportsmanship and fair play. Eline von Borries' (chairman of the Women's Basketball Committee) remarks in the 1931–32 *Guide* illustrate the importance of fair play:

> Coaches and Officials should always bear in mind that in the final analysis, it is the *spirit* of the rules that should govern the playing of the game rather than the adherence or non-adherence to the highly technical rules and regulations, of which there are such an unavoidable number. In the minds of the Committee this means the spirit of play for play's sake, even when competition is at its highest. It means that the safeguarding of the health of the players is of greater importance than the temporary glory of winning a game.[65]

In the previous year's 1930–31 *Guide*, von Borries admonished coaches in her editorial that the Committee "deplores the fact that. . .the game sometimes deteriorates into a battle of wits between coaches who quibble over technicalities. . .and who in every way do anything but set up an ideal for sportsmanlike conduct on the part of the players."[66] She concluded by urging all to "observe the spirit of the rules and thereby place basketball on the high plane where it deserves to be."

In the 1936–37 *Guide* the editor, Marie L. Simes, also referred to the battle of wits and urged that those playing basketball match "wits and skills on the court, rather than by thumbing the rule book in an effort to find possible loopholes. . . ." She also emphasized playing under the "spirit of the rules."[67]

DISCUSSION OF DEBATABLE POINTS IN THE RULES

The New Guarding Rules

At the A.P.E.A. convention in Philadelphia, in April, 1932, in co-operation with the Women's National Officials' Rating Committee, the Basketball Committee staged demonstration games showing basketball as played under the 1931-32 rules and under modifications now incorporated in the Guide. Immediately after the demonstration a discussion meeting was held at which some sixty persons were present. This was followed by a larger one of approximately 600 persons, who were practically all in favor of trying the suggested liberalized guarding for at least two years. Since a large majority of the State Chairmen felt similarly, the Committee felt justified in reading into the Guide changes which to some may seem too radical. The basic principles upon which women's basketball has been built—avoidance of contact with opponent and undisputed possession of ball after it is once secured—still remain intact. The player with the ball will need to pass or shoot more quickly than heretofore and will need to become more adept in the individual tactics of pivoting, bouncing and juggling. Contact is to be strictly interpreted.

Three Seconds

is still the limit for holding the ball while in-bounds. Lengthening the time would have been a step toward allowing "stalling."

With every major suggested rule change, there was experimentation and questionnaires about the new rule. In fact, the Committee even had a subcommittee on questionnaires who solicited and tabulated opinions about changes. For example, before guarding on any plane was made legal, opinions were mostly negative. The Committee decided "the experiment resulted in much bodily contact and rough play and was discarded as incompatible with the intent of the rules."[68] Times and ideals change, so by 1932 the physical education women favored a liberal guarding rule.

When the radical change was made from a three court to a two court game, the Committee explained the change this way: "This change was made because of the demand for it and because the committee feels that this is in the best interests of the game." The statement ended, "someday it is hoped basketball rules will not need to be changed every year."[69]

For many years each *Guide* had an annual article entitled "Change the Rules? Yes and No." New rules were not only described, but the rationale for the change was given. Most articles began with an introduction such as, "The Basketball Committee has welcomed all suggestions on the rules and *Guide* and *has considered them carefully* one by one." The deliberations of the Committee were reinforced by the statement that "experience in the past has indicated that it is unwise to change rules without due experimentation. . . ."[70]

At times the Committee solicited help from the people involved in the game. A typical plea appeared in the 1972–73 *Guide*:

> The Committee needs the help of coaches and teachers in solving the problems related to the "blind pick" and "act of shooting." Several attempts have been made to write rules to alleviate the crises, but each effort seems to cause more problems or have too many loopholes. Please write to Jill Upton (Chairman) if you have any ideas which might help the committee in its deliberation regarding these issues.[71]

Generally the Committee explained the changes succinctly. For example, in 1968, when coaching from the sidelines was no longer a foul, they stated that "calling encouragement or admonitions to players on the court does not materially affect play. . . ."[72]

Rarely did the Committee focus on themselves and the work they did. An exception was this excerpt from the 1956–57 *Guide*:

> The members of the Committee, all serving voluntarily, act not as individuals but as representatives of girls and women playing basketball all over the country. . . . The Committee members bring to the Rules Meeting, in written form the desires of the people they represent in regard to NSGWS Rules.[73]

Previously, in the 1950–51 *Guide* there had been an article about the Women's Basketball Committee which explained that the Committee was composed "of 15 persons and any number of advisory members." The mission of the Committee was described in this manner:

> The work of the committee is directed toward arriving at one set of basketball rules for girls and women. . . and conducts studies in order to secure information concerning controversial issues, and. . . works toward the improvement of standards for participation in basketball in the United States.[74]

Following are examples of statements made by our women leaders who, when they had drastically changed rules, would through their writings plead for visionary acceptance of the new rule(s). Longtime committee member, Fran Koenig, does just that in a 1971 article, "30-Second Clock. . .A Step Forward!" when she remarked:

> What does make a difference is that those who teach and coach the sport are always ready to accept rules changes that contribute toward making basketball the best possible game for the girls and women who participate. The 30-second clock does just that by doing something no other rule has done to date![75]

When the five player game was in its experimental phase, an article in the *Guide* urged a positive attitude:

> Players and coaches may initially undergo a few moments of panic at the thought of possibly changing from a six player to a five player game. But perhaps the differences are not as great as they might appear at first and in a short time the new rules and strategy will be as familiar as the old.[76]

Unquestionably, men's basketball rules influenced many women's rule changes. Also unquestionably, the women's basketball committee attempted to readjust their rules and the format and wording of the rules to comply with the boys and men's rule books. Addressing those who were skeptical about the similarities between the men's and women's games, a committee member wrote, "a rule is not bad just because the boys use it."[77]

Finally, an article in the 1947–48 *Guide* succinctly explains why the development of women's basketball and its rules for this first 100 years had such a long, complex, and colorful history. The author of "Why Play Girls' Rules in Basketball?" remarked:

> Women's rules have been developed for women by women. Women and girls all over the country have participated in rule changes, making the game better suited for girls. Ever since the first rule change. . . [the] three court game. . . women have been making the rules more adaptable and more suitable for women and girls. Women's basketball is a women's game. It is their own game; they made it and developed it for themselves. . . .[78]

Thus, girls and women's basketball after a colorful, deliberate process has come full circle back to the game designed by Naismith. His fundamental principles are in force today in the women's game. Basketball is the most popular girls and women's sport. It certainly is the most popular intercollegiate sport. Consequently, it has the biggest budgets and the highest paid coaches and is the most visible, thanks to media and TV exposure. Today, outstanding women players who have finished their collegiate eligibility are receiving six-figure salaries to play professional basketball in Europe, Japan, and Scandinavia. Hopefully, one day professional basketball will return for women athletes in this country.

It may be an overused cliché that "We have come a long way, ladies" in many aspects of American life. But it is descriptive of women's basketball history. For example, in the early days many games were closed to spectators. There were 178,000 spectators at the 1990 Division I Women's National Basketball Championships, including 40,000 for the Final Four.[79]

So, we have come a long way and a big thank you to James Naismith, the many women who guided the game, and the thousands of girls and women who played the game from the three division court, to the two division court, to the rover, and to the fast-paced sport played today as originally invented 100 years ago.

Notes

1. James Naismith, *Basketball: Its Origin and Development* (New York: Association Press, 1941), 62.

2. Senda Berenson, "Basket Ball for Women," *Physical Education* (September 1894): 106–109.

3. Senda Berenson, "Editorial," in *Basket Ball for Women* (New York: American Sports Publishing Company, 1901), 6. The committee members included Senda Berenson; A. Bertha Foster, Oberlin College; Ethel Perrin, Boston Normal School of Gymnastics (listed as the chairman); and Elizabeth Wright, Radcliffe College.

4. Senda Berenson, "Are Women's Basket Ball Rules Better for Women Than Men's Basket Ball Rules," *Spalding's Official Women's Basket Ball Guide* (New York: American Sports Publishing Company, 1908), 31–41.

5. Berenson, *Basket Ball for Women* (1901), 28–43.

6. Senda Berenson, "Preface," *Spalding's Official Women's Basket Ball Guide 1905–06* (New York: American Sports Publishing Company, 1906). The members of the new Executive Committee on Basket Ball Rules were: Julie E. Sullivan, chairman, Teachers College, New York; Luther Halsey Gulick, director, Physical Training, Public Schools of Greater New York; Elizabeth Burchenal, Teachers College, New York; George T. Hepbron, editor, Men's Of-

ficial Basket Ball Guide; Elizabeth A. Wright, Radcliffe College; Harry Fisher, editor, Official Collegiate Basket Ball Guide; Ethel Perrin, Boston Normal School of Gymnastics; and Senda Berenson, Smith College.

7. Berenson, *Basket Ball for Women* (1901), 28–43; Berenson, "Preface," *BasketBall for Women* (1903), ed. Senda Berenson (New York: American Sports Publishing Company, 1903), 66–85; Senda Berenson Abbott, *Spalding's Official Basket Ball Guide for Women* (1914–15) (New York: American Sports Publishing Company, 1914), 9–49.

8. Berenson, *BasketBall for Women* (1903).

9. Berenson, *Basket Ball Guide* (1905–06), 9, 21.

10. Berenson, *Basket Ball Guide* (1908), 8–27. Fouls were listed as General and Specific (players may be disqualified). The guard may stand firm and guard rigidly, the forward must bounce around her opponent. This is the beginning of the concept of charging.

11. Berenson. *Basket Ball Guide* (1908), 23; Florence D. Alden, Elizabeth Richards, and L. Raymond Burnett, eds., *Official Basket Ball Guide for Women* (1918–19) (New York: American Sports Publishing Company, 1918), 15.

12. Senda Berenson, ed., *Spalding's Official Women's Basket Ball Guide 1910– 1911* (New York: American Sports Publishing Company, 1910), 18; Berenson, ed., *Spalding's Official Basket Ball Guide for Women* (1913–14) (New York: American Sports Publishing Company, 1913), 31; Berenson, "The Significance of Basket Ball for Women," in *Basket Ball for Women* (1901), 26.

13. Berenson, *Basket Ball Guide* (1913–14), 9.

14. Berenson Abbott, *Basket Ball Guide for Women* (1916–17), 57, 58.

15. Helen M. McKinstry, Florence D. Alden, and L. R. Burnett, eds., *Official Basket Ball Guide for Women* (1917–18) (New York: American Sports Publishing Company, 1917), 49, 17, 58.

16. Florence D. Alden, "Editorial Comment," in *Official Basket Ball Guide for Women* (1918–19), 5.

17. Alden, *Basket Ball Guide* (1918–19), 5–6, 13, 37, 17, 48–50. Rule 8, Section A explained the new jump ball position. The players must have one hand held behind their back as they executed their jump.

18. Elizabeth Richards, ed., *Official Basketball Guide for Women* (1921–22) (New York: American Sports Publishing Company, 1921), 38, 45, 15–17. (Note that this is the first year in which "basketball" appeared as one word in the *Guide* title.) Grace E. Jones, ed., *Official Basketball Guide for Women 1925– 26* (New York: American Sports Publishing Company, 1925).

19. Christine White, ed., "Official Playing Rules," in *Official Basketball Guide for Women and Girls* (1939–40) (A. S. Barnes and Co., 1939), 32; Bernice Finger, ed., *Official Basketball and Officials Rating Guide for Women and Girls* (1949–50) (Washington, D.C.: American Association for Health, Physical Education, and Recreation, 1949), 105.

20. Carin Degermark, ed., *Official Basketball Guide for Women* (1922–23) (New York: American Sports Publishing Company, 1922), 7, 13.

21. Emma F. Waterman, Helen Frost, and L. Raymond Burnett, eds. *Official Basketball Guide for Women* (1923–24) (New York: American Sports Publishing Company, 1923), 50–51; Grace E. Jones, Emma F. Waterman, L. Raymond

Burnett, eds., *Official Basketball Guide for Women* (1924–25) (New York: American Sports Publishing Company, 1924), 7, 30; Alden, *Official Basket Ball Guide* (1918–19), 43; Grace E. Jones, ed., *Official Basketball Guide for Women* (1925–26), 37; Grace E. Jones, ed., *Official Basketball Guide for Women* (1927–28) (New York: American Sports Publishing Company, 1927), 40–41.

22. Marie L. Simes, ed., "Official Playing Rules," in *Official Basketball Guide for Women and Girls* (1935–36) (New York: American Sports Publishing Company, 1935), 24–25; Christine White, ed., "Official Playing Rules," in *Basketball Guide* (1936–37), 33.

23. Eline von Borries, ed., "Official Playing Rules," in *Official Basketball Guide for Women and Girls* (1932–33) (New York: American Sports Publishing Company, 1932), 15–16, 17, 22; Eline von Borries, ed., "Official Playing Rules," in *Official Basketball Guide for Women and Girls* (1933–34) (New York: American Sports Publishing Company, 1933), 38; Marie L. Simes, ed., *Official Basketball Guide for Women and Girls* (1936–37) (New York: American Sports Publishing Company, 1936), 33.

24. Wilhelmine Meissner, ed., *Official Basketball Guide for Women and Girls* (1938–39) (New York: A. S. Barnes and Co., 1938), 3–5; Marie L. Simes, ed., "Experimental Rules," in *Basketball Guide* (1935–36), 71–72.

25. Marie D. Hartwig, ed., *Official Basketball and Officials Rating Guide for Women and Girls* (1947–48) (New York: A. S. Barnes and Co., 1947), 72; Grace E. Jones, ed., *Basketball Guide* (1927–28), 19.

26. Josephine Fiske, ed., *Official Basketball and Officials Rating Guide for Women and Girls* (1942–43) (New York: A. S. Barnes and Co., 1943), 19, 113; Rachel J. Benton, "Change the Rules? Yes and No," in *Official Basketball and Officials Rating Guide for Women and Girls* (1945–46) (New York: A. S. Barnes and Co., 1945), 20.

27. Bernice Finger, ed., *Basketball Guide* (1949–50), 113, 115; Miriam Gray, "Experimentation on Basketball Rules, 1947–48," in *Basketball Guide* (1947–48), 9, 19.

28. Gwen Smith, ed., *Official Basketball and Officials Rating Guide for Women and Girls* (September 1951–September 1952) (Washington, D.C.: AAHPER, 1951), 70.

29. Gwen Smith, ed., "Preface," in *Official Basketball and Officials Rating Guide for Girls and Women* (September 1952–September 1953) (Washington, D.C.: AAHPER, 1952), 5.

30. "An Explanation of the Rule Changes," in Grace Fox, ed., *Official Basketball and Officials Rating Guide for Girls and Women* (September 1953–September 1954) (Washington, D.C.: AAHPER, 1953), 43–46.

31. "Rule Changes 1955–56," in Helen B. Lawrence, ed., *Official Basketball and Officials Rating Guide for Girls and Women* (September 1955–September 1956) (Washington, D.C.: AAHPER, 1955), 120.

32. Ibid., p. 119.

33. "Rules Changes 1960–61," in Irma Schalk, ed., *Basketball Guide for Girls and Women* (September 1960–September 1961) (Washington, D.C.: AAHPER, 1960), 119, 120.

34. "Rule Changes," in Irma Schalk, ed., *Basketball Guide for Girls and Women* (September 1959–September 1960) (Washington, D.C.: AAHPER, 1959), 118.

35. "Comments on Rule Changes 1961–62," in Shirley Winsberg, ed., *Basketball Guide* (September 1961–September 1962) (Washington, D.C.: AAHPER, 1961), 117, 118, 138.

36. "Comments on Rule Changes 1964–65," in Barbara L. Drinkwater, ed., *Basketball Guide* (August 1964–August 1965) (Washington, D.C.: AAHPER, 1964), 117–120, 143.

37. "Comments on Rule Changes," in Mildred J. Barnes, ed., *Basketball Guide* (August 1966–August 1967) (Washington, D.C.: AAHPER, 1966), 117–118.

38. "DGWS-AAU Joint Basketball Rules Committee, "You Decide," in Aimee Loftin, ed., *Basketball Guide* (August 1969–1970) (Washington, D.C.: AAHPER, 1969), 34–35, 38–60.

39. Ruth Gunden, ed., *Basketball Guide* (August 1971–August 1972) (Washington, D.C.: AAHPER, 1971), 152–153.

40. Joint DGWS-AAU Women's Basketball Rules Committee, "Try it, you'll like it!" in Norma Boetel, ed., *Basketball Guide* (July 1974–July 1975) (Washington, D.C.: AAHPER, 1974), 80–81; "Experimental Basketball Rules for Girls and Women," in *Basketball Guide* (1974–75), 82–119.

41. "Summary of Basketball Rules Changes for 1975–76," in Norma Boetel, ed., *Basketball* (August 1975–August 1976) (Washington, D.C.: AAHPER, 1975), 87–88.

42. "Preface," in Jill Hutchison, ed., *Basketball* (July 1983–July 1984) (Reston, Va.: AAHPERD, 1983), 18.

43. Mosher and E. Hanson, "Why the Smaller Ball Is Needed," *Women's Court* 1 (1984): 5.

44. M. Flanney, "The Small Changes," *Women's Court* 2 (1984): 10; "Summary of Major Rule Changes and Clarifications 1984–85," in Jill Hutchison, ed., *Basketball* (July 1984–July 1985) (Reston, Va.: AAHPERD, 1984), 20–22.

45. Michelle A. Pond, ed., *1988 NCAA Men's and Women's Basketball Rules and Interpretations* (Mission, Kans.: NCAA, 1987), 10; Michelle A. Pond, ed., *1989 NCAA Men's and Women's Basketball Rules and Interpretations* (Mission, Kans.: NCAA, 1988), 11; Michelle A. Pond, ed., *1990 NCAA Men's and Women's Basketball Rules and Interpretations* (Mission, Kans.: NCAA, 1989), 10–11.

46. "Women's Rules Committee Report," in *1988 NCAA Men's and Women's Basketball Rules and Interpretations* (Mission, Kans.: NCAA, 1988), 9–11.

47. Eline von Borries, ed., *Official Basketball Guide for Women* (1930–31) (New York: American Sports Publishing Company, 1930), 28.

48. Evelyn Logan, "Basketball Officiating," *Guide* (1930), 61.

49. Eline von Borries, ed., "Basketball Official Playing Rules 1934–35," in *Official Basketball Guide for Women and Girls* (1934–35) (Washington, D.C.: AAHPER, 1934), 17; "Discussion of Debatable Points in the Rules," in *Guide* (1934), 14.

50. Ruby L. Brock, "Effect of the New Guarding Rule," in *Guide* (1934), 43.

51. Senda Berenson Abbott, ed., *Guide* (1913–14), 41.

52. Dorothy Tapley, "Thirty Years of Girls' Basketball Rules," in *Guide* (1936–37), 50.

53. Jane Morrison, *The Major Changes in the Philosophy Underlying Women's Sports and Their Influence on Basketball Rules* (unpublished master's thesis, Ohio State University, 1963), 18.

54. Alice Frymir, *Basket Ball for Women* (New York: A. S. Barnes and Company, 1928), 46, 56.

55. Florence D. Alden, ed., *Guide* (1918–19), 49–50.

56. Senda Berenson, *Basket Ball* (1903–04).

57. Senda Berenson, *Guide* (1908), 23.

58. Frymir, *Basket Ball for Women*, 10.

59. Eline von Borries, ed., *Guide* (1930–31), 18.

60. Gwen Smith, ed., *Guide* (1952–53), 112.

61. Jill Hutchison, ed., *Guide* (1984–85), 26.

62. Eline von Borries, *Guide* (1931–32), 4–5.

63. Shirley Jameson, "Smaller Ball for Smaller Hands," in *Guide* (1960–61), 37.

64. Tapley, "Thirty Years of Girls' Basketball Rules," 49.

65. "Editorial Comment," in *Guide* (1931–32), 5.

66. "Editorial Comment," in *Guide* (1931–31), 4.

67. "Editorial Comment," in *Guide* (1936–37), 11.

68. Eline von Borries, ed., *Guide* (1930–31), 55.

69. "Editorial Comment," in *Guide* (1938–39), 10.

70. Marie Hartwig, "Change in Rules? Yes and No," in *Guide* (1947–48), 65.

71. "Comments on Rules," in Nan Nichols, ed., *Basketball Guide* (July 1972–July 1973) (Washington, D.C.: AAHPER, 1972), 116.

72. "Comments on Rules," in Janette S. Sayre, ed., *Basketball Guide* (August 1968–August 1969) (Washington, D.C.: AAHPER, 1968), 118.

73. "Rule Changes, Clarifications and Explanations," in Catherine Snell, ed., *Official Basketball and Officials Rating Guide for Girls and Women* (September 1956–September 1957) (Washington, D.C.: AAHPER, 1956), 119.

74. "The Basketball Committee at Work," in Bernice Finger, ed., *Official Basketball and Officials Rating Guide for Women and Girls* (1950–51) (Washington, D.C.: AAHPER, 1950), 73.

75. Fran Koenig, "30-Second Clock . . . A Step Forward!" in *Guide* (1971–72), 40.

76. Patricia H. Lawson, "A Basic Defense and Offense for the Five Player Game," in *Guide* (1970–71), 26.

77. June D. White, "Basketball Fast and Fifty," in Cal Papatsos, ed., *Selected Basketball Articles* (Washington, D.C.: AAHPER, 1953), 10.

78. Miriam Gray, "Why Play Girls Rules in Basketball?" in *Guide* (1947–48), 35.

79. Lilley, T. J., "Sara Lee Corp. Pledges Funds for Women's Athletics," *NCAA News* (September 24, 1990), 2.

Section 2
Cultural and Medical Influences

6

The Domestication of Basketball

Steveda Chepko

The evolution of women's basketball rules has been influenced by many complex social and cultural factors.[1] The rules of any game do not develop in a vacuum, and women's basketball is no exception. Rather its rules clearly reflect the changing society and culture in which they were written over time. As Carroll Smith-Rosenberg points out: "We cannot understand the public acts of a few women without understanding the private world that produced them."[2] This work examines that broader historical framework, using the articles from the *Spalding Women's Basketball Guides* 1901 to 1917. The *Guides*, from the first *Basket Ball for Women* in 1901 until the *Guide* of 1916–17, when Senda Berenson ceased editing them, are replete with evidence of its authors' personal belief systems.[3]

The *Spalding Guides* are examined from the perspective of the authors' views about the women's basketball game, and the rule changes made in order to make the game applicable and acceptable for young "ladies" to play. The approach is to view the prevailing themes of social historians about what women of the late nineteenth and early twentieth century were like, and what their attitudes and behaviors were that prevailed in the American culture. The articles are examined to determine their consistency with these prevailing perspectives of noted social historians.[4]

Since 1970 there has been a proliferation of research on women, but little of this research has specifically dealt with women's sporting experiences. The *Spalding Guides* supply an inestimable historical record of the attitudes, values, and philosophies of the women who formulated and modified the basketball rules. In addition they supply, through the basketball articles, the rationale for the rules and actions of the physical educators. As Roberta Park notes: "It is only recently that we have

109

begun to understand that sports are cultural artifacts, and as such are very likely to reflect the dominant social structures and salient values of the societies in which they exist."[5] These guides provide valuable historical insight into the women physical educators who laid the foundation for women's sporting experiences based on the "dominant social structures and salient values" of their day.

The two decades, 1900–1920, have been identified by historians as a particularly significant period for women's sport.[6] This epoch saw the rise of contemporary sport and the establishment of sex roles based on perceived differences between men and women. These definitions of what is male and what is female, established at the turn of the century, continue to set parameters for men's and women's sporting experiences.

As society continued to wrestle with the question of what is manly and what is womanly, James Naismith invented basket ball. The same winter of its invention, Senda Berenson adapted the game for her women students at Smith. The question of what to do about basket ball served as the catalyst for women in physical education to seek to adjudicate girls and women's sporting experiences.[7] How these women adapted and tamed this wild, rough, and physically demanding game, invented for men but embraced by women, reveals much about themselves, their culture, and the American women's sporting experience.

Biology as Destiny

Gender is a powerful classification system in society. As Ruth Hubbard states: "From the moment of birth, each of us is admitted to a social club whose membership . . . has been fixed for life. The rules of this membership are often the most stringent that will ever be invoked to govern our conduct."[8] The perceived innate biological differences between men and women were the bases for the rules of membership to the club called "women."

By the 1890s, Darwinism was at its apex. Charles Darwin's theory of evolution provided a conceptual framework for the division of roles based on sex. His biological determinism provided a "scientific explanation" of the differences between men and women. According to Darwin, women were lower on the evolutionary scale and therefore biologically inferior to men.[9] By the turn of the century, researchers in the new social science fields, reformers, and feminists began to challenge parts of Darwin's theory. They rejected his contention that women were inferior and lower on the evolutionary scale, but accepted his premise that biology linked them to social development.

William I. Thomas was one of several sociologists who disputed the evolutionary based inferiority of women. In an article titled "The Mind of Woman and the Lower Races," Thomas carefully documented the differences in cultural experiences that lead to perceptions of intellectual inferiority. In this 1907 article, he placed women's lack of ability on their lack of opportunity. "Scientific pursuits and the allied intellectual occupations are a game which women have entered late, and their lack of practice is frequently mistaken for lack of natural ability."[10] As enlightened as Thomas's views were, he still did not completely reject biological determinism. In an earlier article he explained: "On account of the necessity of protecting her young, she is cautious and cunning, and in contrast to the open and pugnacious methods of the more untrammeled male. . . . In women, also, this tendency to prevail by passive means rather than by assault is natural, and especially under a system of male control."[11]

Thomas's ideas were elaborations of concepts put forth by Helen Thompson (Whoolley) and later expounded upon by Elsie Clews Parsons. But all concepts fell short of explaining sex differences beyond the biological boundaries. Rosalind Rosenberg points out that all theorists assumed that social development was in some way limited by biological forces and that personality development, in particular, derived from physiological conditions.[12] The acceptance of these biologically based differences mandated a different set of rules for men and women in life and in basketball.

The fact that as soon as Naismith invented basketball Berenson adapted it for women speaks volumes about women physical educators' accepting biologically based differences. In an editorial in the first *Guide*, Berenson referred to one of these differences. "It is a well known fact that women abandon themselves more readily to impulse than men. Lombroso tells us that women are more open to suggestion, more open to run to extremes than men."[13] Alice Bertha Foster, the first chair of the National Women's Basketball Committee, took a less extreme view in the same *Guide*. She comments: "Six years' observation of college play has convinced me that the game, as played by men, is just a little beyond women's physical power."[14] This concept of women's biological makeup provided the justification for Foster's and Berenson's "special rules" for women's basketball.

The innate differences between men and women is a recurring theme that appears time and time again in the early basketball guides. In the 1908 *Guide*, for example, Agnes Wayman, an early prime mover in women's physical education, argued against men coaching women on the basis of innate differences. "They fail to realize that girls are more delicately adjusted than boys."[15] Berenson restated a similar concern in the 1910–11 *Guide*. "Brute strength, physical combat, is not essential for women. Her organism is different from that of man."[16]

In the last *Spalding Guide* published during Berenson's tenure as the editor (1916–17), Elizabeth Burchenal summarized the stance Berenson and her committee took from the outset: "Hence, girls' athletics are to my mind of equal importance with boys', but based upon entirely different fundamental principles. . . . Two separate groups of athletic exercises for boys and girls chosen with this principle in mind might incidentally overlap each other . . . and yet men are men, and women are women."[17] The biologically based difference between men and women served as the foundation for a uniquely "female" sporting experience.

Motherhood and Morality

Embedded in the acceptance of biological differences was the acceptance of female uniqueness. Social Darwinism had furnished scientific evidence of the differences in temperament between men and women. Men were egotistic, aggressive, competitive, and dominant, while women were altruistic, passive, cooperative, and maternal. The unique temperament of women made them ideal mothers and guardians of culture and morality. From 1870 to the 1920s, feminists and Progressive Era reformers combined the concept of women's rights with the traditional values of the women's culture.[18] Rosenberg believes that neither feminists nor antifeminists were yet willing to challenge the ancient belief in feminine uniqueness. She concludes: "Indeed, this uniqueness was so much at the core of the idea of American womanhood that liberation could only be conceived in terms of it."[19] Women reformers drew on the values associated with female uniqueness to justify their involvement in the public sphere. They used motherhood and morality as a political strategy.

Motherhood and morality defined two parameters of the "separate female sphere." The ideal of the "moral mother" has a long tradition in America. Ruth Bloch traces the rise of the ideal of motherhood from 1785 with the nadir occurring by the mid-nineteenth century. Her concept is that women, in keeping with the prevailing Victorian image, were supremely virtuous, pious, tender and understanding. They gained social influence as the chief transmitters of religious and moral values by being mothers.[20] Daniel Scott Smith contends that the ideology of woman as "wife-and-mother" undoubtedly raised the status of women within the family.[21] But as Vern Bullough, Brenda Shelton, and Sarah Slavin point out in *The Subordinated Sex*: "The new mystique of motherhood granted women special status but at the same time guaranteed them inferiority."[22] This special status associated with their role as mothers gained women access to education, work, and citizenship, but only within clearly defined boundaries.

At a basketball game played at Oberlin College in the late 1890s, both the spectators and the players could consider themselves representatives of the women's "separate sphere."

Women at the turn of the century not only accepted the concept of female uniqueness, but embraced it as a political device. As Nancy Cott documents in *The Grounding of Modern Feminism*: "Nineteenth-century feminists could (and did) argue on egalitarian grounds for equal opportunity in education and employment . . . while also maintaining that women would bring special benefits to public life by virtue of their particular interests and capacities. In part the duality was tactical."[23] Women employed their role as the keeper of morality and culture to justify their involvement in the public sphere. As long as the cause remained closely associated with the moral and domestic responsibilities of women, the more likely it was to be accepted by society in general. Women had a unique and special role to play in society and they defined this role in terms of a "separate sphere."[24]

The doctrine of "separate sphere" is a well-supported historical concept. Women gained access to the larger political and public sphere through single-sex voluntary associations whose issues were germane to home and children.[25] For example, Paula Baker notes that women soon expanded the definition of home to "anywhere women and children were." In her article "The Domestication of Politics," Baker distinguished the differences in the political activity of women in the late nineteenth and early twentieth centuries. "Women's political activities were characterized by voluntary, locally based moral and social reform efforts. Many women had a stake in maintaining the idea of separate spheres. . . . Separate spheres allowed women to wield power of a sort."[26]

The price of the autonomy they enjoyed within this "separate sphere" was the acceptance of polarized and rigid sex roles.

The acceptance of these sex roles assured women autonomy within their "sphere" and assured social respectability.[27] As women in physical education began to legislate the rules of basket ball, they confronted the issue of how to "play the game" within the boundaries of these sex roles.

The acceptance of "female uniqueness" and a "separate female sphere" is apparent from the very first *Guide*. In Berenson's article, "The Significance of Basket Ball for Women," she referred directly to the "women's sphere" and the need for a different game for women. "Shall women blindly imitate the athletics of men without reference to their different organizations and purpose in life; or shall their athletics do such as shall develop those physical and moral elements that are particularly necessary for them?"[28] Subsequent *Guides* continued to emphasize the need for a different game for women, but until the 1908 *Guide* there was not a clear manifestation of the "women's sphere."

The Preface in the 1908 *Guide* set the tone for the next decade: "The noteworthy thing about this special conference [Second Annual Congress of the Playground Association of America] was that the consensus of opinion was almost entirely toward the side of differentiating the sport of girls and boys. . . . The paper on the subject, advocating the Women's Rules for girls when played with strict supervision under the direction of women coaches, met with unanimous approval."[29] In the same *Guide*, Edward B. DeGroot, outstanding leader of physical education in California, tackled the issue head on in his article "Should Girls' Teams be Coached or Managed by Men?" The answer was a resounding NO! He succinctly stated his case. "Teams coached and managed by men almost invariably defeat teams coached by women. . . . In one case there is a group of players representing girls' ideals and practices in athletics and in the other case there is a group representing boys' ideals and practices in athletics." His solution was simply: "The practical course for any girl to pursue is not to play on any team that is not coached and managed by a woman trained in such work." In his conclusion to the article he called for "women's complete control of their sex in all physical training work."[30] With the full support of men, women in physical education began to separate and control women's sporting experience.

In 1910, James E. Sullivan, secretary-treasurer (later president) of the Amateur Athletic Union, added his voice to the chorus. "Girls' athletics, from a coaching or managerial standpoint, should be absolutely directed by women. . . . I am strongly and unalterably opposed to having a man in a girl's gymnasium, or having him coach or direct girls in their athletic exercises." He opposed not only men coaching women, but also women competing in any public forum. "Girls should be kept in their own group and not be permitted to take part in public sports." He completes his article by stating the position of the Amateur Athletic Union in 1908: "The Amateur Athletic Union . . . will not register a female competitor and its registration committees refuse sanction for a swimming contest or a set of games where an event for women is scheduled. . . ."[31] As long as Sullivan was alive this continued to be the policy, but within a couple months of his death women did compete in AAU swimming.

From 1908 on the *Guides* continued to champion women's control of basket ball. Article after article called for the elimination of men as coaches and for women to control the game. As the Introduction of the 1917–18 *Guide* asserted: "The Basket Ball Rules Committee recognizes and wishes to emphasize that as 'woman is not undeveloped man, but diverse,' so is Basket Ball for Women not a modified, expurgated, imitation of Basket Ball for Men, but a different game."[32] Woman's role as mother defined and delineated the women's game in terms of acceptable role behavior and legitimate roles.[33]

An unusual number of the articles under study sought to associate the participation of women in basket ball with motherhood and morality. These were, after all, acceptable roles for women and helped to legitimize female participation in basketball and other sports.

Edward Hitchcock, first president of the American Physical Education Association, in the 1905–06 *Guide* made a direct connection between basket ball and motherhood. "The training of our girls in basket ball, under perhaps a little more careful watch of coaches and the Department of Physical Education, cannot fail to give us better women for the mothers of the next generation."[34] Wayman too referred to the "better development of women and incidentally, of the race."[35] Elizabeth Burchenal, chair of the Women's Athletic Committee, in the 1916–17 *Guide* asked the question: "What [activities] will contribute to her health and vitality and help to fit her for a normal woman's life?"[36] Motherhood and cooperation defined women's normal life.

Right Spirit of Play: Play Days

Luther Gulick, chairman of Springfield College (perhaps the most outstanding physical educator of the era), discussed the benefits of the game for women in terms of increasing their ability to cooperate. In the initial *Guide* his article, "The Psychological Effects of Basket Ball for Women," elaborated on women's maternal instinct and their altruism in reference to husband and children. However, in his view, players needed to develop "a kind of loyalty to each other, of loyalty to the groups in which they naturally are formed, that is greater than obtains at present."[37] He suggested that basket ball would foster this spirit of cooperation. Senda Berenson, too, addressed the issue of cooperation by noting, "Basket ball . . . is by far the best to teach the importance of team play; to teach co-operation; to teach the value of subordinating one's self for the good of the team—for the cause—most necessary traits to develop in woman of to-day."[38]

Consistently throughout the first twenty years of the basketball articles, the authors emphasized the spirit of cooperation while the spirit of competition was de-emphasized. Competition was a male trait and, as such, unacceptable as a desirable outcome for women participating in sport. Women physical educators faced the dilemma of how to make a competitive game appear noncompetitive. The women adopted a "cookies and milk" strategy, which stressed cooperation and the social value of the basketball experience for women.

From the outset the *Guides* discussed basket ball rules in terms of fair play, morality, honor, courage, self-control, and subordination of one's own glorification for the good of the team. The leaders and *Guide* authors downplayed winning and losing, featuring instead participation. One of the early articles identified the primary purpose of the game for women: "to make health and recreation the primary cause for games. . . ."[39] The 1908 Preface referred to playing the game "in the right spirit." This spirit was different from the spirit of the men's games, as explained by Berenson in the same year. "She cannot go into competitive games in the same spirit with men without developing dangerous nervous tendencies and losing the grace and poise and dignity and self-respect we would all have her foster." She expressed her concern that men's rules might be dangerous to the girls' character. "They also contain elements of roughness that are bad for her social and moral character." Berenson concluded her article by recounting the value of the game "played in the right spirit." "If the coaches emphasize the recreative side of the game and make the players conscious of the joy of play—the modified game of basket ball not only proves safe but is the most valuable of all the sports to develop healthy, graceful, dignified, sane and happy women."[40] The "right spirit of play" conformed to the gender boundaries set by the culture.

E. B. DeGroot identified some of the desirable traits for women and the place of athletic skill in their education. "Women's greatest charms are health, grace, cheerfulness and harmonious physical development. These attributes, or the lack of them, are apparent in the gymnasium, home and school, while athletic skill is so seldom apparent or needed it should be given a subordinate place in the training of women." He went

The University of Minnesota women's basketball team in the era when basketball was designed to foster womanly graces rather than competition. (*Official Women's Basket Ball Guide, 1905–06*)

on to explain the price that competitive basket ball might exact from women. "It is possibly worst for any girl to cheat herself of any of the womanly graces, health, lasting cheerfulness (invariably based on health) in order to exhibit basket ball skill at the time." In the same article he offered this advice to women athletes: "Rather than have your photograph in the newspapers at the time because you are a 'skillful' basket ball player, it is far better to train carefully for such health, lasting cheerfulness and womanly dignity and grace that there will be a demand for your photograph in other quarters than the sporting page."[41] In DeGroot's world, women belonged on the society page and not the sports page.

Another concept is added to the purpose of basketball when in the 1910–11 *Guide*, Berenson advocated that women begin to emphasize the social side of participation in organized games. "Members of both teams should be given an opportunity to meet each other socially after the game." The "cookies and milk" strategy was born as she explained: "Immediately after the game the winning team gives a dinner to the defeated team, and the girls who have played against each other sit next to each other at the dinner." She maintained that the benefits of this kind of competition were many. Among those benefits she noted: "Athletics that are thoroughly supervised, in which the elements of loyalty and courtesy and unselfishness are developed, which bring out enthusiasm without hysteria, and the love of play for its own sake, cannot help but be a great factor in the real education of our women."[42] It seems that the real education of women did not include competition.

Roughness of the Game—Unwomanly Behavior

A recurring theme in the first two decades of the *Guides* is the "fear" of the effect competition would have on women. Overt competitive behavior was unacceptable because it violated the strict code of conduct for their gender. Open competition in games and sport might lead to conduct unbecoming a woman. This "fear" of unwomanly behavior is perhaps the most dominant theme throughout the early years.

In the first years of basketball, Berenson expressed her concern about the behavior of the players. "Unless a game as exciting as basket ball is carefully guided by such rules as will eliminate roughness, the great desire to win and the excitement of the game will make our women do sadly unwomanly things." She further emphasized the different needs of men and women in society. "Rough and vicious play seems worse in women than in men. A certain amount of roughness is deemed necessary to bring out manliness in our young men. Surely rough play can have no possible excuse in our young women."[43] Confronted with this issue of roughness, women physical educators sought to "domesticate" and "tame" the game with the modified rules.

Agnes Childs cites one such behavior problem in the 1905–06 *Guide*:

> A game in which the ball is "muffed" is bound to be scrappy and untidy, for there is an irresistible temptation when the ball is rolling along the floor for the players in the vicinity to go sliding after it; and nothing makes a game more rowdyish in appearance or causes more adverse criticism than this most natural tendency to get after the ball by the quickest means.[44]

Her solution was for coaches to encourage players to surrender once in a while a contested ball.

In the 1907–08 *Guide*, Julie Ellsbee Sullivan, a member of the basketball committee, elaborated on the need to control roughness in the game. "Rough playing is neither necessary nor desirable. The rules for women are planned against the possible display of any exaggerations of the normal instincts either of pugnacity or of grasping at certain objects." She articulated a concern of many women in physical education: "So long as officials will continue to overlook this element of rough playing, just so long will there be criticisms against woman's playing the game at all."[45] The leaders had a legitimate concern that if they did not control the game, women would not be allowed to play at all.

Berenson possibly summarized best the concerns of women physical educators: "They often drag in their wake rowdyism, girls became careless in dress and speech and lost their dignity and womanliness. . . . Our college physical directors came out in the press with the cry that basket ball is a menace to the growing girl—that it unsexes her—it was at least a wholesome cry of warning." She believed the modified women's rules

Critics of women's basketball believed the game was too rowdy, and their concerns resulted in modifications of the game. Evidence of players' enthusiasm and competitiveness appears in this illustration from *Athletics & Outdoor Sports for Women*, edited by Lucille E. Hill and published by Macmillan Company in 1903.

Fig. 176. — A problem for the umpire.

would save the game. "It does away with personal contact and the evil passions that may thus be aroused in the heat and excitement of the game." But she acknowledged that even with modified rules the game still had critics. She admitted that "a reaction had set in, and many people thought that basket ball even with the changed rules should be abolished."[46] The critics that Berenson referred to were parents, especially mothers.

In the article "Danger of Unsupervised Basket Ball," Elizabeth Wright expressed a growing anxiety about basketball. "The last few years there has arisen a strong sentiment against it [basketball] in the minds of a considerable number of parents and teachers. Each year not a few apparently strong athletic girls fail to come out for basket ball practice because they have been forbidden to do so by their parents." Wright issued a dire warning that basketball with all its unrivaled possibilities for good might perish in disgrace, for the lack of "right bringing-up." The "right bringing-up" meant maintaining proper decorum at all times.[47]

Any behaviors that the teachers perceived as a threat to proper decorum were subject to scrutiny. Women's participation in sport was always on the fringe of proper female behavior and therefore especially subject to criticism. Agnes Wayman spoke to one such criticism. "Many a mother objects to having her girl play basket ball or enter into athletic competition of any kind, because she claims it makes her daughter unladylike, careless in dress and habits and speech." Wayman offered solutions that included "neatly combed hair, no gum chewing or slang on the field, never calling each other by last names, and never lying or sitting down on the floor."[48] Kathryn A. McMahon in the 1912–13 *Guide* reminded the players of their manners: "Politeness—Remembering that the same rules of etiquette hold good whether on a basket ball court or in a drawing room."[49] Physical educators allowed women to play the game as long as the women could maintain their drawing room behavior.

James E. Sullivan's article expressed an additional anxiety. He warned his reader about the exploitation of women athletes and the consequences of such action. "They [women] must not be exploited, however, as female Sheppards, Sheridans or Sandows, or as show girls . . . something will surely happen, and parents will refuse to allow their daughters to take part in athletics in any form." He cited examples of the fate of sports where women were exploited. "This applies particularly to public competition among girls in cycling, base ball and pedestrianism, as a result these sports, for girls, were discredited."[50] Kathryn E. Darnell cited another concern with the public display of basketball. "When teams are permitted to play in open games, before an indiscriminate crowd, we cannot deny that the game is making girls 'unwomanly,' which is another common censure."[51] Any "unwomanly" behavior would not be tolerated and the cost of this behavior was social ostracism.

By the last *Guide* under Berenson's editorship, Dudley R. Sargent, who ran a Normal College for women, declared the women's rules to be victorious. He exclaimed:

> Fortunately for the preservation of basket ball, some of us who saw its good points over twenty-odd years ago realized that in order to adapt it to the use of women and girls certain modification would have to be made in the rules and regulations then governing the game. The hair pulling, face slapping, clinching, striking and kicking contests that led up to this decision are all vividly in mind. . . . All of this barbaric rudeness, ill temper and unsportsmanlike conduct was largely eliminated by adopting what is known as the line game.[52]

Sargent believed that the adoption of the "line game" had preserved the game for girls and women.

By 1917, F. F. Mace proclaimed that basketball was a game which had not a single unladylike feature.[53] Women physical educators had successfully domesticated basket ball. They had removed all vestiges of rough play and had replaced competition with cooperation. This new game was safely within the boundaries of acceptable behavior for women. By staying within the polarized gender role, they assured themselves control of women's collegiate basketball experiences.

The cost of crossing those invisible boundaries of social convention could be very high indeed for women in physical education. The "fear" of losing the game of basket ball was very real and rooted in the middle-class morality that dominated the era. As Donald J. Mrozek explains: "Any departure from the most restrained and proper behavioral code could be interpreted into a start down the road to depravity."[54] Women in physical education could not take that chance. Instead they constructed a game that would remain safely within the "separate female sphere" and reassure their critics. As Estelle Freedman claims: "At certain historical periods, the creation of a public female sphere might be the only viable political strategy for women."[55] Women physical educators, already on the academic and cultural fringes, did not dare risk challenging the male domination of sport. Their alternative solution was to domesticate the game of basket ball and keep it in the main stream of social convention.

Conclusion

The first seventeen years of the women's basketball *Guides* laid the foundation for the female's opportunity to experience sport in the United States. This foundation stayed intact through two world wars, a depression, and women's suffrage. Firmly rooted in the "female sphere" it offered women an opportunity to control their sporting destinies, as long as they adhered to social convention. The beliefs of the period shaped the Women's Basketball Committee decisions on basketball rules, but once in place, they served as a socializing agent for the next generation of women athletes. As Carroll Smith-Rosenberg concludes about this generation of "New Women": "We can learn much from their errors—and their successes. Our first lesson must be to understand and not to blame them."[56] The survival of the game of women's basketball became the physical educators' overwhelming concern. They did, indeed, find a way to keep basketball a part of girls and women's sporting experience for the next generation.

Notes

1. Any discussion of women during this era must include the perceived physiological differences and how these differences influenced women's cultural roles. Since this topic is being covered in another chapter, it will not be included in this chapter.

2. Carroll Smith-Rosenberg, "Politics and Culture in Women's History," *Feminist Studies* 6 (Spring 1980): 55.

3. Senda Berenson ceased editing the guides in 1918. By this time, she and her committee had clearly set parameters for women's sports participation at the collegiate level. These first 17 years of guides provided the infrastructure for all the guides that followed. An examination of these first years is crucial for any understanding of the women's sporting experience at the turn of the century.

4. For documentation on the prevailing themes identified by social historians check William L. O'Neill, *Everyone Was Brave: A History of Feminism in America* (Chicago: Quadrangle Books, 1969); Nancy F. Cott, *The Grounding*

of Modern Feminism (New Haven: Yale University Press, 1987); Carl N. Degler, *At Odds: Women and the Family in America from the Revolution to the Present* (New York: Oxford University Press, 1980); Rosalind Rosenberg, *Beyond Separate Spheres: Intellectual Roots of Modern Feminism* (New Haven: Yale University Press, 1982); Barbara Miller Solomon, *In the Company of Educated Women: A History of Women and Higher Education in America* (New Haven: Yale University Press, 1985); Aileen S. Kraditor, *The Ideas of the Women Suffrage Movement, 1890–1920* (New York: Columbia University Press, 1965); Mary P. Ryan, *Womanhood in America: From Colonial Times to the Present* (New York: New Viewpoints, 1983); Sara M. Evans, *Born for Liberty: A History of Women in America* (New York: Free Press, 1989).

5. Roberta J. Park, "Sport, Gender and Society in a Transatlantic Victorian Perspective," in J. A. Mangan and Roberta J. Park, eds., *From "Fair Sex" to Feminism: Sport and the Socialization of Women in the Industrial and Post-industrial Eras* (Totowa, N.J.: Frank Cass and Co., 1987), 70.

6. For a discussion of the importance of this time period, see, for example, the introduction in Mangan and Park, *From "Fair Sex" to Feminism: Sport and the Socialization of Women in the Industrial and Post-industrial Eras*.

7. For an informative discussion on women physical educators' impact on basketball see Joan S. Hult, Chapter 3 in this volume; Eline von Borries, *History and Function of the National Section on Women's Athletics* (Washington, D.C.: AAHPER, 1941); Ellen Gerber, "The Controlled Development of Collegiate Sport for Women, 1923–36," *Journal of Sport History* 2 (Spring 1975): 1–28.

8. "Introduction," in Ruth Hubbard, Mary Sue Henifin, and Barbara Fried, eds., with collaboration of Vicki Druss and Susan Leigh Star, *Women Look at Biology Looking at Women: A Collection of Feminist Critiques* (Cambridge: Schenkman Pub. Co., 1979), 3–5.

9. For a discussion on Darwin's influence see Hubbard et al., "Have Only Men Evolved?" in *Women Look at Biology Looking at Women*, 7–35.

10. William I. Thomas, "The Mind of Woman and the Lower Races," *American Journal of Sociology* 12 (January 1907): 466.

11. William I. Thomas, "Adventitious Character of Woman," *American Journal of Sociology* 12 (January 1906): 37.

12. Rosalind Rosenberg, "In Search of Woman's Nature, 1850–1920," *Feminist Studies* (Fall, 1975): 140–154.

13. Senda Berenson, "The Significance of Basket Ball for Women," in *Spalding's Official Women's Basket Ball Guide, 1901*, ed. Senda Berenson (New York: American Sports Publishing Company, 1901), 23.

14. Alice Bertha Foster, "Official Note," in *Spalding's Official Women's Basket Ball Guide, 1901*, ed. Senda Berenson (New York: American Sports Publishing Company, 1901), 9.

15. Agnes R. Wayman, "Hints Along General Lines" in *Spalding's Official Women's Basket Ball Guide, September 1908*, ed. Senda Berenson (New York: American Sports Publishing Company, 1908), 65.

16. Senda Berenson, "Athletics for Women," in *Spalding's Official Women's Basket Ball Guide, 1910–1911*, ed. Senda Berenson (New York: American Sports Publishing Company, 1910), 31.

17. Elizabeth Burchenal, "Athletics for Girls," in *Spalding's Official Basket Ball Guide for Women, 1916–1917*, ed. Senda Berenson Abbott (New York: American Sports Publishing Company, 1916), 82.

18. For a discussion of women and social housekeeping see Ryan, *Womenhood in America*, 198–220; Evans, *Born for Liberty*, 145–156; Degler, *At Odds*, 144–166.

19. Rosalind Rosenberg, "In the Shadow of Dr. Clarke," in *Beyond Separate Spheres*, 14.

20. Ruth H. Bloch, "American Feminine Ideals in Transition: The Rise of the Moral Mother, 1785–1815," and "Untangling the Roots of Modern Sex Roles: A Survey of Four Centuries of Change," *Signs: A Journal of Women in Culture and Society* (1978): 237–252.

21. Daniel Scott Smith, "Family Limitation, Sexual Control, and Domestic Feminism in Victorian America," *Feminist Studies* (September 1973): 40–57.

22. Vern L. Bullough, Brenda Shelton, and Sarah Slavin, *The Subordinated Sex: A History of Attitudes Toward Women* (Athens: University of Georgia Press, 1988), 250.

23. Cott, *Grounding of Modern Feminism*, 20.

24. Carl N. Degler, "The World Is Only a Large Home," in *At Odds*, 298–327.

25. For documentation of the doctrine of "separate sphere" check Rosenberg, *Beyond Separate Spheres*; Estelle Freedman, "Separatism as Strategy: Female Institution Building and American Feminism, 1870–1930," *Feminist Studies* (Fall 1979): 512–529; Gerda Lerner, "Politics and Culture in Women's History," *Feminist Studies* (Spring 1980): 49–54.

26. Paula Baker, "The Domestication of Politics: Women and American Political Society, 1780–1920," *American Historical Review* (January 1984): 634–635.

27. Sara M. Evans, "Women and Modernity 1890–1920," in *Born for Liberty*; Carroll Smith-Rosenberg, "The New Women as Androgyne: Social Disorder and Gender Crisis, 1870–1936" in *Disorderly Conduct: Visions of Gender in Victorian America* (New York: Aldred A. Knopf, 1985), 245–296.

28. Senda Berenson, "The Significance of Basket Ball for Women," 22.

29. "Preface," *Spalding's Official Women's Basket Ball Guide, 1908*, 5.

30. E. B. DeGroot, "Should Girls' Teams Be Coached or Managed by Men?" in *Spalding's Official Women's Basket Ball Guide, September 1908*, 75.

31. James E. Sullivan, "Should Men Manage or Coach Girls in Athletics?" in *Spalding's Official Women's Basket Ball Guide, 1910–1911*, 36, 37, 39.

32. Helen McKinstry, "Introduction," in *Spalding's Official Basket Ball Guide for Women, 1916–1917*, ed. Senda Berenson (New York: American Sports Publishing Company, 1916), 5.

33. For an interesting discussion on women and competition see Valerie Miner and Helen E. Longino, eds., *Competition: A Feminist Taboo?* (New York: Feminist Press, 1987).

34. E. Hitchcock, "Games for Women," in *Spalding's Official Women's Basket Ball Guide, 1905–1906*, ed. Senda Berenson (New York: American Sports Publishing Company, 1905), 33.

35. Agnes R. Wayman, "Hints Along General Lines," 59.

36. Elizabeth Burchenal, "Athletics for Girls," 84.

37. Luther, Gulick, "The Psychological Effects of Basket Ball for Women," in *Spalding's Official Basket Ball Guide for Women, 1901*, ed. Senda Berenson, 11–14, p. 12–13.

38. Senda Berenson, "Are Women's Basket Ball Rules Better for Women than Men's Basket Ball Rules," in *Spalding's Official Women's Basket Ball Guide 1908*, 33.

39. Senda Berenson, "Preface," in *Spalding's Official Women's Basket Ball Guide, 1905–1906*, 5.

40. Senda Berenson, "Are Women's Basket Ball Rules Better for Women than Men's Basket Ball Rules?" in *Spalding's Official Women's Basket Ball Guide 1908*, 31–41.

41. E. B. DeGroot, "Should Girls' Teams be Coached or Managed by Men?" in *Spalding's Official Women's Basket Ball Guide 1908*, 73, 75.

42. Senda Berenson, "Athletics for Women," in *Spalding's Official Women's Basket Ball Guide, 1910–1911*, 32, 33.

43. Senda Berenson, "The Significance of Basket Ball for Women," in *Spalding's Official Women's Basket Ball Guide, 1901*, 23, 24.

44. Agnes C. Childs, "A Few Suggestions About the Actual Playing of Basket Ball," in *Spalding's Official Women's Basket Ball Guide, 1905–1906*, 81.

45. Julie Ellsbee Sullivan, "A Plea for Basket Ball," in *Spalding's Official Women's Basket Ball Guide, 1907–1908* (New York: American Sports Publishing Company, 1907), 77, 79.

46. Senda Berenson, "Are Women's Basket Ball Rules Better for Women than Men's Basket Ball Rules?" in *Spalding's Official Women's Basket Ball Guide 1908*, 35, 37, 39.

47. Elizabeth Wright, "Danger of Unsupervised Basket Ball," in *Spalding's Official Women's Basket Ball Guide, 1908*, 55, 57.

48. Agnes R. Wayman, "Hints Along General Lines," in *Spalding's Official Women's Basket Ball Guide, 1908*, 65, 67.

49. Kathyrn A. McMahon, "Basket Ball as a Means of Developing Character and Efficiency," in *Spalding's Official Basket Ball Guide for Women, 1914–1915*, ed. Senda Berenson Abbott (New York: American Sports Publishing Company, 1914), 69.

50. James E. Sullivan, "Should Men Manage or Coach Girls in Athletics?" in *Spalding's Official Women's Basket Ball Guide, 1910–1911*, 37.

51. Kathyrn E. Darnell, "Abuse of Basket Ball," in *Spalding's Official Basket Ball Guide for Women, 1913–1914*, ed. Senda Berenson Abbott (New York: American Sports Publishing Company, 1913), 57.

52. Dudley R. Sargent, "Basket Ball," in *Spalding's Official Basket Ball Guide for Women, 1916–1917*, ed. Senda Berenson Abbott (New York: American Sports Publishing Company, 1913), 67, 68.

53. F. F. Mace, "Basket Ball in West Texas," in *Spalding's Official Basket Ball Guide for Women, 1916–1917*, ed. Senda Berenson Abbott (New York: American Sports Publishing Company, 1916), 92–93.

54. Donald J. Mrozek, "The 'Amazon' and the American 'Lady': Sexual Fears of Women as Athletes," in *From "Fair Sex" to Feminism*, 286.

55. Estelle Freedman, "Separatism as Strategy: Female Institution Building and American Feminism, 1870–1930," *Feminist Studies* 5 (Fall 1979): 513.

56. Smith-Rosenberg, "The New Woman as Androgyne," 296.

7

"The Sacrifice of Maidens" or Healthy Sportswomen?

The Medical Debate Over Women's Basketball

Nancy Cole Dosch

Every day girls playing basketball filled the courts of a typical American community. They moved and ran, pivoted and jumped. As the game progressed, tension increased and play yielded to competition. Smiling faces strained. Perspiration drained into players' eyes. Mouths opened, gasping for breath. Basketball was a fight, a desperate fight to win.[1]

From 1892 until the end of World War II, a more important fight took place, not on the basketball courts, but in doctors' and principals' offices, among physical educators, at educational conferences, and in the home. Should girls play basketball? How should they play? Who should coach, officiate—control this game?

The medical issues were debated among physicians, especially those who were physical educators, in the pages of the *American Physical Education Review*, the women's basketball *Guides*, other professional journals, and at professional meetings. Was basketball harmful or helpful? For those who favored the game, basketball developed health and character; for those opposed, the game represented "the sacrifice of maidens."[2]

By the middle of the nineteenth century, physicians attempted to assume authority over a woman's body and physical behavior. The male medical conception of women's physiology and sexuality reinforced a conservative view of women's social and domestic roles. Genitals determined gender; gender determined social roles.[3]

The theory of women's weaknesses rested on basic physiological law: (1) "conservation of energy"—each human had a set amount of vital energy, which was allocated throughout the body as needed; (2) reproduction was the basis of a woman's biological life—the reproductive organs demanded an unequal share of the limited energy and, as a result, took almost total control of a woman's life. Medicine equated women's weakness with sickness. Physicians considered it natural and almost commendable for women to break down under all imaginable varieties of strain. The prescription that prevented a woman from doing anything active or interesting was for her own good. Using a mixture of evolutionary theory and societal stereotypes, physicians explained and reinforced notions of female form and frailty.[4]

Anatomy and Physiology

Anatomically, physicians understood that girls were handicapped when compared to boys. The girls had smaller and shorter bones, smaller and shorter arms and legs. Girls had more body fat, larger thighs, and a lower center of gravity. The girls also had smaller hearts, narrower chests, and more visceral organs than boys. It was obvious to some physicians that girls were not adapted for physical activity, especially for one as vigorous as basketball.[5]

There were physiological differences that influenced the participation of girls in basketball. Muscular strength was of particular concern. Evidence suggested that girls had considerably less strength in the arms and shoulder girdle than boys. The study by Clelia Duel Mosher, M.D. and E.G. Martin on "The Muscular Strength of College Women and Some Consideration of Its Distribution" concluded that sex differences in strength were due to "differences in the use of the muscles brought about by conventional limitations of activities or by dress."[6] Girls were limited because they did not use their muscles.

Since girls had smaller hearts and lungs and did not push their bodies as actively as boys, they had poorer physical endurance. The lack of endurance resulted in excessive fatigue while playing basketball. Overfatigue combined with the presence of germs made the body more susceptible to disease. Some physicians made a connection between the general body weakness, smaller and weaker lungs, and the greater occurrence of tuberculosis among adolescent girls. The fear that the excessive strain and fatigue of playing basketball facilitated the development of lung diseases deterred many from playing the game.[7]

Girls were also limited by their clothing. Dr. Edward Morton Schaeffer wrote in 1896 that admirers of women should educate them to use their own taste and common sense to develop a healthy and artistic standard of dress.[8] Dresses were tight and constricting and when dresses were not restricting activity, corsets were. Dr. Schaeffer despaired of physicians using their influence to convince women to "burst all confining fetters and curtail unnecessary impedimentia of costume." He believed that someday:

> If the barber's pole with its red and white stripes reminds us of the time when doctors were bleeders and emptied folk of pretty much all that they possessed, the world will some day regard the corset as the crest of the gynecologist's patronage, for this figure- and health-wrecking contrivance indicates the candidate for his services as unmistakably as it does the devotee of fashion and deformity (p. 79).

Schaeffer did not want women to imitate the way men dressed, but

> in assuming the divided skirt, or even the bloomer, for purposes of exercise or ease of locomotion, it should be acknowledged that women are simply recovering stolen property, for the women of the East invented the trousers, and the conquering Persians thought it such a good idea that they took them from her, giving her a sound lecture on her proper sphere. . . (p. 79).

Men were always intruding upon women's sphere. They had a propensity for dodging important questions to keep a woman "revolving in a petty circle of which they are the radius." While woman's sphere was inactivity and dependency, stated Schaeffer, man's sphere was "baseball."

If baseball was the sphere of men, basketball was **the** athletic sport for women. According to Alice Bertha Foster of Bryn Mawr, first chair of the Women's Basket Ball Committee, most of the arguments used to justify football for men applied to basketball for women.[9] Yes, she agreed, the game was a physical strain and no woman or girl should be allowed to play without a physical examination. Some conditions should disqualify a woman from competing—a weak heart, pelvic trouble, back problems, history of a sprained knee, or a history of "extreme excitability." At Bryn Mawr, they virtually ignored sprained ankles and "a number of our players wear bandages."

Accidents did happen. Foster believed that strict umpiring and public support for the umpires should limit injuries. The debate was whether the risk of injury should condemn the game. Foster heard "the President of one of our prominent universities say . . . that it mattered nothing if a few men were killed" playing football when compared with the good it did for the thousands who survived. While life-threatening injuries had not occurred at Bryn Mawr, Foster guarded against that danger by allowing only those fit enough to play and by still experimenting to see whether women should continue to play by the men's rules.[10]

At the beginning of the twentieth century, competing medical views concerning basketball emerged. Dr. Theodore Hough noted that even when the ball was in another part of the court, preparing to move involved simultaneous actions of the large muscles. In a game situation, girls, not being aware of the energy expended, ignored their fatigue and increased the strain on their hearts. Recognizing that exercise was important to maintain health and rather than prevent girls from playing basketball, Dr. Hough suggested that girls be trained before being allowed to play basketball.[11] Based on observation, Dr. Harry Eaton Stewart noted that studies on women's physical endurance showed that their physical powers were much greater than originally perceived. Stewart's work proved that given proper training girls could participate in vigorous activities including basketball without any ill affects.[12]

Physical training was a key for physicians' approval of girls and women playing basketball. Dr. Stewart pointed out that family physicians often ruled that girls should not play basketball, without knowing anything about the game itself, the conditions under which it was played, or the effect of the sport on the heart.[13] Dr. Dudley Sargent believed that athletics, sports, and games should be encouraged, that they were beneficial to the individual and to the race. In his view, all athletic sports or games could be played by women without fear of injury, if they were properly trained. He did propose some modifications in the men's basketball game before women attempted to play it. "Divide the field of play by lines and insist upon players confining themselves to the space prescribed for them," Sargent reasoned. "This insures that everyone shall be in the game and prevents some players from exhausting themselves."[14] If the field was large enough, seven or nine players could be on a side, which was preferable to the five players as required by men's rules. The games should be shorter than those of men and there should be more time allowed for rest.[15]

Senda Berenson Abbott, whose Smith College students were among the first women to play basketball in the United States and who was responsible for the initial development of the women's game, recognized that playing basketball could cause excessive fatigue. Playing too long and too often caused the problem. Symptoms of malnutrition and listlessness alerted the teacher that the players were tired. According to Abbott, the girls should never be allowed to play more than thirty minutes for any one period or more than twice a week.[16]

In spite of the increased support that playing basketball received from physicians, parents found it difficult to believe that the health issues could be easily solved through physical training. Disturbed by an exaggerated account of injuries and by what seemed to be a lack of supervision, parents often forbid their daughters from trying out for basketball. Danger existed in a game which required no physical examination, often had unrestricted playing time, where weak girls were not warned to take precautions, and the after-effects of playing were not taken seriously by the participants.[17]

As basketball grew in popularity,[18] women physical educators recognized the legitimacy of parental concerns. In the editor's preface to the 1912–13 women's basketball guide, Senda Berenson Abbott wrote that it was important for each player to have a medical examination. A medical exam provided an indication of organic health or weakness. Since basketball was a vigorous game, the exam should include an evaluation of the heart, lungs, and kidneys and a height-weight ratio. A girl too slender relative to her height was considered malnourished and should avoid strenuous exercise. Excess weight strained the heart and the lungs, so a girl who was overweight should be prohibited from playing.[19]

"Peculiar Diseases"

Other physical problems existed that affected all girls, not just those playing basketball. Girls had the additional burden of their "peculiar diseases": menstruation, pregnancy, labor, and menopause. Instability marked these phases when a girl was most susceptible to mental and physical dangers. If these dangers were ignored, according to Dr. George J. Engelmann:

> Many a young life is battered and forever crippled in the breakers of puberty; if it cross these unharmed and is not dashed to pieces on the rock of childbirth, it may still ground on the ever-recurring shallows of menstruation and lastly, upon the final bar of menopause where protection is found in the unruffled water of the harbor beyond the reach of sexual storms.[20]

Her biological nature limited a girl's capacity for physical activity.

For physicians, the delicacy of women precluded any form of vigorous exercise. Basketball, particularly, could further weaken a woman's already inadequate vital force, a force needed for her most important function—reproduction.[21]

Women physicians and physical educators believed that playing basketball during the period threatened a girl's health. Yet there was always the temptation for most girls to play. Dr. J. Anna Norris recommended that strict rules should be adopted to prevent girls from playing during at least the first three days of the menstrual cycle. The team captains should enforce the rules and the public should support them.[22]

The concern about playing during the menstrual period was an important factor in the recommendation that only trained *women* be used to supervise girls basketball. While there were a lot of other problems with men coaching girls teams, a man could never understand the physiology of girls as well as a woman. Limiting playing until after the first three days of the period was difficult for a woman, but it was seen as impossible for a man. Since the health of the players was dependent on the person in charge, women believed it imperative that a trained woman be available who understood the girls, "their problems and troubles; a woman in whom the girls can confide."[23]

The attitude about girls playing during their period changed very slowly. In the 1940s, Dr. Edna Schrick wrote that although there was no specific rule against playing basketball during the menstrual period, it seemed best that girls should not play games of any kind during the first two days. She did not see any physical harm from playing during the period; her objection was that the psychic and emotional element of competitive sports exacerbated an already unstable condition.[24]

Dr. Margaret Bell agreed. The monthly period was one reason why girls should play girls rules in basketball. She believed that the average girl could play sports right through her period. She was opposed, however, to playing during the first two days of the period. For Dr. Bell:

> The obvious reason is that competition adds nervous or emotional strain. Emotional strain, excitement, worry and nervousness are capable of causing menstrual irregularities.[25]

Dr. Bell was one of the more progressive physicians in her view of participation during the period. She realized through observation that most girls tolerated even strenuous exercise well during menstruation. She preferred that the issue be left to the individual, but there was pressure, professional and societal, to limit participation at least at the beginning of the cycle.[26]

While women physicians and physical educators slowly changed their views of participation during the period, some male physicians and physical educators believed that physical activity might even alleviate menstrual pain. Beginning in 1907, Dr. E.H. Arnold studied the effect of school work on menstruation. In addition, he looked at how physical activity might affect productivity, fatigue, regularity, and pain of the menstrual cycle. In all measurements, he found physical activity (which included regular participation in outdoor basketball in the fall) reduced pain and fatigue and increased regularity and productivity. He was cautious in his conclusions as to whether such improvements would eventually benefit the female.[27]

Not all male physicians were as conscientious as Dr. Arnold. Dr. George Engelmann implied that women were totally incapacitated by their life cycles, almost to the point where he thought they should go to bed at puberty and get up at menopause.[28] Dr. Emil Novak had even less sympathy. He recommended that medical men encourage girls to keep up regular physical activity throughout their periods rather than go to bed. For Dr. Novak, this suggestion made perfect sense. Girls were not endangered by being active during their periods, because menstrual pain existed only in their minds.[29]

Beliefs about not participating in vigorous activities such as basketball during the menstrual period changed very slowly. As recently as 1959, a report by the Research Committee of the Division of Girls and Women's Sports included recommendations of women physicians and gynecologists on participating in sports during the menstrual period. The study cited eight gynecologists (male) and nine women physicians. While the doctors generally agreed that there should be no restrictions on activity or competition during the premenstrual and second half of the menstrual periods, the women physicians suggested limited participation during the first half of the period. In the opinion of authors Marjorie Phillips, Katharine Fox, and Olive Young, the women physicians were consistently more conservative in their views than the male gynecologists.[30]

Separate Rules

In addition to physiological reasons, there were psychological reasons why women wanted to control the women's game. Miriam Grey noted that "ever since the first rule change, when a women's school misinterpreted the meaning of the dotted lines on Dr. Naismith's diagram of the basketball court and thus unwittingly initiated the three-court game," women have adapted the rules and made them more suitable for girls and women.[31] It was a woman's game, they made it, they developed it. Both the men's and women's game originated from the same peach-basket mass game that Naismith first conceived, but they evolved in a completely different way.

The differences in the game eliminated the temptation for women to compete against men. When men and women compete against each other, the women invariably lose. Such an experience would be frustrating and would discourage women from competing at all. The lack of familiarity with the rules diminished the chance that women could compete against men. While women could compete on a nearly equal basis in other sports, they could not compete successfully against men in basketball. "Her anatomical structure says no; her physiological functions say no, and her psyche says no."[32] Women were more emotional than men, more inclined to hysteria, and took their defeats more seriously than men. There was no need for women to be subjected to the sure disappointment that competition against men would bring, especially when they can play a better and more highly skilled game against their own sex, argued Grey. Success in the form of winning was important to a woman, psychologically.

The structural and functional differences between men and women reinforced the belief that separate rules were healthier for women. The man's broad shoulders, narrow hips, and long legs increased his efficiency in running and jumping, while a woman's broader pelvis and oblique femur decreased her ability to run and jump. For a woman to achieve the same running and jumping ability as a man, she had to work harder. Even twelve to thirteen year old girls risked permanent injury if they competed against boys. From a health view point, it seemed a reasonable position that there should be separate rules for girls and boys, and for men and women.[33]

Post World War II

Views toward women and girls participating in sports in general and basketball in particular changed following World War II. Physical exercise became recognized as an important adjunct to a healthy life. Sports developed strong, active muscles, smooth coordination, and quick reflexes. With sports participation, vital capacity increased, a strong heart able to cope with sudden activity developed, digestion and posture improved.[34]

Sports were also important to women psychologically. They increased mental stability, self-reliance, self-confidence, and the interdependence of body and mind. As a means of relaxation, physical activity acted as a "mental catharsis to the overwrought system, inducing normal fatigue, normal sleep, and a rational approach to the irritation of life."[35] Girls benefited not only from the development of skill, but also from the value of health of the body, mind, and spirit.

In the 1950s some teachers and coaches expressed concern that the players were not getting enough rest during the game, even though the number of time-outs allowed was increased from three to four. Thomas K. Cureton disagreed with that view. He cautioned against allowing too much rest during the game to avoid cooling the muscles. Girls should be taught to warm up gradually before going into the game and to shower immediately after. For rest periods during the game, Cureton recommended from one to two minutes between the first and second, and third and fourth periods, and ten minutes between halves. He suggested that players keep walking and deep breathing to keep up the circulation during that time.[36]

The players' welfare became a keynote of the mid-1950s. The position statement of the National Section for Girls and Women's Sports emphasized that "the one purpose of sports for girls and women is the good of those who play."[37] Basketball was to be an educational experience for the players. Coaches held group meetings to discuss (1) *why* eat nutritive food for vigorous exercise, (2) *what* is a balanced diet, (3) *why* regular sleep and rest are needed to compete, (4) *how* they might be obtained, (5) *why* conditioning and warm-up exercises are important, and (6) *what* a girl should do for exercise. A medical exam was still important before the season started but now it must include a chest X-ray to check for tuberculosis. Another check-up was required following an injury or illness. Parental permission was also necessary to play. For safety reasons before the game, fingernail length must be checked and jewelry, such as rings, watches, bracelets, earrings, and ID tags, could not be worn. Glasses guards should be worn for protection unless the glasses had unbreakable lenses.[38]

Athletic Training and Conditioning

By the 1960s, health issues shifted away from the nature of the game to the individual. With the debate over women's endurance, strength, and psychological stability all but won, athletic conditioning became the central goal.

The two basic requirements for peak performance in girls and women's basketball were strength and endurance. Conditioning programs emphasized both. Coaches scheduled training sessions outside of practice, many using circuit training as a method to condition the player. Approximately 10–30 minutes were allotted to complete the circuit, which included rope jumping, leg lifting, bench stepping, wall passing, jump starts, push-ups, sit-ups, and forearm rolls. Patsy Neal advised strengthening the wrists and arms by using a weighted ball for passing and shooting drills. She also suggested using a broomstick with a two–three pound weight tied to the center. Rolling the weight up strengthened the wrists through flexion and extension.[39]

Circuit training became more sophisticated with the transition to the five player, full court game. In addition to jumping, push-ups, and sit-ups, wind sprints, distance runs up to two miles, and stair running became part of the conditioning program. Student-athletes wore weighted jackets and wrist and ankle weights as they did their regular basketball drills.[40]

Weight training also increased strength and endurance. Women coaches were sometimes reluctant to implement the program because weight training was thought to produce bulky, unfeminine bodies. Rhonda Fleming pointed out that while the muscles became stronger through weight training, they did not increase in bulk. Because training loads for females had not been established by 1974, Fleming suggested using a 110-pound weight set to discover a one repetition maximum (1 RM—the heaviest weight an individual can use to complete one repetition), adopting 50–80% of 1 RM and limiting the repetitions to between 8 and 16. She believed this routine would fulfill the objectives of weight training for female basketball players. Fleming found that once initial reservations were overcome, most girls enjoyed lifting weights because they appreciated its effectiveness and efficiency.[41]

As basketball enters its second century, physicians, coaches, parents, and players accept that a woman's place is on the basketball court. A female can run fast and long, be both feminine and strong. Women's physical limitations are no longer the sole basis for rule modifications. A woman can train vigorously for world competition without worrying that the strain might affect her "peculiar diseases" or her mental stability. She is free to play whatever she wants to play, and she wants to play basketball.

Notes

1. Marjorie Bateman, "Health Aspects of Girls' Basketball," *Mind and Body* 42 (April 1935): 21.

2. Ibid.

3. Joan Hult, "The Strange and Wondrous Story of Women in Intercollegiate Athletics," unpublished paper presented at the Seminar on Sport in Higher Education, Institute for Higher Education, University of California, Berkeley, November 13, 1989, p. 4; Carroll Smith-Rosenberg, *Disorderly Conduct: Visions of Gender in Victorian America* (New York: Alfred A. Knopf, 1985), 23.

4. Barbara Ehrenreich and Deidre English, *Complaints and Disorders: The Sexual Politics of Sickness* (Old Westbury, N.Y.: The Feminist Press, 1973), 5, 15, 18, 22–3, 27; Hult, "Strange and Wondrous Story," 4.

5. Miriam Gray, "Why Play Girls' Rules in Basketball," *Official Basketball and Officials Rating Guide for Women and Girls, 1947-1948*, ed. Marie D. Hartwig (New York: A. S. Barnes and Company, 1947), 34.

6. Clelia D. Mosher and E. G. Martin, "The Muscular Strength of College Women and Some Consideration of Its Distribution," *Journal of the American Medical Association* (January 19, 1918) in Roy B. Moore, "An Analytical Study of Sex Differences as They Affect the Program of Physical Education," *Research Quarterly* 12 (October 1941): 595.

7. N. W. Barnard, J. B. Amberson, and M. F. Loew, "Tuberculosis in Adolescents," *American Review of Tuberculosis* 23 (April–June 1933) in Moore, "Analytical Study of Sex Differences," *Research Quarterly*, 601.

8. Edward Morton Schaeffer, "The Hygiene of Bodily Culture," *Report of the Tenth Annual Meeting of the American Association for the Advancement of Physical Education* (Concord, N.H.: Republican Press Association, 1896), 79–80.

9. Alice Bertha Foster, "Basket Ball for Girls," *American Physical Education Review* 2 (September 1897): 153; also "Physical Education Society of New York and Vicinity," *American Physical Education Review* 2 (March 1897): 44–45.

10. Ibid.

11. Theodore Hough, "The Physiological Effects of Basket Ball," *Line Basket Ball or Basket Ball for Women*, ed. Senda Berenson (New York: American Sports Publishing Company, 1901), 16.

12. Harry Eaton Stewart, "Basket Ball in the Normal Schools of Physical Education," *Official Basket Ball Guide for Women, 1918–19* (New York: American Sports Publishing Company, 1918), 72; Harry E. Stewart, "The Effect on the Heart Rate and Blood Pressure of Vigorous Athletics in Girls," *American Physical Education Review* 19 (February 1914): 129.

13. Stewart, "Effect on the Heart Rate," 119.

14. Dudley Allen Sargent, "What Athletic Games, If Any, Are Injurious for Women in the Form in Which They Are Played by Men?"*American Physical Education Review* 11 (September 1906): 174–179.

15. Ibid., 179; Hough, 17.

16. "Preface," in *Spalding's Official Basket Ball Guide for Women*, ed. Senda Berenson Abbott (New York: American Sports Publishing Company, 1912), 5.

17. Elizabeth Wright, "Danger of Unsupervised Basket Ball," in *Spalding's Official Women's Basket Ball Guide*, ed. Senda Berenson (New York: American Sports Publishing Company, 1908), 55.

18. At one time, basketball was the *only* sport popular with college girls. See Ruth Elliott, "Modern Trends in Physical Education," *Research Quarterly* 1 (May 1930): 84.

19. *Basket Ball Guide*, 1912–1913, 5; Frances H. Schiltz, "A Medical Examination is Essential," in *Official Basketball Guide for Women and Girls*, 1940–1941, ed. Christine White (New York: A. S. Barnes and Company, 1940), 35–36.

20. Geo. J. Engelmann, "The American Girl of Today. Modern Education and Functional Health," *American Physical Education Review* 6 (March 1901): 29–30.

21. Hult, "Strange and Wondrous Story," 4.

22. J. Anna Norris, "The Beneficial Results and Dangers of Basket Ball," in *Official Basket Ball Guide for Women*, 1918–1919, eds. Florence D. Alden, Elizabeth Richards, and L. Raymond Burnett (New York: American Sports Publishing Company, 1918), 71.

23. Bateman, "Health Aspects of Girls' Basketball," 23.

24. Edna Schrick, "A Doctor Looks at Basketball," *Official Basketball and Officials Rating Guide for Women and Girls*, 1940–1941, ed. Josephine Fiske (New York: A. S. Barnes and Company, 1941), 30.

25. Margaret Bell, "The Doctor Discusses Basketball," *Official Basketball and Officials Rating Guide for Women and Girls*, 1947–48, ed. Marie D. Hartwig (New York: A. S. Barnes and Company, 1947), 39.

26. Margaret Bell, "The Doctor Advises," *Official Basketball Guide for Girls and Women*, 1938–1939, ed. Wilhelmine Meissner (New York: A. S. Barnes and Company, 1938), 27.

27. E. H. Arnold, "The Effect of School Work on Menstruation," *American Physical Education Review*, 19 (February 1914): 118.

28. Engelmann, "The American Girl of Today," 55–56.

29. Emil Novak, *The Woman Asks the Doctor* (Baltimore: Williams and Wilkins Company, 1935), 138.

30. Marjorie Phillips, Katharine Fox, and Olive Young, "Sports Activity for Girls." *Journal of Health, Physical Education, and Recreation* 30 (December 1959): 25, 54.

31. Gray, "Why Play Girls' Rules," 27.

32. Ibid.

33. Jesse Feiring Williams and Dorothy S. Tapley, "Why Be Different—or Why Not," *Official Basketball Guide for Women and Girls*, 1937–38, ed. Wilhelmine Meissner (New York: American Sports Publishing Company, 1937), 20.

34. Claire King Amyot, M.D. "Basketball Contributes to Health," *Official Basketball and Officials Rating Guide for Women and Girls*, 1946–47, ed. Rachel J. Benton (New York: A. S. Barnes and Company, 1946), 40.

35. Ibid.

36. Thomas K. Cureton, "Rest Periods During Game Time," *Official Basketball and Officials Rating Guide for Girls and Women*, September 1953–September 1954, ed. Grace Fox (Washington, D.C.: American Association for Health, Physical Education, and Recreation, 1953), 47.

37. Mary Buice, "Let's Consider the Player's Welfare," *Official Basketball and Officials Rating Guide for Girls and Women*, September 1954–September 1955, ed. Grace Fox (Washington, D.C.: American Association for Health, Physical Education, and Recreation, 1954), 25.

38. Ibid., 23–24; Louella M. Daetweiler, "Safety: A First!" *Basketball Guide for Girls and Women*, September 1958–September 1959, ed. Catherine Snell (Washington, D.C.: American Association for Health, Physical Education, and Recreation, 1958), 29.

39. Kaye McDonald, "Conditioning for Better Basketball," *Basketball Guide, August 1965–August 1966*, ed. Mildred J. Barnes (Washington, D.C.: American Association for Health, Physical Education, and Recreation, 1965), 37–8; Elaine Smith, "Circuit Training in Basketball," *Basketball Guide, August 1968–August 1969*, ed. Janette S. Sayre (Washington, D.C.: American Association for Health, Physical Education, and Recreation, 1968), 35–6; Earlaine Young Dandavol, "Circuit Training for Basketball," *Basketball Guide, August 1971–August 1972*, ed. Ruth Gunden (Washington, D.C.: American Association for Health, Physical Education, and Recreation, 1971), 48–9; Patsy Neal, "Strengthening the Wrists and Arms," *Basketball Guide, August 1965–August 1966*, 25–6.

40. Sue A. Hager, "Conditioning . . . the Key to Success," *Basketball Guide, July 1972–July 1973*, ed. Nan Nichols (Washington, D.C.: American Association for Health, Physical Education, and Recreation, 1972), 28–29.

41. Rhonda K. Fleming, "Weight Training for Basketball," *Basketball Guide, July 1974–July 1975*, ed. Norma Boetel (Washington, D.C.: American Alliance for Health, Physical Education, and Recreation, 1974), 14–15.

Section 3
High Level Competition

8

Hoops and Skirts
Women's Basketball on the West Coast, 1892–1930s

Lynne Fauley Emery and Margaret Toohey-Costa

When James Naismith created the game of basketball for the Young Men's Christian Association in the winter of 1891–92, probably the farthest thing from his mind was the suitability of the game for women. However, within a month of its invention women were playing and by the beginning of the 1892 school year the game had traveled 3,000 miles and was being played on the West Coast.

The Early Years: 1892–1899

The rapidity of the game's spread and its instant popularity among women was astonishing. One California newspaper was caught so off-guard that it called the game feminine football.[1] A November 1892 article in the *Berkeley Daily Advocate* described the game:

> . . . it is football modified to suit feminine capabilities. It is played in the gymnasium, and instead of goals there are baskets hung at either end of the room. The players line up, nine on a side. The umpire tosses the ball between the two lines, and then a general scramble begins to get it in the baskets.[2]

The first recorded women's basketball game on the West Coast occurred on November 18, 1892 when the University of California, Berkeley women played the first in a series of three games against Miss Head's School, a private girls preparatory school. After a hard fought first half the score was tied 4 to 4 and the Berkeley captain, aptly named Miss Bloomer, tried to rally her team. The players' mothers and sisters who

137

gathered at California's Harmon Gymnasium found the game exciting, cheered and screamed, but to no avail as the visitors won the game, 6 to 5.[3]

There is no record of the other two games in the series being played nor are there records of any other games between 1892 and 1896. An article in the *Seattle Post-Intelligencer* noted that Ellensburg State Normal School (now Central Washington State) first formed a team in 1893 but there was no mention of any game against another school.[4]

Of the early years of western basketball the biggest by far was 1896 for it was in this year that two important women's intercollegiate contests were played. One of the games was in California, the other in Washington, and both are remembered for the great interest and media coverage generated.

> Who made the basket?
> Why do you ask it?
> Sure, it was Stanford,
> Without half a try.
> Berkeley cannot win,
> Without our permission,
> She'll make a goal
> In the sweet by-and-by.[5]

This was the cheer which rang out at the conclusion of the first women's intercollegiate basketball game ever played on the West Coast. It was played on April 4, 1896 between the University of California, Berkeley and Stanford University. The *San Francisco Chronicle's* report of the game stated:

> When the next California Venus is modeled in marble she will have a thirty-two-inch waist, for the wasp-like young woman has gone out of fashion. With the waspish waist has also passed a certain waspishness of temper, as 700 women who witnessed the basketball game between the girls of the University of California and Stanford at the Page-street armory yesterday will testify.[6]

This seems a favorable comment on a sport which was later to cause such controversy. Of course the article was written by a woman since only women were allowed to see the game. The stipulation that the game be played in the presence of *women only* was one of Berkeley's conditions when accepting Stanford's challenge.

A letter to the editor of *The Berkeleyan* praised California's tact and good judgment in refusing to play in the open before a mixed audience. In an attempt to explain this position, the author wrote:

> . . . but as to playing in the open, before a lot of college men, it seems to us to be lowering a certain standard of womanhood. It is the place of the co-ed, with her high education, to advance wom-

anhood toward the ideal. Does she do this in an open contest? There is a quiet undertone around the college which is decidedly against the reputation of our University being put in jeopardy by such a display of advanced womanhood.[7]

In preparation for the big game, Berkeley played at least one practice game with Miss Lake's School whom they beat 3–2.[8] They may also have played against Miss West's School.[9] Stanford, on the other hand, held but two practice sessions in the week before the game because of injuries to two key players.[10] Their previous experience showed, however, as at the end of two twenty-minute halves, Stanford was ahead and won the game, 2–1. In its report of the game, *The Berkeleyan* called the game a success, noted it was free of roughness, and "the conservative few cannot say that there was anything displeasing to the supposedly retiring nature of womankind." [11]

Less than two weeks after the Berkeley-Stanford game, another intercollegiate contest was held. This was the game played on April 17 in Seattle between the University of Washington and Ellensburg State Normal School, purported to be the first meeting of these teams.

Won by Washington 6–3, the game was not without controversy. First there was a problem with the ball. The Washington ball measured 33 ¼ inches in one direction and 34 inches in the other while the Ellensburg ball was 32 ¼ inches in circumference. Since the Washington ball was a "Victor" and considered standard size it was named the official ball. There was also a problem with rules since the Ellensburg team used "rules which were gotten up for women, while the university girls play under the same rules that the S.A.C. [Seattle Athletic Club] and Y.M.C.A. teams use."[12] While both teams consisted of nine players, each playing in her own one-ninth of the court, the rules controversy centered around knocking the ball from an opponent's hands. The University's rules allowed this while the women's rules did not. The Washington rules were used much to the chagrin of the Normal School team. An article in the *Ellensburg Capital* noted that the team felt:

> . . . they were not quite fairly treated in being compelled to play in accordance with the rules of '92. They think they should not be compelled to be three years behind in their sports simply because the university pupils are. They were also compelled to play by the rules for the boys instead of the rules for the girls. Next time those preliminaries will be arranged before hand.[13]

Whether or not there was a next time is unknown.

Berkeley was involved in several more intercollegiate contests prior to the turn of the century. There are no records of games played in 1897 due, perhaps, to the overabundance of publicity surrounding the game with Stanford. The year 1898 was a different matter entirely as Berkeley began the season with a 13–1 victory over Mills College.[14] A challenge was issued to Stanford but problems regarding the site and spectators led to the game's cancellation. As a replacement, Berkeley promptly scheduled a game with the University of Nevada, Reno.

To prepare for Nevada, Berkeley played several practice games and was victorious over Lowell High School, Miss West's School, and the Irving Institute.[15] Their last practice was against the Mission Young Women's Christian Association team, whom they defeated 10 to 1.[16]

The game with Nevada was played on April 9, 1898 and was won by Berkeley 14–1. While not an exciting game for spectators, several interesting and stereotypical comments appeared in the *San Francisco Chronicle* coverage. Regarding the style of play, the article suggested that Berkeley had as many tricks and as much "guile as a Stanford football team. A favorite maneuver was to lure the opposing team into a bunch . . . and then suddenly throw the ball between the feet." Also referred to was the roughness of play, falling on the ball, "piling themselves up several deep," and crashing into chairs which "would have crushed into fine powder those Dresden shepherdesses who had the honor to be their grandmothers." The Nevadans were described as young (the average age was 16) and blonde, "with a halo of light hair standing out from the oval of their faces." The players "waltzed and capered with glee" after making a basket and the gymnasium resounded with shrill shrieks.[17]

Because of the distance between Berkeley and Reno, the out-of-staters arrived the day before the game and were treated to lunch at one of the dorms. They stayed overnight at the homes of the players, returning to Reno shortly after the game. Apparently the game was considered a great success since the rivalry was renewed the next year.

Preparation for the culminating 1899 game with Nevada included the defeats of Mills College 14–0 and Stockton High School 12–0. These two games were again played in the presence of women only, although following the Stockton game it was discovered that "eight High School boys disguised in dresses, gloves, heavy veils and other apparel had run the gauntlet of the doorkeeper. They witnessed the entire game."[18]

California found Nevada greatly improved under the tutelage of Ada Edwards, who had been an assistant coach at Stanford and an official in the 1896 Cal-Stanford game. The April 8, 1899 game was played in San Francisco's Odd Fellows Hall. It was a hard fought battle in which Cal was pressed to finally defeat Nevada 7–3. The headline in the *San Francisco Chronicle* proclaimed "One Broken Nevada Nose and a Hard-Fought Victory for California at Basket Ball." Myrtle Montrose, who played left center for Nevada, suffered the injury, which occurred when "several fell in a wriggling heap, and one of the athletic Berkeley girls administered a sort of an uppercut in her efforts to free herself."[19]

Probably because of Coach Edwards' former association with Stanford, Nevada scheduled a game with the Cardinals, beating them 3 to 2 before returning home after five days on the road.

During these early years other groups besides the colleges were playing basketball. High schools in northern California were involved in the sport as evidenced by Berkeley's practice games. Miss Head's, Miss Lake's, and Miss West's Schools were but three of these. Castelleja Hall in the Palo Alto area was another and, in fact, a section of the *San Francisco Examiner*'s coverage of the 1896 Cal-Stanford game was written by the captain of Castelleja's team, Ella Wing. Wing was termed an expert by the *Examiner*. Her account was a technical play-by-play description of the game and she called the players "men"—as in "the Stanford men seemed to show a better sporting spirit than the others. The Berkeley men were inclined to be technical."[20]

Castelleja apparently maintained its team in the years following 1896 since an account was found of them losing 5–0 to Stanford in 1899. This particular game was played on an outdoor court in front of a mixed audience as the *Chronicle* reported that there was a force of university men present. The author then made the following cryptic comment: "the cheering and yelling were done in true feminine style and formed not the least interesting of many amusing features."[21] Interestingly, the Castelleja team included a *Mrs.* Younger on the roster.

A married woman was also on the team of the San Francisco YMCA when they met the Atlantas of Girls' High School in 1899. Playing the right forward position, Mrs. Dietz of the YMCA was named a star player in the defeat of the high school 10–5.[22] At least eight of the Y players were also members of the San Francisco High School team while Mrs. Dietz served as its manager. One article described SFHS's defeat by Oakland High School 4–2. It appears that the extra playing time did not guarantee success in this instance.[23]

Reviewing the early years, women's basketball in the West centered around the colleges/universities and high schools, both private and public. Not surprising, considering its invention, is the fact that both the YM and YWCA fielded women's teams, at least in the San Francisco Bay area.

Basketball in Southern California

Unlike the rest of the West Coast, the first recorded basketball game in Southern California did not involve teams associated with educational institutions or the YM/YWCA. It was, instead, a game played by "society" as the culminating event of the 1897 Southern California Lawn Tennis Association's annual tournament. The tourney was played on the casino courts in Santa Monica and the grand finale for the players was "a basket-ball game in a secluded spot where horrid men cannot encroach."[24]

Despite the admonition concerning men, the game was contested on August 3, 1897 between the three male tennis victors (Barry, Freeman, and Picher) and seven unnamed tennis-playing women. One of the women undoubtedly was the women's single titelist, Marion Jones, who eventually won the United States championship and placed third in the 1900 Paris Olympic Games. Reports of the game are revealing about the caliber of the game. The *Pasadena Daily Evening Star* wrote that the three men lined up on one side and the seven women on the other. One blonde jumped into the air, "made a wild clutch at Freeman's scalp lock and fell on the ball as it came down." When they were knocked down "the girls pluckily got up again, hitched up their bloomers and sailed into the scrimmage with a melodious whoop." The article's final paragraph provides additional flavor:

> And such a crowd as they appeared afterwards! Picher was so thoroughly winded that a pair of bellows was needed to supply him with the necessary air; while Freeman shed so much perspiration that the lawn is forever protected against drouth. As for the girls, they are best described in Kipling's way, being virtually, "A rag and a bone, and a hank of hair." Large chunks of anatomy were missing from various members of the teams.[25]

This first game was not typical of early women's basketball in Southern California since no other reports of co-ed games were found nor were there other accounts of games played outside of school sponsorship. On the other hand, the picture presented of healthy young women involved in outdoor sports is typical of the Southern California lifestyle.

Public and Private Schools

Early settlers of Southern California, many of whom were the well-to-do, desired to project an image of progress and innovation. They accomplished this partially by broadening the experiences allowed young girls. Among these experiences were more and advanced education and participation in sports. Southern Californians early developed physical education programs in the schools for both boys and girls. It was believed by many that exercise of the proper sort would benefit the health of females and thereby allow them to bear sturdier youngsters. Boosters of Southern California raved about the healthy climate and especially noted the effects of this climate on women and children.

In the forefront of physical education programs for women were the private schools. Westlake School for Girls promised "gymnastics work and certain classes . . . conducted in the open air."[26] Orton School for Girls had a gymnasium where Indian club swinging took place and basketball was played while Marlborough School required daily physical activity of all its students.[27] Pasadena's private coeducational Throop Polytechnic Institute (the forerunner of California Institute of Technology) also had a compulsory gymnasium class for girls. The purpose of this daily exercise was to "attain correct carriage, grace, ease of posture, muscular reserve, depth in breathing, and best of all, the rosy bloom of health."[28]

In the late 1890s four Los Angeles area schools organized girls basketball teams. Three of these schools were in the city of Pasadena: Marlborough (just prior to its move to Los Angeles), Throop Polytechnic Institute, and Pasadena High School. The fourth team was formed by the young women of Los Angeles High School. The student newspaper of Throop Institute observed that "for brutality the young ladies of the basketball team are close seconds to the average football team." All four of these schools played each other several times before the turn of the century. The game became so popular that its image was used for product identification of the area's citrus industry.[29] The College Heights Orange Association depicted a Pomona College basketballer on their navel orange label, calling the oranges basketballs.

What was this game that was to get so much attention? In the early years it was played both indoors and out with a round leather-covered

The girls basketball team at the Marlborough School in Pasadena (shown at practice above) was one of four in the Los Angeles area engaged in high level competition in the late 1890s.

rubber ball 30″ to 32″ in circumference. The field or court was divided into three, the players being confined to their respective divisions. Three forwards tried to put the ball into the basket, three guards tried to prevent the other team from doing the same, and the three centers passed the ball to the forwards. The game for women was primarily one of passing and catching with no dribbling or running with the ball. Two 20-minute halves was the norm, although there were many reports of 15-minute halves followed by a 10-minute third and later three 10-minute sections. Fouls included tackling, tripping, shouldering, hacking, striking, and unnecessary roughness of any sort.[30] While the games already mentioned were played with a nine-person team, by 1900 teams appeared composed of less than that number.

One of the most prominent of the early Southern California teams was Pasadena High School. In 1900 Pasadena had three sisters on its undefeated team: Violet, Florence, and May Sutton. These three achieved long-lasting fame for their participation in tennis and May, the youngest sister, won the United States singles title in 1904 and was the earliest

The Pasadena High School girls basketball team in 1901 included the Sutton sisters, who gained fame as both basketball and tennis stars. May and Violet are in the first row, center, and Florence is far right on the second row. When the Sutton sisters played, it was claimed, Pasadena could not lose.

American to win Wimbledon, first in 1905 and again in 1907. The *Los Angeles Times* discussed the championship basketball team:

> The Pasadena High School girls did not meet a team that was really a good match for them. Their first game was with the girls of Throop Institute of Pasadena and was very one-sided, as Throop was not in very good practice, the score being 28–3.
>
> The next game was won by default from Occidental College, score 2 to 0. The hardest fought game was with Marlborough School of Los Angeles, but this game was won by Pasadena by a score of 14 to 3.[31]

In all of the games, May and Florence played as forwards while Violet played center. In the final game of the 1900 season, the team met Citrus High School of Azusa. The *Pasadena Daily News* reported that Citrus played much better in the second half, while Pasadena was primarily concerned with passing and teamwork, but the final score was 25 to 2 in favor of Pasadena. The local paper ended its article with "Rah! Rah! Rah! Once for all, Pasadena high school beats them all."[32]

The 1901 season began in December 1900 when Pasadena met San Diego's Russ High School, both squads playing with only five players. The final score was 22 to 5 in Pasadena's favor. In the Suttons' honor, a poem, written with apologies to the author of "When Johnny Comes Marching Home," was published in the March issue of the school paper. It was entitled "When Sutton Sisters Play."

> The San Diego girls play well, That's true—they do.
> At basket ball they all excell, But we—do too.
> They are worthy the steel of our High School team,
>   Well matched were these foes—but they didn't dream
> That basket ball's not what 'twould seem
>   When the Sutton Sisters play.
>   All hail to you, our noble five! 'Tis done—you've won.
> This verse may keep your deed alive, 'Twas fun—'twas fun,
> It's just this way—you can't be beat,
> This truth we now and again repeat,
> Our team will never know defeat
> While the Sutton Sisters play.[33]

During the season of 1902, Pasadena met Marlborough School again and the paper reported "the forwards on our team were May and Florence Sutton. The former played a very good game, scoring thirteen, but the latter did not play in very good form and scored only one goal."[34] The final score of the game was 15 to 8 and while the team consisted of five players, it is obvious that they were not playing a full-court game since only the forwards shot for the basket. In a second game with Marlborough, Pasadena was again the winner, 7–4. The third game was the charm for Marlborough, however, as they won 6–4. The yearbook explained that this third game was exceptionally close; in fact, "it was very nearly a tie as our team made a goal five seconds after time was called."[35] This comment is indicative of the looseness with which the rules of the game were interpreted during this time period. However, since Pasadena won two of the games they were named Southern California champions.

Interest in basketball increased in 1903 as 33 young women came out for the Pasadena team. Practices were held twice a week and each athlete was required to pay dues of ten cents a month for the privilege of playing.[36] After try-outs, May Sutton was chosen to play right forward on the first team. Two games were played with Throop Institute, which Pasadena won 14–2 and 14–5. In March Pasadena defeated Monrovia High 22–7 and Pomona College 52–10. An interesting practice game was also played in March against the "All Pasadena Team," a team composed of former team members. Florence Sutton played right forward while Violet Sutton played left forward. The All Pasadena Team also went down in defeat 28–14.[37]

Because of the increased interest and the growing ease of transportation, the first league, the Girls Basketball League of Southern California, was formed in 1903. Eight teams were members and the championship went to the team with the best percentage. Girls' Collegiate, Marlborough, Monrovia, Ontario, and Pasadena High Schools were members as well as Pomona College, Throop Institute, and the Normal School. Other schools in Los Angeles, Santa Ana, Riverside, Santa Monica, Alhambra, and San Diego participated in nonleague games.[38]

One of the most unusual games was against Los Angeles High School in April 1903. In an understated headline, "Los Angeles Girls Were Never In It," the local paper remarked that "the high school basketball team defeated the Los Angeles high school team Saturday afternoon by a score of 95–0—which, it is hardly necessary to suggest, is rather unusual."[39] The final game of the 1903 season saw Pasadena defeat their nemesis of the previous year, Marlborough, 25–15 and thereby become champions of Southern California again. Pasadena's success led to a general discussion of the suitability of the sport for women:

> Where are the people who think that basketball athletics are not for girls? I wish they might have seen this game and the results to disprove their idea. The game teaches school patriotism quicker than anything else. . . . Besides it gives good healthy complexions and teaches quickness of thought.[40]

By 1905 another team had risen to prominence, the team from Long Beach High School. When it was victorious against Glendale High School in March, the game was hailed as the roughest game of basketball ever played:

Except the center position, the teams are evenly matched, but while Glendale's center, Emily Smalley, weighs 205 lbs., Minnie Sessions will tip the scale at 125, so that the encounter today was like a pebble hitting a boulder, and the slender local center was pushed and shoved until her back and front hair came loose, and then she turned the tables. First Miss Smalley got a jolt on the chin, accidentally, that jarred her front teeth, and a few minutes later in a scrimmage struck the hard ground with a dull thud.[41]

In succeeding articles the *Times* continued to note the roughness of the Long Beach style of play. "Sweet Things Have A Scrap. Hence Local Misses Claim Default Championship. Too Many Fouls, One Row and Some Faces" were the headlines when an undefeated Long Beach team walked out of a game against Los Angeles High at the neutral University of Southern California court. Much of the blame was placed at the feet of the two officials who had been chosen by each team.[42] Long Beach was not the only team to use aggressive tactics. In a game between Los Angeles and Polytechnic High Schools, hair pulling, tumbling, and sliding over the court was the norm. A reporter noted that "there was something disquieting in the grim and murderous determination with which the young ladies chased each other over the court."[43]

Highly competitive players and rough play, biased officials, and an unusually high number of fouls apparently continued. By June 1907 those in charge of women's basketball decided that the game had sufficiently degenerated to call for a drastic modification of play. Citing bitter, hard-fought matches, numerous fouls, and favoritism by officials, the Executive Board of the County League made the following changes:

> There shall be three thirds, consisting of ten minutes each, with a ten-minute rest between thirds. Goals and ball shall be changed at the middle of the game (middle of the middle third). There shall be six players on each team—two forwards, two guards and two centers.

Officials were to be outsiders rather than partisan. "A post-graduate or an alumnus of an institution is not considered an outsider."[44]

Not to be outdone by the local high schools, Los Angeles area grammar schools began fielding teams in 1904. By 1905 they were playing for the prestigious *Los Angeles Times* trophy. A sign of the times was noted in the grammar school competitions when in the third round, a player was reported as having "sassed" the umpire.[45] By 1907 the grammar school league had expanded to the point where two separate divisions became necessary.

The Los Angeles playgrounds, which had officially joined the playground movement in 1904, also added basketball competition. A trophy for the winning team was provided, again by the *Los Angeles Times*. In

1907 the *Times* noted that Violet Street playground played Echo Park playground as part of the *Times* Cup competition.[46]

As a result of all the various levels of interest in basketball with hundred of teams competing in front of large audiences, local and county winners began to look farther afield for competition and higher rewards. The *Times* peaked such interest by reporting on the competition in other leagues. The champions from each of seven Southern California leagues played each other. The Los Angeles High School team finally declared themselves state champions after having played a team which had previously beaten the northern champion.[47] Long Beach also continued winning and in 1911, having won the championship of Southern California for the third time, was allowed to keep the trophy.

Colleges and Universities

In Southern California and the West Coast in general basketball was considered a game for women; few men, other than members of the YMCA or various Turnvereins, were involved in it. A 1905 *Los Angeles Times* article explained this phenomenon:

> Probably in the entire category of sports there is none more generally misunderstood than . . . basketball. Owing to the fact that girls take quite readily to it, an idea has become prevalent that basketball is a "sissy" game, and unworthy the efforts of athletes. There could hardly be a greater mistake, inasmuch as basketball is one of the most exciting games, physically, that men play.[48]

Because of the misconception, there is no mention of basketball being played by men in schools and colleges until 1903 and the sport did not become popular in educational institutions until 1907.

While men were not playing basketball, college women were going wild over the game, particularly in Southern California. One of the earliest colleges to organize a team was the small liberal arts school east of Los Angeles, Pomona College, whose first team was formed in 1900. The college yearbook, *The Metate*, included a photo of ten women in bloomers and middy blouses and noted that basketball "is the only branch of college athletics belonging exclusively to the girls. It is not generally popular, but is the favorite game of those who play." Further, "if the spirit of college loyalty flourishes still among the girls, if the Faculty and onlookers support the game, if a coach can be found, Pomona will win the championship of Southern California next year."[49] While Pomona did not win it in 1901, they were undefeated in 1902.

Shortly after Pomona organized, so did their prime rival, Occidental College, then the University of Southern California, Woodbury Business College, and the Normal School (which was to become the University of California at Los Angeles). The first intercollegiate game in Southern

California was between Pomona and Occidental Colleges in 1904. Pomona won this first game 19–15[50] but the next time the two met, in 1906, Oxy was victorious 28–8.[51] The perennial basketball powers in the area were these two teams and the University of Southern California, who first fielded a team in 1904. Several games were played among these three teams between 1904 and 1908 with no one team dominating.

One of the features which becomes apparent when reading the accounts of West Coast women's basketball is the randomness with which teams were fielded. This is not surprising when one realizes that the early teams were organized by the players. Some years, for example, Pomona College had a strong team and a year or two later there was no mention of basketball at all. Another interesting occurrence is that high schools and colleges competed against each other. An example of this is USC, who in 1905 had a 12–0 record but only one intercollegiate game, against Occidental whom they beat 26–13.[52]

Popularity of basketball grew tremendously in the early 1900s and several women who were star high school players continued to play in college. As interest grew, more women tried out for college teams and by 1905 so many women came out that interclass games became a method of selecting the varsity team. Both Pomona and Oxy held interclass tournaments during the fall and selected their varsity for intercollegiate games which were played primarily in the spring. In 1907 the president of Occidental donated a silver cup for the winner of the interclass tournament. The interest in interclass play was so great that Oxy decided not to play any off-campus games.[53] A clearer view of Oxy's refusal to play outside games was presented in a *Los Angeles Times* article which noted "the freshman girls received a challenge from the U.S.C. first year team yesterday, but as the college management does not countenance intercollegiate sports for women, the Presbyterian young women did not accept the offer to play the Methodists."[54]

An indication of the importance of women's basketball as a collegiate sport is shown by the fact that in 1906, Occidental College awarded the first varsity letter "O" to five women athletes, all basketball players.[55] After years of indecision, Pomona College followed suit and granted the "P" to seven women basketballers in 1909 and an additional five in 1910.[56] The last intercollegiate women's game played in Southern California in the early years occurred in 1909 when Southern Cal beat Pomona 17–13.[57]

By 1911 a noticeable decline in the enthusiasm for women's basketball was evidenced. Newspaper reports which declared basketball for both men and women more dangerous than football or baseball did not help matters. Nor did some medical professionals. Dudley Reed, medical examiner of the University of Chicago, received attention when he claimed that participation in such a violent sport led to slightly enlarged, irritable, and overactive hearts.[58] Al Treloar, from the Harvard Summer School and physical director of the Los Angeles Athletic Club, also declared that competitive sports were not only dangerous for girls but suicidal to the race![59] Other factors may have been that women's basketball was too successful, too athletic, too much fun, and received too much publicity for the time period. It was also about this time that college men began serious competition in the sport.

Predictably, in 1910, 1911, and 1912 some colleges and high schools began noting in their yearbooks that they had adopted a different form of competition, interclass play. Interschool and interclass competition was sporadically revived through the thirties, but the media coverage for basketball in educational institutions was not to prevail again.

Examined in the light of national experts' prescriptions for team sports, the Southern California women's experience appears quite daring and bold. Most of the women's teams were coached by men. All of them played not "just for fun" but to win in the true spirit of competition. Most of the games were played in front of mixed audiences and many teams traveled as far away as San Diego and Sacramento. The women were continually praised in the college and school yearbooks for their dedication, their contributions to school loyalty, and the positive media attention resulting from success in competition. Rarely was any mention made in the media of the bloomers which they wore or the occasional baring of a limb. Nor was there any hint after the first years that the women lacked the necessary stamina for intense competition.

It would be easy to overlook the fact that at the most, the schools and colleges probably fielded two teams encompassing 20 women. Perhaps basketball was so popular and well regarded that more women wanted to play it competitively. Hence the interclass mode of competition would appear to be a logical alternative.

The tone of the school newspapers changed dramatically however. Hiking clubs, indoor baseball, and wall scaling were just some of the events which began to garner more print than basketball. Newspaper articles described the scenery and the dress of women rather than the mode and quality of play. The high schools and colleges had thus begun to conform to a mode of physical activity which was more in line with the national experts' prescriptions for women.

The 1920s and 1930s

Basketball as a sport for women was much too popular to disappear entirely; it was still played in schools and colleges on an interclass level or as part of the Girls' Athletic Association or Women's Recreation Association. Teams were put together for play and sports days but varsity competition came to an end for the time being. It was almost as if basketball went underground from 1911 until the mid-1920s.

In the 1920s an interesting phenomenon occurred. Basketball re-emerged, but not in the schools and colleges; rather it reappeared as a club sport. One of the first mentions of this reemergence was a 1922 article in the *California Eagle*, the Los Angeles African-American news-paper, which announced that the Los Angeles YMCA invited all girls to attend basketball practice.[60] Several games were played during the 1920s by the Girl Reserves of the Los Angeles and Pasadena YM/YWCAs and the two were great rivals. Since the sport was invented for use in the Y, it is not so strange that the game would continue to be played within the organization.

What was interesting, however, was the emergence of basketball in the private athletic clubs, the bastion of tradition and feminine activities for members' wives and daughters. In 1925 the Pasadena Athletic and Country Club formed a women's basketball team composed of nine local high school athletes who also competed on the club's track team. An announcement of the team's formation explained that scheduling games was a problem since the women had "accepted a new A.A.U. ruling that provides that girls shall play the same fast game as do the men, except that a longer rest shall be permitted between halves."[61] Edward Laurenson, coach of the Pasadena High School boys team, was retained to prepare the women for their major game with the traveling Edmonton Grads. While Pasadena lost to the Grads 27–7, the team contained two women who were members of the 1928 and 1932 United States Olympic teams. Both of the women, Maybelle Reichart and Lillian Copeland, were discus throwers. Copeland won the gold medal in the 1932 Los Angeles Olympics.

Because the Pasadena Athletic Club hosted a successful AAU national women's championship in track and field in 1925, they were granted the first national senior basketball championships for women on April 8 and 9, 1926. In an announcement of the tournament, the *Los Angeles Times* headlined "Amazons Here From All Over Country" and noted that one of Pasadena's star players "is quite capable in the kitchen or cleaning house, but her game of basketball is equal to her ability in more feminine traits."[62] The final results of this first national tournament were the Pasadena Athletic Club first with the Anaheim Athletic Club and Goodyear Tire and Rubber Company second and third respectively.

During the 1927–28 season, an athletic club league was formed with teams from Pasadena, Glendale, Hollywood, Santa Ana, and Whittier playing under "girls rules." After playing all league games with these rules, a new series of games using men's rules began in January 1928 for the Pacific Coast Championship.[63] No further mention was made of basketball after this season and the club appeared to concentrate on track and field, placing five women on the 1928 Olympic team. However, by this time industrial and church leagues had been formed for women as well as a YWCA league. Basketball seemed alive and well even though there was a scarcity of coverage by the media.

The 1930s witnessed a tremendous resurgence of interest in basketball among women in the Los Angeles area. In 1931 a group of Chinese-American women founded the Mei Wah Club for the purpose of playing basketball. The Mei Wah's last game of the 1931 season was against a group of Japanese-Americans from the Los Angeles' Lincoln High School and Mei Wah won handily, 15–8.[64] African-American women also organized club teams; among the most successful was the Athena Athletic Club founded in 1930. By 1934 the Athenas had played over fifty games losing but four of them.[65]

From 1934 to 1939 there was a huge amount of women's basketball in the Los Angeles basin. Hispanic, Russian-American, and the previously mentioned African-, Chinese-, and Japanese-American teams played many regular season and all-star games. Industrial teams also became prominent and in 1938 the Southern California championship was won by the Sunfreeze Ice Cream team who defeated the *California Eagle's* all-star Eaglettes, 66–14.[66] The same Eaglettes returned in 1939, however, to edge the league champs, the Queen Esther Japanese, 29–27.[67]

From the evidence presented it is obvious that basketball on the West Coast has had a long and interesting history. It has been played by thousands of girls and women from its beginnings in 1892 to the present day. Race, religion, social class, age, and ethnicity were unimportant when it came to just playing the game. The number of women who played basketball and then became internationally recognized for their athletic prowess in other sports is astonishing. From the grammar schools to the universities, the YM/YWCAs to exclusive athletic clubs, industrial to church leagues, women on the West Coast were involved with the game. Basketball is truly a part of the western lifestyle and James Naismith is smiling, with Clara Baer and Senda Berenson nodding their approval.

Notes

1. *The Occident*, October 7, 1892, cited by May Dornin in "Basketball at the University of California from Its Beginning in 1892 Until Its Acceptance as a Major Sport" (unpublished paper, University of California Berkeley Archives, 1957), 1.

2. "Feminine Athletics," *Berkeley Daily Advocate*, 19 November 1892.

3. Ibid.

4. "Girls at Athletics," *Seattle Post-Intelligencer*, 17 April 1896, p. 3.

5. Mabel Craft, "Co-eds in Red Beat at Ball," *San Francisco Chronicle*, 5 April 1896, p. 26.

6. Ibid.

7. He, "A Communication," *The Berkeleyan*, 9 March 1896, p. 1.

8. "Basket Ball," *The Berkeleyan*, 27 March 1896, p. 1.

9. "Berkeley Co-eds Rebel," *San Francisco Chronicle*, 27 March 1896, p. 11.

10. "On the Eve of Battle," *San Francisco Chronicle*, 4 April 1896, p. 16.

11. "Basket-Ball. Stanford Wins, 2–1—The Game a Success," *The Berkeleyan*, 6 April 1896, p. 1.

12. "U. of W. Girls Win," *Seattle Post-Intelligencer*, 18 April 1896, p. 3.

13. Nemo, "Notes of the Normal," *Ellensburg Capital*, 23 April 1896, p. 1.

14. Dornin, "Basketball at the University of California," p. 4.

15. Ibid.

16. "Berkeley Girls Ready to Meet Fair Nevadans at Basket Ball," *San Francisco Chronicle*, 7 April 1898, p. 5.

17. "California Co-eds Win," *San Francisco Chronicle*, 10 April 1898, p. 32.

18. "Berkeley Co-eds Win at Stockton," *San Francisco Chronicle*, 5 March 1898, p. 25.

19. "One Broken Nevada Nose and a Hard-Fought Victory for California at Basket Ball," *San Francisco Chronicle*, 9 April 1899, p. 32.

20. "Waterloo for Berkeley Girls," *San Francisco Examiner*, 5 April 1896, p. 11.

21. "Stanford Girls the Winners," *San Francisco Chronicle*, 12 March 1899, p. 20.

22. "Ladies at Basketball," *San Francisco Chronicle*, 10 April 1899, p. 8.

23. "Oakland Victorious," *San Francisco Chronicle*, 30 April 1899, p. 21.

24. "On Its Last Legs," *Los Angeles Times*, 31 July 1897, p. 5.

25. "Boys and Girls Play Basket Ball Down at Santa Monica," *Pasadena Daily Evening Star*, 4 August 1897, p. 4.

26. Westlake School for Girls *Catalogue*, 1909–10.

27. "Health Giving Exercise," *Pasadena Daily Evening Star*, 2 May 1897, p. 1.

28. *The Polytechnic*, Throop Polytechnic Institute newspaper, December 15, 1899, cited by Victoria Bissell Brown, "Golden Girls: Female Socialization in Los Angeles, 1880 to 1910" (Ph.D. diss., University of California, San Diego, 1985), 433.

29. Brown, "Golden Girls," 475–476.

30. "Basket Ball," *Los Angeles Times*, 5 August 1900, sec. IV, p. 3.

31. Ibid.

32. "Winners Again," *Pasadena Daily News*, 25 June 1900, p. 4.

33. "When Sutton Sisters Play," *Pasadena High School Item*, March 1901, p. 13.

34. Chas. White, ed., "Athletics," *Pasadena High School Item*, April 1902, p. 12.

35. Chas. White, ed., "Athletics," *The Item Annual*, June 1902, p. 25.

36. "Athletics: Basket Ball," *The High School Item*, November 1902, p. 13.

37. Fannie Furman, ed., "Girls' Athletics: Basketball," *The Item Annual*, June 1903.

38. "Basket Ball," *The High School Item*, April 1903, p. 12.

39. "Los Angeles Girls Were Never In It," *Pasadena Evening Star*, 6 April 1903, p. 8.

40. Furman, "Girls' Athletics."

41. "Long Beach Girls Win," *Los Angeles Times*, 26 March 1905, sec. 3, p. 2.

42. "Sweet Things Have a Scrap," *Los Angeles Times*, 7 May 1905, sec. 3, p. 2.

43. "Fair Maids in Brain-Storms," *Los Angeles Times*, 1 June 1907.

44. "Rough Playing Is Eliminated," *Los Angeles Times*, 6 June 1907, p. 7.

45. "Thirtieth by Three Points," *Los Angeles Times*, 6 June 1905.

46. "Public Playgrounds Teams in Condition," *Los Angeles Times*, 13 September 1907.

47. "L.A. Girls Win Snappy Contest," *Los Angeles Times*, 5 May 1907.

48. "Basketball Now on Tap," *Los Angeles Times*, 1 January 1905, sec. 3, p. 4.

49. *The Metate* (Pomona College), 1900.

50. "Athletic Comment. Intercollegiate Basket Ball," *The Student Life* (Pomona College), 25 March 1904, p. 429.

51. "College Basketball. Occidental Beats Pomona," *Los Angeles Times*, 11 March 1906, sec. 3, p. 4.

52. "Men Ordered Off the Court," *Los Angeles Times*, 19 March 1905, sec. 3, p. 3.

53. "Girls Tourney Opens," *Los Angeles Times*, 20 February 1907, p. 6.

54. "Basketball Activities," *Los Angeles Times*, 23 November 1907, p. 7.

55. " 'O' Women in College," *La Encina* (Occidental College), 1906, p. 85.

56. *The Metate* (Pomona College), 1909; *The Metate*, 1910.

57. "Girls Basket Ball," *The Metate*, 1909, p. 132.

58. "Basketball Is Risky Pastime," *Los Angeles Times*, 18 February 1912, sec. 7, p. 8.

59. Al Treloar, "Swimming, Fancy Dancing and Rowing Give Health to Girls," *Los Angeles Times*, 31 December 1911, sec. 4, p. 8.

60. "Y.M.C.A. Notes," *California Eagle*, 7 January 1922, p. 6.

61. "Girls' Basketball," *P.A.C.C.* (Pasadena Athletic and Country Club), January 1925, p. 11.

62. "Women Cagers Meet for Title. Amazons Here From All Over Country," *Los Angeles Times*, 6 April 1926, sec. 3, p. 1.

63. "Athletic Notes," *Pasadena Sportland* (Pasadena Athletic Club), January 1928, p. 13.

64. "Lincoln High: Star Players Seen at Casaba Practice," *Rafu Shimpo*, 9 April 1931, p. 1.

65. Arie Lee Branch, "Girletics," *California Eagle*, 24 December 1934, p. 11.

66. "Chinese Quintet Hold M.D. Five to Close Score," *California Eagle*, 3 March 1938, p. 3-B.

67. "Eaglettes Top League Champs," *California Eagle*, 6 April 1939, p. 5-B.

9

Basketball Texas Style, 1910–1933
School to Industrial League Competition

Roxanne M. Albertson

Between 1910 and 1933 Texas girls and young women competed in basketball games and tournaments at all levels of play. On farms and ranches and in small towns and cities girls practiced putting the round ball into iron hoops. On dirt patches behind barns or in playgrounds, in small school rooms or in large converted warehouses girls practiced skills, planned game strategies, and competed against teams from across Texas and the nation. School leagues, recreation and industrial leagues, college teams, and Sunday school leagues all provided competitive opportunities for these young athletes.

High school state basketball championships had been contested since 1906 with invitational regional tournaments beginning in 1910. Initially, leagues used Spalding's Official Women's Rules with six players on a team but by 1910 some teams played using a combination of men's and women's rules.[1] There was a well-developed interest in women's basketball in San Antonio, Waco, Fort Worth, Dallas, Corsicana, Galveston, Corpus Christi, Austin, and Georgetown.[2]

Community and industrial leagues developed for young women who had learned basketball in school and who wished to continue playing after school years. Cedar Spring Avenue playground, Dallas, organized a girls team that alternated use of the basketball court with the local boys team; "the girls have the grounds Monday, Wednesday, and Friday evenings."[3] Sanger Department Store began a gymnastic and basketball club for 20 of its female employees.[4] Fort Worth Masonic Home, Summit Play Park, San Antonio Sunday School League, Fort Worth Girls Recreation League, and Corpus Christi YWCA sponsored basketball teams and endorsed competitive activities for school girls and young women.[5]

155

The Corpus Christi girls defeated the Robestown girls 34–11 in a well played basket-ball game Friday evening. The team was in excellent condition for playing and exciting for all to watch.[6]

Summit Play Park girls basket-ball team defeated Trinity Play Park 14–1. After the game the Summit girls entertained the Trinity girls with a dance.[7]

The Carpenters Union sponsored an exhibition of fancy swimming and diving and swimming contests for women only. After the exhibition, the Union ladies participated in basketball games on the outdoor court next to the union hall. The game was fast and clean and enjoyed by all.[8]

Before the founding of the University Interscholastic League in 1917 little distinction was made among school, college, or nonschool basketball teams.[9] Teams scheduled contests against a variety of teams within traveling distance during the season. At the end of the seasons, teams divided into school, commercial, industrial, and Sunday school leagues to determine league and state champions. In larger cities, the administrators of the leagues divided non school leagues into a major loop and recreational loop to accommodate competitive and skill levels.[10]

This interest in basketball competition by girls and women of all skill levels and the organizations formed to accommodate and control competitions during the early twentieth century set the framework for the

Women's basketball practice at the University of North Texas, Denton, in 1921. (Courtesy UNT files) During the basketball frenzy of the 1920s in Texas, college teams competed against schools and community-sponsored teams as well as other college teams.

basketball frenzy during the 1920s. Though basketball competitions and news coverage of sports events were curtailed during WWI, interest in basketball by women and sponsoring organizations continued unabated.[11] In 1910 AAU's policy concerning women's sport competitions was "not to register a female competitor and its registration committee refuses sanction for . . . a set of games where an event for women is scheduled."[12] This policy changed as girls and women increasingly requested permission to have AAU sanctioned tournaments at state and regional levels. In 1920 AAU reported that 962 women in Texas had applied to AAU headquarters for permission to take part in sanctioned basketball tournaments.[13] The University Interscholastic League determined competition rules for high school teams and organized means of determining state championships, but the AAU controlled nonschool competitions plus regional and national invitational tournaments.[14]

During the 1920s competition levels became increasingly diverse from neophyte to highly skilled. Interested teachers formed school teams and taught the girls skills. Kathleen Peace recalled:

> The reason we won the National [high school] tournament was . . . the coach that came that year to teach gymnastics . . . asked the boy's coach about basketball and he told her how to coach and worked out some drills for her. Every afternoon she'd have us run through these plays.[15]

Claudine Petty remembered that at Seagoville High School they played basketball outside. Even when her school team won the state tournament they did not have a gymnasium, and thus made their plays in the classroom. The superintendent of schools was interested in their team and taught them "things about basketball . . . we skinned lots of knees playing outdoors, but I learned to play well enough to score 87 points in one game."[16] In Mingus, a small town in central Texas, the girls practiced and played all their home games on an outdoor dirt court. Marie Berbino, Mingus jump center, contended that "playing on the dirt court only made the team better."[17] The calibre of the Mingus team's play was high enough for it to be invited to a national tournament.

College teams competed against schools, colleges, and community-sponsored teams. A few colleges recruited and offered scholarships to promising basketball players. Rubye Mansfield and Claudine Petty received scholarship offers from Randolph College. In a letter to Petty the coach of the Randolph Kittens indicated she was interested in having her attend Randolph because she was "very anxious to build up a strong basketball team . . . a girl attending Randolph College that has the ability of a basketball player has the opportunity to distinguish herself that no other college can offer."[18] Other colleges in Oklahoma, Arkansas, and Texas also were actively recruiting players with promises of housing and tuition assistance.[19] Though recruiters did not mention athletic scholarships, the recruited athletes did have financial aid available to them.

For talented young women who did not want to go to college or who wished to continue playing after college, opportunities to combine basketball and jobs in large towns and cities became increasingly available during the 1920s. Young women from rural areas moved to cities to seek employment. Basketball was a popular recreational activity for many of these new employees and they sought opportunities to showcase those basketball skills learned in school.[20]

Showcasing Women's Basketball

Coinciding with the influx of women basketball players in the workforce was the growing interest of companies in broadening their advertising base beyond newspaper advertisements. One of the methods used for increased advertisement was sponsorship of local sport teams. Sanger Department Store, Franklin Motor Car, Schepps, Sunoco Oil, Employer's Casualty, Sproles Transfer, Huey and Philip, Trezerant and Cochren, and Piggly Wiggly Groceries sponsored women's basketball teams and tournaments.[21] Most companies sponsored community-based recreational league teams, but a few companies formed teams of their own employees. This marriage between sport and advertising, though utilized by men since the inception of trade guilds and fraternal organizations, was a new phenomenon for women. The idea of getting paid to work and sponsored to play basketball was a lure that many highly skilled athletes and willing workforce learners considered an ideal association of convenience.

Women showcasing basketball skills in public arenas did not have universal appeal. There were increasing rumblings by some physical educators that athletics for women was getting beyond control. Concerned opponents of the basketball frenzy advocated broadening opportunities for all females to participate, using female coaches, and tightly controlling spectatorship to invited guests.[22] James Sullivan contended that male coaches tended to "exploit [girls] as female Sheppards, Sheridans, or Sandows, or as show girls."[23]

The efforts of some physical educators in Texas and throughout the nation to control girls and women's basketball competitions may have had an impact in some schools and colleges but their admonitions went unheard or unheeded in many parts of Texas until after 1936.[24] Lalia Warren and other All American players indicated that they were not aware of any social stigma to playing highly competitive basketball either in school or on community or industrial teams.[25] Women's teams competed in leagues, and AAU invited them to AAU-sponsored state, regional, and national tournaments. Men and women coached the teams, and the teams often charged admission to contests and encouraged the public to attend the games. Neither players nor coaches reported concerns that others considered these actions detrimental to participants or to companies they represented.

City newspaper coverage of these concerns was nonexistent or minimal. By 1930 Dallas newspapers were covering 48 girls/women's basketball teams. At the height of basketball seasons, press coverage included feature articles, pictures, box scores, game descriptions, interviews, and announcements for future games.[26]

Four types of women's basketball leagues—girls school, commercial, industrial, and Sunday school—received extensive press coverage. If a school team showed exceptional talent AAU invited the team to sanctioned regional and national tournaments. Kathleen Peace recalled that her high school team lost the state tournament but received a special invitation to go to the national tournament in Wichita, Kansas in 1928.[27] Agnes Iori and her high school team received invitations to the national tournament in 1927 and her teammates selected her to captain the All American team while she was still a high school junior.[28]

At these tournaments, colleges and companies recruited talented players for their sponsored teams. Dallas companies accomplished some of the most successful recruiting efforts. Athletic directors of Dallas companies recruited talented stars from Kansas, Pennsylvania, Louisiana, Oklahoma, Colorado, Missouri, and Texas. They promised prospective player/employees job training plus opportunities to show off their basketball talent. Lalia Warren indicated the major enticement for her to join a Dallas company and team was an increase in salary from $36 to $65 per month as a secretarial trainee.[29]

Between 1925 and 1932 two of the most talented commercial and industrial league teams in Dallas were the Sunoco Oil Company Oilers and the Employer's Casualty Company Golden Cyclones. The Oilers, as members of the major industrial league loop, was an independent team sponsored by various companies throughout its seven year existence: 1925–1928 Trezerant and Cochren, 1928–1929 Schepps, and 1929–1931 Sunoco Oil.[30] This team of talented players did not lose a game in league or tournament play from 1927 to 1929. It captured the National AAU Tournament Championship in 1928, 1929, and 1930.[31] At the height of their popularity in the Dallas region 1,000 to 2,000 fans crowded the bleachers in the Fair Park Automobile Building to watch and cheer each game.

> The dash and spirit of the contestants, the picturesque uniforms and the enthusiasm around the swift maneuvers of the opposing teams all combine to give the spectators all the thrills they can stand in one evening of athletic contests.[32]

Gypsy Williams and Carrie McLeroy were two Oiler All American forwards providing height and scoring leadership to the team.[33] Oiler team members had been recruited and the company provided traveling and housing stipends from gate receipts and company sponsors. Unfortunately, because of the lack of long-term sponsorship or job commitments, team stars joined other teams and companies that enticed them with job security.

The Oilers' first defeat occurred on January 6, 1929 at the hands of their city rivals, the Golden Cyclones, while over 2,000 spectators crowded the Fair Park Automobile Building cheering their favorite team.[34] The Oilers were able to gain revenge during the AAU national finals by defeating the Cyclones by one point before 5,000 spectators.[35] The rivalry between these two talented basketball teams continued until the Oilers disbanded in 1931. Though sports writers and fans admired the skill of the Oilers players and the teamwork exhibited, the charisma of the Cyclones captured the enthusiasm of Dallas and North Texas fans as no other sport team, men's or women's, could until the 1950s.

The Rise of the Cyclones

Who were these charismatic, talented basketball players who captured the hearts of Dallas and the ranking of Dallas top sport team in 1929? What were the circumstances influencing the Cyclones' rise to local, regional, and national prominence and then their demise after the 1932 season?

M. J. McCombs, athletic director, recruiter, organizer, publicist, and periodic coach, was the dominant force behind the development of the Golden Cyclones into a national championship team and advertising agent for the Employer's Casualty Insurance Company.[36] McCombs was manger of the company's safety engineering department. In 1927, he convinced the advertising department to increase financial backing for the athletic program sponsored by the company, primarily to increase funds for women's basketball and track and field teams.[37] McCombs believed that one method of achieving national recognition as an excellent insurance company was to develop a nationally ranked women's basketball team.[38]

Business competitors, colleges, high schools, and the rival Oilers recruited All American players. The company interviewed each potential player for a position within the engineering department's clerical or secretarial pool.[39] After 1928 it was against company policy to hire married women but at least one Cyclone player combined marriage, basketball, and job. Claudine Petty roomed in Dallas with other players during the week, then returned home to her husband in Seagoville on weekends. She indicated that team members and coaches knew about her marriage, but she did not discuss it during work hours.[40]

By 1929 McCombs had convinced ten All American athletes with skills in both basketball and track and field to join the Cyclones. He then recruited star high school players to complete the team's roster.[41] The company provided tutors to finish their education plus close supervision during leisure hours.[42] This galaxy of Cyclones All American stars included guards Agnes Iori, Lucy Stratton, Kathleen Peace, and Claudine Petty, jump center Belle Weisinger, and forwards Rubye Mansfield, Babe Didrikson, Lalia Warren, Nadine Neith, and Gypsy Butcher. Other members of the team included Mary Huckabee, Jackie Maxwell, Augusta Coleman, Jessie Nivens, Addie East, Lillian Waits, Mary Carter, Fay Langford, Isla Rhea Leister, Oma Thornburt, and Leona Thaxton. Each of these reserves had been a star on other teams but usually had to assume a supporting role with the Cyclones because of its depth of talent.[43]

To coach this group of players, the company hired Danny Lynch, professional baseball pitcher. A business manager, chaperon, trainer, and mascot rounded out the Cyclone organization. This team and extensive supporting cast developed into such a dominant force in basketball by 1930 that few teams in the nation could provide a challenging contest.

During the Cyclones' five years as a major industrial league team it won 36 loving cups for tournament championships and 361 individual medals. The team played more than 40 games per season averaging 38 points per game while holding its opponents to an average of 11 points. It was the only team in the nation at that time to hold national records in two sports, basketball and track and field. It reached the AAU National Tournament semifinals or finals in each of the five years between 1927 and 1932, losing in the finals by one point in each of three years and winning the championship by one point in 1931. It held the highest score record made in a national AAU tournament, 97 points, and the defensive record of holding its opponents to 4 points.[44]

The AAU tournament games used the Spalding rules for the two division court game. During the 1931 season AAU tested experimental rules involving the two division court, three second passing, and one dribble rules. The basketball committee abolished technical fouls for close guarding and center circle restrictions changed permitting movement through the circle by designated players.[45] These rule changes aided the Cyclones' quest for national prominence since the team specialized in passing and defensive strategies.[46]

The Cyclones practiced passing, shooting, and endurance skills three times per week in Highland Park High School gymnasium. The coaches stressed year-round conditioning as vital to the team's success. Any player who appeared to be dogging it was given extra running drills. When opposing teams began to tire during the fourth quarter of a game the highly conditioned Cyclones would put on an offensive and defensive spurt.[47]

Home contests, played on center court in the Fair Park Automobile Building, drew 1,000–4,000 spectators. During city league season the preliminary contests featured the men's league games with the gold and white plaid shorts Cyclone team scheduled as the main attraction.[48] During regional and national tournaments crowds would swell to 3,500–5,000 with bands playing and halftime entertainments.[49] During the 1931 national finals between the Oilers and Cyclones newspapers reported that cheering was so loud residents could hear the excitement a mile away.[50]

Published negative reactions to the competitiveness and athletic prowess of the Cyclones or any other women's basketball team in Dallas were not found. Players could not remember any instances of social pressure from their families, peers, or press to pursue different goals during their basketball careers. Families supported them and the press

The Golden Cyclones of Dallas, Texas, rose to local, regional, and national prominence in the years 1929–32. Among the many talented, charismatic players were: left, Claudine Petty Glenn, and below, Agnes Dori Robertson.

Employers' Casualty Company, like many commercial companies in Texas, promised prospective employee/players job training and opportunities to show off their basketball talents. The Company's best known recruit was Babe Didrikson (right), who achieved fame not only as a Cyclone but also in the 1932 Olympics and the amateur and professional golf circuit. She was selected as the outstanding female athlete of the first half of the twentieth century. (All three photos of the Cyclones courtesy of Claudine Petty memorabilia)

lauded their performances. Though few Cyclone players' parents traveled to Dallas to watch their talented daughters play, team members did indicate that their mothers and fathers listened to the games broadcast on radio.[51] Lalia Warren's father and brother encouraged her to participate in basketball.[52] Rubye Mansfield remembered the press was very favorable, covering most games home or away plus all tournament games. She noted that at times the team did not deserve the praise or lead story coverage.[53] Some Employer's Casualty employees did complain that a few players were not working as hard as necessary, but most players received high evaluations on both work and basketball.[54] Employee-players may have been conscientious about performing their jobs because, except for one player, they looked upon basketball as a short-term interlude between school and career necessities.

The reasons for the disbandment of the Cyclone basketball team after the 1932 season were varied. Retrenchment at Employer's Casualty Insurance Company, because of the depression, reduced the advertising budget that financed athletic events as well as available jobs for talented athletes but learning workers.[55] The use of Babe Didrikson after her 1932 Olympic achievements as the company's publicist reduced the need to support an entire basketball team.[56] McCombs' preoccupation in basketball waned as his attention turned to track and field, then to managing press relations for Babe Didrikson.[57] A final reason may have been the loss of the Cyclones to the Durant Cardinals in the 1932 AAU finals. No longer were the Cyclones the reigning queens of the hard court.[58]

The Cyclone members were highly skilled women athletes dedicated to the pursuit of two goals. They wanted to participate in competitive basketball on a challenging and exciting level; they also wanted to obtain a job with a reputable company. Employer's Casualty Insurance Company provided an opportunity for these women to fulfill both goals. The company's primary goal was to produce a nationally recognized women's sport team thus gaining positive advertising benefits through sponsoring sport excellence. Neither team nor company felt exploited in the pursuit of these goals.

After 1932 fewer Texas companies provided financial resources for basketball teams for their female employees, but companies continued to sponsor commercial and recreational league teams and Texas women continued to play competitive basketball. The patterns of competitive play initiated in basketball spread to other sports, including tennis, bowling, track and field, boating, golf, and riding. As one avenue of sponsorship declined, women found other avenues to continue their interest in sport participation. These avenues were increasingly found in community and church recreation leagues. School girls and young women of Texas enjoyed competitive sports, especially basketball. They demanded opportunities to participate. Schools, colleges, communities, and companies provided resources for their participation. Families, community residents, and press encouraged their participation and supported local teams. Between 1910 and 1933 girls basketball in Texas, whether on an outdoor dirt court or in a large auditorium, was an exciting sport to play and dominant agent for developing community cohesiveness.

Notes

1. J. E. Lombard, "Basketball for Women in the South," *Spalding's Official Basket Ball Guide for Women* (1910–1911) (New York: American Sports Publishing Co., 1910), 59–61.

2. Ibid., 60.

3. *Dallas Morning News*, 11 November 1914.

4. Ibid., 14 November 1914.

5. Ibid., 18 February 1916; *San Antonio Express*, 11 January 1914; *Fort Worth Star Telegram*, 15 February 1916; *Corpus Christi Caller*, 6 January 1915.

6. *Corpus Christi Caller*, 14 January 1920.

7. *Dallas Morning News*, 18 February 1916.

8. *Dallas Times Herald*, 11 October 1917.

9. "Minutes of the University Interscholastic League Executive Board, 13 March 1917," Papers of the Texas University Interscholastic League, University of Texas, Austin.

10. League schedules, records, and games of both the major loop and recreational (commercial) loop leagues were reported in *Dallas Morning News* and *Fort Worth Star Telegram* from 1918 through 1933.

11. During WWI, newspapers reduced their descriptive coverage of regular league games to reporting only game statistics, except for major contests. During the war, teams curtailed travel to out-of-state invitational tournaments, but inner city and inner league contests continued.

12. James E. Sullivan, "Should Men Manage or Coach Girls in Athletics?" *Spalding's Official Basketball Guide for Women* (1910–1911), 36–39.

13. *Dallas Morning News*, 13 June 1920.

14. "Minutes of the University Interscholastic League Executive Board, 3 April 1920," Papers at University of Texas.

15. Kathleen Peace, interview, 4 May 1985.

16. Claudine Petty, interview, 2 March 1985. Other women reported playing basketball on dirt courts in schoolyards, using three division courts for high school games, and even playing against boys teams for practice.

17. Kevin Sherrington, "Bootlegging and Basketball," *Dallas Morning News* Supplement, 8 July 1990.

18. R. H. Garrett to Claudine Perry, 7 July 1930, Petty memorabilia.

19. Rubye Mansfield Terrell, interview, 18 March 1985; "Ruby Terrell is still an All-American Lady," *Athens Daily Review*, 25 February 1985.

20. Agnes Iori Robertson, interview, 22 April 1985; Terrell, interview, 18 March 1985.

21. *Dallas Morning News, Dallas Times Herald*, and *Fort Worth Star Telegram*, 1920–1933.

22. Daniel Chase, "Suggestions for Safeguarding Girls Who Participate in High School Athletics," *Official Basketball Guide for Women* (1925–26) (New York: American Sports Publishing Company, 1925), 68.

23. Sullivan, "Should men manage or coach girls in athletics?" 36–39.

24. A description of Anna Hiss's contention that school-vs.-school basketball competition eliminated too many girls from the sport experience was detailed by Mary Stuart in Brad Bucholz, "Basketball, White Gloves and Espionage," *Dallas Morning News*, 31 August 1990.

25. Lalia Warren, interview, 29 April 1985.

26. Press coverage of women's basketball was extensive in North Texas newspapers, often dominating the sport section January through March each year from 1927 through 1933.

27. Peace, interview, 4 May 1985.

28. *Wichita* (Kansas) *Beacon*, 28 March 1927.

29. Warren, interview, 29 April 1985; "Lalia Recalls Her Days with Babe," *Pay Sand* 7 (August 1982): 14–16.

30. Oilers is the team name used throughout this paper to avoid confusion. This team changed names to coincide with sponsoring group changes: 1925–1928 T & C; 1928–1929 Aces; and 1929–1931 Sun Oilers.

31. Memorandums in Sunoco Oil Employee Recreation File, 1930–1935, Dallas City Library.

32. *Dallas Morning News*, 3 January 1928.

33. Ibid., 11 January 1928.

34. Ibid., 7 January 1929.

35. *Wichita Beacon*, 30 March 1929; *Dallas Morning News*, 31 March 1929.

36. M. J. McCombs, memorabilia, Lamar University; William O. Johnson and Nancy P. Williamson, *Whatta-Gal* (Boston: Little, Brown and Company, 1975), 74–79.

37. Golden Cyclone Basketball and Track File, Texas Employers' Insurance Association Archives, Dallas.

38. McCombs memorabilia, Lamar University.

39. Warren, interview, 29 April 1985.

40. Petty, interview, 2 March 1985.

41. Mildred Didrikson Zaharias Papers, Babe Didrikson Memorial Library, Lamar, Texas.

42. Peace, interview, 4 May 1985.

43. Ann Caldwell to Roxanne Albertson, 16 February 1981.

44. "The Employers' Casualty Company Golden Cyclones" Circular, circa 1932; Warren, interview, 29 April 1985.

45. Dorothy S. Tapley, "Thirty Years of Girls' Basketball Rules," *Official Basketball Guide for Women and Girls* (1936–37) (New York: American Sports Publishing Company, 1936), 49–53.

46. Petty, interview, 2 March 1985.

47. Peace, interview, 4 May 1985.

48. *Dallas Morning News*, 1 February 1928; *Dallas Dispatch*, 30 December 1930.

49. AAU Women's Basketball Committee, "Rules Governing Tournaments," Circular (1931); *Shreveport Times*, 6 June 1930.

50. *Dallas Dispatch*, 27 March 1931.

51. Petty, Peace, Terrell, Warren, and Robertson, interviews, March–May 1985.

52. Warren, interview, 29 April 1985.

53. Terrell, interview, 18 March 1985.

54. Warren, interview, 29 April 1985.

55. Golden Cyclone Basketball and Track File, Texas Employers' Insurance Association Archives, Dallas, Texas.

56. Peace, interview, 4 May 1985.

57. McCombs memorabilia, Lamar University; Zaharias Papers, Babe Didrikson Memorial Library, Lamar, Texas.

58. *Wichita Beacon*, 26 March 1932; *Dallas Morning News*, 27 March 1932.

10

The Early Years of Basketball in Kentucky

Peggy Stanaland

No other game captured the interest of girls or roused the enthusiasm of spectators as did the game of basketball during the first decades of the twentieth century. Moreover, no other game caused faculty and athletic committees to hold so many special sessions and dispense so many regulations as did the game of girls basketball during the same time period. There is probably no logical or scientific explanation for the popularity of basketball for distaff Kentuckians from its early years on through ensuing decades. But no sport has ever caused the aligning of opposing camps for five or six decades like the game of basketball for girls and women.

At the turn of the century, women had never manifested any playing interest in football—it was, indeed, too rough and predicated on physical contact, and therefore, not appropriate; baseball was too manly and oh so firmly entrenched in professionalism; and softball had not been invented yet. So when basketball came on the scene in 1892, it seemed tame enough and was not fraught with physical contact. It was no wonder the women were intrigued. One Kentucky school administrator noted that in an attempt to start basketball in his school in 1910, boys were not particularly interested. The girls, however, took to basketball like a thoroughbred at the starting gate.[1] The modification of rules by Berenson and others to make the game safe and suitable for girls was an even greater attraction.

Kentucky girls, however, found the game quite suitable as invented and proceeded to play (basically) by boys rules for well over two decades. Without question, basketball was a visible and effective part of athletics and physical culture for Kentucky women and girls during the first decades of the twentieth century.

Dominant Themes

In researching old records, colleges and academy catalogs and year-books, newspapers, and photographs, three recurring themes were observed throughout the two decades. The first of these themes concerned the social barriers and Victorian attitude that placed restrictions on the extent of women's and girls' participation. This condition included such notions as constraints in clothing, limitations on spectators, and concern for stamina or physical conditions of female players. In the early years, women were limited, either by choice or circumstance, to only a few games per year. The records revealed that in some years only one or two games were played. Seldom were there over five or six games in a season.

The second theme was related to the first. It dealt with a philosophical ambivalence on the part of school officials, women directors, and leaders, not just in Kentucky but in other parts of the country as well. Early in the century, Lucille Eaton Hill, Elizabeth Burchenal, and Florence Offutt (of Kentucky) began to make statements about the harmful effects of intense competition. Even the eminent Luther Halsey Gulick wrote in 1906 that athletics for women should be confined to intramural-type sports. He further stated that strenuous training of teams tends to be injurious to both body and mind.[2] The diatribes of these leaders seemed always directed at basketball, not at other sports.

Their criticisms, however, did not stem the tide of competitive basketball among schools and colleges in Kentucky during the first two decades of the century. Colleges and high schools continued to play each other in basketball. This pattern existed in Kentucky on in to the decade of the twenties despite an increase in criticism on the part of women leaders and administrators.

The third theme so visible in the literature on competitive basketball for girls and women in the state was that curriculum designers and teachers in the earliest years of the twentieth century tended to favor basketball as an appropriate activity for classes and even for intramural-type competition. Colleges and academies consistently mentioned basketball as an activity for physical culture classes. For example, under the leadership of Florence Offutt, the 1901 *Catalogue of the State College of Kentucky* (now the University of Kentucky) made the following statement about basketball for girls: "Social games like basketball have a definite purpose in Physical Education. Players require quickness of thought, judgment and self-control under excitement. They learn to sacrifice self for the sake of the team as a whole. Girls who have had one year's training in the gymnasium or have played the game before are permitted to practice for a place on the team."[3]

The December 1903 issue of the *Hamiltonian*, a quarterly magazine of Hamilton College in Lexington, referred to the increased enrollment for basketball that year.[4] The 1914 catalog of Kentucky College for Women (now Centre College at Danville) first mentioned "sports" as a part of the physical education program. It is conceivable that basketball was included, for the school had been enjoying competitive basketball for its women students since 1904.[5] The *Eastern Kentucky Review*, Kentucky State Normal School's catalog, described a five term physical education requirement in 1911 that included Swedish gymnastics and activities that were seasonal. Basketball was one of these activities.[6] The 1908 Campbell-Hagerman College Bulletin stated that "Basketball is one of the regular gymnastic exercises, and is found to be both attractive and healthful."[7]

Basketball as an activity never fell out of favor in the state of Kentucky. Herein lies a paradox. Its critics always referenced intense intercollegiate or interschool competition, yet always cited basketball as an appropriate activity for women's physical culture or physical education classes.

Role of Schools

The coming of competitive basketball to Kentucky women was by and large in the hands of the school systems. There was little evidence that the sport was available to girls and women through the YWCA (or YMCA) or any other agency in the early part of the twentieth century. The only agencies or institutions that girls/women had access to in Kentucky in the 1800s and early 1900s were the schools.

At the turn of the century, for example, there were at least four thriving schools in Lexington tending to the educational needs of young women—State College of Kentucky (now the University of Kentucky), Kentucky University (now Transylvania University), Campbell-Hagerman College, and Hamilton College. The latter two were rival "finishing schools" for young ladies, and both were eventually absorbed by Transylvania University. Nonetheless, all four schools had popular basketball teams during the first decade of the century. There was not a preponderance of evidence indicating that basketball was played in Kentucky prior to 1900 either by men or women in private schools or public institutions. College and academy catalogs and bulletins cited exercise programs, Swedish gymnastics, and men's sports of football, baseball, and track but had nothing to say about basketball. The Kentucky State University catalogs from 1897 to 1901 mentioned the above sports as clubs that were led and managed by the students themselves.[8] Caldwell College (for young ladies) in Danville had no records of sports being played in the nineteenth century.[9]

The First Records

The first intercollegiate basketball game for men in the state of Kentucky is reputed to have been in 1901 between Centre College in Danville and Transylvania University in Lexington.[10] The first reported intercollegiate basketball game for women in the state was between the University of Kentucky and Transylvania University, both in Lexington, on February 21, 1903. According to a Lexington newspaper, the game held on that date was "the first intercollegiate game between girls' basketball teams that Lexington has seen." There were 500 enthusiastic spectators crowded into the gymnasium to see the action. They "kept the air ringing with their songs and yells." The paper went on to say that the enthusiasm was not unlike the spirited atmosphere of the Thanksgiving football game between these same two schools. The gridiron heroes were all but "forgotten at the sight of the skill of the basketball heroines."[11]

The Kentucky State College (now University of Kentucky) women's basketball team was the 1903 champion, in an era when many Kentucky schools limited spectators to women only. (All photographs in this chapter courtesy of Eastern Kentucky University)

Actually, the first intercollegiate basketball game for women in Kentucky likely occurred earlier. *Echos*, the student yearbook at the University of Kentucky, paid tribute to the 1904 team and implied in the process that basketball had its inception in 1902. "Successful from the start—two years ago—basketball as played by girls caught not only the student, but the public favor as well, and every game played drew enthusiastic houses which packed the standing room to the doors—an appreciative crowd of fellows—mad, riotously mad, over contests abounding in snappy spectacular plays."[12]

Whether the year was 1902 or 1903 is really a moot point. Competitive basketball for women had indeed arrived in Kentucky, only a few years after its invention and only a year or so after the men's first intercollegiate contest.

The Game Played On

A few years later, a number of schools had terse statements in their catalogs saying that only women spectators could watch the games. This presidential decree in at least two institutions indicated that only under "certain circumstances" were men permitted to watch. The Hamilton College yearbook of 1905 reinforced this idea in describing a game with Kentucky University:

> About two hundred students and friends witnessed the game and much college spirit abounded. It was not a public game and only ladies were admitted with the exception of the officials, a surgeon, and a few members of the K.U. faculty. The Hamilton College faculty and students were all out in full force.[13]

Thus, the wildly cheering crowd described in the 1903 newspaper account and the 1905 Hamilton College yearbook may well have precipitated the presidential decrees in the first place and a more stringent enforcement of the spectator presence through the years.

The January 1915 issue of the *EKSN Student*, Eastern Kentucky State Normal College, presented continuing evidence of the spectator limitation factor:

> The Athletic Editor sincerely regrets that he cannot write an account of what the girls are doing; but since he is a man, since men are not admitted to the gym while the girls are practicing, and since peeping through the key hole would be impolite, it seems inevitable that the public remain ignorant on that point.[14]

Nevertheless, as was the case in decades to follow, women seemed to quietly have their sport contests, with or without spectators, and with or without a lot of publicity and hoopla.

From 1900 to 1920 there is much evidence that basketball for women and girls in the school setting was a popular and attractive activity in Kentucky. Team pictures abound in bulletins and yearbooks. Team records and evidence of travel to other schools were unearthed and accounts of games and coaching personnel were retrieved.

Not much has been said about competitive basketball at the public high school level. Actually, the state of Kentucky made no provision for public high schools until 1908.[15] However, in the first two decades of the twentieth century, it was not uncommon for college teams to play against high school teams. In 1910, for example, the University of Kentucky played Paris, Somerset, and Maysville, all high schools.[16] In 1911, Eastern Kentucky State Normal College played Caldwell High and Model High.[17] In 1916, Kentucky College for Women at Danville played a nine game schedule, and three of the opponents played were high school teams.[18] These examples demonstrate that basketball competition between colleges and high schools did exist. In general, the scores recorded for these contests indicated that the level of play was not out of proportion. Sometimes the college teams won; sometimes the high school teams won.

When Richard A. Edwards went to Bedford, Kentucky in 1910 to organize a high school, he also introduced basketball. The boys in that area were not particularly interested in the game, but the girls eagerly responded. Since the game of croquet was about the only outdoor game

In 1917 the Kentucky College for Women played the University of Louisville. Short bloomers were appropriate wear for both officials and players.

The State University of Kentucky women's basketball team in 1916 wore red scarves to hold their hair in place since short hair was not yet in vogue.

the girls had played, they took up basketball with enthusiasm. Their uniforms were blue serge bloomers, white middy blouses, black cotton stockings, tennis shoes, and red bandanna handkerchiefs around their heads. Short hair was unheard of for girls or ladies at that time, so the bandanna held their hair in place. During the next three or four years, the Bedford girls' team played basketball games with neighboring high schools of LaGrange, Eminence, Pleasureville, New Castle, and Carrollton.[19]

It is not known whether basketball for girls was already in those Kentucky towns or whether Edwards was instrumental in initiating the game in those places. His manuscript, however, offered more evidence for the existence of high school basketball in the state during the first decade of the century.

Criticized but not ostracized, exercised but not publicized, basketball for girls and women in Kentucky was a viable sport during the 1900 to 1920 period. A Hamilton College student wrote on the occasion of a 1910 basketball game between her school and Kentucky State College: "Of all sad words of tongue or pen, the saddest are these—fifty to ten."[20] Their scores may have been a bit comical—50–10, or 9–5, or 17–8; their uniforms of dark serge and black stockings may have been cumbersome; their spectators may have been few in number; and their well-meaning protagonists may have shortened their season, but women's basketball teams did exist and were alive and well in Kentucky during the first two decades of the twentieth century. The popularity of the game could not be quashed. As Kentucky basketball vaulted into the roaring twenties, it took with it a two-decade legacy of successful competition, even if the scores were sometimes 50–10.

The Roaring Twenties

The decade of the twenties brought to light girls basketball teams from every hill, creek, crossroad, and fork that could claim a high school. This decade represented a zenith in basketball for Kentucky females, particularly at the high school level. Small schools in isolated hollows all over the state bragged on their girls' teams. Yearbooks, local papers, and local histories attested to the boast.

The Kentucky High School Athletic Association (KHSAA) was organized in 1917 and staged the first State Boys Basketball Tournament the following year. True to form, a girls tournament followed several years later. In 1921, KHSAA sponsored the first girls basketball state championship. As early as 1922, there were some 51 girls teams participating in district tournaments. From its very beginning, the Kentucky High School Athletic Association had included girls in its policies and plans.[21]

Ashland, Hazard, and Woodburn high schools dominated play in the state as well as in the state tournament during the twenties. Tiny Woodburn High School with a total student population of 66 finally won the state tournament in 1930; it had been runner-up to Ashland in 1929 and went to the state tournament three years in a row.[22] Despite favorable support of girls teams in the small towns and some administrators' obvious pride in their teams' accomplishments, the KHSAA saw fit to abandon the girls state tournament in 1932. The KHSAA Board seemingly bowed to the prevailing philosophy among women educators of the early 1930s that intramural type programs rather than varsity athletics would better serve the girl participants.

At the college level, there is evidence that intercollegiate basketball was also in full swing during the twenties. The University of Kentucky women's basketball team (called the Kittennettes) in those days played such schools as Western Normal, Peabody, Kentucky Wesleyan, Chattanooga, and Georgetown (Kentucky). Their 1921 coach was Sarah Blanding, who went on to become president of Vassar College. In 1923 the University of Kentucky girls team was coached by the enigmatic A. B. ("Happy") Chandler who later became governor of the state and then baseball commissioner.

In 1926, a note in the college yearbook said the University of Kentucky had prohibited girls basketball.[23] There were no more pictures of the girls intercollegiate team after that year.

In another area of the state, Eastern Kentucky State Normal School depicted ten years of girls basketball teams, 1920–1929, in its yearbooks.[24] Through the decade they played other Kentucky schools such as Georgetown, Western State Normal School, Cumberland College, Kentucky Wesleyan, Transylvania and Union College, University of

The first girls basketball state championship in Kentucky was held in 1921 and as early as 1922 more than 50 girls teams participated in district tournaments. The 1924 team pictured above followed popular custom and labeled its ball.

Louisville, and the Paris YWCA. The women's varsity basketball team at Eastern State Normal School gave way to the intramural concept in 1930. Like the flapper, collegiate basketball teams seemed to fade from the public eye with the coming of a new decade.

The Conservative Thirties

School sports and the opportunities to play on highly skilled competitive teams, particularly basketball, were curtailed for the distaff population in Kentucky during the decade of the 1930s. Changes in competitive sports chances for girls and women were not so much products of the depressed economic times as they were products of changing philosophic postures on the part of strategic school leaders in the state. If the twenties represented a zenith in basketball competition at college and high school levels, then the thirties represented its nadir.

Antagonism toward highly competitive sport for girls had been fomenting for several years. In 1923 this concern was clearly voiced in the creation of a women's division of the National Amateur Athletic Federation. The platform accepted at the 1923 meeting of leading women physical educators from all over the country represented a rejection of intense, competitive varsity-type experiences for the highly skilled in favor of participation experiences for many. The platform was intended to protect women athletes from such constraints as commercialization, spectator exploitation, overt gaudy awards, publicity, gate receipts, and dominating male leadership. Its statements left few stones unturned in promoting a safe playing environment, conservative costumes, and good health for the girls who played.[25] The philosophic posture of this manifesto served as a model for leaders in college programs for decades to come.

After 1929, there were no pictures of women's varsity teams (namely basketball) in college yearbooks. The decade of the 1930s pictured women's intramural teams (mostly basketball). Without exception, college yearbook staffs placed these pictures in their "athletics" section, just after men's intercollegiate football, basketball, and baseball teams. At the University of Kentucky, Centre College, and Berea College, for example, these intramural activities were directed by an elected council of women students known as the Women's Athletic Association (WAA) or the Women's Recreation Association (WRA). These councils assumed the leadership responsibility in organizing and directing various sports programs for women students.

The councils were under the faculty supervision of a woman in the physical education department. During the thirties, these faculty advisors in Kentucky represented one of the more stable components of college programs. Several held their posts (or related positions in the physical education departments) the entire decade. They directed, via the WAA/WRA councils, what was perceived to be right in school sports for Kentucky women. These women leaders were the philosophic core of school sports programs for women in the 1930s.

They were officers and active members of the state health and physical education association. Their presence was known at meetings of this organization throughout the state. Many of them attended national meetings and reported to the state the information they gleaned and the trends they perceived. They were influential in bringing people like Ann F. Hodgkins of the Women's Division of the National Amateur Athletic Federation to the state of Kentucky to speak on the beliefs and accomplishments of that organization.[26]

The influence of these women was far-reaching to fellow professionals (men and women) and to high school teachers and coaches throughout the entire state. Their support of the concept of participation of many instead of intense training of a few was unwavering.

The road to diminishing or deemphasizing interschool and intercollegiate competition for girls and women was quite clear in Kentucky in the early thirties. Rebecca Averill, University of Kentucky faculty and state chairman of the Women's Division of the National Amateur Athletic Federation, and Jessie Keep, physical education faculty at Centre College and a member of the state basketball committee, reported on a study they conducted on girls' interscholastic basketball in Kentucky. They stated that "the fever of interscholastic basketball for girls has reached an alarming degree and has raged in its worst form, that is: girls' teams coached by men, girls' games using boys' rules and girls participating in regional, sectional, and state tournaments." They further averred that the consensus of opinion of authorities on the subject supported these concerns. Averill and Keep gave a preliminary report of their study at the 1931 meeting of the Kentucky Health and Physical Education Association and published their findings in the *Kentucky School Journal* in 1932.[27]

In May 1932, Julie Guthrie reported on her study of girls basketball in Kentucky high schools. Her survey of some 279 schools revealed that a majority of the respondents believed a girl's health could be harmed by playing boys rules. Her study also tended to discredit the holding of tournaments for the enjoyment of fans. Guthrie's own response to that was, "surely the health of the girls concerned is of more value than the amusement of a crowd."[28] Earlier in the decade, Charles J. Turck, president of Centre College, wrote a letter to the college presidents in the state of Kentucky, pleading for support in refusing to sanction basketball tournaments for girls playing under boys' rules. Eliminating girls' tournaments altogether appeared to be his ultimate goal.[29]

An ironic twist to the negative position held by women in charge of physical education and some administrators in the early thirties was the abrupt decision of the Kentucky High School Athletic Association (KHSAA) in 1932 to abolish the state basketball tournament for girls.[30] This decision, by a vote of 70 to 45 at the annual banquet meeting of KHSAA, was surprising in that for the last 12 years (1920–1932) this organization had promoted the popular district, regional, and state competitive basketball tournaments for girls. During this time the KHSAA had paid little heed to the stand of college presidents and women physical educators throughout the state. A further ironic twist was in KHSAA's alleged reason for abolishing the girls tournament. The reason was simply that men coaches did not want to coach the girls teams any longer. Over 80 percent of the girls teams in the state were coached by men who also coached the boys teams.[31] So the vote against girls basketball appeared to be favoring convenience and a work-load reduction rather than making a statement of philosophy.

Although modest amounts of varsity basketball competition remained in the state in the thirties, gone was the emphasis on collegiate teams; gone was the excitement of district and regional championships; gone was the state tournament for girls; and gone was the leadership and administrative support for any highly competitive interschool or intercollegiate sports programs for girls and women in Kentucky. The movement away from intense competition toward voluminous participation for all displayed a philosophic posture that influenced decision makers in sports for several ensuing decades.

An Epilogue

On a detached and sobering note, interviews made in the 1980s with old-timers who played competitive basketball in the twenties and early thirties revealed that no players remembered basketball as too strenuous, or unladylike, or ruinous to their health. They all remembered their basketball playing experiences as fun, exciting, and exhilarating. They were glad they had played and were proud to have been a part of it all. They dispelled the notions fostered on them by women leaders and administrators that basketball competition was bad for young women, that it ought not be so intense, and that it could harm them physically and emotionally for years to come. Yet for 43 years, support for girls' competitive basketball via state, regional, and district tournaments by the Kentucky High School Athletic Association lay dormant. Colleges and universities in the state were little different. It was well into the 1970s before their lip-service support changed to scholarships and visible financial backing.

Notes

1. Richard A. Edwards, *Looking Back*, original manuscript, Richmond, Ky., 1972, Eastern Kentucky University Archives, 84.

2. Luther H. Gulick, "Athletics from the Biologic Point of View: Athletics Do Not Test Womanliness," *American Physical Education Review* 11 (September 1906): 157–160.

3. *Catalogue of the State College of Kentucky 1901*, Lexington, Ky., 87–88.

4. *The Hamiltonian*, December 1903, Hamilton College, Lexington, Ky.

5. *Catalog of Kentucky College for Women, 1914*, Kentucky College for Women, Danville, Ky.

6. *Eastern Kentucky Review*, 1911, Kentucky State Normal School, Richmond, Ky., 15.

7. *Campbell-Hagerman College Bulletin, 1908*, Campbell-Hagerman College, Lexington, Ky.

8. *Kentucky State University Bulletin, 1897–1901*, Kentucky State University, Lexington, Ky.

9. Kitty R. Baird, *Women in Physical Education and Sports at Centre College, 1854–1978* (unpublished specialist in education thesis, Eastern Kentucky University, Richmond, Ky., 1978), 26.

10. Edwards, *Looking Back*, 84.

11. *The Morning Herald*, Lexington, Ky. (22 February 1903): 7.

12. *Echos*, Student Yearbook, Kentucky State College, 1904, Lexington, Ky., 93.

13. *The Hamiltonian*, March 1905, Hamilton College, Lexington, Ky., 101.

14. *EKSN Student, 1915*, Eastern Kentucky State Normal College, Richmond Ky., 18.

15. Barksdale Hamlett, *History of Education in Kentucky*. Bulletin of Kentucky Department of Education, vol. 7, no. 14, 1914, Kentucky Department of Education, Frankfort, Ky.

16. *The Kentuckian, 1910*, Student Yearbook, Kentucky State College, Lexington, Ky., 253.

17. *EKSN Student, 1911*, vol. 4, Eastern Kentucky State Normal College, Richmond, Ky., 11.

18. Baird, *Women in Physical Education and Sports*, 31–32.

19. Edwards, *Looking Back*, 84–85.

20. Ellen Moore, "Hagerman Notes," *Idea* (17 February 1910): 7 (Syndicate of the State University of Kentucky, Lexington, Ky.).

21. Kentucky High School Athletic Association Records, Eastern Kentucky University Archives.

22. L. A. Beck, "Woodburn: A New Champion," *Kentucky Progress Magazine* (August 1931)3: 45.

23. *The Kentuckian 1926*, Yearbook, University of Kentucky, Lexington, Ky., 113.

24. *The Milestone*, 1920–1929, Eastern Kentucky State College, Richmond, Ky.

25. Ellen Gerber, Jan Felshin, Pearl Berlin, and Waneen Wyrick, *The American Woman in Sport* (Reading, Mass.: Addison-Wesley Publishing Company, 1974), 81–82.

26. Minnie M. Macaulay, *Kentucky Association for Health, Physical Education and Recreation Progress, 1909–1973*, mimeographed, 15–48.

27. Rebecca Averill and Jessie Keep, "Interscholastic Basketball for Girls in Kentucky," *Kentucky School Journal* 10 (May, 1932): 9–10.

28. Julie Guthrie, "Girls Basketball in Kentucky High Schools," *Kentucky School Journal* (October 1932): 35–37.

29. Charles Turck, Letter to Presidents, Kentucky Colleges, Berea College Archives, Berea, Ky.

30. Minutes Series, Box 105, Kentucky High School Athletic Association Records, Eastern Kentucky University Archives, Richmond, Ky.

31. Kentucky High School Athletic Association Records, Eastern Kentucky University Archives, Richmond, Ky.

The Iowa Agricultural
College (now Iowa State
University), Ames, 1896 girls
basketball team.

11

Iowa, the Longtime "Hot Bed" of Girls Basketball

Janice A. Beran

Women in Eastern colleges were the first to play basketball while the first intercollegiate competition occurred in California. It was in the midlands of the country, however, where basketball reached its zenith. On March 5, 1893, less than a year after women first played, women in Chicago played a demonstration game.[1] That same year Max Exner, James Naismith's Springfield College roommate, introduced the new game to Carleton College coeds in Minnesota.[2] A Sargent College graduate taught it to Denver, Colorado school girls. Basketball quickly became popular in other universities throughout the midwest. Once high school girls saw or heard about basketball they scrambled to play. The sport caught on especially in Iowa, which came to be called "a hot bed of basketball."

From its genesis until the present day, little girls, high school students, college coeds, and even mothers play basketball in Iowa. Whether played by bloomer clad students on dusty outdoor courts or in cracker box size gyms, as in the early 1900s, or in today's modern gyms under the glare of television lights, girls basketball in Iowa is important. Regarded as remarkable because of broad participation, community support, and spectacularity, basketball remains a major sport for Iowa women and girls.

Basketball has enabled tens of thousands of Iowa girls to have a highly competitive athletic experience, while high school females in most states in the 1930s–1960s missed such experiences. High school girls teams in Iowa have many fans and the girls state tournament draws more spectators than does the boys tournament. The television contract for the girls tourney is the most lucrative of any high school sport, girls or boys, in the United States. Tug Wilson, president of the United States Olympic Committee, remarked in 1963, "Ten years ago, those directing women's physical education would not vote for women's athletics, but that has changed. We give thanks to the state of Iowa for changing all that." He went on to predict that soon each state would permit competitive athletics for girls and that "the Olympic Committee literally is reaching out to shake the hand of Iowa."[3]

First Teams, First Games, First Tournaments

The YMCA at Iowa State College in Ames first introduced basketball to Iowans in 1893.[4] The first male players learned the game when they attended the YMCA Camp at Lake Geneva, Wisconsin. The Iowa State College women soon organized teams with such picturesque names as Ish-koo-dahs, Shengodohnees, Tadpoles, Pygmies, Kickapoos, and No Eyes. They played in the center of campus on a makeshift grass court with net baskets suspended from upright poles.[5] By the next year, students at Grinnell College played basketball and by 1900 the game had been introduced in several other Iowa communities.[6] Teachers trained at Springfield College, Boston Normal School of Gymnastics, and the New Haven School of Gymnastics started to include basketball in their curricula in some Iowa high schools and colleges. Other girls learned to play basketball by reading the rules or from sisters and brothers.

The number of players on a team ranged from five to nine. One team "coached" by a man who had never seen a game instructed his girls' team to line up in a football formation.[7] Often, the girls played boys rules but shortened the playing time. Some teams used the full court, others the two court game, and still others the three division court. As was the trend in most girls games in Iowa, they played before male spectators. In fact, they even played against teams of male students. At Highland Park College in Des Moines the girls' team played a faculty team. A faculty member of that team recalled later, "every time they wanted money for uniforms . . . they played us . . . and took the receipts. . . . I remember those girls had sharp fingernails."[8]

The first games were of short duration with ten-minute halves. A newspaper article publicizing a forthcoming game in Dubuque advised players that scratching and slugging would be prohibited.[9] Gyms or other playing sites, such as church basements, were as small as 24 by 48 feet and many had low ceilings. Home town teams had real advantages in those gyms. They knew just how to "bank" the ball against the walls for the most effective passing. They could shoot without having the ball hit the ceiling. Old-time players told of the hazards of playing in a gym with a pot belly stove in the center of the floor. An errant pass hitting the stove meant a spray of soot blanketing the players. One old-timer, Emma Wilmarth, reminisced that as a sixth grader playing in 1900 in Humboldt, Iowa, she and the other players kept their playing clothes in the school attic, played outdoors, and traveled in a kind of horse-drawn bus to small towns nearby for competition. She recalled playing the full court game at a pace that was leisurely compared to today's girls basketball.[10]

There were mixed reactions to the new game of basketball, but players from the early years recall having parental approval. The Dubuque papers noted that "female players catch the spirit of the game more easily than their masculine friends" and that after a few games the girls had as much stamina as the boys.[11] The players "were heartily applauded by the spectators for the cleverness with which the baskets were thrown."[12] A 1902 newspaper reported a high school game as being "one of the best contests ever seen in Marshalltown" and in Ames, "basketball girls are blooming these early spring days."[13]

The game rules, number of players, and the court division gradually became standardized. By 1910 the Iowa game reflected the rules established by the National Basketball Committee of the American Physical Education Association. It was played on a three section court with from five to nine players, but most frequently the teams consisted of two forwards, two guards, a jumping center, and a side center. Players were limited in their dribbling and could hold the ball just three seconds. They were not allowed to snatch the ball from an opponent. Although described by some as a slow game, girls basketball maintained a positive image as illustrated in the 1920 Davenport High School newspaper: "The players exhibited unusually brilliant playing and this denotes the versatility of the American girl. She is such an all around sport, good in athletics and good in her studies . . . we give our heartiest congratulations to the girls' basketball team."[14]

The standardization of the basketball rules along with its increasing popularity led to the first state 24-team tournament in 1920. For the first 14 years of the tournament the high school girls played three division court rules. Each time a team scored, the ball would be returned to the center circle for a center jump. Each jumping center would attempt to tip the ball to her teammates. A good jumper could control the game. A 1926 jumping center reminisced that "the coach told me to stay in the air and in the second half the ball didn't get past the center court. The other team scored only one point. The score of the game was 100–2."[15] Low scores could be attributed to the return of the ball to the center court and the fact that the two shooting forwards stopped and passed before shooting. An overhead shot counted one point while the two-handed underarm free throw, the chest shot, and any other shots scored two points.

A charge aimed at early girls high school interscholastic basketball was that it, in fact, was rough and tumble. In the early days it was rough and tumble with occasional hair pulling, tripping, and pushing. Often coaches had their girls play against boys to develop more aggressive play. However, as girls continued to play they became more skilled and stopped the illegal pushing, tripping, and ball grabbing.

A 1979 survey was conducted by the author among 72 living members of the Iowa Girls Basketball Hall of Fame, including several who played in the first decade of tournament play, 1920–1930.[16] The survey, with an 89 percent return, provided extensive information on basketball between the years 1915–30. It seems that several Hall of Famers had played before they were high school students. These former elite competitors played with brothers and older sisters even before the tournaments began. To gain a more representative view of basketball during the first half of the twentieth century, the author also interviewed 20 old-timers whose playing years spanned the years 1904–30, 12 coaches and officials who were active between the 1920s and 1940s, and students who did not play basketball.

The players from the 1920s acknowledged the game was slower, but made such comments as "we were tough," "we never took a pass standing still," and "we used certain signals for play."[17] Some of the players conditioned by running hurdles winter and summer. From the girls who tried out for their school teams, usually only ten were selected. The

In 1926, the first year of leadership by the Iowa Girls High School Athletic Union, 159 schools fielded girls team. (From *Palimpsest*, April 1968, published by the Iowa Historical Society)

players had to be not only skilled but also strong enough to play the entire game.

The first invitational Iowa Girls High School Basketball Tournament in 1920 was very successful. It continued from 1920 to 1925 under the auspices of the all-male Iowa High School Athletic Association (IHSAA). But in 1925, the Association decided at its annual meeting that athletic competition before crowds that paid admission was good for boys but not for girls in Iowa.[18] By that time, the growing popularity of boys basketball and their need to use the high school gyms was undoubtedly an important factor in ousting the girls basketball.

Citizens, educators, and students debated whether competitive basketball was harmful to girls' health and moral habits. The dissension voiced at the 1925 IHSAA meeting reflected the controversy that was raging among professional women physical educators. After debate the majority of the IHSAA members, representing 259 schools, agreed they would no longer sponsor basketball tourneys for females.

Due to the effort of four male high school superintendents and the support of the *Des Moines Register and Tribune* newspaper, basketball for girls in Iowa was not relegated to interclass competition as it was in the 1920s in many other states and in large cities. The initial four men were joined by twenty-one other superintendents who organized the Iowa Girls High School Athletic Union (IGHSAU). It was their purpose to provide sponsorship of county, sectional (district), and state tournament competition.[19]

In 1926, the first year of IGHSAU leadership, 159 schools fielded girls teams. Sixteen of those teams won their district championship and competed in state tournament play. The organizational pattern established in 1926 continues today, making it the longest lasting still functioning high school athletic association exclusively for female athletes.

In the 1920s and early 1930s approximately half of the coaches of girls basketball teams were women physical educators. The games were officiated by both women and men. If there was a difference in a call, the women's call would take precedence over the men's. However, in the 1930s and 1940s increasingly more male coaches and fewer women physical educators coached, and most officials were men.

The pattern of small school participation that began in the late 1920s continued into the 1930s and 1940s. During the 1940s, 70 percent of the teams came from schools with less than 100 students. Because there were few female students in the smaller schools, some players reported joining the team as early as seventh grade. In the 1950s, 70 percent of the girls in Iowa high schools played basketball—an amazing statistic![20]

In 1985 significant changes occurred when the Iowa Girls High School Athletic Union, after long deliberation, gave high schools the option of playing the full court five player basketball game or the traditional six player divided court style. The changeover to the five player game was not rapid and far from universal. In fact, five years later, 329 high schools still play the six player divided court game and 99 teams play the five player full court game.[21] The state tournament competition culminates in championships for both five player and six player teams.

Iowa Girls Basketball Tournaments

The girls basketball tournaments held each year are one of the stellar attractions in Des Moines, the capital of Iowa. Hotels are completely booked months in advance. Fans purchase tickets seven or eight months before the tournament begins. Radio and television contracts are signed months before the March competition. From the very first tournament in 1920 until the present day vast numbers of Iowans attend the tournaments.

While small schools were the principal proponents of girls basketball from 1926 until the 1960s, that did not mean that few Iowans followed the competition. In the 1940s, half of those years during wartime, regular season games attracted paid attendance of a million spectators. Added to this number were the 225,000 who attended the five day tournament. This total was twice the number of fans who watched the St. Louis Cardinals during the same period. On a 1945 national radio broadcast, sportscaster Red Barber informed his audience, "the towns that produce the teams are small, but the interest is great."[22]

In 1955 the combined town population of the "Sweet Sixteen" teams in the tournament was 13,611—that's just about the number to fill the Veterans Auditorium where the tourney is held. In fact, often, the attendance by loyal fans is inversely proportionate to town population and school size. Tiny Napier with a town population of 40 and a school population of 22 once appeared with 450 fans to support their team.[23]

Television coverage started in 1951. Nonetheless, 15,290 fans broke all sport attendance records when Goldfield defeated Holstein 53–51 in overtime.[24] In 1953, E. Wayne Cooley began his more than 35-year tenure as executive secretary of the Iowa Girls High School Athletic Union. Among the many changes he made was to pattern television coverage after that of the Houston Astros.[25] He instigated pregame and halftime shows featuring Iowa high school students with musical, dance, and athletic talents. Cooley's innovations are a major reason for the continuance of sell-out audiences at the state tournaments.

Cooley explained his action by noting that prior to 1957 "the only halftime entertainment was visiting the concession stands. It was dull. For years I'd been amazed at the amount of high school music talent in the state. It seemed a wonderful opportunity to put it to work."[26] In 1957 he invited a high school choir to sing before the title game. From then on, bands, choral groups, and drill groups had an increasingly larger part in the state tournament extravaganza.

Stage bands, choirs, and high school drill and dance groups vie for the chance to perform at the tourney in Veterans Auditorium. Performing groups along with a 17-minute Parade of Flags provide color and culture and help to ensure a capacity crowd. The final evening competition of the five day-night state girls tournament is featured in a four-hour televised program. Professionally directed, half-time pre- and postgame shows entertain both fans in the Veterans Auditorium and the television audience. Each of the 17 other high school girls sports champions are featured in the Parade of Champions, which is held between the consolation and championship games. The winning teams parade onto the floor under the spotlight and are introduced by teams—softball, track, swimming, volleyball, and so forth. It is a thrill for each champion team to be recognized in front of the large audience. It is also a thrill to the audience to see their winning hometown team being honored.

The jubilant Gladbrook High School team celebrates its 1959 win at the state championship, with a trophy and flowers representative of the fanfare that marked the annual event. Gladbrook won the state title in 1960 also.
(Photograph by Henry E. Bradshaw, West Des Moines, Iowa)

The entertainment continues with the induction of the latest four or five former players selected for the Iowa Girls Basketball Hall of Fame. Each woman's high school and post-high school basketball achievements are announced. Every year the Hall of Fame committee selects one or two friends of basketball who are also introduced during the ceremonies. Following the championship game, the winners receive their trophies and flowers. The traditional red jacket is presented to the winning coaches. Last, the all-tourney team is announced.[27]

The winning team customarily attends church together the morning after the championship game. This is followed by a triumphant school bus ride home where they are joined by a car caravan of jubilant fans. Elaborate ceremonies at the school welcome the players home. Special programs and newspaper and media coverage add to the excitement of the championship title.

In conclusion, the Iowa girls basketball tournament attracts more followers and more media attention and arouses more enthusiasm than the Iowa boys tourney. As one of the tournament cleanup crew noted, "The girls have a lot of pageantry, the boys just play basketball."[28] It is that winning combination of pageantry and basketball that draws crowds to the state girls tournament. It brings in revenue that enables the Iowa Girls High School Athletic Union to be completely self-supporting.

Significance of Girls Basketball in Iowa

It is not possible to capture the aura, the ambiance, and the significance of this female sport in a few paragraphs. Some facts attest to its importance: Every school in Iowa competes in girls basketball. More than a million females have played interscholastic basketball since 1900.[29] Girls basketball draws roughly 3 percent of the state's population to the games. This is more fans in one season than intercollegiate male and female athletics attract. The girls basketball tournament has brought in enough revenue over the past 20 years to support 17 other interscholastic sports for high school girls. The games are important enough to bring many state and local politicians to the arenas. The state championship tournament "bumps" Saturday night television. All of these factors combine to verify the athletic, socio-economic-political, and entertainment value of girls basketball over the years.

In 1925, John Agans, one of the four superintendents who founded the IGHSAU, told his co-administrators: "Gentlemen, if you attempt to do away with girls basketball in Iowa you'll be standing in the center of the track when the train runs over you."[30] That statement made almost

A Kamrar High School forward goes airborne for a jump shot in a 1948 state tournament game in Des Moines, Iowa.

70 years ago is as true today as it was then. A significant factor in the continued success of six player basketball is that it has been an acceptable vehicle for athleticism for young women, in part because it is distinct from boys basketball.

Iowa players and fans are generally undaunted by criticism of the six player game. In the 1940s and 1950s when physical educators were still not in favor of interscholastic ball, it was quite common to find "testimonials" by players, former players, school administrators, and even parents praising the value of basketball for themselves, students, or children. The testimonials were not so much to defend basketball competition as to explain its value to individuals.

In 1951 a group of 11 former high school players who were students at Iowa State Teachers College defended vigorously their playing days. Mona Van Steenbergen and Janet Payne, former high school stars, led the players in listing advantages and disadvantages of playing basketball. They had a list of 10 positive influences from competing in basketball while they could identify only four possible disadvantages. The former players agreed that through basketball they developed social poise, sportsmanship, and friendship and that the positive things more than offset the possibility of overemphasis on winning and the chance of injury.[31]

Findings from the survey conducted by this author supported the contention that basketball play was acceptable and valued. All of the Hall of Fame former players credited basketball with developing their fitness, strength, and self-reliance and a larger majority felt it developed self-confidence. Half of the respondents reported it increased their popularity with girls and their teachers; only 30 percent felt it increased their popularity with boys.

The female basketball players have through the years been highly respected. Families take pride in their basketball players. There are basketball family dynasties; often three and even four generations of women in one family have played. During the state tournament time grandmothers, sometimes great-grandmothers, mothers, aunts—all former players—cheer on the present family members. In 1956 a newspaper featured a mother who had been a basketball mother over a 20-year span—seven of her eight daughters had played but none of her boys.[32] Many coaches have coached their own daughters. With this long tradition of family involvement in basketball it is not surprising that there has been little discussion in basketball communities as to whether competitive athletics is appropriate; of course it is appropriate!

Considerable community support and prestige have been attached to the accomplishments of the hometown team. As one reporter expressed it: "They're just ordinary little towns that nobody knows about most of the year—then all of a sudden . . . these towns are on the minds and

State champions, Wellsburg, are welcomed home on a chilly day in March 1949, with almost the entire student body in the caravan of school buses and cars. Townspeople line the streets in tribute and then move to the school gym for an elaborate celebration, testimony to the significant role played by girls basketball in the state of Iowa.

lips of everyone in the state."[33] Small schools undistinguished in other ways garnered much attention in tournament play as area newspapers and the statewide media increasingly publicized girls basketball between 1950 and 1970.

Publicity has come principally through the *Des Moines Register*, the newspaper with the largest circulation in the state. This newspaper has been a principal reason for the popularity of girls basketball. Prior to, during, and following the state tourney it features stories about small towns playing teams from schools with a much larger enrollment and devotes many column inches to on and off court stories about the players, their academic performance, their hobbies, their superstitions, their future career choices, and even their team mascots.[34]

A *Des Moines Register*'s sports writer, Bert McGrane, actually managed the IGHSAU basketball tourney when it first sponsored competition in 1926. Jack North, sports editor for the *Register*'s sister evening paper, *Des Moines Tribune*, assisted in the tournament management. In the early years, he and another sports writer not only wrote about the tournaments they had created but officiated all games. While it was an accepted practice for sports writers to earn extra money this way, there was some question about "vested interest."[35] North, in later years, worked for the IGHSAU and was responsible for the selection of the all-tournament teams.

This somewhat informal cooperative arrangement between the girls athletic union and the newspaper existed until the 1950s. The affiliation then abruptly ended because the newspaper editor decided it was not wise to be so closely entwined with a news source. It was an amiable parting because by that time the IGHSAU preferred to handle the tournament themselves. The *Register* and *Tribune*, nonetheless, continued to give extensive coverage to girls basketball. Local newspapers also devoted much space to coverage of girls teams. In 1946 all the newspapers that comprised the Iowa Daily Press Association began to select a yearly all-state team.

Statewide radio coverage by WHO, the major Des Moines station, and WMT of Cedar Rapids gives identical coverage to the girls and boys state basketball tournaments, broadcasting all the games live. Of course, local stations also cover their favorite teams' play.

The first filming of the basketball tourney occurred in 1947. The films were often purchased and repeatedly viewed so coaches and players could study winning teams. With the advent of television coverage, more Iowans and residents in neighboring states were able to view the girls play.[36] So, from the time the *Des Moines Register* ran the tournament as a circulation builder until the present, with both print and electronic media, coverage has been extensive.

The media is just one of the businesses that gains from basketball. From the largest businesses in Des Moines to the small town merchant who pasted this announcement in his window:

CLOSED
AT 1:00 O'CLOCK
FOR BALL GAME
UNTIL COMPLETED

businesses both supported and profited from girls basketball. As Babe Bisignano, a Des Moines restauranteur, remarked, "The Girls' Tournament is second only to Christmas when it come to spending. Cooley (IGHSAU Executive Secretary) is another Santa Claus for Des Moines."[37]

High School Girls Competition in the Midwest

As was the case in Iowa's large city schools until the 1960s, basketball varsity competition was not held in many states. Women physical educators looked for substitute types of competition. They had interclass intramurals and "play days." For example, Illinois instituted telegraphic meets wherein the girls competed against "certain standards."

Iowa has its own Girls Basketball Hall of Fame and each year, during the state championship, former players are selected for induction. The 1967 designees, above, are heralded in a special ceremony and their basketball achievements announced. (*Palimpsest*, April 1968, Iowa Historical Society)

Other states that did hold state or regional basketball tournaments included Missouri, Maryland, Mississippi, Texas, Wyoming, North Dakota, Oklahoma, Arkansas, and Tennessee.[38] In the southeastern part of the country, Georgia (with 400 school teams), South Carolina, and Maryland all held interschool contests and tournaments into the 1940s.

Iowa's first interstate game occurred in 1923 when an Oklahoma team from Guthrie defeated the Iowa champs, Audubon, on two successive nights, 47–7 and 27–17.[39] Guthrie eventually claimed the mythical national championship after also defeating the state champions of New York and New Jersey in three games each. During the 1920s and 1930s the IGHSAU assisted Texas, Tennessee, Oklahoma, South Dakota, Arkansas, New Mexico, and Wyoming to develop their girls basketball programs.[40] The union corresponded with the basketball leadership in those states, sent rules information, and occasionally held clinics.

Texas initiated a statewide girls basketball program in 1938, a time when most states hesitated to have varsity competition. Ten years later there were 357 Texas high school girls basketball teams.[41] The Texas rules were similar enough to Iowa rules to permit interstate competition. Both states played the two division court and six player basketball.

Kamrar, the 1948 Iowa champions, defeated 36–33 the Texas champions, Mesquite.[42] In 1950, however, Texas evened the score. The Iowa champion team Slater, exhausted after the train ride to Dimmitt, Texas via Amarillo, lost to Dimmitt by the whopping difference of 47–20.[43]

Dimmitt, as three-time Texas champs, journeyed to Iowa to play the 1951 Iowa champions, Hansell. At a banquet for the two teams a fan remarked, "You're friends tonight and arch enemies tomorrow." "No," responded the Dimmitt star player, Lometa Odom, "We're friends all the time." The Dimmitt players were awed by the size of the crowd. One of them said in a courtside interview, "this is more people than we ever saw at a ball game in our lives."[44] That year Dimmitt won again but Hansell's score was more respectable (38–30).

Iowa and Texas were just two of the 30 states with high school girls interscholastic basketball competition in 1951. At least nine of those states had statewide tournaments. There was some rule variation between states, but the majority used the rules written for Iowa girls basketball.

Teams from other states were sometimes rewarded for their successful seasons. One such was a Macon, Missouri team who visited the Iowa tournament in 1951.[45] The trip was in celebration of their 20–4 season record. Community fans in Gardner, North Dakota rewarded their champion team for a perfect season's record of 32 wins with an all-expense trip to Minneapolis and St. Paul the same year.[46] The number of games played by these teams illustrates clearly that there were many teams competing in basketball in the early 1950s.

Oklahoma had, undoubtedly, one of the largest programs. In the mid-fifties the state had 650 active teams. Oklahoma teams played the same divided court, six player rules as did Iowa, except they did not limit the number of dribbles. Their state tournaments were held together with the boys and schools were grouped by size of enrollment into Class A and B. Bertha Frank Teague, of Oklahoma, was named the "winningest coach" with a record of 633 wins and 34 losses in her 20 years of coaching.[47] She was an early author of a basketball book for women and lectured at coaching clinics conducted by the IGHSAU. She was among the first three women inducted into the National (men's) Basketball Hall of Fame in Springfield, Massachusetts.

These brief highlights of girls basketball during the 1930–60 period demonstrate that basketball was widely played throughout the country. The specific illustrations contradict the historical literature in physical education, which indicates few secondary schools in the country had interscholastic girls basketball during the 1930s–60s. This extensive competition occurred at the same time that leading women physical educators spoke out strongly regarding the "dangers" of highly competitive sport for girls, especially basketball and track. There were, however, many younger physical educators who were beginning to criticize the anti-varsity, anti-Olympic stance of their leaders. These younger physical educators had experienced the positive aspects of girls' experiences in interschool athletics and wanted to provide such programs for their students.[48]

Iowa high school girls traveled to other states for high level competition. The Slater High School team, 1950 state champions, are officially welcomed to Waco, Texas, for an interstate game.

The Iowa Girls High School Athletics Union Board of Directors were totally aware of the arguments. The *Iowa Girls Basketball Yearbook* often included articles during the 1940s and 1950s extolling the values of basketball for high school girls. The Yearbook editors conducted a survey in 1955 among Iowa physicians, educators, ministers, parents, and players, and results showed respondents favored girls playing interscholastic basketball.[49] A notable physical educator and research professor, Charles H. McCloy of the University of Iowa, reported in a 1952 *Iowa Girls Basketball Yearbook* article that, based on his and others' scientific research, there was little physical or psychological evidence that a girl should not engage in relatively strenuous exercise of the nonbruising type. Although McCloy sidestepped endorsing competitive girls basketball, he said he had presented the facts and suggested that the reader could decide for or against basketball based on the scientific facts.[50] An osteopathic surgeon stated, however, that basketball play was beneficial, improving muscle tone, stamina, and posture and bringing out physical faults which could be corrected. His statements were based on studies of girl athletes by several noted osteopathic research specialists.[51] Floyd Taylor, a longtime follower of girls basketball in Iowa wrote in 1951 that basketball was not too hard on girls, pointing out that "80,000 girls had played basketball in the last twenty years without one sustaining serious injury."[52]

The scientific facts presented by McCloy and the laymen's conclusions drawn by Taylor led the college students (former players) at Iowa State Teachers College to decide in 1953 that girls basketball was not too strenuous or injurious. It would take the physical education world another two decades to actively support and join Iowans in their love affair with interschool basketball.

Iowa's Post High School Basketball

Basketball was such a vital part of high school life for girls in Iowa that it is no surprise they did not just stop playing once they graduated. Many players went to work at banks, businesses, and industries that sponsored teams. Others chose to go to school at one of several business or beauty schools that fielded teams. Many high school basketball players chose to attend Iowa Wesleyan College (the oldest college west of the Mississippi River) because it was the only liberal arts college to consistently recruit and field women's basketball in the post WWII years.

Most of the schools and businesses used basketball as a "recruiting" tool to entice high school players to study or go to work for them. Each *Iowa Girls Basketball Yearbook* published from 1943 to 1964 carried advertisements about these business and school teams. Samples include this 1948 ad: "Regardless of your career choice it is fun to play basketball at Iowa Wesleyan. It's a major sport on campus. Top competition— travel—the national tournament, an exciting schedule, and trips to Pittsburgh, Baltimore, North Carolina, Atlanta, Nashville, Kansas City, Oklahoma, Arkansas, Peoria, Oklahoma."[53] The American Institute of Commerce for Stenographers (AIC Stenos) in Davenport, Iowa enticed players starting in 1952: "The Stenos received a good educational tour traveling in 22 different states."[54] Bankers Life, a large insurance company, sponsored teams as early as the late 1920s. They invited players to work for them, where "basketball is just one of the pleasant activities that Bankers Life girls enjoy outside of working hours. They make friendships and find common interests that last a lifetime."[55] Meredith Publishing in 1948 told high school girls, "if sports and outside activities interest you, you'll enjoy working at Meredith, the members of our basketball team are still chalking up victories."[56]

Business and schools provided high school graduates career opportunities along with the pleasure of playing basketball. In turn, the company and school teams garnered recognition for the sponsors. The teams competed in city leagues, against teams from other parts of the state and from other states, and in AAU district, state, and national competition. The best teams played internationally.

Iowa Wesleyan Tigerettes

Iowa Wesleyan, in Mt. Pleasant, pioneered women's college ball in 1943.[57] The inception of Wesleyan's program came from voiced needs and demands from former players, their parents, and school superintendents. Girls wanted to continue to play after high school graduation. The school realized there was a need to train women to coach. They also saw the potential of women's basketball for recruiting students.

The 12-member Wesleyan Tigerette Team was strong even in its first year, 1943. They finished their season with a 13–14–1 record against five independent teams (two from Indiana), one business school team, eight high schools, and Parsons College of Fairfield, Iowa. In 1948 they played the Westinghouse Electric Company team in Philadelphia and teams in Baltimore, North Carolina, Nashville, Kansas City, Oklahoma, Illinois, Arkansas, and Omaha. In 1952 they placed fourth in the AAU tourney defeating the highly favored perennial powerhouse team, Wayland College. They spent Christmas vacations playing in such places as the Smokey Mountains and Georgia. There they were regular competitors in the "Battle of Atlanta" tournament, which surely must have included the highly regarded Atlanta Tomboys.[58]

Wesleyan's contribution to basketball was significant not just because of their high standard of play but for their services to girls and women's basketball. They held clinics and tournaments for players, coaches, and officials. They also worked for better cooperation between the IGHSAU and the AAU. Beginning in 1945 they were one of the first four-year colleges to compete in AAU national tournaments.[59] The Wesleyan teams continued in the 1960s and 1970s to field national calibre teams and placed third in the first National Invitational Collegiate Basketball Tournament in 1969.

Twenty-five Wesleyan players were All-Americans between 1952 and 1962.[60] During those years many Tigerettes were chosen for national teams. They played in World Tournaments, Pan-Am Games, and with touring teams in Chile, the Soviet Union, Sweden, and the United States. A highlight for the team, school, and community was Wesleyan being chosen to play the Russian national team in Mt. Pleasant in 1963. Although ranked third in the United States at the time, the Tigerettes were no match for the Russians, who won 83–38. The players believed the experience they gained compensated for the loss. It was a thrill for the small town of Mt. Pleasant to be the host of this international event centering on basketball. It also featured the Russian men's team playing a select team from the National Association for Intercollegiate Athletics.[61]

Tigerette Coach Olan G. Ruble, the first women's basketball coach inducted into the Helms National Hall of Fame (1965), twice coached American teams on European tours. He coached the 1971 Pan-American USA women's basketball team. For 25 years he was an active member of the United States Olympic Committee's Basketball Committee and had a major role in establishing women's basketball as an Olympic sport.[62]

Davenport AIC Stenos

The Davenport AIC Stenos organized in 1937 was another Iowa team that made a tremendous impact on basketball. In 1942 and 1943 they won the national women's basketball championship. By then they were experienced competitors, having won the national AAU consolation competition in 1938 and in 1940 placing second in the Iowa AAU tourney and reaching the AAU national quarterfinal.[63]

The Stenos played in Toronto, Canada before 15,000 people in 1942 during World War II. They helped the Red Cross raise $40,000 to be used to house homeless British children. The next year they were guests of the Mexican government as they played different teams in Mexico during their 21-day tour. Proceeds from the games were used to buy sewing machines for needy Mexicans. The Stenos traveled 7,000 miles in 1948 on an international goodwill tour to South America and Mexico.[64] An account of the trip in the United States *Congressional Record* noted the Stenos' contribution toward improved relationships with Mexico, El Salvador, Nicaragua, Puerto Rico, and Costa Rica. The Stenos related how impressed they were with the South Americans' eagerness to learn the fine points of basketball. Evidently, the Stenos' play and basketball clinics contributed to the improved caliber of play. Two Mexican teams eliminated the Iowa Wesleyan Tigerettes from the 1951 AAU championship. Politas of Mexico City defeated them 34–22 and Coahuila Tintorearias, also from Mexico City, crushed their championship hopes by a score of 38–34.[65]

American Institute of Business Team

The third significant school to be recognized in Iowa is the American Institute of Business (AIB). They organized a team in 1930 and in 1934 had a 22–0 record against the best Iowa high school teams. They also were the first Iowa team to play in the National AAU tournament.

Because AIB as well as other teams in the Des Moines YWCA league had been playing three court basketball they were "badly handicapped as the AAU tournament was played under two court rules." Bert McGrane of the *Des Moines Register*, then still manager of the IGHSAU tournament, accompanied the Stenos. After returning from the AAU tournament, McGrane suggested that two court basketball should be introduced in Iowa. So AIB invited Steve Beck, coach of the National AAU champion Tulsa Stenos, to conduct the first coaching clinic on two division court basketball. By 1936 Iowa high school and post high school teams played two court ball instead of the traditional three court game. The AIB pioneered the two dribble rule and introduced the present guarding rule allowing the guard to tie up the ball in the act of shooting. They were also the first Iowa team to play outside the United States when they played the "world champion" Edmonton Commercial Grads in Canada, in 1935, 1937, and 1939. After the War, they made trips to the east coast and all sections of the midwest.[66]

Other Iowa schools with basketball programs between 1928 and 1950 were the Des Moines Lutheran Hospital of Nursing, Pitzer Waterloo School of Beauty College, and Iowa Success School in Ottumwa. William Penn College fielded a team in 1928, the first college women's team in Iowa. That team continued until 1930. Again between the years 1948–52 and 1958–61 the college sponsored teams, and resuming basketball play again in 1973, they won the AIAW Division III championship in 1980.[67]

Post-high school players also played for Omaha, Nebraska Business School, the Commercial Extension School of Commerce. This All-Iowa team regularly competed in the midwest and national AAU tournaments. They played a 20 game season. They, too, competed against a touring Russian team in 1960.[68]

For the Iowa high school graduate who wanted to continue playing basketball there were still other opportunities. Those who did not go to one of the schools described above could join town teams, independent teams, and business-sponsored teams. Age, marriage, motherhood, and work did not prevent these women from playing. There were industrial leagues and YWCA leagues which included teams sponsored by churches, factories, labor management councils, towns, and businesses. The players had fun and the industries who paid the bill were happy because the girls "have a good clean time and the entire company personnel feel close to the contest."[69] The level of competition and skill varied but teams such as the Marshalltown Gasoline Alley, Hardin County All Stars, Van Zee of Oskaloosa, Centerville, and two from Sioux City played in national AAU tournaments in the 1950s and 1960s.[70]

Converting from high school rules to AAU rules was difficult for Iowa players during those years. The AAU game was faster paced because it used a rover player system. The guard who passed from her defense court to the forward court could then enter the forward court play. In order to balance the court, one forward on that team would then go to the guard in the defense court to help on defense. This made for more complex play. Still, at the time, only one dribble was allowed and no tie-up of the ball was permitted except in the act of shooting. The Iowa players found AAU ball so much to their liking they did not want to play Iowa high school girls rules again.

The AAU tournament enabled Iowa players to demonstrate and compare their skill with players from around the United States. It also presented the possibility of being chosen on the All-American team and of being selected for an American international team. The Iowa players in the AAU tournaments were outstanding. An all-time record was set in 1964 when 48 of the 288 players were former Iowa high school players.[71]

Between 1940 and 1960 at least 20 percent of the first team All-Americans were Iowans. Among those were eleven from Iowa Wesleyan, ten from AIB, nine AIC Stenos, eight Omaha Comets, and in one year three from the Dr. Swett's Des Moines team.[72] The 1963 Pan American team included four former Iowa high school players. The USA team that played in the 1964 World Tournament included one Iowan.

Conclusion

Athleticism, color, and emotions are all a part of basketball for females in the Midwest. In Iowa, particularly, basketball has a continuous and remarkable history since 1893. Community support and pride, several generations of players, post high school play, and the connection between the media and the sport have all contributed to girls basketball's enduring central position in schools and communities. A 1950s coach may best explain Iowa girls special brand of basketball. When asked the secret of his success he lightheartedly responded, "I tell my girls, you be ladies, make people proud of you, but when you play basketball, you play like boys."[73] That is a dated admonition, but it was the key to Iowa's successful program. It probably is not incidental, therefore, that in a late 1970s survey conducted by the Project on Equal Rights, Iowa ranked first in the United States in the percentage of high school athletes who were females.

Once largely the domain of smaller schools, by 1985 girls interscholastic basketball teams were fielded by nearly 500 schools of varying sizes. The rapid increase during the 1960s and 1970s in large schools' teams was due to the expressed desire of female students for basketball. Their desires were made reality by the impetus of Title IX of the Educational Amendments of 1972. Girls basketball is certain to continue in Iowa whether it is the traditional six player two division court as played by the majority of the teams or the five player full court game as played by increasingly more teams. As a Midwestern sports writer observed in 1976, "It is only in Iowa where the high school athlete is queen."[74]

Notes

1. George A. Moore, "From Springfield, to Edmonton, to Montreal, A Comparative Study of Women's Basketball." 5th International Symposium for Comparative Physical Education and Sport (Vancouver, Canada, 1986), 4–5.

2. Max Exner, personal communication, Ames, Iowa, 28 July 1990.

3. *Iowa Girls High School Yearbook*, ed. R. H. Chisholm (Des Moines: Iowa Girls High School Athletic Union, 1963), 142.

4. *Iowa State Daily*, 30 August 1990.

5. *The Student*, 1895 (Yearbook of Iowa State Agricultural College, Ames); *Bomb*, 1894 (Yearbook of Iowa Agricultural College, Ames).

6. Mabel Lee, *Memories of a Bloomer Girl* (Washington, D.C.: American Alliance for Health, Physical Education and Recreation, 1977), 58.

7. William J. Petersen, "Beginnings of Girls' Basketball," *The Palimpsest*, ed. William J. Petersen (Iowa City: State Historical Society of Iowa, April 1968), 121.

8. Maury White, "Girl Cagers—1898 Style," *Des Moines Tribune*, 22 February 1951.

9. Petersen, "Beginnings of Girls' Basketball," 120.

10. Emma Tellier Wilmarth, personal communication, Ames, Iowa, December 1983.

11. "Girls Play Ball," *Dubuque Herald Tribune*, 12 December 1901.

12. White, "Girl Cagers—1898 Style."

13. *Ames Tribune*, Ames, Iowa, 4 April 1903.

14. *Davenport Blackhawk*, 1920. Quoted by William J. Petersen in "Iowa Girls High School Athletic Union," *The Palimpsest* (April 1968), 121.

15. Mrs. Everett Black, personal communication, 6 April 1979.

16. Janice A. Beran, survey of 72 members of Iowa Girls Basketball Hall of Fame, 1979 and data gathered by personal interview with former players, 1920–30s students, teachers, and coaches, 1980–1990.

17. Gladys Mead, Louise Gillespie, and Leona Brandt, personal communication, Ames, Iowa, 1981.

18. For more on the 1925 situation, see Janice A. Beran, "Playing to the Right Drummer: Girls Basketball in Iowa, 1893–1927," *Research Quarterly for Exercise and Sport* (Centennial Issue, 1985), 78.

19. Iowa High School Athletic Association, Bulletin 14, December 1925. "John Agans—Father of Iowa Girls Basketball," *Iowa Girls Basketball Yearbook* (Des Moines: Iowa Girls High School Athletic Union, 1949), 49–55.

20. E. Wayne Cooley, "Aims and Objectives of the Iowa High School Athletic Union," *Iowa Girls Basketball Yearbook* (Des Moines: Iowa Girls High School Athletic Union, 1955), 3.

21. Iowa Girls High School Athletic Union, personal communication, Des Moines, Iowa, 6 September 1990.

22. "From Coast to Coast with Gene Shumate," *Iowa Girls Basketball Yearbook*, ed. R. H. Chisholm (Des Moines: Iowa Girls High School Athletic Union, 1947), 6–7.

23. Brad Wilson, "Auditorium Would Seat All Girls' Townfolk," *Des Moines Register*, 16 March 1955.

24. "Girls State Finals First High School Sport in Iowa to Receive Live Telecast," *Iowa Girls Basketball Yearbook*, ed. Rod H. Chisholm (Des Moines: Iowa Girls High School Athletic Union, 1951), 85–152; Maury White, *Des Moines Register*, 13 March 1985.

25. Jim Duncan, "Girls' Basketball—1950–68," *The Palimpsest* (Iowa City: State Historical Society of Iowa, April 1968), 155.

26. Jim Enright, *Only in Iowa* (Des Moines: Iowa Girls High School Athletic Union, 1976), 28.

27. For a fuller discussion see Janice A. Beran, "The Iowa High School Girls High School Basketball Tournament Viewed as an Institutionalized Ritual," *Play as Context*, ed. Alyce Cheska Taylor (West Point, N.Y.: Leisure Press, 1981), 149–158.

28. John Karras, "Vets Quiet During Rest Between Tournaments," *Des Moines Register and Tribune*, 17 March 1979, 3A.

29. George Turner, personal communication, Des Moines, Iowa, 5 September 1990.

30. R. H. Chisholm, "Iowa Girls High School Athletic Union," *The Palimpsest* (Iowa City: State Historical Society of Iowa, April 1968), 125.

31. Mona Van Steenbergen and Janet Payne, "Girls at Iowa State Teachers College Claim Sportsmanship, Social Poise, Understanding, and Friendship Result From Basketball," *Iowa Girls Basketball Yearbook*, ed. R. H. Chisholm (Des Moines: Iowa Girls High School Athletic Union, 1951), 59–60.

32. Earl O. Berge, "There's a Cole Shortage in Seymour," *Iowa Girls Basketball Yearbook*, ed. R. H. Chisholm (Des Moines: Iowa Girls High School Athletic Union, 1932), 50–52, 163.

33. Valerie Monson, *Des Moines Register*, Des Moines, Iowa, 16 March 1979.

34. E.g., Nick Lamberto, "Iowa's Sweet Sixteen and a Bit of Hoop History," *Des Moines Register*, 7 March 1978.

35. Interview, Maury White, *Des Moines Register*, 2 February 1990.

36. "State Tournament Builder," *Iowa Girls Basketball Scrapbook* (Des Moines: Iowa Girls High School Athletic Union, 1947), 17.

37. Enright, *Only in Iowa*, 35.

38. *Iowa Girls Basketball Yearbook*, ed. R. H. Chisholm (Des Moines: Girls High School Athletic Union, 1948), 64, 66.

39. Fred Hawks, "First Intersectional Games Played in 1933, Audubon East to Guthrie, Oklahoma," *Iowa Girls Basketball Yearbook* (Des Moines: Iowa Girls High School Athletic Union, 1948), 62.

40. "Girls Basketball in Other States," *Iowa Girls Basketball Scrapbook* (Des Moines: Iowa Girls High School Athletic Union, 1946).

41. "Texas Moves Iowa Into Girls' Basketball Limelight," *Iowa Girls Basketball Yearbook*, ed. R. H. Chisholm (Des Moines: Iowa Girls High School Athletic Union, 1947), 48.

42. "The Texas Game," *Iowa Girls Basketball Yearbook*, ed. R. H. Chisholm (Des Moines: Iowa Girls High School Athletic Union, 1948), 58–60.

43. *Iowa Girls Basketball Yearbook*, ed. R. H. Chisholm (Des Moines: Iowa Girls High School Athletic Union, 1951), 45.

44. *Iowa Girls Basketball Yearbook*, ed. R. H. Chisholm (Des Moines: Iowa Girls High School Athletic Union, 1951), 105.

45. "Macon, Missouri High School," *Iowa Girls Basketball Yearbook*, ed. R. H. Chisholm (Des Moines: Iowa Girls High School Athletic Union, 1951), 129.

46. "Gardner Consolidated, North Dakota Champs, Wins 32; Fans Award Vacation," *Iowa Girls Basketball Yearbook*, ed. R. H. Chisholm (Des Moines: Iowa Girls High School Athletic Union, 1951), 106.

47. "A Woman Coach Is Oklahoma's Winningest," *Iowa Girls Basketball Yearbook* (Des Moines: Iowa Girls High School Athletic Union, 1955), 88–89, 91–92.

48. Joan Hult, personal communication, Ames, Iowa, 30 August 1990.

49. "Capper's Farmer Reveals Facts About Girls' Basketball," *Iowa Girls Basketball Yearbook*, ed. Hank and Vera Bradshaw (Des Moines: Iowa Girls Basketball Yearbook, 1955), 92.

50. C. H. McCloy, "Evidence Proves Girls Able to 'Take' Basketball in Stride," *Iowa Girls Basketball Yearbook*, ed. R. H. Chisholm (Des Moines: Iowa Girls High School Athletic Union, 1952), 66–69, 82, 123.

51. H. C. Friend, "Osteopaths Find Girls' Basketball Helps Physique," *Iowa Girls Basketball Yearbook*, ed. R. H. Chisholm (Des Moines: Iowa Girls High School Athletic Union, 1952), 102–103, 106.

52. Floyd Taylor, "Iowa's No. 1 Girls' Basketball Fan Has Time of His Life," *Iowa Girls Basketball Yearbook*, ed. R. H. Chisholm (Des Moines: Iowa Girls High School Athletic Union, 1951), 93, 122.

53. "Basketball Coaching as a Career," *Iowa Girls Basketball Yearbook*, ed. R. H. Chisholm (Des Moines: Iowa Girls High School Athletic Union, 1948), 28.

54. "AIC Stenos," *Iowa Girls Basketball Yearbook*, ed. R. H. Chisholm (Des Moines: Iowa Girls High School Athletic Union, 1952), 244.

55. "Basketball at Bankers Life," *Iowa Girls Basketball Yearbook*, ed. R. H. Chisholm (Des Moines: Iowa Girls High School Athletic Union, 1948), 48.

56. "Still Chalking Up Victories," *Iowa Girls Basketball Yearbook*, ed. R. H. Chisholm (Des Moines: Iowa Girls High School Athletic Union, 1951), 38.

57. Olan G. Ruble, "Girls Basketball in a Liberal Arts College," *Iowa Girls Basketball Yearbook*, ed. R. H. Chisholm (Des Moines: Iowa Girls High School Athletic Union, 1948), 81–82.

58. "We Did It," *Iowa Girls Basketball Yearbook*, ed. R. H. Chisholm (Des Moines: Iowa Girls High School Athletic Union, 1952), 180–181, 184.

59. "1944–45, Girls Basketball," *Croaker* (Mt. Pleasant, Iowa: Iowa Wesleyan College, 1945), 39.

60. Nancy Duffy, personal communication, Mt. Pleasant, Iowa, 4 September 1990.

61. "Tigerettes 62–63," *Croaker* (Mt. Pleasant, Iowa: Iowa Wesleyan College, 1963), 95.

62. Olan G. Ruble, Citation, Iowa Wesleyan College, Mt. Pleasant, Iowa, 1982.

63. "AAU Basketball for Girls," *Iowa Girls Basketball Yearbook*, ed. R. H. Chisholm (Des Moines: Iowa Girls High School Athletic Union, 1946).

64. Leo Schultz, "A Girls Team Tours Central America and Mexico," *Iowa Girls Basketball Yearbook*, ed. R. H. Chisholm (Des Moines: Iowa Girls High School Athletic Union, 1948), 49, 78.

65. "Iowa Wesleyan Plays in 7th National Meet," *Iowa Girls Basketball Yearbook*, ed. R. H. Chisholm (Des Moines: Iowa Girls High School Athletic Union, 1951), 131.

66. Rube Bechtel, "Business College Basketball in Iowa," *Iowa Girls Basketball Yearbook*, ed. R. H. Chisholm (Des Moines: Iowa Girls High School Athletic Union, 1948), 57.

67. John Eberline, personal communication, Osceola, Iowa, 6 September, 1990; History of Lady Statesman Basketball Pamphlet, William Penn College, 5 September 1990.

68. "C. E. Comets Spend Year Rebuilding With All Iowa Build-Up," *Iowa Girls Basketball Yearbook*, eds. Homer and Vera Bradshaw (Des Moines: Iowa Girls High School Athletic Union, 1960), 115; "C. E. Comets Travel to Eight States in Playing 23 Games," *Iowa Girls Basketball Yearbook*, eds. Homer and Vera Bradshaw (Des Moines: Iowa Girls High School Athletic Union, 1961), 120.

69. "Senior Girls . . . You Can Continue Playing Basketball at Bankers Life," *Iowa Girls Basketball Yearbook*, eds. Homer and Vera Bradshaw (Des Moines: Iowa Girls High School Athletic Union, 1959), 17.

70. Gene Agee, "Wesleyan Third, Omaha Fourth in National AAU Championship," *Iowa Girls Basketball Yearbook*, eds. Homer and Vera Bradshaw (Des Moines: Iowa Girls High School Athletic Union, 1959), 128–129.

71. E. F. Agee, Jr., "Forty-Eight Iowa Girls in National Tourney," *Iowa Girls Basketball Yearbook*, eds. Homer and Vera Bradshaw (Des Moines: Iowa Girls High School Athletic Union, 1964), 134.

72. Gene Agee, "Iowa Wesleyan Finishes Second in National AAU; Des Moines Civic Rading (Look) Wins Consolation," *Iowa Girls Basketball Yearbook*, eds. Homer and Vera Bradshaw (Des Moines: Iowa Girls High School Athletic Union, 1958), 118.

73. Bill Norris, "Be Ladies! . . . But Play Like Boys," *Iowa Girls Basketball Yearbook*, ed. R. H. Chisholm (Des Moines: Iowa Girls High School Athletic Union, 1951), 67–68, 78–87.

74. Enright, *Only in Iowa*.

PART II

THE SECOND FIFTY YEARS OF BASKETBALL
1940s–1980s

Greenville College (Ill.) Lady Panthers 1959 Team

Wayland Baptist College (Texas) Flying Queens (white uniforms), a
powerhouse from the 1950s through the 1970s

1984 USA Olympic Women's Basketball Team (Photo credit, USA
Basketball)

12

Introduction to Part II

Joan S. Hult

Dramatic changes in the American culture from the 1940s to the 1980s influenced women's basketball experiences. The articles in Part II of this collection are best understood in the context of women's experiences in the general culture, which affected women athletes, physical educators and their programs, and governance and questions of control. Two distinct eras emerged for women both in sport and in general society: the "age of transition" (1940s and 1950s) and the "age of liberation, revolution, and reform" (1960s through 1980s).

During both eras, but particularly in the latter, what feminists refer to as "gender travel" transpired, that is, movement in and out of the traditional roles of men and women. Delight in competition was the impetus for female athletes who experienced "gender travel" as they experimented with intensely competitive sporting experiences. As Jean F. O'Barr comments in *Signs: Journal of Women in Culture and Society*, "Unlike androgyny, which is associated with conformity to a settled model, gender travel implies a fluidity of life experiences and sanctions a wide spectrum of experiences that allow overlap and commonality between genders . . . it does recognize that any particular individual at any particular time can negotiate between these norms. The biological base of gender roles can dissolve away."[1] Gender travel for the female athlete became commonplace by the 1980s. Further, the evolution of culture's gender relations patterns expressly affected the governance and control of women's basketball.

The Age of Transition—1940s–1950s

The effect of the Second World War on culture. The 1940s triggered the modern evolution of gender roles. Despite some regression during the 1950s to their former roles compatible with the "cult of true wom-

207

anhood," women remained influenced by the new lifestyles they had discovered during the Second World War.

The 1940s culture severely tested and stretched to the limits the last vestiges of the "cult of true womanhood." As the war created a great demand for production workers, a liberal transformation of gender roles, responsibilities, and behavioral expectations took place. With the new values came a new vocabulary for the attributes the American woman needed to exhibit during the war. She had to be strong, courageous, sturdy, healthy, and stoic. "Rosie the Riveter," a popular referent to the hundreds of thousands of females who worked in war plants in war-related positions and new nontraditional jobs left vacant by men, demonstrated fortitude, physical strength, endurance, and relatively little frailty or outbursts from emotional stress. She surprisingly manifested fewer than expected "female problems." Never again would women who worked in three-shifts-a-day plants or gave thousands of hours in volunteer organizations for war efforts feel superfluous, weak, or fragile. Their self-esteem and self-confidence soared.

At the same time, another band of mostly single professional women entered the armed forces or supported them, joined Red Cross teams, or took USO positions at home or abroad. Married professional women performed similar tasks on the home front. Civil defense created a demand for women in leadership roles. These roles called for women to be physically fit for potential war emergencies. A hardy constitution was a prerequisite to exerting authority when warranted. These activities further expanded women's role expectations. Yet women understood clearly that they were not to extend "gender travel" beyond the duration of the war.

Physical education.   Women physical educators who did not seek war-related occupations filled new decision-making roles beyond their separate female sphere. At both the high school and college levels they built new fitness programs and tests to fulfill the U.S. Office of Education's objective of fitness for war. That office recognized vigorous competitive sports as an important means to achieving the now desirable fitness goals. Physical education programs reflected the exercise component, adding the usual team sports with greater emphasis on competition. In addition, a few lifetime sports became common offerings.

Some physical educators also ran fitness programs for service women who trained on various college campuses and Army or Navy bases. Thus they acquired expertise at all competitive levels. They, in turn, provided competitive opportunity for not only servicewomen but also Red Cross workers and USO personnel. Basketball and softball were most often the sports selected to meet fitness objectives.

Undeniably, the women physical educators adjusted their values to include heretofore unacceptable female competition. Participants who enjoyed the sporting experience returned home favorable to competition as an avenue to fitness and convinced of its social and democratic objectives.

Anna Espenschade (chairman of the Women's Section during the war years), in a 1946 speech before the National Section on Women's Athletics called "Women's Sports Today and a Glimpse of Tomorrow," stressed the importance of teachers putting to use their learnings from the servicewomen's competitive sport experiences. Furthermore, she proposed that women in schools, industry, and all across post-war America needed to recognize competition "as the natural inherent impulse of all red-blooded Americans; to accept it for its true value, then to guide and direct it into desirable channels of functioning in the everyday life of American girls and women."[2] She advocated natural competition via vigorous competitive programs under controlled development. Espenschade's "glimpses" encouraged changes in physical educators' attitude toward competition. She fully endorsed the new fitness objectives, but continued to subscribe to the traditional values of socialization and democratic ideals inherent in team sports.

Culture of the 1950s.   As production demands subsided after the war, the cultural message was for women to leave the labor place and return home. Society now mandated that women yield their jobs to returning servicemen. Women were expected to reestablish the narrow cultural definition of "woman"—primarily wife and mother and, in fact, a wife and mother who ought to build a strong nuclear family. "In response to the reconversion to a peacetime economy, the tensions of the Cold War, and the antifeminist Freudianism, a 'feminine mystique' enforcing domesticity, motherhood, and sexual suggestiveness subordinate to men came into being."[3] The ideal of beauty and femininity harkened back to the mid-twenties or even to the voluptuous woman of the early 1900s. The appearance of the cute cheerleader rather than the athlete was the new ideal mothers shared with daughters.

Thousands of women, however, stayed in the workplace (at reduced salaries). They worked in order to assist their husbands in college under the GI Bill. They postponed child-raising or struggled to maintain both family and career. This group seemed to remain the exception to the typical 1950s woman, as did a modest number of other women who simply wished to work. Also atypical were most single women already in paid positions or those returning from war jobs or military service. Typically they returned to their professional jobs in education, nursing, or social work. Many more women, however, returned to low paying clerical jobs. Some were themselves eager to attend college, but colleges already filled by male GIs frequently denied access to women.

Physical education women were uniquely exempt from pressure to conform to an "ideal woman" role. They returned to, or had maintained, positions in the separate sphere of physical education. Because of the new importance of women's physical fitness, colleges established many major programs in the 1950s. A growing demand for women physical educators at all levels of education created some tensions between the genders. An over-abundance of male physical educators were anxious to work and teach in women's programs if they could not find positions in men's. In some combined physical education programs, men did occasionally teach women's activity classes and, more frequently, theory classes. Thus the door to the "women's sphere" opened slightly.

The woman so aptly symbolized by Rosie the Riveter had experienced the freedom and excitement of the workplace, financial success, purchasing power, independence, and status as head of the household. She tried to readjust to her homebound lifestyle. However, there were three interacting quandaries: boredom with suburban life, desire for additional income given the general affluence of the 1950s, and a wide range of appealing job opportunities. An important substitute for paid employment was volunteerism, then at its high point, or leisure and fitness pursuits. But many women did in fact return to the labor force, thereby threatening the gender division that assigned women to work without pay. As more and more women acquired some degree of financial independence, divorce was increasingly sanctioned.

The age of transition brought women to the edge of the modern feminist movement. In those decades the behavioral patterns, the opening of the job market, and the fitness surge all spoke to the emergence of a freer, more independent woman.

Physical education.   The education environment was ready for the women physical educators' new programs involving fitness for peace, vigorous activity, and acceptance of the new competitive values. The Korean War further contributed to a new physical education motto, "fitness to live, fitness to work, and fitness to fight." This time the fitness motto involved men and women.

The younger generation of women physical educators all shared common experiences in play days and sports days. But many had also enjoyed competitive and leadership opportunities in a wider diversity of settings, including the armed services, varsity teams, and public recreation leagues. This larger experience brought to physical education leadership and athletics a new breed of liberal physical educators—the future proponents of varsity competition directed by women.

School physical education classes (the base in the pyramid model) included basketball and other team sports as in the past. However, by the end of the 1950s additional program content encompassed more lifetime sports and emphasis on fitness for life. Slowly programs again began to include gymnastics and track and field. The pyramid model had classes at its base, with intramural and extramural activities in the form of sports days in the middle building block. The apex of the pyramid would now include varsity sports. Each of the program blocks (base, middle, and top) used basketball, generally the first varsity sport offered in new programs.

Most high school girls and college women in the 1950s seemed far more interested in being cheerleaders or pompon girls than athletes, a role which yielded status for presumed beauty of appearance rather than physical ability. Nonetheless significant numbers of girls and women did select the new athletic programs in education or the public domain.

Age of Liberation, Revolution, and Reform— 1960s–1980s

Eleanor Roosevelt's commission report on *American Women* along with Betty Friedan's *The Feminine Mystique* put words to the dissatisfaction women of the 1950s had been experiencing in their lives.[4] Having their frustrations described, explained, and validated and knowing others had similar feelings prompted some women to form women's organizations. The National Organization for Women (NOW) and Women's Equity Action League (WEAL) became catalysts in revitalizing the women's liberation movement. Together these elements brought transitional women to the dawn of women's liberation, revolution, and reform.

Culture.   The 1954 Supreme Court decision *Board of Education vs. Topeka, Kansas* required racial integration. It was the first of many legislative actions in the fight for equality. The new application in the 1960s of the Fourteenth Amendment (Equal Protection Clause) broadened its protection provisions to include gender. The Equal Pay Act of 1963 (and its 1972 amendment) and the 1964 Civil Rights Acts (including Title VII and Equal Employment Opportunities section) prohibited sex discrimination. Similarly, the Executive Order enacted in 1965 demanded equal opportunity practices in hiring and promotion for those with federal grants and contracts. The order affected most colleges and universities. All of the civil rights legislation collectively energized the gender and racial revolutions of the 1960s. The legislation was the first legal tool to combat race and sex discrimination in education. It foreshadowed a decade of struggle by women and African-Americans to change their subordinate status. The human rights legislation affected attitudes and progress of women in physical education, who began to realize that conceivably they had a responsibility to furnish new opportunities for highly skilled female athletes. Unquestionably, the women's liberation movement contributed to awakening a quest for equality by young female student-athletes as well as by their mentors.

Congress enacted the Equal Rights Amendment (ERA), but not enough states ratified it. Nonetheless, the ERA effectively redressed many blatant cultural inequities on the way to its defeat. It also prompted many states to legislate their own ERAs.

Title IX of the 1972 Education Amendments was the benchmark legislation for parity in education. The amendment states: "No person in the United States shall, on the basis of sex, be excluded from participation in, be denied the benefits of, or be subjected to discrimination under any education program or activity receiving federal financial assistance."

All the legislation opened two avenues of access to equality—legal access and social access. This combination led to reforms in the job market, education, economics, and family life and hastened gender equality.

Women physical educators played a new role when Title IX opened the door for equality in sports, and many took an active part in such political statements as this 1979 rally in Washington, D.C.

NOW and WEAL were the two most important organizations in redressing gender inequities through legal channels. Jointly with many other women's organizations and coalitions, they kept feminist goals ever present in the culture, offering workshops and support networks and working to raise the consciousness of both men and women about race and gender-related injustice.

Women during the age of liberation, revolution, and reform were a mixture of conservatives, liberals, women's rights advocates, status quo advocates, defenders of traditional family values, and others more difficult to label. On the whole, more women moved to the workplace, married later, controlled the "when" of pregnancy, had fewer children, and after child-bearing returned to work sooner. In education, more women graduated from high school, went to college, completed college, and moved to nontraditional careers. With increased work options, leisure and personal lifestyle options expanded as well. For example, greater economic independence permitted women to divorce or to live as emancipated single women or single heads of household. At the same time, greater freedom in social choices permitted women alternative lifestyles.

The financial gains of women college graduates rose steadily in the era. College graduation offered more women opportunities in middle management and more promotions in education. Gains for nonprofessional women workers were generally much slower. For this latter group, except for women in unionized nontraditional jobs, earnings were disproportionate from men's.

The feminist movement in this era, unlike any other, was not just a political statement. It was a unique new way of life. The traditional family life was reformed. A key objective in the modern feminist struggle was to achieve equality not only in the public forum but within the family as well. The subordination of women in the home was a central issue affecting family division of labor, motherhood and childrearing, wifely role, and freedom for leisure. A woman had to contemplate new ways of looking at herself and her place in the world. She did so often in the face of male resistance to what he saw as encroachment of his territory. Unlike any previous era of war, women reacted to the secondary status they had been forced to take in the anti-war movement during the Vietnam War, and many joined the women's movement.

Each woman's pride in female identity and ownership of her body became fundamental tenets of the feminist movement. Women's liberation conveyed the realization of discrimination in pay, business, and the professions and unfair practices in the family. The feminist platform asked women to make choices—for example, whether to use contraception, whether to change family role expectations and practices—and to adopt new thinking patterns.

These new ways of viewing experience had the potential to change women's power base. Facing the truth of these realizations and using power to change, the feminist believed, empowered woman. The feminist movement dispelled much over-emphasis upon physical beauty, a concept based on sexual suggestiveness and subordination to men's view of beauty. The physical appearance ideal changed from "cosmetic" to natural beauty.

Sound medical judgment about healthy bodies influenced standards of beauty. The trim look, but with muscle tone, became the ideal. The redefinition of beauty concurrent with women taking responsibility for their own bodies in the era of revolution and reform resulted in an elevated self-image and self-esteem, just as health and fitness had the reciprocal effect of being conducive to exploring new ventures. Countless more women felt free to enjoy jogging, aerobics, exercise programs, and new sporting experiences for their own sake. Fitness objectives, for perhaps the first time, were personal and not for war, motherhood, or males. No longer were these physical activities associated with a loss of femininity. Daughters of liberated women accepted sport involvement as natural, without concern for gender.

The feminist movement lost some of its power in the 1980s and conservatism reasserted domesticity as an ideal for women. The healthy body concept, however, did not change, established as it was on solid medical knowledge. The feminist march toward gender equality in all facets of life did continue, but the pace was slower. The pro life/pro choice controversy, however, spoke to the heart of the question of autonomy over one's body. The conservatives' narrowing of Title IX's implementation procedures also brought grave concern to feminists as did the retrenchment from affirmative action cases.

Power relations are integral to revitalization and revolution of gender parity. Power relations have historically determined that men would and should dominate. The women's revolution was about changing that relationship to make it equal—equal in work, equal in play, and equal in marriage.[5] The struggle for feminists, then, was to take that power away from men by empowering women. Gender equality would, of course, achieve that goal, but the reforms had to be the vehicle through which women attempted to break power relations. Such gender equality is in no way complete. Work toward equalizing power relations through litigation, legislation, and social action is unfinished. Change in attitudes, a task of the culture itself, also remains an objective not yet achieved.

Athletics.   In the 1960s the American Medical Association (AMA) modified its stand on the value of competitive athletics for girls and women. The AMA shifted from cautioning about the dangers of vigorous competition for girls to strong endorsement of the benefits. Women had traditionally subscribed to the authority of the AMA. Thus its new stance encouraged women to develop varsity programs and actively support the Olympic movement.

Sport for women benefited significantly from legal action and social change strategies. Women gained access to a far wider choice of sporting experiences that, in turn, promoted a broader concept of femininity. Of greatest consequence in legislation and litigation were the Fourteenth Amendment, Title IX, and state ERAs. Their premise was that the historical male model of athletics was the ideal model and that model should be made available to women. The Office of Civil Rights' Title IX Guidelines and its ensuing investigations substantiated use of the male model for defining equity. Using the male norm as the gauge for equality made Title IX a double-edged sword for women. Title IX made it difficult for women to preserve their alternative model of athletics.

The struggle for women's rightful place in society and equalization of power relations was intensified in women's athletics because women had invaded the sacrosanct male domain. The more subtle power relations in sport could not be litigated. Only changed attitudes and behavior patterns could accomplish gender equality in power relations in athletics. The struggles between men and women in the sports domain challenged the historical reality of male domination in all social institutions in the sport order. Further, a residual of the sporting tradition had long been the "rite of passage to maleness and manhood." Thus men understandably considered sport ownership an inherent male right. While the influx of women dispelled myths about manliness, attitudes about sport being male territory did not subside easily. Yet sport was an important tool in reconstructing gender roles. Women's sport reforms confronted the issue of femininity too, and by the 1980s the culture accepted women's participation in most sports with prehaps only the heavy contact sports still considered as truly male territory.

One tenacious and pervasive social value that remained in sport was that men should display strength, power, and might, whereas women ought to display grace, form, and beauty. This bias was apparent when women competed with the same aggressive competitive spirit as men, or when they dared to invade the "truly" male sports. As women adopted the same goals and norms as men, they began to dispel the convictions about what gender behavior patterns really were "correct." Only with the breakdown of this dichotomy will female athletes have achieved acceptance without the rigidity of gender norms.

Athletics for collegiate women underwent a revolution spurred by the confluence of Title IX, the women's rights movement, and the founding of the Association for Intercollegiate Athletics for Women. Further, the "state's interest" in the success of women in the Olympics also granted women greater sport opportunities. The Amateur Sports Act of 1978 added immeasurably to the female athlete's options from the grass roots level through elite competition. A more detailed discussion of the growth of athletics after the establishment of AIAW and Title IX is contained in Part II articles.

Physical education.   The actions of women in physical education to design and conduct intercollegiate athletic programs paralleled the women's liberation movement and cultural reforms. Reform in physical education and athletics involved redesigning competitive programs so an alternative model of women's athletics would become reality. A review of the process through the 1960s and early 1970s reveals the profound role performed by a volunteer army of women physical educators. They were the mainstay in developing athletic programs at each secondary and collegiate institution.

The issues of athletic control and how to secure financial support were two central concerns at schools in the 1960s and early 1970s. In many colleges women's and combined physical education departments accepted the burden of funding girls and women's athletics. Most often the participants themselves had to help support the teams. They held bake sales, candy drives, and car washes, sold raffle tickets, and conducted a multitude of other money-making projects. In addition, in most collegiate situations in these years, the woman physical educator/coach used her own money for transportation, food, entry fees, and even officiating. She had to drive her own car full of students to the events. Uniforms typically were physical education outfits with "pinnies." The school might have supported buying one set of uniforms for all sports, but just as likely, however, the teams earned money to buy uniforms. The coaches received no release time from teaching, and rarely received any extra pay. Once the programs had been established they often received funding from the student body as an extracurricular activity on campus. In other situations the intercollegiate programs used the women's already small recreation or intramural funds. (Similar experiences can be found on the high school level, although they were quicker to provide the basic funding for girls' programs.)

At the same time, many well-established interscholastic and intercollegiate programs operated throughout the age of transition and liberation. Generally speaking, the era of the 1960s did bring athletic revolution and reforms, although there was inconsequential financial support from *the* athletic department.

In schools where men's athletics became responsible for supporting women's programs in the 1970s, the athletic directors began to demand control of the program as well as the budget. While many schools had

Vivian Stringer, head basketball coach at the University of Iowa, typifies the coach of the 1990s—professional and intensely involved with motivating players to exhibit high levels of competitive spirit as well as excellence in athletic skills. (Photo courtesy University of Iowa Sports Information)

a small but separate women's budget under women's control, when the funding came partially from monies designated for men's athletics women began to lose control of the program. By the mid-1970s the mandate of Title IX made greater funding an important priority, for nominal funding would not fulfill the Title IX requirements. In spite of Title IX, funding for women's programs increased from less than 2 percent to only 16–18 percent. By the end of the 1980s, few separate women's athletic departments existed. Mergers had moved women's athletics under the leadership of the former men's athletic director.

Women's and men's physical education departments also merged. With few exceptions, in these situations males became the chair of the department. The coeducation requirements of Title IX changed the physical education program offerings drastically. Physical education teachers attempted to offer classes that would not demand physical contact. In the process, many schools selected to drop basketball from the program. Fitness continued to hold high priority in the classes. However, this time fitness was unrelated to any nationalistic goals; this time fitness was for "self." Students favored courses in lifetime sports instead of team sports. New courses in aerobics, self-defense, and outdoor activities became preferred classes.

While women in physical education and athletics were building competitive programs, a parallel happening in the culture also favorably influenced women's freedom to pursue sport. Billie Jean King burst into national consciousness strong, spirited, fiercely competitive, and successful at the right time in history, the late 1960s and early 1970s. As *Women Sports* magazine successfully commercialized the new interest of large numbers of women, King inspired children and masses of women to follow her lead to the tennis courts. Billie Jean's win against Bobby Riggs in "the battle of the sexes" was especially gratifying to women since Riggs had declared that no female could beat a world class male such as himself. Thus King's victory seemed to build confidence in the power of women in sport.

Together all of the events described for the 1960–1980 era were central to redefining femininity to include active sporting experiences. The women's movement, along with a new sporting enthusiasm, challenged the traditional notions of femininity and endorsed sport. Competitive sport simultaneously with fitness, jogging, and concern for nutrition and health produced multitudes of new converts to physical activity. A reversal of medical views of sport dispelled female fragility myths and promoted vigorous competitive athletics. The state's interest in Olympic and international competition lent wholehearted support to women's participation. All of this together kindled the initiation and groundswell of women's interscholastic and intercollegiate competition.

Summary

The depiction of basketball's cultural context is intended to enhance the following articles and personal reflections. Investigation of basketball in light of women's struggle for autonomy of her body, changes in power relations, and changes in behavior patterns and gender role expectations establishes meaningful connections between basketball and the culture. There are reciprocal linkages between the culture's influence on basketball and basketball's influence as a change agent on the culture. The effects of basketball on the culture are less obvious than the effects of the culture on basketball. Nonetheless, basketball has indeed influenced the culture. For example, the degree of intensity in basketball competition, its popularity, and the significance and design underlying basketball competition all have impacted on gender roles. Understanding women's changing roles in the culture from the 1940s through the 1980s enables the reader to appreciate the story of basketball in dynamic relationship to the context in which it unfolded.

The writings in Part II include a discussion of women's sport governance organizations in education, accounts by coaches, an account of a leader, and narrative histories of leaders about what occurred in collegiate basketball and officiating the last fifty years. The final section looks at women's basketball's most recent history and examines present governing bodies for intercollegiate and interscholastic basketball.

Needed Research

The articles in Part II reflect selected topics based, in part, on availability of research data and the authors' knowledge about the collegiate basketball scene. As a result of this selection process at least two significant contributors to basketball in the two eras are wanting. The first and most serious gap is the sporting experiences of African-American basketball players and the predominantly black institutions of higher education.

There is a dearth of research and published articles on African-American women's basketball expriences before their general acceptance on intercollegiate teams as players and coaches after the mid-seventies. The unique saga of their contributions and the role of basketball in their lives is not yet told.

Lost in the traditions of African-American communities, institutions, and individuals are tales of struggles, hopes, and dreams of women basketball players and coaches striving for an opportunity for elite competition. For example, not until the decade of the 1980s was there anything beyond token recognition for national caliber predominantly black schools (Cheyney State, Federal City College, and Virginia Union).

Vivian Stringer, Marion Washington, and Betsy Stocker are examples of outstanding coaches who received little recognition until recently. Lynette Woodward and Lusia Harris are the only two exceptions to the lack of notice (before the end of the 1970s) afforded the many outstanding black female basketball athletes. Until the mid-1970s, few major collegiate basketball powers included more than one or two black players, and half had none.

The second significant contributor to girls and women's basketball missing in our discussion in this collection is the Catholic Youth Organization (CYO). Its basketball program provided participants vigorous competitive opportunity for the ten years before college age. The CYO is unique because it served thousands of young girls from eight to eighteen years of age. The CYO leagues were active in large cities of the East, including New York, Baltimore, Washington, D.C., and Philadelphia, and as far west as Chicago.

CYO teams competed in leagues and tournaments both locally and regionally. Leagues consisted often of both parochial schools and parishes and provided competition at different skill levels. Former women players, coaches, and officials participating in the 1950s and 1960s described the excitement and fierce competition of the CYO program, which effectively functioned as a feeder system not only for Catholic colleges but for other colleges and universities as well. The tradition of basketball in parochial high schools and CYO leagues deserves much credit for the caliber of players on the three-time National Championship teams of the "Mighty Macs" of tiny Immaculata College (Pennsylvania).

These two missing links in the story of women's basketball demonstrate a need for additional research to uncover the buried past. New evidence will not only make the invisible women visible, but will also rectify remaining distortions in how we understand women's basketball.

Notes

1. Jean F. O'Barr, "Editorial," in *Signs: Journal of Women in Culture and Society* (Chicago: University of Chicago Press, Spring, 1989), 531.

2. Anna Espenschade, "Women's Sports Today and a Glimpse of Tomorrow," *Proceedings of AAHPER Convention, April 9–13, 1946, St. Louis*, 87–88.

3. Lois W. Banner, *American Beauty* (Chicago: University of Chicago Press, 1983), 283.

4. Commission on Women, "The Report of the Commissions," in *American Women* (Washington, D.C.: U.S. Government Printing Office, 1963); Betty Friedan, *The Feminine Mystique* (New York: Delaware Publishing Company, 1963).

5. Patrica Madoo Lengermann and Ruth A. Wallace, *Gender in America: Social Control and Social Change* (Englewood Cliffs, N.J.: Prentice-Hall, 1985).

Select Bibliography

Listed here are the writings that have been of major use in development of this essay, indicating the nature and range of reading which helped form its ideas. It is intended to serve as a convenience for those who wish to follow the topic of women in sport through recurring themes of our culture.

Banner, Lois W. *American Beauty*. Chicago: The University of Chicago Press, 1983.

Beneria, Lourdes and Catharine R. Stimpson, eds. *Women, Households, and the Economy*. New Brunswick, N.J.: Rutgers University Press, 1987.

Birke, Lynda. *Women, Feminism and Biology: The Feminist Challenge*. New York: Methuen, 1986.

Boston Women's Health Book Collective. *The New Our Bodies, Ourselves*. New York: Simon and Schuster, 1984.

Boutilier, Mary A. and Lucinda SanGiovanni. *The Sporting Woman*. Champaign, Ill.: Human Kinetics, 1983.

Cary, John H., Julius Weinberg, and Thomas L. Hartshorne. *The Social Fabric: American Life From the Civil War to the Present*. Boston: Little Brown and Company, 1987.

Chafe, William H. *The American Woman: Her Changing Social, Economic, and Political Role, 1920–1970*. Oxford: Oxford University Press, 1972.

Chafe, William H. *Women and Equality: Changing Patterns in American Culture*. Oxford: Oxford University Press, 1981.

Dyer, K. F. *Challenging the Men: Women in Sport*. New York: University of Queensland Press, 1982.

Freeman, Jo. *The Politics of Women's Liberation*. New York: Longman, 1975.

Friedan, Betty. *The Feminine Mystique*. New York: Delaware Publishing, 1963.

Friedan, Betty. *The Second Stage*. New York: Summit Books, 1981.

Geadelmann, Patricia et al. *Equality in Sport for Women*. Washington, D.C.: AAHPER, 1977.

Guttmann, Allen. *A Whole New Ball Game: An Interpretation of American Sports*. Chapel Hill: The University of North Carolina Press, 1988.

Gluck, Shera Berger. *Rosie The Riveter Revisited: Women, the War, and Social Change*. New York: New American Library, 1987.

Hoepner, Barbara J., ed. *Women's Athletics: Coping With Controversy*. Washington, D.C.: American Association for Health, Physical Education, and Recreation, 1974.

Jaggar, Alison and Paula Rothenberg Struhl. *Feminist Frameworks: Alternative Theoretical Accounts of the Relations Between Women and Men*. New York: McGraw-Hill Book Company, 1978.

Kennedy, S. E. *If All We Did Was to Weep At Home: A History of White Working-Class Women in America*. Bloomington: Indiana University Press, 1979.

Kerber, Linda K. and Jane DeHart Mathews. *Women's America: Refocusing the Past*. Oxford: Oxford University Press, 1982.

Lapchick, Richard E., ed. *Fractured Focus: Sport as a Reflection of Society*. Lexington, Mass.: Lexington Books, 1986.

Lengermann, Patricia Madoo and Ruth A. Wallace. *Gender in America: Social Control and Social Change*. Englewood Cliffs, N.J.: Prentice-Hall Inc., 1985.

Mangan, J. A. and Roberta J. Park. *From Fair Sex to Feminism: Sport and the Socialization of Women in the Industrial and Post-Industrial Eras.* London: Frank Cass and Company, 1987.

Matthaei, Julie A. *An Economic History of Women in America: Women's Work, The Sexual Division of Labor, and the Development of Capitalism.* New York: Schocken Books, 1982.

Miller Lite Report on American Attitudes Toward Sports. New York: Research and Forecasts, Miller Brewing Co., 1983.

Sage, George. *Power and Ideology in American Sport.* Champaign, Ill.: Human Kinetics Books, 1990.

Scott, J. W. *Gender and the Politics of History.* New York: Columbia University Press, 1988.

Sena, A. M. "The Administration Enforcement of Title IX in Intercollegiate Athletics," in *Law and Inequality: A Journal of Theory and Practice,* 2(1), 1984.

Twin, Stephanie L. *Out of the Bleachers: Writing on Women and Sport.* New York: McGraw-Hill Book Company, 1979.

Section 4
Governance of Women's Basketball

13

The Saga of Competition
Basketball Battles and Governance War

Joan S. Hult

The Second World War precipitated great alterations in traditional beliefs, as large numbers of women took formerly all-male jobs in heavy industries or joined various branches of the women's armed services. The options available to American women in the 1950s, while still far fewer than those available to men, were, nonetheless, more numerous than in previous decades. In sport, indications of change were beginning to be seen.

The postwar era of economic prosperity and increased freedoms for women was in its infancy when America entered into the Korean War conflict. Once again in the 1950s the physical education profession responded to the "war effort" by gearing up for an emphasis on fitness in their programs. The motto became "fit to live, to work and to fight." This time girls and women, as well as men, were expected to be prepared through fitness. The National Section on Women's Athletics (NSWA)*

The reader can assume the discussion about sports, athletics, and basketball deals with girls and women unless otherwise specified.

*As the organization underwent change, its name also changed several times: 1932–1953, National Section of Women's Athletics (NSWA); 1953–1957, National Section for Girls and Women in Sport (NSGWS); 1957–1974, Division for Girls and Women in Sport (DGWS); and 1974–present, National Association for Girls and Women in Sport (NAGWS). In this article, depending on the year under discussion, NSWA or DGWS is used for the 50s; DGWS for the 60s; DGWS or NAGWS for the 70s; and NAGWS for the 80s. The parent organization was the American Association for Health, Physical Education and Recreation (AAHPER) 1950–1979. It became the American Alliance for Health, Physical Education and Recreation (AAHPER) in 1974 and the American Alliance for Health, Physical Education, Recreation and Dance (AAHPERD) in 1979.

joined in the effort to develop programs that emphasized fitness through sporting activities. Basketball was only one of the major sport activities deemed appropriate for girls and women's fitness goals within the school curriculums. While teaching basketball skills and strategies was also a part of women's physical education, the NSWA emphasized policies, standards, and rules for extracurricular activities in the school and in the public sector. Throughout this era and the next, NSWA focused more on controlling intramural and extramural sports than the day-to-day physical education programs. Certainly, most schools and levels of education had basketball classes; however, these programs posed no control problems to the physical educators because they were already in charge of their separate female domains unchallenged until the 1970s.

The *Basketball Guides*[1] of the period demonstrate clearly the close interaction and relationship between teaching and coaching. The women saw basketball, for example, as part of a total program for students. So the struggles and controversies came from forces outside the cloistered girls gymnasium. The arena was in small and rural schools that had no girls program, and in the athletic programs in the public sector. No matter the issues and problems, basketball seemed inevitably at the hub.

The end of the 1940s through the 1960s was a period of transition for women's competitive athletics. Women physical educators returning from work with the armed services had experienced highly competitive athletic programs, either as participants, officials or administrators. They were well aware of the new joys in basketball and other sports under proper supervision. As suggested in the article on governance, the end of the 1940s saw ideological changes that affected the new leaders of the 1950s and 1960s.[2] There was a resurgence of high level competition for the younger women physical educators as well as the returning service women. Both appreciated their new opportunities to compete. Though well grounded in the play day attitudes of their foremothers, their own experience yielded different attitudes about competition. The period would indeed be the progression from the social play days attitude to sport days toward varsity competition for women. Basketball would continue in the vanguard of sport changes and would, in fact, lead the revolution in women's athletics.

NSWA/NSGWS/DGWS—1950s

The most important role of the organization was setting standards, policies, and modification of rules. Basketball was at the center of most rule controversies because several groups were vying for control of the "official" women's rules. Especially the National Federation of State

High School Athletic Associations (National Federation) and Amateur Athletic Union (AAU) were the bane of existence for the NSWA. Each wanted to determine the set of rules to be used for basketball. The only other major rules controversy involved volleyball when the United States Volleyball Association (USVBA) proclaimed the single-hit power volleyball game for all girls and women to replace the "pitter-pat" two-hit game.[3] In retrospect, this action foreshadowed the basketball rules changes.

During the 1950s, two conferences addressed the issues surrounding women's elite competition, the National Leadership Conference on Girls and Women's Sport and the National Conference on Social Changes and Implications for Physical Education and Sports Programs. Also, three women's organizations established the Tripartite Committee to evaluate the National Collegiate Golf Championship. Finally, the NSWA attempted to negotiate with the National Federation and the AAU for one set of women's basketball rules.

The National Leadership Conference, planned in June of 1954 to address women in leadership roles in NSWA, took place at Estes Park, Colorado, in June 1955. Among the major topics that evolved from discussions was concern about standards for various levels of competition. Participants' concern was that patterns for girls in sport seemed to be moving toward boys rules and boys patterns of organization. This led to the conclusion that they should seek leadership roles in all sport organizations, even those which advocated varsity and Olympic competition for girls and women.[4]

From their discussions about standards, participants agreed to consider all levels of competition for women, but the basic program should revolve around intramural competition. *The Story of the National Leadership Conference on Girls and Women's Sport* sold over 1,000 copies. This demonstrates clearly the broad interest in the competition topic to individuals beyond those selected to attend the conference.[5]

The DGWS and NAPECW Social Change Conference. In June of 1958 the National Conference on Social Changes and Implications for Physical Education and Sports Programs attracted over 200 participants. The central focus was the role of high level competition in the development of sporting opportunities for girls and women. Basketball was an important focus of discussion because of its popularity, the opportunity for women to compete, the rule controversies, and the worrisome femininity issue. Participants also addressed concerns about the established golf and tennis championships. The conference resulted in a stronger commitment to the highly skilled female athlete. A second outcome was encouragement of cooperation with other sport organizations controlling girls and women's athletics. The resulting publication sold 2,000 copies, again demonstrating the importance of the topic of competition.[6]

The Women's National Collegiate Golf Championship.   In 1941 Ohio State University, under the guidance of Gladys Palmer, initiated an intercollegiate Golf Championship. Although it was not acceptable to many women physical educators at that time, nonetheless by the 1950s it was an acceptable tournament. Yet the members of DGWS and the National Association of Physical Education for College Women (NA-PECW) felt there was a need to form a group to oversee the conduct of this event. So in 1956 the Tripartite Golf Committee representing DGWS, NAPECW, and the Athletic and Recreation Federation of College Women (ARFCW) evaluated the total championship experience by attending the tournament at Purdue University.[7] As a result the more permanent National Joint Committee on Extramural Sports for College Women (NJCESCW) became the vehicle for considering future national championships. They explored the pros and cons of national competition in sports other than the traditionally acceptable individual sports of golf and tennis.[8] Ultimately the DGWS would develop the Commission on Intercollegiate Athletics for Women (CIAW) for sanctioning and sponsoring regional and national competition.

The National High School Basketball Committee   was the major challenge from high school athletics. In 1952 a liaison project with the National Federation failed. In the spring of that year a splinter group of members from nine state athletic associations created their own code for basketball. They used most of the language and organization of the boys' basketball rules to write their own girls' rule book. The group became the Girls National Basketball Rules Committee for Secondary Schools. While the National Federation did not approve these rules, the group met at the Federation meetings. All or portions of the following states used these new rules: Arkansas, Georgia, Louisiana, Missouri, North Dakota, Ohio, Oklahoma, and Tennessee. Texas and Iowa wrote their own basketball rules.[9] In each of these states some districts used the NSWA rules, and the rest used other rules. Some used the same rules as for boys. All of these states had anywhere from 100 to over 500 teams competing in basketball. Obviously this meant there were thousands of girls varsity basketball teams using rules not sanctioned or developed by the Women's Section. It also suggests the large numbers of high school girls competing in varsity basketball. A national survey in 1954–56, however, found that over 220,000 girls were playing basketball using the NSWA rules.[10]

During the 1950s changes were made that brought girls rules closer to those of the boys, but the leadership of NSWA/DGWS encouraged members to continue to fight for separate rules. Women physical educators were altering their conception of high level competition but it took the entire decade to move toward governance power that would include varsity athletics.

The leaders of NSWA attempted to deter the Girls Basketball Committee by adjusting the rules in the 1953–54 *Guide*. There were at least 17 different rule changes that year. The committee changed all nonessential rules to more nearly conform to the boys' rules. The changes were to remove "lack of clarity," and to use language more in keeping with boys' rules so men coaches would accept the rules. This was to no avail as the splinter group continued to insist on their own rules.[11] The NSWA leadership encouraged women physical educators in state associations to assist in the development of varsity programs, but to fight for the women's rules in basketball.

The NSWA Basketball Committee received a good deal of criticism from their conservative membership about the new 1953–54 rules. The committee explained the new changes this way: It was an attempt to change all rules which differed from the men's and yet were unimportant in preserving the spirit and degree of strenuousness deemed appropriate for rules changes. "No change has been made or will be made at the sacrifice of the players, regardless of the confusion that differences between boys and girls games might cause among coaches, officials, timers, scorers or spectators."[12] To further defend their changes, the Basketball Committee commented that the changes had been made to alleviate, somewhat, conditions existing throughout the United States where few women were available to direct the girls' games. In consideration for men coaches the rules had been reviewed and reconciled, in part, to make them read as the men's rules did. The committee probably made the changes not only to appease the high school groups, but in an effort to bring the AAU and NSWA rules closer together.[13]

The AAU and the NSWA had more congenial relationships as they moved toward one set of women's basketball rules. While the decade was mostly an exploration stage in the cooperative efforts to develop one set of rules, there were some important compromises. For example, the wording changes for the high school Basketball Committee were in keeping with the AAU rules, as were some of the rule changes. By the end of the 1950s more women physical educators moved to work in the AAU on local levels.[14] Also in the 1950s the AAHPER Division for Men's Athletics (DMA) and the Women's Section applied for membership in the United States Olympic Committee (USOC) multiple membership category. At the same time, they requested memberships on various AAU committees. This was important in that it confirmed adoption of a more favorable stance about high level competition.

Summary

Women physical educators were altering their conception of competition and their service to amateur athletics throughout the postwar years. However, it was to take the entire 1950s to complete the process of change and move toward governance power that would include varsity athletics. When the NSWA became a division, The Division for Girls and Women in Sport (DGWS) of The American Association for Health, Physical Education and Recreation (AAHPER) rather than just a section, it gained power and prestige. The DGWS now had stature to reach out to different sports organizations and to develop cooperative relationships with other sporting establishments.[15] This process, that continued through the early 1960s, might be called the "age of transition." For the nation's high schools, it would mean turning to the boys' athletic organizations for control of girls' athletics. This was not the case for the college level because the women of DGWS closed ranks and formed an organizational structure that would control women's collegiate athletics until the early 1980s. In the public domain the DGWS worked with AAU to develop basketball rules, officials, and rule modifications.

Basketball in the 1950s, as in the 1920s, provided the impetus for developing interscholastic and intercollegiate athletics. It drew the most attention and took much of the time and energy of the DGWS. Phebe Scott commented on the era: "So goes women's basketball; so goes women's sports." Basketball grew by leaps and bounds. This was especially true in AAU-sponsored teams, in small high schools and colleges, and even in well established colleges under women's leadership. While play days had completely given way to sports days, the sports days steadily moved toward varsity basketball teams. First the women physical educators started "coaching" in sports days, then they competed in "informal scrimmages" with nearby schools, and finally they participated in acknowledged varsity competition.[16]

The question of the 1950s was about DGWS's fundamental position regarding competition for girls and women. In the 1920s they had maintained the stance that they were not "anti-competition," but only concerned about the "right kind of competition." In the 1950s the burning issue was who should control the "right kind" of competition, rather than ought there to be high level competition at all. The answer had to be "for the good of those who play."

DGWS — 1960s

In the early years of the 1960s decade, President John F. Kennedy formed a Commission on the Status of Women to explore the function and to expand the role of women in our democratic society. As chair of the committee, Eleanor Roosevelt stated in June of 1962:

> I feel confident that in the years ahead many of the remaining outmoded barriers of women's aspirations will disappear. . . . Americans will have a better chance to develop their individual capacities. . . .[17]

The Commission's report, *American Women*, along with Betty Friedan's *The Feminine Mystique*, ushered in the modern era of the women's liberation movement.[18] Several important civil rights actions contributed to expanding the rights of women. These included the Equal Pay Act of 1963 and the 1972 Education Amendments; Title VII of the Civil Rights Act of 1964 as amended by the Equal Employment Opportunity Act of 1972; and the Executive Order enacted in 1965. The Executive Order required educational institutions with federal contracts to comply with equal opportunity practices. Federal intervention in concert with the women's liberation movement awakened a quest for equality by young female student-athletes and inspired their leaders and teachers to act.

In the 1960s (and 1970s) DGWS was a powerful organization in the growth of athletics. It provided the leaders for the new CIAW/AIAW organization and took control of rules modification, standards, and officiating for most team sports. Though not an enforcement agent, it continued publishing rules and maintaining liaison relationships with most sport governing bodies and cordial interactions with AAU and the USOC. DGWS was in control of women's college athletics and contributed guidance and expertise for development of girls high school varsity programs.

The decade included a study Conference on Competition, a National Conference on Sports Programs for College Women, changes in policies and guidelines to aggressively encourage varsity athletics, the formation of the Commission on Intercollegiate Athletics for Women (CIAW), and enthusiastic cooperation with the Olympic Development Committee of the USOC. The Women's Division pledged itself to intramural, varsity, and Olympic competition. The organization offered guidance and encouragement to women in secondary schools to participate in the state associations for girls' championships. The DGWS's most pivotal decade ended with dramatic changes in their basketball rules.

Move toward high level competition.   Two of the most outspoken physical educators in the early 1960s were Phebe Scott and Katherine Ley. They favored opportunities for the new breed of skilled female athletes anxious to find self-expression and unlimited competitive opportunities. Although both experienced criticism from their mentors and peers, they nonetheless tried to convince the DGWS membership that through controlled athletics they could provide necessary athletic experiences. In 1961 Scott reminded the DGWS Executive Council that girls were going outside the school setting for competition not available at school. Further, she commented,

> Whether we like it or not, we have educated a whole generation of women to believe that somehow there was something slightly evil or immoral in competition for the highly skilled girl. The time has come to decide if the highly skilled girl is our responsibility or not. If we decide she is, then it is time to do some re-evaluation of our policy statements and standards. . . . We cannot be bound by the traditions and thinking of the past.[19]

Ley followed in 1962 by asking the DGWS women to do two things in relation to the Olympic movement:

> Train the best we have to perform to the best of their ability. At the same time, promote all sports for all girls and women so that eventually we will have more prospects [for the Olympics] from which to choose the best.[20]

DGWS/DMA Values Conference.   The DGWS and Division for Men's Athletics (DMA) planned a joint conference called Conflicts in Values— Implications for Sports at the National Music Camp in Michigan in June 1962. The two organizations' goal was to seek answers to cultural changes while probing the needs and values of high level competition for men as well as women. The participants explored not only what were the values of competition but what was the role of competition for women and men. The discussion led to recommendations of changes that ought to occur in men's athletics. They also agreed about how women ought to proceed with the growth and development of girls and women's athletics. Because of the extensive interest in this topic, there was a great demand for the publication *Values in Sport* that resulted from the conference.[21]

New Policies and Guidelines.   Other women's voices joined Scott and Ley asking that DGWS take new directions and develop new policies. The 1963 *Policies and Standards* publication actively encouraged varsity and elite competition. Certainly these policies reflected a new philosophical commitment to competitive athletics. This landmark policy dramatically changed the direction of sport programs for girls and women.[22] A Study Conference on Competition in 1965 led to the first publication of guidelines for conducting interscholastic and intercollegiate competition.[23] Soon after this the Extramural Joint Committee dissolved and the DGWS created the CIAW. The desire for self-determination in female athletic governance prompted the Division to support the formation of the CIAW.

Formation of the CIAW.   The Commission on Intercollegiate Athletics for Women was primarily the "brainchild" of Phebe Scott. She saw an immediate need for national championships and control of athletics that should be under the leadership of women. The CIAW's mission was to expand the number of national collegiate sport championships to sports other than golf and tennis. Its function was (1) to establish a framework and organizational pattern to control competition and set standards, (2) to encourage the formation of local and regional governing bodies for women's athletics, (3) to sanction tournaments, and (4) to sponsor national championships. The CIAW sponsored national championships in six different sports in 1970–71 before the decision to become a formal organization with an institutional membership.[24] This new structure was called the Association for Intercollegiate Athletics for Women (AIAW).

Olympic Cooperation.   Capitalizing on the renewal of interest in high level competition, DGWS and the Women's Board of the USOC's Olym-

A fruitful cooperative relationship was solidified between DGWS and the Women's Board of the U.S. Olympic Committee through their joint sponsorship of National Sport Institutes in the 1960s. As DGWS began to expand its governing functions to cover varsity athletics, its leadership became increasingly aware of the lack of trained coaches. With help from the U.S. Olympic Committee, women were able to gain skills necessary for higher level teaching and training in a variety of Olympic sports. Because of the great need for officials, the Fifth National Institute included basketball officiating. In January 1969, experienced women basketball officials were able to work on floor practice under expert guidance and were then critiqued on their officiating techniques.

pic Development Committee co-sponsored a series of five National Sports Institutes.[25] As a consequence of having turned their backs on high level competition most physical educators were left with insufficient expertise to coach or officiate high level competitors. Thus the purpose of the institutes was to improve the quality of teaching and coaching advanced skills in many of the Olympic sports.

The first institute in 1963 was for track and field and gymnastics. Public schools had neglected teaching both of these sports and the United States had recently performed poorly in the Olympics (1948–56 Olympics). Each institute participant (about 200 per institute) was responsible for sharing their new knowledge by conducting workshops in their state or county. In this way an estimated 25,000 additional teachers benefited from the advanced teaching techniques for skilled women. In 1966 and again in 1969, the Development Committee selected basketball for emphasis in the institutes. Because of the desperate need for more highly qualified women officials, the 1969 institute also included basketball officiating.

Significantly, the co-sponsorship of institutes by USOC/DGWS did much to lesson tensions between the USOC and women physical educators. It was the beginning of an alliance that is still bearing fruit.[26]

AAU/DGWS Basketball Rules.   In 1961 the DGWS Rules Committee incorporated the roving player (part of AAU's rules for nearly 20 years) and an experimental rule on dribbling. These new rules represented a major step toward the final consolidation of rules and a truly joint DGWS/AAU Rules Committee. The basketball committee's rationale for this change was as follows: "It seemed necessary and propitious to make compromises for the good of women's basketball due to the present problems as well as to forestall anticipated ones."[27] Some others suggested an additional reason was to favor the highly skilled female athlete. As was usual for major rule changes, there was a lengthy trial period and a survey of opinions by the Basketball Committee. Had the Basketball Committee actually abided by the data from a majority of the members who answered their survey, they would not have changed the rules to the "rover" game.[28] There is much evidence in the literature insinuating that the major changes in basketball occurred in order to minimize differences with AAU and to eliminate the two sets of rules. The conservative physical educators complained bitterly that "we were ruining girls' and women's sport because now we are letting the rules turn out to be more like the men's game than the women's game."[29]

Sara Jernigan, an officer of the DGWS, claimed to receive 1,000 letters protesting the 1961 experimental rules. "They simply were too much like the boys' game" the protesters complained. Furthermore a typical response hints at the underlying tone of the letters: "the measuring stick seemed always to turn to the boys' rules to compare their likenesses and the evils which might result."[30] Certainly the question of men coaches and men officials was partly one of control, and the new rules catered to men and their control. So many of the letters seem to suggest, "If men control the sport, how can women control the welfare of the female athlete?"[31]

Basketball's most dramatic changes   for girls and women actually occurred between 1966 and 1970, not with the rover player game. In 1966 the unlimited dribble became official. In 1969 the five player full court game was experimental. The experimental rules became the official rules in 1971. One fact is clear: The three major rule changes effectively destroyed Baer's and Berenson's rules, returning the game more to Naismith's rules.

Given the difficulty the National Basketball Committee experienced in the change to the rover game, it is ironic that the anticipated criticism about the five player game simply didn't occur. Because the committee had envisioned major difficulties there was a lengthy trial period and several questionnaires of opinions. Teachers, coaches, players, and officials received questionnaires asking their views of the rule changes. Strange as it may seem, although these rules were drastic changes, over 90 percent of the respondents favored the five player game. The women were not upset at the five player game, but some were not sure they approved the unlimited dribble, or the 30-second clock. There were a few strong voices of protest about the potential roughness that would surely result from a full court game, and that the new game clearly was the men's game.[32]

In response to the survey, the charges, and the rule changes, the Basketball Committee reminded the membership that their decision always centered on the welfare of the individual female athlete, and these rules were no exception. They further defended this decision based on the backing of the medical community and most of the public sector of the sports milieu. The American Medical Association had gone on record that girls and women were strong and healthy enough for the new vigorous game and that the public demanded it.[33] "The public as spectators didn't understand the differences between girls and boys basketball rules and why the girls couldn't cross the middle line and why charging was different. They would boo and that would upset the players, because the spectators would think that the officials had called it wrong."[34] The committee stood united and firm: women would play the five player full court game. The DGWS/AAU Joint Basketball Committee would function as the official Women's Basketball Rules Committee. It was a new era and athletic revolution. The aggressive fast paced five player, full court, 30-second clock, and tie ball rules seem to symbolize the women's reform movement. The organization was ready for the modern game of women's basketball.[35]

Summary

The decade of the 1960s came to a close with the DGWS's new directional pathway clear. Their pyramid concept of athletics would now include highly competitive athletics for girls and women in the educational domain. At the same time DGWS offered support for the non-school agencies that fostered elite competition through the Olympic movement. In addition, the National Girls Athletic Association, a substructure in the AAHPER, encouraged its members to sponsor play days and sport days and to move toward varsity athletics.[36] Similarly, DGWS encouraged women high school teachers, coaches, and administrators to work cooperatively with their high school athletic associations, to assist in the development of competitive programs, and to use DGWS rules. The DGWS continued its traditional services through the 1960s, including the publication of the *Guides* with their accompanying rules, strategies, skills, and officiating techniques. A strong Affiliated Board of Officials (over 11,000 officials) responded to the needs of girls and women participating throughout the nation. State representatives in basketball and other sports and chairs of various sport committees became part of the ever growing network of volunteer workers within the association's 13,000 membership.[37] During this period, research, standards, publications and officiating training and rating continued to be the range of services offered. The association also maintained strong liaisons with sport-governing bodies.

The era ended with the first national AAU championship using the five player game and the first National Collegiate Invitational basketball championships (held at West Chester College). Carol Eckman, basketball coach at West Chester College, initiated and directed the first National Intercollegiate Championship. She orchestrated selection of teams from many parts of the country who represented the nation's best. The championship was sanctioned by the CIAW.[38] By then 80 percent of the colleges and universities had some form of basketball extramural competition, as did well over 50 percent of the high schools of the country. So on the eve of Title IX, varsity competition, at least in basketball, was found at all levels and within both educational and public domains. The AAU/USOC and women's international basketball teams were competing and schools were providing a majority of the coaches, managers, and players for the teams.

DGWS/NAGWS — 1970s

In the 1970s struggle for equality, the women's movement, particularly the Women's Equality Action League (WEAL) and the National Organization of Women (NOW), contributed immeasurably to the sports movement. The women's groups used two approaches. One was to gain legal access to equality and the other was to gain social access to equality. Local feminist groups were extremely active and successful both in dealing with sexism as a social disease and addressing the wrongs in sports through litigation. A multitude of legal actions resulted in giant strides on behalf of competitive athletics. The court cases that dealt with the DGWS/AIAW scholarship issue (which forced athletic scholarship upon AIAW), girls' access to Little League, and opportunity for access to boys' teams or single sex teams provided a legal basis for sex equity within the sport movement. The headway made in these court cases has had lasting effects on women in sport.[39]

Because NAGWS's national headquarters was in Washington, D.C., with a full complement of paid staff and many volunteer workers, it was a prime mover in lobbying Congress. The most important task was to monitor the development of the Guidelines, compliance regulations, and enforcement of the Education Amendments of 1972 (Title IX). Together with the work of the women's organizations discussed above, the NAGWS/AIAW lobbied for women in sport regularly.

The traditional services of the DGWS/NAGWS continued through the period. These services included publishing the *Guides*, maintaining a strong affiliated Board of Officials, focusing (with a new emphasis) on research and liaison relationships, and the initiation of national coaches conferences throughout the country. The association devoted much of its work to forming the AIAW.

In 1974 the division became an association, the National Association for Girls and Women in Sport. This status permitted greater autonomy in the alliance (AAHPER) and enabled the Association to provide broader services through its substructures. Coinciding with this new freedom was the Association's work with the Olympic movement, Title IX, and the Amateur Sports Act. Also, secondary school and college athletics experienced phenomenal growth. Mergers of men's and women's physical education and athletic departments were to change the face and mission of NAGWS. They would also contribute to the demise of AIAW. All of these events are integral to the story of NAGWS in the 1970s.

Research endeavors were particularly significant, as illustrated by the three NAGWS volumes titled *DGWS/NAGWS Research Reports*. Vital social and psychological issues about women in sport appeared in two other publications sponsored by NAGWS, *Coping with Controversy* and *Equality in Sport for Women*. These publications signify a commitment to understanding the physiological, sociological, and psychological aspects of women in sport and to understanding the critical issues of equality present in women's sport.[40]

Coaching Clinics. The creation of National Coaches Conferences was an important activity of the NAGWS which would be a central focus for the next decade. The purpose was to prepare teachers and coaches for the highly skilled elite athletes as well as the improved skills of the regular students in classes. The Conferences had the top women basketball coaches as staff with locations throughout the country. While basketball was taught at a majority of the Conferences, other sports also received attention.[41]

Association for Intercollegiate Athletics for Women. By the late 1960s it became painfully clear to the DGWS leadership that it could not both expand opportunity and control athletics on the collegiate level through its CIAW volunteer individual membership structure. Thus, the leaders developed a unique vision of competition based on an alternate educational model of athletics designed to avoid the commercialization of

Sue Gunter, of Stephen F. Austin State University (Texas), serves as clinician to prepare physical education teachers and coaches for improved basketball skills during the NAGWS Coaches Conference held at Boise State University (Idaho) in September 1978.

the men's model by focusing primarily on the athlete as a student. While the story of AIAW cannot be fully told here, it deserves more than a passing comment because of its influence upon the entire athletic community.

As in the past, the focus of the new intercollegiate governance structure remained on the individual participant in her primary role as a college student. The justification for such athletic programs was their educational value. The AIAW developed rules, policies, and procedures with these philosophical tenets in mind. It also had an active student representation in all major functions of the Association, including the Executive Board and Appeals Board. The AIAW, then, as an outgrowth of DGWS's vision, provided an experimental educational model of competitive athletics. The model had an egalitarian rather than a major/minor sport concept. Its regulations were initially framed on the DGWS/CIAW Procedures, Guidelines, and Standards. In order to have complete autonomy, AIAW became a separate legal entity from NAGWS in July 1979. It nonetheless maintained a close affiliation with NAGWS/AAHPERD.[42]

At the height of its influence, 1980–81, over 99,000 female athletes participated in AIAW events. Furthermore:

> AIAW offered a program of 39 national championships in 17 different sports to more than 6,000 women's teams in 960 member colleges and universities. The same year institutions of higher education provided more than $30 million in financial aid to able female athletes.[43]

Throughout its short life (1971–82), the AIAW provided leadership and development of intercollegiate programs well beyond its founders' dreams. Its success, however, was in a real sense central to its demise, as the National Collegiate Athletic Association (NCAA)/National Association of Intercollegiate Athletics (NAIA) "took over" the role of conducting championships for women at all NCAA/NAIA institutions. The leadership of the AIAW were forced to relinquish their dream of an alternative educational model of athletics. They had to reconcile themselves to a piece of the existing NCAA pie of privilege, power, and prestige. In the process of NCAA's "take-over," women in athletics irrevocably lost control of women's athletics.

Olympic Movement and Amateur Sports Act. Perhaps the most significant united effort by NAGWS/AIAW in the Olympic movement was to demand that the President's Commission on Olympic Sports devote attention to the needs of female amateur athletes. The NAGWS/AIAW spent a great deal of time, energy, and funds lobbying for enactment of the Amateur Sports Act (ASA) of 1978.

The original Olympic report by the President's Commission did not include discussion of women's sports. The AIAW/NAGWS reacted to the report with such vigor that the Commission undertook a study of women's sports. Its final publication addressed the needs in women's sports and ultimately led to the ASA.[44] As a result of the AIAW and NAGWS objections, the Act passed by Congress contained important concessions for women in the Olympic movement. It mandated $16 million to completely revamp the USOC. The Act provided funding and empowerment for individual National Sport Governing Bodies (NGBs) to control their own Olympic sport. The Act also set up fairer representation including more female Olympians and women leaders on NGB boards and in the USOC House of Delegates. It provided seed money for elite athletes and a yearly sports festival for junior and national team competitions. Colorado Springs became the headquarters for the USOC and any NGB wishing to maintain its offices there. The site also serves as an Olympic Training Center for all Olympic sport programs. Important ASA provisions that impact on women include mandated grassroots developmental funds for all women's Olympic sports, more funding for research on women athletes, and more training opportunities for female athletes at Olympic Training Centers. The financial support and opportunity for elite competition, such as for women basketball players in national and international play, are results of the Amateur Sports Act.[45]

The 1970s are rich in cooperative efforts between the USOC/NGBs and NAGWS/AIAW. Especially basketball has benefited by sharing college players and coaches of national and international basketball teams. The National Sports Festival, with junior and national basketball teams, international junior and senior tours, and championships increase opportunities for women athletes.

Basketball, of course, is also a sport in the Pan Americans Games, the World University Games, and the Olympics. In all of these events the country has profited by the intercollegiate programs in colleges and universities. All coaches for these teams come out of the college ranks, as have most of the players on the U.S. Women's Olympic basketball teams.

Title IX of the Education Amendments of 1972. This Congressional action states: "No person in the United States shall, on the basis of sex, be excluded from participation in, be denied the benefits of, or be subjected to discrimination under any education program or activity receiving federal financial assistance."[46] This unusual governmental intervention in education and sport demanded full compliance by secondary schools and colleges by July 21, 1978, with the guidelines and implementation regulations published in June 1975. This was the most significant single piece of federal legislation to affect the growth and expansion of girls and women in sport first in education, and then in the public sector.

Title IX was a two-edged sword which ultimately led to the male dominated governance of women's athletics. Yet it proved to be the catalyst for "A Golden Age of Sport for Girls and Women." Equality through Title IX was an aspiration first of the women's movement and then the cry of women within the sports domain. While criticized for their aggressive political stance on behalf of equality for women in society, female leaders of the NAGWS/AIAW saw the issue of equal rights as central. They began to define equality, however, not only as a participation question but in terms of the male model of athletics. The AIAW suspended, in part, their focus on an alternative athletic model as they won the battle for implementation of Title IX guidelines.[47]

The success of NAGWS/AIAW on the issues of Title IX has led to unbelievable growth in high school and collegiate athletics. (Recreational sports also grew by leaps and bounds.) The National Federation, for example, reported a growth in the number of female participants from 294,000 in 1971–72 to over 1,800,000 in 1981. The number of sports available to girls at the high school level increased from 14 in 1971 to over 30 in 1980–81. By the 1980s, 35 percent of the high school participants on varsity teams were female.[48]

Mergers of Physical Education Departments.   Title IX was also detrimental for the NAGWS, as it had been for AIAW and high school athletic programs. With Title IX came the merger of men's and women's departments of physical education and men's and women's athletic departments in all educational institutions. With each new merger, women administrators and directors of physical education and women's athletics were demoted to secondary positions. Men athletic directors and heads of physical education departments were almost automatically given control of the merged departments. The mergers not only affected women physical educators and coaches in thousands of school systems, but caused NAGWS to lose its authority over rules and officiating and most of its jurisdiction over women's athletics.[49]

A concurrent series of events in collegiate athletics was closely paralleled in the state athletic associations. Men's high school athletic associations began offering state championships for girls. Women were most often included only in advisory roles and rarely held decision making positions in these associations. They, too, moved down from positions of authority when physical education departments merged. Men took over coaching, officiating, athletic directorships, and, through the National Federation, began publishing girls' rules in basketball. The

The title game for women's basketball during the 1978 National Explorer Olympics is an example of the expanded opportunities for competition opened to women in the 1970s.

Federation became the dominant figure in governance of girls' athletics. State by state, women lost control over athletics, and often physical education as well. With the mergers in departments and the mandate for coeducational classes, basketball was often cut out of the programs because it seemed too difficult to teach coeducational basketball classes.

After the mergers, the primary role of NAGWS for the secondary school systems was that of an advocacy organization. It offered direction and advice on leadership strategies for the teachers. The NAGWS leaders encouraged the women to move into the male dominated state associations to gain leadership roles and to use the NAGWS rules.

Summary

The decade of the 1970s saw no major basketball rule controversies or changes in rules, after the initial reaction to the five player game, the 30-second clock, and the issue of using international rules. However there were drastic changes in the area of officiating (see Koenig's article) and loss of dominant leadership roles for NAGWS members. AIAW, however, did have a greater role in modification of the basketball rules. The AAU/NAGWS Joint Basketball Committee expanded to include several other basketball organizations. The battle for use of the NAGWS rules continued state by state. Most states and individual school systems used the National Federation's rules. The NAGWS achieved in great measure the aims set forth by the leadership of the 1960s and 1970s— the dual aims of improving sport performance and participation for girls and women. Furthermore it established a governance structure for collegiate athletics. The Association had affiliations with all the major sport governing bodies.

Perhaps its greatest accomplishment was in the passage and monitoring of Title IX. Basketball profited enormously from the federal legislation that mandated equality and opportunity for female athletes. Certainly basketball was the most popular varsity sport for girls and women. Its rules were fairly stable, and except in the high schools, issues about the control of rule changes had been temporarily resolved.

NAGWS—1980s

The decade of the 1980s had a new agenda for women. Women moved to the marketplace in larger numbers. The new work demographic seemed to be leading to a new form of male-female equality as "fully human" beings in family, economy, and sports life.

By the end of the 1980s AIAW was "taken over" by NCAA/NAIA. Women's basketball rules were no longer published by NAGWS. The National Federation published the high school rules and the NCAA the collegiate rules. However, before NCAA started publishing the women's basketball rules, NAGWS and the Women's Basketball Coaches Association (WBCA) worked together to gain adoption of the smaller basketball for collegiate women. The National Coaches Conferences and the work of the Affiliated Boards of Officials (ABO) continued to be important functions of the Association. A major role of NAGWS was as an advocacy organization. Another important NAGWS role was to maintain strong liaisons with the USOC/NGBs and other sport organizations. A third major effort was generation of a network with other women's sport groups (e.g., Women's Sport Foundation (WSF), WBCA, and a Coalition for Women in Education).

The NAGWS joined with the USOC and the Women's Sport Foundation (WSF) in a major conference on a New Agenda for Women's Sport. Members of NAGWS cooperated with Miller Lite in an extensive *Lite Sports Report*. Title IX left untouched pervasive inequalities in leadership so NAGWS accepted the task of addressing these inequalities.

The NAGWS is no longer a true partner in the development of sport opportunities. Instead, it provides through networking the information essential for service to the membership and it trains coaches and leaders. It also provides a horizontal link to the grass roots. The primary change in focus of the NAGWS is its concentration on advocacy rather than a governance structure. Its goal is to regain leadership positions and to support women coaches, officials, and athletic personnel for schools and the nonschool agencies, as well as to continue to support opportunities for girls and women in competitive athletics.

New Agenda Conference.   In keeping with this new goal, the NAGWS joined with the USOC and the WSF to sponsor a conference in 1983, which gathered together an impressive array of influential men and women. The conference, "The New Agenda: A Blueprint for the Future of Women's Sports," was a milestone event, setting the tone and direction for the future. It had excellent visibility and planned follow-up programs, which have enhanced the opportunities for female athletes and encouraged inclusion of women in leadership roles. The Conference steering committee announced its purpose/goals:

> With increased participation levels, our society has undergone a major change in attitude toward the women in sport. Woman's ability to compete, her potential prowess, her wish to be recognized, and her desire to be a lifelong participant needed to be discussed in light of these changed attitudes and perceptions. The motivated, highly skilled athlete was not the only concern of the new age. Of equal importance was the continuing support of sport and fitness opportunities for all women from the cradle to grave."[50]

The spin-off from the Conference not only led to other conferences, but cemented a network of women's sport organizations that were able to work together to successfully lobby Congress for a yearly National Women in Sport Day. The network also triumphantly supported the Restoration Act of 1988, which restores the original intent of Title IX.

The Conference report, together with the Miller Lite sports report, substantiates society's acceptance of the female athlete.[51] Over 88 percent of the population sampled is willing, for example, for a daughter to be a professional athlete. Over 82 percent of all respondents indicate participation in sports does not diminish a woman's femininity. In addition, nearly 50 percent want equal funding, and an additional 32 percent believe girls in school sport programs should have more funding. Equally important to the future of sports for girls and women is the fact that the same group believes that pay for professional female athletes should not differ from the pay for male athletes in the same sport.

Current Status.   Title IX has left untouched pervasive fundamental inequities in leadership, decision-making authority, coaching systems, and role models for girls in all athletic situations. Within educational athletics, for example, the current ratio of female to male athletes is

1:2. The same is true of female Olympians. Uhlir notes that "despite widespread belief that women have arrived in the sacrosanct bastions of athletic power and privilege within the university the reality is otherwise."[52] Acosta and Carpenter substantiate this loss of administrators, adding that just barely 50 percent of coaches of women's teams are women, compared to nearly 80 percent a decade ago. In 38 percent of collegiate institutions, there are no female administrators.[53] The NCAA maintains 93 percent male voting representatives, while committee, legislative, and executive status has not increased beyond the quota system. According to Lopiano, there is little expectation this will change significantly.[54] NCAA has not only taken over officiating, but now publishes the women's *Basketball Guide*. The high school athletic programs for girls function entirely under the auspices of the male dominated state athletic associations, who use the Federation rules. The success of Title IX has led to male governance power in all amateur sports from high school competition to college, nonschool agencies, and the Olympic movement.

Summary

The NAGWS has traditionally been the defender of women's rights to participate in a diversity of sports, and that role continues. Its emphasis has shifted now toward eradicating the inequalities in women's sport leadership. In addition to the political goals, the NAGWS membership is a true network and has been since the 1920s when state basketball representatives and officials rose through a mentor system into positions of national leadership.

In the 1980s, and hopefully in the future, the NAGWS membership is unrelenting in their commitment to sport for girls and women. As such, the NAGWS has a unique mission: To join other sports organizations to shape the future according to the new values and sport enthusiasm emerging from "A Golden Age of Sport for Women." This mission promotes the NAGWS's dual mottoes: "A sport for every girl and every girl in a sport" and "The one purpose of sports for girls and women is for the good of those who play."

Notes

This paper is a revision and expansion of previously published articles: Joan S. Hult, "Women's Struggle for Governance in U.S. Amateur Athletics," *International Review for the Sociology of Sport*, 24 (November 1989); Joan S. Hult,

"NAGWS: 1960–1985," *Journal of Health, Physical Education, Recreation and Dance* 56 (April 1985, Centennial 1885–1985 Issue). Acknowledgement is gratefully given to Carol Jackson for her work as editorial consultant.

In conducting the research, extensive use was made of the archives of the National Association for Girls and Women in Sport in the American Alliance for Health, Physical Education, Recreation and Dance Archives, Reston, Va. Unless otherwise noted, materials cited are from archives. The archives also include the basketball sport guides used in this study.

1. The *Guides* used in this article are *Official Women's Basketball Guides* for different years. The *Guides* were edited by National Section for Women's Athletics (NSWA)/National Section for Girls and Women's Sport (NSWGS)/Division for Girls and Women's Sport (DGWS)/National Association for Girls and Women in Sport (NAGWS). From 1950 to 1979 the *Guides* were published in Washington, D.C. by the American Association for Health, Physical Education, and Recreation. From 1979 to 1985 the *Guides* were published in Reston, Va. by the American Alliance for Health, Physical Education, Recreation and Dance (AAHPERD).

2. Joan S. Hult, "The Governance of Athletics for Girls and Women: Leadership by Women Physical Educators, 1899–1949," *Research Quarterly for Exercise & Sport* (Centennial Issue, 1985): 64–77.

3. Division for Girls and Women in Sport (DGWS), *Official Women's Volleyball Guide 1957–1958* (Washington, D.C.: AAHPER, 1957), 88.

4. National Section for Girls and Women's Sports (NSGWS), *The Story of the National Leadership Conference on Girls and Women's Sport* (Washington, D.C.: American Association for Health, Physical Education, and Recreation, June 1955), 45; "How Was the Estes Park Conference?" *Journal of Health, Physical Education, and Recreation* 26 (September 1955): 17–18.

5. NSGWS, *The Story of the National Leadership Conference*, 17–19. See also Christine White, "Extramural Competition and Physical Education Activities for College Women," *Research Quarterly* 19 (October 1954): 244–363; Naomi Laura Leyhe, "Attitudes of the Women Members of the AAHPER Toward Competition in Sports for Girls and Women" (DPh. diss., Indiana University, 1955). See also National Section for Girls and Women's Sport Eastern District, "Leadership Conference Report" (Held in Northampton, Mass.) (March 1957).

6. Division for Girls and Women's Sport (DGWS) and National Association of Physical Education for College Women (NAPECW), *National Conference on Social Changes and Implications for Physical Education and Sports Program* (Washington, D.C.: AAHPER, June 1958), especially Jane Mott, "Implications of Estes Park Conference for DGWS," 102–104.

7. "Golf Minutes of the Executive Committee of NSGWS" (Chicago, December 27, 1956); "Report of the Golf Tripartite Committee to NJSECW" (June 1959).

8. "Report of the Tripartite Council on Extramural Sports Competition for College Women," Athletic and Recreation Federation of College Women, Division for Girls and Women's Sport, National Association of Physical Education for College Women (June, 1957): 6–11.

9. Lee W. Anderson, "The Development of Basketball Rules for Girls" (A Supplement, 1&2, n.d.), in *The History, Organization, and Function of the Division for Girls and Women's Sports, 1940–62*," Paulajean Searcy (Master's

Thesis, Smith College, 1962), 36; Letter from Rachel Bryant to Frances McGill "Re:NFSHSAA," March 20, 1969 (committee correspondence).

10. Helen B. Lawrence, "Survey of Number of Girls and Women Playing Basketball and the Rules Used," in *Official Basketball Guide September 1956–1957* (Washington, D.C.: AAHPER, 1956), 27–28.

11. Lee Anderson, "The Development of Basketball Rules"; National Basketball Committee of NSGWS, "An Explanation of the Rule Changes," in *Official Basketball Guide 1953–54* (Washington, D.C.: AAHPER, 1953), 43–46; Jane A. Mott, personal interview in Searcy, *History, Organization, and Function of DGWS*, 11.

12. Basketball Committee, "Explanation of Rule Changes," 43.

13. National Basketball Committee, "NBC Minutes and Report" in Board of Governors NSWA Minutes, 13. See also letter from Dorothy McQueen, School District of Philadelphia, to Grace Fox, n.d.

14. National Section for Girls and Women in Sport, "January Newsletter," (January 1950): 2; idem, "Minutes of the Legislative Board Meeting" (Chicago, 1952), 1; Letter from Josephine Fiske to Pauline Hodgdon, 25 April 1953.

15. Thelma Bishop, "DGWS: A Permanent AAHPER Division?" *Journal of Health, Physical Education, and Recreation* 28 (October 1957): 56.

16. Joan S. Hult, personal observation and interviews of peers in institutions in Minnesota, North Dakota, and California and personal interviews of colleagues throughout the country in the 50s and 60s.

17. *American Women*, The Report of the Commission (Washington, D.C.: Government Printing Office, 1963), vi.

18. *American Women*; B. Friedan, *The Feminine Mystique* (New York: Delaware Publishing Company, 1963).

19. Phebe Scott, "DGWS Minutes of the Executive Council," Special Report of "Competitive Discussion, March 21, 1961," 20–21, December 1961.

20. Katherine Ley, "A Philosophical Interpretation of the National Institute on Girls Sports," in *Proceedings: First National Institute on Girls Sports* (Washington, D.C.: AAHPER, 1964), 12.

21. Division for Girls and Women's Sport/Division of Men's Athletics, "Report of a National Conference on Values in Sports" in "DGWS Executive Meeting" October 1962; DGWS/DMA, *Values in Sport* A Joint Conference, DGWS/DMA, June 1962 Interlocken, Michigan (Washington, D.C.: AAHPER, 1962).

22. Division for Girls and Women's Sport, "New Policies Report" in "Minutes of the Executive Council" (Washington, D.C., December 1962), 28–30.

23. Division for Girls and Women's Sport, "Statement of Policies for Competition in Girls and Women's Sports," *Journal of Health, Physical Education, and Recreation* 34 (September 1963); Katherine Ley, "Are you Ready?" *Journal of HPER* 34 (April 1963): 20–22.

24. Phebe M. Scott and Celeste Ulrich, "Commission on Intercollegiate Athletics for Women," in *Sports Programs for College Women*, DGWS National Conference, June 1969 (Washington, D.C.: AAHPER, 1970), 50–52; Commission for Intercollegiate Athletics, "Procedures for Women's Intercollegiate Athletic Events," (n.d.), 1–8.

25. Sara S. Jernigan, "The Institute Challenge," in *Proceedings: First National Institute on Girls Sports*, University of Oklahoma, November 4–9, 1963 (Washington, D.C.: AAHPER, 1964), 3–4.

26. Sara S. Jernigan, interviewed by author on "DGWS Women in the Olympic Movement," at National AAHPERD Convention, Anaheim, Calif., March 29, 1983. See also *Proceedings* of the five DGWS Institutes on Girls Sports (Washington, D.C.: AAHPER).

27. National Basketball Committee, "Comments on Rules Changes," in *Official Women's Basketball Guide September 1961–September 1962* (Washington D.C.: AAHPER, 1961), 117–118.

28. National Basketball Rules Committee, "Basketball Rules Changes Proposed Experimentation," in a memo in Correspondence of the Basketball Committee (n.d.); Basketball Committee, "Comments on Rules Changes 1961–62," in *Basketball Guide 1961–62*, 117–118.

29. Shirley Winsberg, "National Basketball Committee, Correspondence File," 1961; idem, "Taking Ball from Opponent," in *Basketball Guide 1962–63* (Washington D.C.: AAHPER, 1962), 54–57.

30. Sara S. Jernigan interviewed by Pauline Hodgdon in "An Investigation of the Development of Interscholastic and Intercollegiate Athletics for Girls and Women from 1917–1970" (DrPE Diss., Springfield College, 1973), 132.

31. Jernigan interview, in Hodgdon, "Development of Interscholastic and Intercollegiate Athletics," 133.

32. National Basketball Committee, "You Decide," in *Basketball Guide 1970–1971* (Washington, D.C.: AAHPER, 1970), 137–138. See also, idem, "You Decided," in *Basketball Guide 1971–72* (Washington, D.C.: AAHPER, 1971), 31–34.

33. National Education Association and American Medical Association, "Joint Resolution on Sports for Girls and Women," Joint Committee on Health Problems in Education, 21–23 April 1968; American Medical Association, "Sports Opportunities for Girls and Women," *Journal of Health, Physical Education, and Recreation* 35 (Nov.–Dec. 1964): 64.

34. Rachel Bryant interviewed by Pauline Hodgdon, 24 May 1972, in "Development of Interscholastic and Intercollegiate Athletics."

35. Janette Sayre memo to Division for Girls and Women's Sports, "What's Going On," 17 January 1968; Mildred Barnes, "From Half Court to Full Court," *Basketball Guide 1971–72* (Washington, D.C.: AAHPER, 1971), 35–37. See also, Harriet Taylor, "Analysis of Data of DGWS Questionnaire," (Newton, Iowa: DGWS, May 1969).

36. The National Girls Athletic Association was a project of DGWS/AAHPER in 1962–63. It merged with DGWS. Similarly, the ARFCW affiliated with AAHPER under the auspices of DGWS with a separate consultant.

37. Rachel Bryant, "DGWS Promotional Information," Report of the consultant, August 1969. See also, for example, Officiating Service Area, "Handbook for Teaching Basketball Officiating"; Aletha Bond, "National Rating Boards: An Attempt at Officiating Consistency," *Journal of Health, Physical Education, Recreation* 49 (September 1978): 26–28.

38. Carol Eckman, "National Invitational Women's Collegiate Basketball Tournament," *Women's Sports Reporter* (Inaugural Issues Jan./Feb. 1970): 1.

39. E. A. Alden, "Feminism and Women's Sports: The Influence of Four Women's Organizations, 1960–1978" (MA Thesis, University of Maryland, 1983), 1–7, 9–13, 52–102. See also, Patricia Geadelmann et al., *Equality in Sport for Women* (Washington, D.C.: AAHPER, 1977).

40. Dorothy V. Harris, ed., *DGWS Research Reports: Women in Sports*, Vol. I *(Washington, D.C.: AAHPER, 1971)*; idem, *DGWS Research Reports: Women in Sports*, Vol. II (Washington D.C.: AAHPER, 1973); Marline Adrian and Judy Brame, eds., *NAGWS Research Reports*, Vol. III (Washington, D.C.: AAHPER, 1977); Barbara J. Hoepner, ed., *Women's Athletics: Coping With Controversy* (Washington, D.C.: AAHPER, 1974); Patricia Geadelmann et al., *Equality in Sport for Women.*

41. Coaches Council Report, "Coaches Conferences for 1973–74," in DGWS/NAGWS "Minutes of Executive Board of Governors." See also, "Report of Coaches Conferences Committee" for each year 1973–1982.

42. Hult, "Governance."

43. A. G. Uhlir, "The Wolf Is Our Shepherd: Shall We Not Fear?" *Phi Delta Kappan* 64 (November 1982): 173. The figures come from research by the AIAW National Office (but differ from later data).

44. Commission on Olympic Sports, *The Final Report of the President's Commission on Olympic Sports, 1975–77*, Vols. I and II (Washington, D.C.: Government Printing Office, 1977).

45. Amateur Sport Act of 1978: "Report of the Senate Committee on Commerce, Science, and Transportation" (Washington, D.C.: Government Printing Office, 1978).

46. U.S. Department of Health, Education, and Welfare, Office for Civil Rights, 1975, "Final Title IX Regulation Implementing Education Amendments of 1972: Prohibiting Sex Discrimination in Education" (Washington, D.C.: Government Printing Office, 1975).

47. A. M. Seha, "The Administration and Enforcement of Title IX in Intercollegiate Athletics," *Law and Inequality: A Journal of Theory and Practice* 2 (1) (1984): 121–325; J. S. Hult, "The Philosophical Conflicts in Men's and Women's Collegiate Athletics," *Quest* 32 (1980): 77–94; Hult, "Women's Struggle for Governance."

48. National Federation of State High School Associations, *Sports Participation Survey 1971–1981* (Kansas City, Mo.: NFSHSA, 1981).

49. C. Lehr, "Women in Sports Management: Fact or Fallacy Since Title IX?" poster presented at "The New Agenda," Washington, D.C., November 3–5, 1983; Uhlir, "The Wolf Is Our Shepherd," 172–76; R. V. Acosta and L. J. Carpenter, "Women in Sport" in *Sport and Higher Education*, J. O. Segrave and B. J. Becker, eds. (Champaign, Ill.: Human Kinetics), 313–325.

50. E. S. Auchincloss, D. V. Harris, and C. A. Oglesby, *The New Agenda: A Blueprint for the Future of Women's Sports* (San Francisco: Women's Sports Foundation, 1984), 3.

51. Auchincloss, *The New Agenda; The Miller Lite Report on American Attitudes Toward Sports* (New York: Research and Forecasts, Miller Brewing Co., 1983).

52. A. G. Uhlir, "Athletics and the University: The Post-Woman's ERA," *Academe* 4, (1987): 17–36.

53. Acosta and Carpenter, "Women in Sport," 313–325.

54. D. A. Lopiano, "A Political Analysis of the Possibility of Impact Alternatives for the Accomplishment of Feminist Objectives Within American Intercollegiate Sport," in *Fractured Focus*, ed. R. Lapchick (Lexington, Mass.: Lexington Books, 1986), 163–176.

14

Rachel E. Bryant

Twenty-One Years of Women's Leadership in Basketball—in Sport

Nancy Weltzheimer Wardwell

Rachel E. Bryant served AAHPER during the most dramatic changes in the conduct and expansion of sports for American girls and women. As the first consultant for physical education and girls and women's Sport (GWS*), she exerted a strong influence in the broad changes in policies and practices in the women's sport arena. Because of her long tenure at AAHPER and the nature and quality of her work, she was a primary figure in the transition from sports days to interscholastic and intercollegiate competition. In addition, because of her liaison role with the USOC she made significant contributions to the progress of American women in international sport. There is no doubt that Rachel Bryant's service to girls and women in sport was central to the organization's control and transition of basketball and collegiate governance of athletics.

This paper is an extension of Nancy Weltzheimer Wardwell, "Rachel E. Bryant: Contribution to Physical Education and Girls and Women's Sports" (Ed.D. dissertation, University of Toledo, 1979).

*"GWS" is used in this paper to simplify reference to the series of names used by the organization. Successively, the organization was known as the National Section on Women's Athletics (1932), National Section for Girls and Women's Sports (1953), Division for Girls and Women's Sports (1957), and National Association for Girls and Women's Sports (1974). Each new name signaled a significant philosophical or structural change for the group.

For 21 years, 1950–1971, Rachel represented GWS to millions of girls who learned and played sports and to the thousands of women who taught and coached sports. All were enriched by the countless numbers of *Sport Guides*, teaching materials, and the many conferences and conventions she engineered. She also *was* GWS to all the organizations that she served in a liaison role. She represented GWS at Amateur Athletic Union (AAU), National Collegiate Athletic Association (NCAA), the U.S. military, and various Olympic organizations. She was a dynamic and forceful professional whose kindness and gentle style influenced her staff, those working at the grass roots, GWS Board members and officers, and the representatives of allied organizations.

An educator from a family of educators, she loved and participated in sport from an early age. Her family loved swimming and were tennis "fanatics" but she grew to love basketball best. In high school at Bowling Green, Ohio, where her father was superintendent of schools, Rachel played on the girls basketball team. As was the tradition in her era, the girls team played before the boys' games, a tradition she later worked diligently to undo. Her position was generally as a side center in the three court game. As a college student at Ohio State, she took a basketball class and played basketball in intramural contests. Her undergraduate major was Romance languages and mathematics but she took many physical activity classes in her college days. "I elected everything I could get," she said.[1] Later, while teaching, she earned her certificate to teach physical education.

After graduation from college in 1928, Rachel taught and coached basketball at a school in Mentor, Ohio. She also joined a semi-professional basketball team sponsored by a taxi company in nearby Painesville. The team traveled all around the Great Lakes area competing against other industrial league teams. On that team she enjoyed at least one moment of glory when she made an appearance in the Cleveland Auditorium against the well-known national championship-calibre team, the Chicago Taylor Trunks. During the early minutes of the game she was fouled and confidently stepped to the free throw line and scored the first point of the game. As one would expect in competition with such a high ranking team as the Chicago Taylors, her team did not win the game. Neither did Rachel finish the season. Her county school superintendent came to observe her play and was very concerned about the brevity of the players' uniforms. Rachel dutifully retired from the team.[2]

In the autumn of 1936, Rachel left public school and began her first job in higher education. She taught eight years at Otterbein College in Ohio. World War II drew most of the men faculty into service and finally Rachel joined the Red Cross Field Service, serving in Italy, North

Africa, and the Philippines. Returning in 1947, she completed her doctorate at Ohio State. She taught two years at Florida State, then accepted the position of director of physical education for women at Mankato State in Minnesota.[3] In the fall of 1950 Rachel Bryant became the first GWS consultant.[4]

The Women's Section (GWS) at that time was a year-round working body making rules, editing *Sport Guides*, advising on policies and programs, conducting research studies, and performing whatever duties and related activities presented themselves.[5] That AAHPER identified the need to have a consultant specific to the interests of girls and women's sports was most timely and could be seen as a harbinger of change. During Bryant's years as consultant, she guided the organizational course of the GWS and represented the organization to others working with girls and women in sport, particularly the United States Olympic Committee (USOC). Because a major GWS activity in its early years was publications, a large portion of Rachel's time was devoted to preparing and publishing the vast numbers of *Sport Guides* and other materials. Perhaps her most lasting contribution was in developing the organization to govern women's intercollegiate sports and sponsor national championships for women.

A. S. Barnes and Company, a publisher that specialized in physical education books, published all the numerous GWS *Guides* for AAHPER. In 1947, the discontinuation of their publishing contract provided the impetus to secure a full-time consultant.[6] The materials for the *Guides* were obtained through an elaborate volunteer system of GWS subcommittees, but Carl Troester, the AAHPER executive secretary-treasurer, was responsible for editing and proofing the *Guides*. While the AAHPER office staff joined Troester in the work of producing the *Guides*, there was simply not enough time to edit and proof the volume of materials beginning to come out of GWS. Thus, Troester asked the AAHPER Board for a new position, and it was granted.[7]

After the details of a new consultant position were worked out by AAHPER, Troester wasted little time in identifying his candidate. "Rachel was the person I had my eye on as the person who could do the *Guides* and develop girls and women's sports."[8]

As soon as Rachel moved to Washington, D.C., she became responsible for Troester's previous tasks of editing, proofing, and publishing the *Guides*. When A. S. Barnes was publishing the *Guides*, the Women's Section received about $3,000 in royalties. By 1953, after Rachel and AAHPER had taken over the venture, they were involved in an operation grossing $60,000 that generated about $8,000 profit![9] Because Rachel worked directly with the printers, skillfully anticipating needs, suggesting and delegating assignments, and urging necessary revisions

Rachel Bryant served as AAHPER consultant for girls and women's sports during two decades of dramatic changes in women's athletics.

and additions, the operations were increasingly successful. Under her guidance and watchful eye, AAHPER's publications flourished.[10]

Rachel realized immediately the need to continually promote the publications, which she knew would concomitantly promote the organization. In 1956, she noted the outdated costumes and activities depicted in the *Guides*. It was obvious to her that they needed to be revised, so she sought and got authorization to develop a new cover and revise the format of the *Guides*. Thanks to her work, in 1958, when GWS had become the *Division* for Girls and Women's Sport (DGWS) the *Guides* in the "Sport Library for Girls and Women" had a new logo and cover format.[11]

At every opportunity, the published materials were displayed at state, district, and national AAHPER conventions. The national office designed the display boards and backgrounds while the GWS chairman had the responsibility of getting the space and setting up the displays. The revision and distribution of display boards fell to Bryant's office. The promotion of the *Guides* led to a constant increase in the number being sold. Figure 1 shows representative annual totals over three decades. The *Basketball Guides* consistently headed the list of titles sold. In addition to *Guides*, physical educators conducting basketball programs for girls and women bought the GWS-published Score Books,

Selected Articles, Technique Charts, outlines for the teaching of basketball officiating, and the filmstrip on basketball skills. Revenue from sales of their publications was a source of pride to GWS members as this was a primary source of income for GWS work and, in fact, for the whole AAHPER organization.[12]

During Rachel Bryant's years of service, teachers, students, coaches, and players purchased over 3,300,000 Sport Guides. The impressive publishing record of GWS dramatically illustrates the magnitude of the contribution made by Rachel and the women leaders of GWS who volunteered their time and talent to the cause of sports for girls and women.

Because of Rachel's total commitment to the GWS philosophy and standards, she believed it was of paramount importance to get up-to-date materials into the hands of women physical educators, other AAHPER members, and other sports providers and governing bodies in the public sector. Her goal was to distribute widely to all these organizations the competitive philosophy, the resultant standards, and GWS rules. In addition, a large part of her consultant role was to act as liaison to "affiliated groups." She worked tirelessly to get GWS rules adopted by sport associations in the public domain. She was successful in getting GWS rules used by the Armed Forces and was instrumental in basketball rules being translated into Japanese and Spanish.

Figure 1
PUBLISHING HISTORY OF GWS SPORT GUIDES
For selected years

Guide	1949–51	1959–61	1969–71
Aquatics	5,263	8,198	12,134
Archery-Riding	X	10,539	13,948
Basketball	99,047	72,834	101,377
Basketball Rules Reprint	X	58,114	40,556
Bowling-Fencing-Golf	X	9,104	14,119
Field Hockey-Lacrosse	18,671	26,114	43,783
Gymnastics	X	X	33,047
Individual Sports	7,675	X	X
Outing Activities and Winter Sports	132	2,862	4,519
Recreational Games	X	X	X
Soccer-Speedball	15,432	23,348	41,160
Softball	X	X	39,655
Softball-Track	13,324	33,815	X
Tennis-Badminton	14,929	29,726	36,257
Track-Field	X	X	36,257
Volleyball	X	43,100	72,994

The National Federation of State High School Athletic Associations (National Federation) was organized in 1920 and performed as a sanctioning service for interstate contests. It protected the athletic interests of high schools, promoted interscholastic athletics (which are educational in both objectives and method), and protected high school boys from exploitation for purposes having no educational implications. Neither AAHPER nor the subsidiary GWS were ever members of the Federation; however, they were allowed representatives at its meetings.[13] At her first National Section Legislative Board meeting in December 1950, Bryant suggested the group work to secure a woman on every state athletic association board affiliated with the National Federation.[14]

A major concern of the women was about the basketball rules that might be used in girls' programs. The GWS Legislative Board instructed Bryant to make contact through the National Education Association and its subordinate agencies such as the Department of School Principals and Superintendents. By April 1952, a joint committee of AAHPER, National Association of Secondary School Principals (NASSP), and the National Federation had been formed at the request of GWS. Bryant served as secretary of its Subcommittee on Standards in Athletics for Girls.[15]

One major project in this connection was the recodification in 1952 of GWS rules so that the language would be similar to that used in the rules for boys. Bryant served on the codification committee, and as a result was invited to speak at the National Convention of the Association of Secondary School Administrators. The topic of the panel was "Girls Athletics in the Educational Program."[16]

In an interview, Bryant recalled that the effort of rule modification was most significant because the boys rules were a jumble of add-ons and amendments.[17] The recodification process allowed some of the principles of the women's thinking to influence the boys basketball programs as well! As Karen Wilkins, a long-time girls basketball coach, explained: "Back when girls didn't compete against other schools, it didn't really matter what rules were used teaching basketball, but all the while we were having input on the Federation rules. What we ended up with were rules in keeping with the spirit of GWS."[18]

The physical education women leaders were concerned not only about school athletics, but equally about the programs in the public sector. The AAU was the major group providing sport opportunities outside the aegis of schools. The women of GWS had long been concerned about the wholesomeness of the programs provided by the AAU. In 1958, Rachel began working with the AAU as an invited observer and liaison. By 1964, the AAU committees included gymnastics, swimming, and track and field. In addition, Rachel served on the Foreign Relations Committee that approved plans for international competitions.[19]

The consultant's role on behalf of GWS in connection with the Olympic Development Institutes is a fascinating page of our history. It is fascinating because for many years the very notion of international competition for elite athletes was antithetical to the efforts of the women physical educators. For a variety of reasons, a GWS Olympic Study Committee was formed in 1947.[20] The committee developed a list of standards and recommendations. A major one was that the Olympic Committee seek the advice of leaders in physical education. Following this statement, the women did not wait for an invitation, but in 1950 applied directly for women's participation on Olympic committees. Patience and persistence would eventually pay off. In 1953, the USOC was still considering applications and would keep GWS advised.

Cooperation with the USOC

In 1956, Rachel attended a USOC Legislative Board meeting with Carl Troester. They had mapped out a strategy by which Troester would submit the GWS request. This time Kenneth "Tug" Wilson, president of the U.S. Olympic Association, spoke in favor of GWS's membership, stating that they had been awaiting it hopefully![21] A major agenda of USOC was their national imperative to prepare women to compete at the highest levels. As GWS moved toward acceptance of the need for high level competition, the USOC and GWS formed important lasting relationships for their later efforts to prepare outstanding world class athletes.

In 1958, the DGWS Executive Board learned that volleyball had been accepted as an Olympic sport in Rome. Since GWS was a member of the United States Volleyball Association, the minutes of the January 1959 meeting proclaimed, "This is the first time we have been so represented on an Olympic Committee."[22] Rachel had been working since 1952 with the USVBA seeking a common set of GWS/AAU Olympic rules. As a result of Rachel's liaison partnership, she was personally invited to serve on the Women's Sports Subcommittee of the Olympic Development Committee. Even after retirement, she maintained her representation with the U.S. Olympic Committee and the U.S. Volleyball Association.

Also in 1959, GWS received a letter from D. T. Nelson Metcalf, chairman of the Committee on Medical Training Services for the U.S. Olympic Committee. He requested names of women trainers who could be recommended for the women's teams at the 1950 Pan American Games at Chicago. Here was another door being opened to provide opportunities in the international sport scene for women. Unfortunately, there were no qualified women—but Rachel suggested it was an important issue. The request did trigger a fruitful discussion about ways the women could upgrade their qualifications and the potential role GWS should take in these matters.

In her March 1961 Consultant's Report, Rachel stated that she and other AAHPER staff had met with Tom Hamilton, chairman of the Olympic Development Committee. Hamilton had requested names of prominent women to serve on the Olympic Development Committee. He asked that the women focus on fencing, gymnastics, swimming, and track and field. In December 1962, Rachel presented a "Report on the International Sports Picture and Implications" to the GWS Executive Committee. She reported that the Women's Advisory Board of the U.S. Olympic Committee had approved in principle the idea of National Sports Institutes to be jointly sponsored by AAHPER and the Advisory Board of the USOC.[23]

A series of National Leadership Conferences were held in 1955 and 1958 at Estes Park, Colorado, and in 1962 at Interlochen, Michigan. At these conferences, the GWS position on competition, culture, and values was carefully examined by the leadership and distinguished consultants.[24] As the next logical step, a series of National Sport Institutes was conducted during 1963 to 1969. Each of the Institutes focused on teaching and coaching specific Olympic sports.

Rachel played a vital role in the success of these Conferences, and significantly in the five National Institutes. She was on the planning committees for all of them. In addition to her prodigious memory and knowledge of members to recruit, she promoted the conferences with a series of advertisements and mailings. In fact, she handled all the invitations, registration, study materials, and "thank-you" letters. She supervised the publication of thousands of copies of proceedings of the Institutes and the Conferences. All of the publications were much sought after by those who could not attend.[25]

Midwife for the CIAW

Katherine Ley was GWS chairman in 1962, the first commissioner of the Commission on Intercollegiate Athletics for Women (CIAW) in 1966, and later president of AAHPER. She noted: "It was Rachel who guided the changeover in the late 50s and 60s and who supervised the formation of the Commission on Intercollegiate Athletics for Women."[26] The CIAW (and later the Association for Intercollegiate Athletics for Women) was a result of the leaders' concern about who would govern women's athletics and how it should be governed to uphold the philosophical tenets and standards of GWS. Throughout this era, the GWS

As a member of association committees that made many important decisions, Bryant exerted a significant influence on the expanding women's sports arena. Shown above is the 1963 Steering Committee for the National Sport Institutes, which were instrumental in improving the teaching of basketball skills. Bryant is seated, second from left.

and its members, having previously resisted, were now eager to fulfill their dreams of an educational and wholesome sport experience for the highly skilled athletes. Because Rachel was deeply involved with each of these elements and orchestrated much of what occurred, she might be considered the "midwife" at the birth of the Commission.

The first meeting of the new CIAW was held June 21, 1966 at the National Intercollegiate Golf Tournament in Columbus, Ohio. Naturally, Rachel was present at that and all subsequent meetings in her capacity as consultant ex-officio.

On December 7, 1967, Rachel Bryant engineered a national press conference, called to announce the birth of the Commission on Intercollegiate Athletics for Women. Key journalists interested in women's sports were invited and Rachel enlisted an old family friend, Wilber Snypp (sports information director for The Ohio State University) to act as master of ceremonies. Katherine Ley officially announced the first schedule of National Women's Collegiate Championships. The membership of AAHPER were informed of the gala event in an article in the February 1968 *JOHPER*.[27]

Basketball is central to the issues surrounding the relationship of GWS to other associations governing men's sports. During the development of CIAW, the NCAA had clearly stated that they had no interest in sport programs for women. Shortly after the CIAW had been formed, however, the NCAA set up a committee to study the feasibility of NCAA's supervising women's intercollegiate sport! These were fighting words not only for CIAW but also for AAU. The AAU worked closely with GWS, but AAU controlled and prepared the women's teams for international competition and the Olympics. Bryant had steadfastly believed that if NCAA could control women's basketball, they would have a wedge for international recognition.[28] Basketball was, indeed, the prize NCAA sought.

To this point, in the dealings with NCAA, Bryant functioned primarily as a resource and clearinghouse for materials and personnel. Now, in a more assertive stance, she wrote a letter to Earl Ramer, president of NCAA, in which she spelled out the concerns of the CIAW and the women it represented. She requested representation for DGWS and CIAW at an August NCAA meeting. She also included a summary of the accomplishments and philosophies of GWS and CIAW.[29] Almost by return mail, Walter Byers invited Bryant to the "NCAA special committee concerning female intercollegiate athletic competition."[30]

In July 1971, the meeting took place with representatives of NCAA, AAHPER, GWS, and the newly formed AIAW. The NCAA plans were clear and both sides engaged in very sharp correspondence. On the eve of her retirement, Rachel Bryant wrote to Walter Byers what may be the most clearly confrontational letter in her correspondence files:

> We were all very concerned with the last line of Mr. Neinas' letter, "we hope that your organization would be the vehicle to fill that need, but if you cannot make the adjustment necessary to accomplish that end, then I suppose we will have to look to some other solution." There is no indication what *adjustments* might be necessary except the indication in the first sentence of that paragraph, "becoming an affiliate member of the NCAA would have no meaning or provide no solution to the problem of the NCAA on the basis of its constitution. . ."

> There is only one inference that can be made from this threat; that AIAW must become the female arm of NCAA or NCAA will set up a competing program to the AIAW in its member schools. I hope I am wrong in making this interpretation, but I would like to advise you that no action the NCAA could take would be a bigger mistake.

> A group of professional women educators have designed an organization and program in accordance with their accepted philosophy and standards to meet the needs and interests of college women students. To have it now threatened by an organization designed for men and controlled by men would cause such a furor that the NCAA would have a real battle on its hands. The possibility of one girl instituting a court suit to participate on a male varsity team would be a very pale issue in comparison.[31]

For twenty-one years, Rachel Bryant worked with and for a succession of talented women dedicated to devising and promoting "desirable athletic practices for girls and women." Rachel served as a constant and stabilizing force in the GWS organization. She was central to publishing and articulating philosophical tenets with affiliated organizations and among the membership of GWS. She retired October 15, 1971. That day, JoAnn Thorpe, chairman of GWS, sent this tribute to Rachel:

> This is your last day of formal service to DGWS. We want you to know that we will never be without you and all that you have given us. You were able to identify and capture that motivating force and spirit which we know as DGWS. It's more than an organization for girls and women's sports. It has a history but it's current. It has a physiology but it's real. Through it we are united. It's your creation which will transcend *you* and *us*—and may it always be happy for you to remember that your departure is marked by respect, devotion and a sense of gratitude that we have had the pleasure of your company and your leadership.[32]

Rachel Bryant was thorough, intelligent, insightful, had a prodigious memory and great skill in human relations. For two decades she exerted steady, continuous, and positive influences in the growth and development of basketball and in the growth and development of girls and women's sports.

Notes

1. Rachel Bryant, interview, 21 September 1978.

2. Ibid.

3. Rachel Bryant, interview, 11 September 1978.

4. For a detailed discussion of the decision to secure a consultant and the selection of Rachel Bryant see Nancy Weltzheimer Wardwell, "Rachel E. Bryant: Contributions to Physical Education and Girls and Women's Sports" (Ed.D. dissertation, University of Toledo, 1979).

5. Eline von Borries, The History and Functions of the National Section on Women's Athletics (Washington, D.C.: NSWA/AAHPER, 1941), quoting Helen Hazelton, Files of NSWA Promotions Committee, 1937, 11.

6. Carl Troester, Jr., interview, 21 June 1979.

7. Josephine Fiske, "Minutes of NSWA Policy and Finance committee," 21–22 March 1950, in AAHPERD Archives, Reston, Va.

8. Troester, interview, 21 June 1979.

9. NSGWS Financial Report for Period June 1, 1947 through May 31, 1955, AAHPERD Archives, Reston, Va.

10. The Annual Consultant's Reports and the GWS Financial Reports included publication and sales reports. These materials are available in the AAHPERD Archives, Reston, Va.

11. Consultant's Report, December 1959.

12. Troester, interview, June 21, 1979; data taken at 10-year intervals from GWS financial Reports and Consultant's Reports.

13. Elinor Crawford, "The DGWS and Allied Sports Organizations," 15 March 1965 (mimeographed), AAHPERD Archives, Reston, Va.

14. Consultant's Report, December 1950.

15. Consultant's Report, April 1952.

16. Crawford, "DGWS and Allied Sports Organizations."

17. Rachel Bryant, interview, 10 September 1978.

18. Karen Wilkins, interview, 16 August 1979.

19. The Annual Consultant's Reports and Updates 1950–71 itemize and describe the consultant's role and accomplishments. DGWS Minutes and Executive Committee Minutes and Reports further document the period.

20. National Section on Women's Athletics, "Official Stand of the NSWA on the Participation of American Women in Olympic games" (mimeographed) (Washington, D.C.: NSWA, 1948), AAHPERD Archives, Reston, Va.

21. Sara Staff Jernigan, "Women and the Olympics," *JOHPER* (April 1962): 25.

22. Minutes of the DGWS Executive Council, January 1959.

23. Minutes of the DGWS Executive Council, December 1962.

24. The proceedings of the National Leadership Conferences were published and widely distributed as: *The Story of the National Leadership Conference on Girls and Women's Sports* (Washington, D.C.: AAHPER, 1955) and *Social Changes and Sports* (Washington, D.C.: AAHPER, 1962).

25. Consultant's Reports, 1966.

26. Letter to Nancy Wardwell from Katherine Ley, 26 June 1978.

27. "DGWS National Intercollegiate Athletic Championships for Women," *JOHPER* (February 1968): 24–27.

28. Rachel Bryant, interview, 8 June 1979.

29. Letter to Carl Ramer from Rachel Bryant, 16 April 1971.

30. Letter to Rachel Bryant from Walter Byers, 21 May 1971.

31. Letter to Walter Byers from Rachel Bryant, 8 October 1971.

32. Telegram to Rachel Bryant from JoAnne Thorpe, 15 October 1971 (in Book of Letters to Rachel E. Bryant).

15

Women's Basketball Officiating

Fran Koenig and Marcy Weston

The need to provide an official for the game of basketball is as old as the game itself. Perhaps the first "official" was the person who climbed a ladder to retrieve the ball from the closed-bottom basket. By the time the National Women's Basketball Committee functioned in 1899 the official Spalding baskets had a chain to pull to recover the ball from the basket. After doing so the referee was to take the ball up the center of the field and toss it up in a plane at right angles to the side lines. He tossed the ball to start the game, begin the second half, and after each field goal. This same referee was the "superior officer" of the game. He "in all cases must be a thoroughly competent and impartial person."[1] That 1901 description of a referee in the first official women's *Guide* is not different from the characteristics demanded of the 1991 referee.

The 1905–06 *Guide* called for more officials than players. A team consisted of five to nine players, but there were to be eleven officials: "a referee, two umpires, two scorers, two timekeepers, and four linesmen."[2] The linesmen called "fouls" that in today's definitions would be "line violations." Since the 1905 rules restricted each player to her own specific small area of the court, undoubtedly linesmen were necessary to keep track of the players' foot positions. As the rules changed, so did the number of officials. The National Women's Basketball Committee, for instance, deleted linesmen from the list of officials by 1922.[3]

The first official *Guide* article to address officiating appeared in 1913–14 when George T. Hepbron listed twelve "Suggestions for Officials." He introduced his suggestions with, "If, among others, the following characteristics are exhibited by the officials, the games this season will be better officiated, and less friction will be manifested." His twelve suggestions follow:

261

1. Instant recognition of a violated rule and the penalty for same.
2. Backbone enough to make a decision and stick to it.
3. Abstinence from fault finding. (The duty of officials is to make decisions—not to lecture the players.)
4. Readiness to explain in the fewest possible words why that particular ruling was made.
5. Willingness to produce the rule as authority for action.
6. Never, under any circumstances, allowing the prolonged discussion of a rule during the progress of the game.
7. Willingness to allow the players the privilege of appeal from their interpretation of the rules to the proper committee.
8. Kindness and courtesy to all and the maintenance of a level head under trying circumstances.
9. A strong purpose to follow the rules in letter and spirit, and a determination not to be susceptible to outside influences.
10. Carefulness never to overstep their authority, appreciating at the same time their full duty.
11. Such knowledge of the rules that a reversal of decision is not necessary.
12. Impartiality in all dealing.[4]

From 1918–19 through 1927–28, L. Raymond Burnett, M.D. of the Sargent Normal School for Physical Education wrote in the *Guide* about "The Duties of Basket Ball Officials." His suggestions served as the basic instructions for the referee and the umpire for those ten years. Among his suggestions was a statement about whistles. "The best make of whistle for women's use is the deep two-toned whistle with short chain for attachment to the clothing. The shrill-toned whistle with cork ball is not so distinctly heard when a feminine group is cheering a fast game, but this sort of whistle may be used by the umpire and linesmen."[5]

Early History

The formation of the first national officiating board occurred in 1928–29.[6] According to Aletha W. Bond in her article "National Rating Teams" in the *Journal of Health, Physical Education, and Recreation*: "The formal organizing occurred several years after boards had formed throughout the East." As early as 1922, Florence Alden, then chairperson of the National Basketball Committee (NBC), suggested that each town or area needed to establish local boards of officials to ensure an adequate and trained supply of officials. In 1925 the National Section on Women's Athletics (NSWA) organized an Officials Committee with Anita Preston from Temple University serving as chairperson. This initial attempt at organization functioned mainly as a resource center for information about how to establish local boards.

By 1928 local rating boards in basketball had already formed as individual units in Pittsburgh, New York, Philadelphia, Slippery Rock, Lehigh Valley, Harrisburg, and Washington, D.C. However, these boards felt a need to establish uniform standards for ratings in order for officials to transfer ratings from one local board to another. Grace Jones, the 1928 chairperson of the NBC, which had become a subcommittee of the NSWA, and Elise Nelson, 1927 chairperson, arranged a meeting attended by all the chairpersons of the local rating boards. The outcome of this meeting was the establishment of the Women's National Officiating Rating Committee (WNORC). It later became the Officiating Services Area (OSA), and in 1974 it became the Affiliated Boards of Officials (ABO). Helen Shedden of Harrisburg, Pennsylvania, was the first WNORC chairperson.

By November 1930, the Philadelphia Board of Women's Basketball Officials was sponsoring an annual interpretive basketball game for officials, coaches, and players. The 1931–32 *Basketball Guide* listed 38 local boards and ten in process and was the first one to carry the words "National Officials' Ratings" on its front cover. By 1932 there was such a demand for ratings that the WNORC announced it would allow a limited number of candidates to take the examinations for a rating at the American Physical Education Association (APEA) convention in Philadelphia that year.

Officials Directing the Game

The WNORC in 1930–31 published the first pamphlet on "Technique for the Woman Official as Referee or Umpire in Girls' Basketball," and the *Basketball Guide* of 1931–32 included "Technique for the Woman Official in Girls' Basketball" for the first time. Although not as detailed, the content was similar to that published in the *Guides* until 1984–85.

In the early days of basketball there was considerable disagreement about whether an umpire was a supernumerary official or a vital part of the game. Both the 1923–24 and 1924–25 *Guides* contained a one-page article on "Making the Umpire of Value to the Game." In 1933–34, it was still permissible to have only a referee call a game. If there were two officials, it was common practice to alternate the duties of referee and umpire at the end of the first half, as a matter of courtesy.

The duties of the referee and umpire were very different; the referee was clearly in charge of the game and the umpire was to remember that she was assisting the referee. The referee watched the ball, tossed the ball for the center toss, or threw it to the player if a center throw occurred (as in the early rules). She also called fouls and violations, administered free throws, called tie balls, recognized the substitutes, and checked the scorebook for accuracy. The umpire watched the backfield and the part of the court to where the ball might be thrown and helped the scorer by repeating the name of the foul and offender after the referee called the foul. She also made decisions when the referee could not see the play, enforced the rule against coaching from the sideline, and watched for lane violations on free throws. By the mid-thirties the umpire became responsible for getting substitutes in the game because her position was on the same side of the court as the teams and the scorers and timers table.[7]

The emphasis in 1933–34 was on cutting the amount and sound of whistle blowing. On a tie ball the whistle was to be blown just loudly enough so the two players involved could hear. There was no whistle for an out-of-bounds ball unless the wrong team tried to put the ball in play. By 1938–39 the WNORC added signals for goal, personal and technical fouls, jump ball, and no goal. They illustrated the new signals in the *Guides*.

The 1946–47 *Guide* was the first to ignore the issue of an advance notice to the official if she was calling alone. For the first time the *Guide* presented a detailed outline of the responsibilities of the referee and the umpire in starting the game, out-of-bounds play, violation, fouls, time-outs, tossed ball, substitution, disqualification, and the end of quarters and the game. Apparently, however, there were still occasions when only one official called a game because the *Guides* listed a rate for a single official until 1975–76 when NAGWS eliminated all mention of suggested fees.

Major Changes in Techniques of Officiating

From 1930–31 when the first generalized techniques of officiating article appeared in the *Guide* until 1950, there were no major changes in the mechanics of officiating. For those twenty years, the referee was *the* official and the umpire *assisted* her. Major and minor modifications in the rules occurred, but the officiating techniques had only minor alterations.

During the 1949–50 and 1950–51 academic years the WNORC experimented with a "double referee" technique. In this new technique, each official called fouls and violations and administered penalties when the ball was in her designated area of the court. After two years of experimentation, with several ways to divide the officials' court responsibilities, the WNORC adopted the final version of new techniques for officiating basketball. The WNORC recommended that as many officials as possible work with the new techniques during 1951–52 to make the changeover easier the following year.[8]

The changes were shown in the "Diagram of Court Responsibilities of Officials" (see below) in the 1951–52 *Guide*. The referee, positioned on the side of the court opposite the timers and scorers table, put the ball in play at the center circle and administered all penalties for fouls. The umpire was positioned on the side with the timers and scorers. Each official called fouls and violations when the ball was in the diagonal half of the court to her right. When the ball was in the diagonal half of the court to her left, the official was to watch players moving into position to receive the ball. One official was to be ahead of the play and the other behind or alongside the play. When the ball was in her area of the court, the "lead official" (the one watching the ball) moved with it toward the basket and took a position along the end line to her right to watch play under the basket. The "trail official" moved down as far as the free throw line and watched "off the ball." The "trail official" had to be ready to see play "on the ball" if play moved suddenly in the opposite direction. Each official was responsible for calling out-of-bounds on her sideline and the end line to her right.

Finally, after *years* of having been a "second class official," the *umpire* had responsibilities more comparable to those of the referee. More

DIAGRAM OF COURT RESPONSIBILITIES OF OFFICIALS

Referee

Umpire

xxxx Timers and Scorers

10. The officials shall change duties and sides of the court at the end of each quarter.

important to the players and coaches, the officials had better court coverage and could position themselves for the best view of the players "on" and "off" the ball.

The Basketball Committee adopted experimental five player rules for the 1969–70 and 1970–71 seasons. Most college teams elected to play the five player game because the Commission on Intercollegiate Athletics for Women (CIAW) had agreed to sanction tournaments that used the experimental rules. The new five player rules, coupled with the free exchange of ideas during the January 1969 Fifth National Institute, led to the next major change in basketball officiating techniques.

The Women's Board of the U.S. Olympic Development Committee and the DGWS co-sponsored the Fifth National Sport Institute. They invited sixty of the best and most experienced women basketball officials to attend the Institute. The group met for five days of discussion, floor practice, and critique of their officiating by the officiating staff. The staff members included Carol Wolter, Milwaukee Lutheran High School; Kaye McDonald, Mesa Community College, Mesa, Arizona; Fran Koenig, Michigan State University; and Fran Schaafsma, California State University at Long Beach. The fifth staff member was Rich Weiler, a National Collegiate Athletic Association (NCAA) official, whose experience was invaluable in helping prepare officials to call the fast-paced five player game.

The 1969–70 technique changes resulted essentially from the discussions at the Fifth National Institute where women from all parts of the country shared their expertise. The 1969–70 *Guide* did not have the terms "referee" and "umpire" in the techniques section. The terms

At the Fifth National Sport Institute, at Urbana, Ill., in January 1969, experienced women basketball officials worked on techniques.

"leading official" and "trailing official" referred to an official's *floor position*. The techniques designated the responsibilities of either official by the terms "on the ball" and "off the ball." The techniques also included new signals to assist the official in better communicating her decisions to players, coaches, and spectators. Also, more flexibility was written into the techniques to enable the official to get in the best possible position at the right time. So thorough was the revision of the techniques that year that few changes have been made since, except to clarify or to reflect rule changes.

When the rules permitted a three point play in 1987–88, the positioning of the trailing official had to be adjusted. That official needed to see foot positions during the three point shot. She had to move more toward the center of the floor when a player passed the ball wide below the free throw line on the lead official's side. This became crucial when the teams began to develop strategies in which the ball would be kicked out for a "trey" and the trailing official had to make the call.

Officials Served All Girls and Women

The WNORC and its successor groups, the OSA and ABO, provided officials for high schools and colleges starting with the inception of WNORC in 1928. The DGWS's National Rated Officials made every attempt to become involved in basketball games wherever they occurred, whether in schools or in the public sector. The organization provided a list of qualified rated officials to help coaches and administrators secure the services of officials. The *Guides* from 1937 to 1957 listed the names and addresses of all National Rated Officials under their Board according to geographical location. The list, although convenient, had to be eliminated because it used too many pages in the *Guides* (50 in 1956–57).[9]

From 1957 until 1974 there was a listing of the names of Boards and their respective chairmen, secretaries, and basketball chairs in the *Guides*. After 1974, coaches or administrators had to contact the National Association for Girls and Women in Sport (NAGWS) to get a list of Boards in their vicinity. The administrators then had to contact the chairperson of the nearest Affiliated Board for a list of currently rated officials. The OSA/ABO also attempted to serve nonschool basketball teams, letting them know the Board in their area so they could request a list of basketball officials from the chair of the Board.

Since there were so many different sets of basketball rules, it was very difficult to offer to officiate other than the DGWS/NAGWS rules. After six years of meetings and discussions, the AAU and the DGWS women's basketball rules committees published identical rules in their 1964–65 *Guides*. One year before, both organizations used the "rover player" rules. Though there were minor differences in the rules, these were not significant enough to prevent DGWS officials from calling AAU games.

A milestone event occurred in the 1964 AAU National Women's Championship. Because the rules were virtually the same, the AAU invited two DGWS national officials, Carol Wolter, Milwaukee, Wisconsin, and Fran Koenig, from River Forest, Illinois, to call games at the 24-team AAU Basketball Tournament in St. Joseph, Missouri, March 9–13, 1964. All the years of struggles for control of basketball rules, compromises, and modifications in rules were worth it as the two associations shared their expertise. No woman official had been used in the AAU tournament before this moment. Many participating teams had never seen a woman official, so the event caused quite a stir among players, other officials, coaches (yes, especially the coaches), and most

Fran Koenig and Carol Wolter (hand on clock) were the first women officials to serve at an AAU National Tournament (1964).

assuredly the press. In the March 4, 1964 issue of the St. Joseph *News-Press* an editorial on the sports page read:

> Women referees for the Women's National AAU Basketball Tournament? It sounds logical. And yet, when two women from Midwestern states show up to help out with the officiating . . . , it will set a tournament precedent. . . . Although most coaches and officials feel that women would have too much trouble refereeing the game, the experiment should prove interesting.[10]

In that first tournament the women called only in the consolation bracket and officiated only with one another. Spectators and players alike had good things to say about the DGWS officials' work. In succeeding years, not only did the original two officials return but other DGWS women officials called the AAU tournament games. It wasn't too long before women called games in the winner's bracket!

Similarly, when the National Federation of State High School Associations (National Federation) started formulating and publishing girls basketball rules, the OSA urged rated officials to learn those rules and officiate whenever possible. By 1967 about nine states were using rules other than DGWS rules. The National Federation did not want to cooperate with the DGWS in making rules. They viewed the cooperation between DGWS and AAU described above as a step toward making rules for the postsecondary school athlete but not for the high school athlete. The National Federation believed that DGWS ignored the skill level and the needs of the high school basketball players and developed its (DGWS) rules for highly skilled players. As a consequence of that stance, the National Federation wrote their own set of girls basketball rules in 1970–71. The first year only seven states adopted the rules. This occurred because the DGWS/AAU rules were for the roving player game, which high schools liked better than the six player two court game as reflected in the 1970–71 National Federation rules. The following season, the DGWS and the National Federation both moved to the five player game. After this, high school athletic associations in state after state switched from using DGWS rules to mandating National Federation rules.

In protest against the National Federation's "take-over" of girls basketball rules, some rated officials felt they should not officiate games for high school teams using the Federation rules instead of the DGWS rules. The OSA, however, did not concur with the protest and reminded each official of the 1967–68 *Guide* statement on the registration of officials. It read:

> A number of states require those who officiate either boys or girls interscholastic contests to be registered with the State High School Athletics Association or other administrative body. Holding a DGWS

rating ordinarily does not exempt an official from complying with this regulation. All DGWS officials who officiate any high school or junior high school games are urged to cooperate fully with their state regulatory body by registering with the proper organization and paying any required fee, by wearing the official emblem in addition to the DGWS emblem and by complying with all requirements for sports officials.[11]

The statement or a similar one remained in the *Basketball Guide* through the final publication of the *Guide*. Many states used DGWS officials while other state associations selected to use their officials. (Many of these were men officials trained within the ranks of the state associations.)

The OSA also attempted to reach out to the Armed Services by giving a military service rating. The OSA rating, initiated in 1954–55, provided for the military services through 1961. It apparently was not being used by the Armed Services because the OSA dropped the rating without any discussion.

National Ratings for Officials

The process of earning a WNORC/OSA/ABO rating was a difficult one to establish. From 1933 the official seeking a national rating had to take both a theoretical and practical examination. The score had to be at least 90 percent on the theoretical examination, and 85 percent on the practical test. The practical test demanded that three national referees observe a candidate during the actual playing of a "set-up" game. By the 1950s the candidate had to score at least 82 percent on the written test and at least 85 percent on the practical test with an average of 85 percent. The highest ranking an official could obtain in basketball was the national honorary. This was earned by having a national rating for ten years. After that time officials did not need to renew their rating as long as they officiated games, trained officials, or acted as a judge for rating sessions. In 1972–73 the ABO dropped the national honorary and initiated a new state rating. The state rating called for 82 percent on the written test and at least 85 percent on the practical with an average of 85 percent. The required scores for a national rating were raised to 88 percent on both the written and practical.

Between 1976 and 1978 the Affiliated Boards of Officials (NAGWS) inaugurated two programs that were to have a significant impact on officiating. The first consisted of alternative methods for practical examinations and the second the establishment of a National Rating Team. By 1976–77 many experienced officials of high school or men's college basketball games expressed interest in officiating women's college games.

Officials seeking a national rating for basketball took both theoretical and practical examinations. A National Rating Team helped to establish consistent and high-level officiating skills until 1985, when NAGWS stopped offering all forms of basketball officials' ratings.

Because of their experience and membership in other officiating organizations, the present system was not appropriate for them. The Boards concurred that clinics and alternative practical examinations were more suitable. These experienced officials could receive a local rating which signified that the holder qualified to officiate interscholastic and intercollegiate contests requiring a competent and experienced official. To receive this rating, they had to achieve a score of 76 percent on the ABO/NAGWS closed book theoretical examination and demonstrate ability to use ABO officiating techniques. Boards could determine the nature of the demonstration but ABO directed boards to recognize the official's experience. Two years later, the ABO authorized boards to apply the alternative method to state ratings. The state rating qualified the official to officiate any contest within the state or region where she/he had received the rating.[12] This new method brought large numbers of men to the women's basketball officiating ranks. This disturbed many women officials who were fearful that men would take over the officiating positions (exactly what has happened).

In 1977–78 the ABO established a National Rating Team for basketball officiating to bring about nationwide consistency. Before this, rules interpretations had differed in various areas of the country, and the expertise of the officials was being questioned. To acquire the new national rating, officials had to apply to attend a national rating session, held in several locations across the United States.

In order to improve the quality of officiating, established criteria had to be met just to apply for the rating session. The individual:

a. Must have officiated with a current state rating for two years or have a national rating.

    b. Must have passed the written test scoring 88 or above, administered and verified by the local officiating board chairperson.

    c. Must have officiated at a state, regional or qualifying tournament in at least one of the two previous years; OR must have obtained signatures of three (3) different individuals who serve in any of the following capacities:

    (1) college or university basketball coach for women (2 maximum)

    (2) basketball National Rating Team member (1 maximum)

    (3) certifying Board Chairperson

    (4) NAGWS-ABO national official with national tournament officiating experience (1 maximum)

    (5) officiating coordinator or tournament director of a state, regional or qualifying women's basketball tournament (1 maximum).[13]

While at the session, the National Rating Team evaluated each official's ability. A national rating signified a truly superior official, and as such the NRT awarded the rating only when warranted by outstanding test scores and officiating skills.

Officiating attire has followed the changing trends in appropriate dress for women basketball participants. "Proper" attire was considered essential to women's basketball rules committees over the years.

The alternative exams, the National Rating Team system for national ratings, and the state rating procedures cited functioned through 1985. After 1985 the ABO stopped offering all forms of basketball officials' ratings because the conferences women joined chose to select their own officials and to develop their own officiating criteria.

Proper Officiating Attire

The attire to be worn by the officials in basketball became a concern in the early years of basketball games. The uniform suggested in the *Guide* as early as 1918–19 was: "Regular gymnasium costume, differing in color from that of the players and allowing perfect freedom, is the most practical dress. Rubber-soled shoes are a necessity."[14] The 1933–34 *Guide* specified that WNORC officials wear navy blue blazers with powder blue piping and a matching powder blue shield and navy insignia on the chest pocket. The 1947–48 *Guide* stated that the blazer be all navy blue flannel with the WNORC shield. A decade later the uniform was changed to a navy blue and white striped shirt with a new shield emblem. A blue skirt and white tennis shoes and socks completed the attire.

By 1971 the official could wear a skirt, culottes, or kilt. The *Guide* of 1973 stated that a kilt, skirt, or slacks could be worn. If kilts were worn, according to the 1976–77 *Guide*, the length had to be between the knee and mid-thigh.[15] That uniform remained the official one until the last NAGWS *Guide* in 1984–85. A few conferences moved to a black and white shirt and black slacks in 1984. Since 1985 the proper attire consists of black and white striped shirt, black dress slacks, black shoes and socks, and a navy blue jacket to be worn until game time. Since the rule books were so definite on attire, it is obvious the committee believed *proper* attire was essential for *proper* officiating!

Fees

When the NSWA established the WNORC in 1928, the new committee set the fee for a national official at $5.00 plus expenses for a single game and $7.50 for a doubleheader. The WNORC retained that specific regulation from the original constitution probably longer than any other regulation. They did not change the maximum rates until the 1956–57 academic year when they raised the fees to $6.00 and $9.00, respectively, if there were two officials. If there was only one official, the fees were $9.00 and $12.00, respectively. There were many times when the oldtimers officiated alone and did *two* Games. Certainly it wasn't the *money* that mattered as much as providing the opportunity for girls and women to enjoy playing basketball under proper officiating.

Some schools hired only one official because it would cost only $12.00 for a double game instead of $18.00. At other times, they simply couldn't find two officials free in the middle of the afternoon. The WNORC changed the fees in 1964–65 to discourage the practice of hiring only one person. They set the rates at $6.00 and $10.00 for two officials calling the game and double that if one official called alone.

In 1969–70 with the experimental five player game, two officials received $9.00 plus travel. If only one official called the game the fee was doubled. The following year when most college teams were using the faster five player rules, the *Guide* didn't mention the possibility of officiating a double game. No one wanted a worn-out official for a second game, even a junior varsity game. Until 1974–75 the *Guide* provided a fee structure for "one official." That rate was $24.00 (the same as the fee for a regular two official game). In 1975 the ABO Executive Board voted to delete any recommendation of fees because of problems in establishing minimums that were fair.[16] In addition to the parity issue, the ABO Board recognized the fact that fees received by various boards throughout the nation differed significantly from one another and from other officiating associations.

Although fees varied somewhat from one AIAW Division to another and from one section of the country to another, most Division I Conferences were paying officials under $100 plus travel for regular season games until the mid-1980s. During the 1988–89 season, the 27 NCAA Division I Conferences paid an average fee of $125 for each official. Most conferences also compensated officials for travel and per diem, although that was not a universal practice. Game fees continued to rise, and in 1990–91 two Division I Conferences paid $200 for officials for regular season contests. The minimum fee in Division I remained at $100 per game.

As regular season game fees rose steadily after 1975, championship game fees increased commensurately. In 1980, AIAW Division I first round officials received $100 plus expenses and quarter-final officials received $125 per game. The pay for officials in the final four (semi-finals and finals) was $150 per game. In the 1982 NCAA Division I National Championship, officials for all rounds received $250 plus travel and per diem. In 1989 NCAA paid a fee of $275 per game for Division I Championship contests; $175 for Division II, and $150 for Division III. With these fee structures, it is not surprising that many more men have moved into officiating on all levels, especially calling games at the college level.

Gender of Officials

Over the years of basketball competition the language used in the women's *Basketball Guides* to denote gender of the official has changed several times. From the first *Guide* in 1901 until 1914–15 the *Guides* used "he" when discussing the officials. From 1914–15 the *Guides* used "she" exclusively when referring to officials.[17]

For a considerable time, WNORC national officials were exclusively female as WNORC permitted only women to get a national rating for girls and women's basketball. However, men could get a local rating. This fact is clearly verified from examining the name and address of the officials listed in the annual *Guides*. In 1956–57 for example, the last year in which ABO published names, there was a list of 1,798 officials, all women.[18] Incidentally, those lists of basketball officials with national ratings read like a "Who's Who" in physical education and athletics, including at least six of the authors in this book.

While the *Guides* from 1957 to 1980 did not list the names of officials, females *did* officiate most of the women's basketball games, at least in the educational domain, through the 1960s and early 1970s. In 1973–74, the last year the *Basketball Guide* listed affiliated boards, all 189 boards had the words "Board of Women Officials" as part of their names. Although the lists of boards had been eliminated, the suggested steps under "How to Establish a Board of Officials" in the 1974–75 *Guide* included, "At a designated meeting of interested women, present plans for forming a board."[19] The following year, the Committee changed the term "women" to "individuals" in the *Guide*.[20]

In the fall of 1977 the NAGWS Affiliated Boards of Officials adopted an official statement of goals. One of the goals was: "To increase the number of competent women officials, not to the exclusion of men, but as needed affirmative action."[21] That statement makes clear that a goodly number of men already were calling girls and women's basketball games.

Starting June 1, 1976 the National Basketball Rating Team was the only group who rated and gave national ratings. The first *Guide* to list names and addresses of NRT national officials was 1980–81. That roster included 59 national officials, 49 percent of whom were female and 51 percent male. By 1984–85 the list of national officials totaled 123, only 37 percent of whom were female.[22] As in all areas of athletics, the men move into the action, and progressively fewer women are among the leaders.

It is interesting to note, however, that since the inception of the NCAA Division I Championships for Women in 1981–82, 40 percent (16/41) of the final four officials were women and 60 percent (25/41) were men. By contrast, the Championship final game has been officiated by a ratio of 56 percent (10/18) females and only 44 percent (8/18) males. Marcy Weston (Michigan) was the first woman to officiate the finals of an NCAA Division I National Championship. In 1982 and 1984 Weston called the game with a male partner. June Courteau (North Carolina) teamed up with a man for the 1985 and 1986 championship game. The sixth Division I NCAA National Basketball Championship in 1987 was the first occasion when NCAA assigned two women to the final game — Courteau and Patty Broderick (Indiana) officiated that contest. The following year the committee paired Broderick with a male partner, and in 1989 they again assigned Broderick and Courteau to the championship game. The fourth woman chosen to officiate the finals was Sally Bell (Georgia), who called with a male partner in 1990.

The number of women officials selected for the women's final four does not give an accurate portrayal of the total number of women working collegiate Division I basketball. While it seems that women officials who do well are moved along and often are assigned to the playoffs, the number of women and men who work the finals are inversely proportional to the numbers calling regular season games. In 1989–90, for example, the Big Ten Conference officials' roster included 85 percent men (22/26), thus only 15 percent women. The Mid-American Conference used 74 percent men (20–27) and only 26 percent women.[23] Yet three of the four women who have officiated the NCAA Division I championship game on ten occasions since 1981–82 call or called for one or both of these Conferences. Despite efforts on the part of NAGWS and other groups to increase the number of women basketball officials, men continue to dominate the officiating ranks today.

Darlene May served as the first woman official for Olympic basketball. May coaches basketball at California State Polytechnic University, Pomona, and her team has won the Division II national basketball championship.

The Inception of Conference Structure

After the initial year of the NCAA Division I Women's Basketball Championship in 1981–82 discussions began about the future of the rating system currently in use for collegiate women's basketball officials. The NCAA questioned the use of ABO and theoretical exams when they took over the reins of women's basketball from the AIAW.

The number of active officiating boards had enjoyed steady growth over the years until NAGWS ceased publishing women's basketball rules in 1985. In the early 1930s, there were 42 boards scattered throughout the United States from Massachusetts and New York to California and Washington, and from Florida and Texas to Wisconsin and Iowa. The number of boards grew slowly in the early years of WNORC because of the limited number of interscholastic and intercollegiate opportunities for girls and women to compete in basketball. In 1945 there were only 53 active boards. As interschool and interagency basketball increased in the 1950s there was a surge in the numbers of boards of women officials. By 1960, there were 162 boards affiliated with WNORC. After the founding of AIAW in 1971–72 competition for the college woman became widely available in collegiate institutions, and by 1975–76 there were 200 boards affiliated with NAGWS. In 1984 the ABO reached an all-time high of 220 basketball boards.[24]

As women's basketball teams began to either affiliate with the conference in which their men's team competed or form their own conference, Affiliated Board jurisdiction gave way to conference policy. Supply and demand seemed to be the rule. For several years (1982 through 1986) officials still referred to their state and national ratings, when in actuality that ranking system was no longer in existence. As conferences developed criteria for hiring officials, very few, if any, had any type, let alone theoretical, evaluation for new officials. In fact, during that time, many conferences were still asking officials what "rating" they had held in AIAW—giving strong credence to the respect many assigners and supervisors had for the NAGWS rating system.

In 1986 the NCAA approved the funding for a series of Regional Basketball Training Clinics for both women's and men's Division I officials. The money earmarked for these fall clinics came from revenue generated at the NCAA Division I Men's Basketball Championships. That effort marked the first time the NCAA had taken measures to deal with officiating for any sport they sponsored. The participants heartily approved of the clinics; therefore, they have continued to be offered in the fall of each year.

Many conferences and independent groups developed training camps for officials during the summer months. This venture was to meet the need for an "instructional setting" where prospective as well as current collegiate officials could be critiqued and trained on deficient aspects of their game.

In conjunction with training camps, most conferences have in place an evaluation system in which officials are given critiques in person or via video analysis on games they work during the actual season. This vital feedback, hopefully done by knowledgeable observers, provides suggestions necessary to the improvement of each official's game. It became apparent to conferences that training of officials was a necessity. If conferences themselves did not provide opportunities where would officials learn, grow, and improve? In the early 1980s, conferences began to hire supervisors of officials for women's basketball, and by 1990 each Division I Conference employed a person designated to hire, assign, and evaluate its women's basketball officiating staff.

NAGWS provided basketball rules and guidelines for officials up until the 1984–85 *Guide*. When the NCAA published its first women's rule book in 1985, there was a localization of guidelines for officials by conference edict. Everything from fee designation to per diem, tournament assignment procedures for conference championships, and format for selection of officials to the NCAA Tournament was left to individual conference discretion.

In 1987–88 the NCAA initiated the Block Grant Program. They distributed $30,000 to each conference that had automatic qualification into the Division I NCAA Women's Championship and $15,000 to conferences without automatic qualification. These monies were to be used in officiating improvement, drug education, compliance, and opportunities for women and minorities. Since its inception, the grant money has had major effect on the improved status of officiating programs for women. As the NCAA specified certain conditions for conferences to receive those funds, national standards for officiating returned. The new training programs in which conferences were evaluating, training, and assigning officials established a commonality of standards. It is amazing that "what goes around, comes around!" NAGWS emphasized standardization through the 1970s, local conference dictate emerged through the mid-1980s, and a national overview and standardization of officiating returned in the late 1980s!

The Women's National Officials' Rating Committee was formed in 1928 for the purpose of helping to provide competent, well-trained officials for competition. The Officiating Services Area followed the same goals and patterns as the WNORC, as did the Affiliated Boards of Officials. While the programs and services of these groups remained virtually unchanged over fifty years, no one would deny that the officiating techniques have come a very long way since 1928.

The referee of the 1920s and early 1930s had one big decision to make that does not concern today's officials. Until 1933–34, the only legal way to guard was with the arms in a vertical plane. From 1921 until 1933 the rules committee permitted guarding only on the vertical plane. As a result, in order to give the guards a fairer chance, the Committee only permitted one point for shots that were difficult to guard in a vertical plane. Officials had to determine if a field goal was worth two points or whether, because the shot was an overhead or a "back-to-the-basket" shot (shots which were difficult in a vertical plane), only one point should be awarded.[25]

Today's basketball officials have many more rules to know, much faster movement to follow, and more on-court judgments to make during the course of the game. Given all these demanding changes for the officials, they at least are not given the additional responsibility of deciding whether a field goal counts one point or two!

Notes

1. Senda Berenson, ed., *Basket Ball for Women* (New York: American Sports Publishing Co., 1901), 30.

2. Senda Berenson, ed., *Spalding's Official Women's Basket Ball Guide*, 1905–06 (New York: American Sports Publishing Co., 1906), 10.

3. "Official Rules," in Official *Basketball Guide for Women* (1922–1923), ed. Carin Degermark (New York: American Sports Publishing Co., 1922), 21.

4. George T. Hepbron, "Suggestions for Officials," in *Spalding's Official Basket Ball Guide for Women* (1913–1914), ed. Senda Berenson Abbott (New York: American Sports Publishing Co., 1913), 55.

5. L. Raymond Burnett, "The Duties of Basket Ball Officials," in *Official Basket Ball Guide for Women* (1918–19), ed. Florence D. Alden, Elizabeth Richards, and L. Raymond Burnett (New York: American Sports Publishing Co., 1918), 65.

6. Helen Shedden, "Women's National Officials' Rating Committee," in *Official Basketball Guide for Women* (1928–29), ed. Grace E. Jones (New York: American Sports Publishing Co., 1928), 8; Aletha W. Bond, "National Rating Teams: An Attempt at Officiating Consistency," *Journal of Health, Physical Education, and Recreation*, 49 (September 1978): 26–28. Acknowledgment is gratefully given to Aletha Bond, on whose article this brief historical section is based.

7. Wilhelmine E. Meissner, ed., "Technique for the Woman Official in Girls' Basketball," in *Official Basketball Guide for Women and Girls* (1933–34), ed. Eline von Borries (New York: American Sport Publishing Co., 1933), 71–78.

8. Dorothy Martin, "New Techniques in Basketball Officiating," in *Official Basketball and Officials Rating Guide for Women and Girls* (September 1951–September 1952), ed. Gwen Smith (Washington, D.C.: American Association for Health, Physical Education, and Recreation, 1951), 141–142.

9. "Affiliated Boards of Officials," in *Official Basketball and Officials Rating Guide for Girls and Women* (September 1956–September 1957), ed. Helen B. Lawrence (Washington, D.C.: American Association for Health, Physical Education, and Recreation, 1956), 41–90.

10. "Editorial," *St. Joseph (Missouri) News-Press*, 4 March 1964.

11. "Registration of Officials," in *Basketball Guide, August 1967–August 1968*, ed. Janette S. Sayre (Washington, D.C.: American Association for Health, Physical Education, and Recreation, 1967), 93.

12. "Alternative Methods for Practical Examinations," in *Basketball, July 1979–July 1980*, ed. Geri Polvino (Washington, D.C.: American Alliance for Health, Physical Education, Recreation and Dance, 1979), 85–86.

13. "National Official in Basketball and Volleyball," in *Basketball, July 1977–July 1978*, ed. Ruth Gunden (Washington, D.C.: American Alliance for Health, Physical Education and Recreation, 1977), 83.

14. Burnett, "Duties of Basket Ball Officials," 62.

15. "Official Uniform for National Officials Rated by the Basketball NRT," in *Basketball, July 1976–July 1977* (Washington, D.C.: American Alliance for Health, Physical Education, and Recreation, 1976), 94.

16. "Recommended Fees," in *Basketball, August 1975–August 1976*, ed. Norma Boetel (Washington, D.C.: American Alliance for Health, Physical Education, and Recreation, 1975), 47.

17. Dorothy S. Tapley, "Thirty Years of Girls' Basketball Rules," in *Official Basketball Guide for Women and Girls* (1936–37), ed. Marie L. Simes (New York: American Sports Publishing Co., 1936), 49.

18. "Affiliated Boards of Officials," in *Official Basketball Guide*, 1956–1957, 41–90.

19. "How to Establish a Board of Officials," in *Basketball Guide, July 1974–July 1975*, ed. Norma Boetel (Washington, D.C.: American Alliance for Health, Physical Education, and Recreation, 1974), 51–53.

20. "How to Establish a Board of Officials," in *Basketball, August 1975–August 1976*, 51–53.

21. "NAGWS Affiliated Boards of Officials," in *Basketball, July 1978–July 1979*, ed. Pat Sherman (Washington, D.C.: American Alliance for Health, Physical Education, and Recreation, 1978), 89.

22. "Roster of National Basketball Officials," in *Basketball, July 1980–July 1981*, ed. Mary Beth Alphin (Reston, Va.: American Alliance for Health, Physical Education, Recreation and Dance, 1980), 93–95; "National Basketball Officials 1984–1985," in *Basketball, July 1984–July 1985*, ed. Jill Hutchison (Reston, Va.: American Alliance for Health, Physical Education, Recreation and Dance, 1984), 93–97.

23. Phone call from Marcy Weston to Patty Broderick, Big Ten supervisor of officials for women's basketball, 10 August 1990; Mid-American Conference Women's Basketball Staff Directory, 1989–1990.

24. "NAGWS Affiliated Boards of Officials," in *Basketball, July 1984–July 1985*, 78.

25. Tapley, "Thirty Years of Girls' Basketball Rules," 50.

Section 5
Collegiate Governance, Championships, and Memories

16

The Legacy of AIAW

Joan S. Hult

In a pageant called "Women in Action: The Story of the Division for Girls and Women's Sport (DGWS), 1892–1958" presented at the 60th Anniversary Convention of the American Association for Health, Physical Education, and Recreation (AAHPER), Eleanor Metheny commented on the history of women physical educators that "always, no matter what we argued about, we were genuinely concerned with the good of those who play . . . this is really the reason for our existence as an organization."[1]

Similarly, the first proposal for the Association for Intercollegiate Athletics for Women (AIAW), first named National Organization for Intercollegiate Athletics for Women, stated:

> The NOIAW is to be composed of member institutions which wish to uphold and promote the highest standards in women's collegiate athletic programs. As in the past, the focus is to remain on the individual participant in her primary role as a college student.[2]

An article reflecting on the actions taken by the 1978 Delegate Assembly opened with the following observation:

> The AIAW maintains as its cardinal principle the belief that the focus in intercollegiate athletics should remain on the individual participant in her primary role as a college student; the justification for such athletic programs is their educational value.[3]

This paper is a revision and expansion of a previously published article by Joan S. Hult, "Women's Struggle for Governance in United States Amateur Athletics," *International Review for the Sociology of Sport* 24 (3) (1989). Acknowledgment is gratefully given to Charles Walcott, Virginia Tech University, for his collaboration on the AIAW vs. NCAA portion of the manuscript.

Whether the dateline was the 1899 first basketball committee meeting to modify rules for women, the 1970 invitation to charter membership in the AIAW, or the 1978 reflections of the AIAW, the refrain was the same. The refrain signified the deep concern of physical education women for the female participant. That deep concern prompted the leaders to revamp the male dominated sports scene to permit implementing a unique model of athletics. The needs and interests of the female athlete were the basis for AIAW's alternative model of athletics.

AIAW Emerges

The AIAW's rich heritage in sports can be traced through AAHPER and the National Association for Girls and Women in Sport (NAGWS) from the first women's basketball committee in 1899 to the present. The legacy is unmistakable as one views the philosophical foundations, policies, purposes, and regulations of AIAW. The first direct roots of AIAW are found in the National Joint Committee for Extramural Sports for College Women (NJCESCW) which began its work by the end of 1957. Two representatives from each of three important organizations for women physical educators comprised the committee. The organizations were the National Association of Physical Education for College Women (NAPECW), Athletic and Recreation Federation of College Women (ARFCW), and Division for Girls and Women's Sport (DGWS).[4]

As the DGWS became more involved in the competitive arena, and as attitudes toward competition for women changed, it became clear that DGWS should control collegiate athletics for women. The young women leaders of DGWS envisioned a new model of intercollegiate athletics. They accepted the desirability of organized competition, but rejected the commercialization rampant in men's athletics (NCAA). From this vision emerged the Commission on Intercollegiate Athletics for Women (CIAW), the direct foremother of the Association for Intercollegiate Athletics for Women (AIAW). The DGWS approved the CIAW in March 1966 and it began to function in the fall of 1967. The Commission sanctioned tournaments and sponsored national championships. By the spring of 1967 it had published its first guideline booklet, *Procedures for Women's Intercollegiate Athletics Events*. The basic functions of the Commission were to establish standards and control competition through sanctioning regional tournaments, encouraging the formation of local or regional governing bodies of women physical educators, and sponsoring national championships.[5]

The original eligibility regulations of CIAW were relatively few and simple. In its early years, AIAW also used most of them. The regulations included: (1) The student must be an amateur. (2) The student must be a full-time undergraduate who maintains the academic average required for participation in all other major campus activities at her institution. (3) Transfer students are immediately eligible for participation following enrollment. (4) A student cannot participate more than four times in the same national championship. However, the first Delegate Assembly of AIAW changed the most controversial CIAW regulation which had stated: "there shall be no scholarship or financial assistance specifically designated for women athletes."[6]

The legacy to AIAW from CIAW is clear; the new Association was an expansion of CIAW. The AIAW provided a structure for a governing body through institutional membership. The proposal for this membership organization passed the DGWS Executive Council and AAHPER Board of Governors late in 1970. The proposal contained the basis for the philosophical tenets of AIAW, the general structure of the association, and the services which would be rendered to the membership. In addition it introduced the functions of regions, committees, and the executive board and the requirements for membership.[7]

In 1971–72 the CIAW became the AIAW, an affiliate organization of AAHPER and a substructure of the DGWS. The association had its

Members of the Executive Board of the first Commission for Intercollegiate Athletics for Women, who envisioned a new model of varsity sports for women. Left to right, seated, are the three commissioners, Phebe Scott, Katherine Ley, and Maria Sexton. Standing are Rachel Bryant, DGWS consultant; Frances McGill, DGWS vice president; and Lucille Magnusson, DGWS vice president-elect.

genesis within the educational domain, so its educational focus was not accidental. Its leaders knew what conflicts they wished to avoid and what educational purposes they wanted to achieve. Although on its way out, the CIAW still conducted the national championships for the 1971–72 academic year. The AIAW took complete control of women's intercollegiate athletics in the summer of 1972.[8]

The AIAW began with a clear vision of its mission, its strategies, and the role of its institutional members. There were four original purposes of the Association as presented to AAHPER/DGWS:

1. To foster broad programs of women's intercollegiate athletics which are consistent with the educational aims and objectives of the member schools.
2. To assist member schools in the extension and enrichment of their programs of intercollegiate athletics for women.
3. To stimulate the development of quality leadership among persons responsible for women's intercollegiate athletic programs.
4. To encourage excellence in performance of participants in women's intercollegiate athletics.[9]

It had a set of procedures for conducting national championships, eligibility rules for athletes, and plans for legislative actions through its Delegate Assembly. It adopted a student-centered, education-oriented model with built-in safeguards designed to avoid abuses observed in the male athletic model. As a substructure of DGWS/NAGWS, AIAW used the division's rules, *Sport Guides*, and rated officials.

The first Delegate Assembly of AIAW in November 1973 voted on its purposes and functions as a segment of its Constitution. It included many specific services to be rendered by AIAW to its membership. In summary these were to: (1) hold national championships; (2) conduct athletics within the "spirit of the game" for achieving educational values from sport; (3) increase public understanding and appreciation of the importance and value of athletics in contributing to enrichment of life; (4) encourage and facilitate research in athletics; (5) offer assistance in development of and improvement of intercollegiate programs; (6) sponsor conferences, institutes, and meetings for member schools; (7) cooperate with other professional groups interested in sports programs and opportunities for women; and (8) provide direction and maintain a relationship with AIAW regional organizations.[10]

Under the threat of a class action suit filed in January 1973 against NEA, AAHPER, DGWS, and AIAW, the Delegate Assembly reluctantly took a most significant action. The delegates voted to permit scholarships for intercollegiate female athletes at its member institutions.[11]

The *Kellmeyer* suit challenged the AIAW scholarship policy, which prohibited women athletes who received athletic scholarships from participating in AIAW sponsored competition. Kellmeyer was seeking entrance to the USLTA National Tennis Championships. The AIAW leaders were more steadfast about not changing the scholarship regulations than were DGWS leaders from 1971 to 1973. At the time of the lawsuit, AIAW leaders wanted to fight the decision in court; the AAHPER/DGWS leaders did not support that position.[12] After several important meetings of all the organizations involved in the decision, a large majority mandated that AIAW change its stance. The AIAW Delegate Assembly vote, therefore, was almost perfunctory. This action resulted in the modification of the DGWS scholarship statement:

> The decision was that the DGWS scholarship statement be modified to reflect that the prevention of possible abuses in the awarding of athletic scholarships to women can be accomplished more appropriately by the strict regulation of such programs than by the outright prohibition of such forms of financial assistance.[13]

AIAW reluctantly issued a statement concerning the new regulation that opened its membership to institutions which had previously been ineligible because they awarded athletic scholarships. The statement included the warning that a college considering the use of a program of financial aid for athletes should be cognizant of potential abuses. The final item on the agenda of the Assembly, about 2:00 a.m., was the Constitution and Bylaws. The delegates wisely accepted the Constitution and a general consensus of the Bylaws with details to be worked out later by the Executive Board and Bylaws Committee. In May 1974, the membership voted on the Constitution, Bylaws, and Interim Financial Aid regulations.[14]

AIAW Structure

The AIAW, unlike the National Collegiate Athletic Association (NCAA), was an all-purpose organization for the total program of women's intercollegiate athletics at its member institutions. The entire intercollegiate sport experience of any female athlete was under the jurisdiction of AIAW, which accepted the responsibility for the control and enforcement of AIAW regulations at *all* member school events. This concept of total program commitment was similar to the National Association of Intercollegiate Athletics (NAIA) policies. Each student had to be eligible for each contest, not just those that led to postseason national championships.

AIAW's governance structure included a paid executive director (the staff increased to eight full-time employees and a lawyer), an elected

Executive Board of officers, national commissioners for championships, and nine regionally elected representatives. By 1976 the board also included one student athlete. Throughout its history, only women served on the Executive Board. The board conducted business, developed policies, procedures, and regulations, and set the agenda for the Delegate Assembly.[15]

Membership in the Delegate Assembly included one voting representative from each institution. Unlike NCAA, NAIA, and NJCAA, AIAW encouraged the institutions' chief executive officer to select a woman athletic director or a coach as the voting representative. There were few delegates, therefore, from outside the athletic department. At the first assembly, over 95 percent of the delegates were women. At the last assembly, AIAW still had 75 percent women representatives, but NCAA's voting delegates were nearly 95 percent men.[16]

Presidents of the Association for Intercollegiate Athletics for Women join for a historic photo. Back row, from bottom of stairs up: Carol Gordon, Carole Oglesby, N. Peg Burke, Christine Grant, Charlotte West, Leotus Morrison, Laurie Mabry. Seated: Judith Holland, Carole Mushier, Donna Lopiano. Not present were Merrily Baker and Virginia Hunt.

While AIAW was a substructure of DGWS/NAGWS, it had a great deal of autonomy even before it severed its relationship with NAGWS in 1979. AIAW started with 206 active charter member institutions (278 active and associate members). It increased to a high of 970 members. Each year AIAW conducted 750 state, regional, and national championships under a unified membership plan with state and regional associations. The Association conducted 39 national championships in 19 different sports during its last full year of operation, 1981–82. In addition, the nine AIAW regions conducted qualifying events in over half of those sports. During its peak year in 1980–81 approximately 99,000 female athletes competed for AIAW member institutions.[17]

AIAW strongly endorsed athlete participation in governance. A student-athlete was a voting member of AIAW's Executive Board and the Ethics and Eligibility Appeal Board Panels. Each sport committee had a student-athlete member. AIAW encouraged each member institution to include students in its delegation to the Delegate Assembly and for each institution to have a student athlete organization. AIAW also sponsored two student leadership conferences to develop leadership skills and inform the students about the association. A student leadership manual was written by the student representatives.[18]

The national commissioners were responsible for the conduct of national championships. Each sport committee conducted championships for its sport. Coaches made up the membership of the sports committee, except for a student athlete member. Each committee had a great deal of autonomy in designing championships. However, major changes, such as moving to "four satellites" and a final four instead of a 16-team format in basketball, did go to the Executive Board. The sport committee of basketball was at the forefront of changes and experimentation of formats. Jill Hutchison, basketball coach at Illinois State, noted: "I've been a member of all ten tournament committees. . . . It's been fun watching the whole thing grow. I can remember the excitement when we set up the first structure and all the qualifying procedures."[19]

There were separate state and regional associations for conducting preliminary tournaments, all of which led to national championships. In the early years, institutions had only to join the regional organization to gain access to national championships. But in the later years the controversial unified membership demanded state, regional, and national membership in order to compete in the nationals. The regional championship, however, was a complete event in itself, that is, it was conducted by the region for a regional champion as well as for future competition.

It was a unique feature of AIAW that its preliminary tournaments were designed to be feeders to the national with the winners of each region being in the national championship. There were only nine regional organizations, but AIAW divided the Eastern Region into Region IA and Region IB, so there were ten regional championships. This resulted in at least ten teams instead of nine who represented regions at the 16-team national tournaments in different sports. The national sport committee selected the additional teams based on two criteria: team or individual season performance and balanced representation from all ten geographical regions. This permitted each area of the country to be represented at the nationals and thereby have the opportunity to build its sport. There were no automatic conference bids. Unified membership along with the preliminary championships and a strength of region factor assured geographical representation and fair opportunity at all tournaments.[20]

Ethics and Eligibility Committee

To understand AIAW's educational focus, its commitment, and consequently its effect on women's basketball, it is essential to examine its procedures of legislation and general control patterns of intercollegiate programs. The most significant arm of the AIAW governance was undoubtedly the Ethics and Eligibility Committee. It assumed both a judicial and legislative function within the association.

AIAW's "self-policing" enforcement procedure differed significantly in purpose and application from the NCAA procedure that included over 14 full-time investigators. The media, and to a lesser extent the membership who favored stronger enforcement, criticized AIAW's self-policing philosophy. As a result of criticism, the E&E Committee proposed legislation to permit more thorough investigation of complaints and more stringent penalties. AIAW's self-policing was one of its alternative model concepts that remained to the end.[21]

As a result of the media and membership criticism, institutions accepted more responsibility to report infractions. Consequently, there were more infractions reported and more in-depth investigations resulting in more sanctions being imposed. As might be expected, given its financial success, basketball had the most infractions and consequently the most sanctions.[22]

Another noteworthy policy of AIAW which differed from other governing bodies was its system of liberal "waivers" for institutions and for individual student-athletes. The procedure permitted any student-athlete or institution to make a request to the E&E Committee if she or the institution believed a rule should be waived. If the committee denied a waiver, there was also a process of appeal available to the student-athlete. This liberal process of waiver requests bears witness to AIAW's genuine concern for the individual student-athlete and member institution. Once again the sport of basketball recorded the largest numbers of transfers and waivers, both denied and granted.[23]

The final noteworthy E&E procedure was the process of an appeal of either a denied waiver or a sanction. An appeal panel permitted due process. The procedure not only prevented several court cases, but more significantly provided a check and balance system in this most sensitive area of the governance.[24]

Representatives from the various AIAW divisions comprised the national E&E Committee. In addition an expanded appeal panel consisted of the nine regional E&E chairs. Each chair, in turn, had a committee to deal with regional issues and some national issues and requests for waivers. By the last few years of E&E, a Rules Standards Committee took over the duties of developing legislation and overseeing compliancy of more restrictive rules by institutions. It enforced AIAW's controversial regulation that an institution could not have rules that were more restrictive than AIAW's *nor* could the institution have rules more restrictive for athletes than for nonathletes. This issue of "infringement on institutional autonomy" was a major controversial issue dividing AIAW in its last few years.[25]

Rules and Regulations

The erosion of the student-centered education-oriented eligibility, financial aid, and recruitment regulations was largely the result of Title IX regulations. Title IX demanded use of the male model of athletics as the norm for determining equity. The discriminatory potential of differing rules seemed to affect all AIAW regulations. Highlights of the eligibility, financial aid, and recruitment rules are discussed in the following section.

Eligibility

AIAW's eligibility rules were consistent with CIAW and AIAW's educational focus on the individual student, while treating the student-athlete as much like other students as possible. As noted earlier, many of the basic participation requirements were the same as those in the first CIAW *Procedures* booklet. The greatest area of criticism about AIAW's eligibility rules was the freedom of athletes to transfer to other institutions without penalty of "red shirting" (sitting out a year). While there was much criticism, the membership generally believed it was essential to permit transfers because student-athletes should have the same freedom to transfer as the regular nonathlete student. In the final analysis, however, AIAW's transfer rule became identical to NCAA's transfer rule.[26]

Financial Aid

There is little question in the minds of the AIAW membership and most observers that the most critical, and controversial, legislation to affect women's athletics was the reversal of the stand on scholarships. The action was a traumatic experience for AIAW's conservative members.

In May 1973, the AIAW Executive Board approved a set of interim financial aid and recruitment regulations for member institutions offering aid. At the first Delegate Assembly the delegates reviewed and commented upon these interim regulations and suggested changes. In addition the assembly voted:

> that the AIAW go on record as approving financial aid only when it is available to all students regardless of talent and sex and that recruitment of athletes through the use of any financial inducements be discouraged by the association on both the local and regional levels.[27]

When a mail vote of the membership in May 1974 approved the final financial aid and recruitment regulations, the first portion of the above motion was not written into the regulations. However, the new regulations did include the recruitment part of the motion.[28]

The new regulations also included procedures for institutional administration of financial aid, number of allowable awards in each sport, recruitment procedures, and the actual financial aid limitation of tuition, fees, room, and board for a student-athlete. In addition, the regulations permitted the loan of books to students but prohibited tutoring services out of athletic funds.[29]

The AIAW first passed a resolution in 1976 and then a regulation in 1977 to limit financial aid to tuition and fees. The 1977 debate on the floor of the Assembly was perhaps the most controversial and emotional one ever experienced by delegates. The final decision, resulting from a roll call vote, to limit aid starting in the fall of 1978 was irrefutably a vote for upholding an education model. The reversal of that 1977 vote the next year returned the aid to tuition, fees, room, and board, passing with few dissenting voices. The reversal stemmed not so much from a philosophical belief in the educational soundness of the "full ride" as from a pragmatic belief that limiting financial aid was, in fact, discriminating to female athletes. While the delegates were in an affirmative action mood, they voted to allow tutoring services for student-athletes.[30]

As a result of the reversal, by 1981 financial aid in basketball, for example, reached an all-time high of over $8 million. Five hundred twenty-nine AIAW institutions provided aid to 4,561 students. This was out of a total of 888 AIAW institutions fielding basketball teams. The same year AIAW institutions spent a total of $32 million on financial aid.[31]

Recruitment

The greatest difficulty for AIAW was in the area of recruitment restraints. While Title IX mandated scholarships, it was not so clear about its intent regarding recruitment. On this issue, therefore, AIAW stood firm on wanting women athletes to attend college as students first, and thus for recruitment to be limited.

In the evolution of the recruitment regulations, there were what appear to be far more drastic changes in attitudes and practices. Legislation led to active recruitment practices that allow institutional funding for some forms of recruitment. The 1978 and 1979 Assembly actions attempted to create a delicate balance between concern for the welfare of the student-athlete, the interest of the institution, and the concern for opportunity without discrimination. To obtain this balance, the membership had to depart from some traditional views on institutional funding for recruitment. The first significant action was to permit collegiate athletic personnel to "assess the talent" of the prospective student-athlete. A second action allowed coaches to receive release time and

Members of the 1972 Immaculata College Mighty Macs, winners of the first "official" national championship for women, sponsored by the CIAW/AIAW. (Photo from Immaculata College Public Relations Office files)

compensation for all expenses incurred while engaged in "talent assessment."[32] The third significant action passed was to liberalize recruitment rules, to allow an institution to pay for on-campus housing, meals, and local transportation for a prospective student-athlete who paid her own way to visit the campus.[33]

The difficulty to Title IX, however, was that it did demand some changes in recruitment efforts. Ultimately recruitment and self-policing were to stand alone among the policies and regulations that maintained a portion of the women's alternative model. Nonetheless, even with some major recruitment traditions broken, the retainment of a low recruitment profile for member institutions had been retained compared to the male model. Even though there was a small vocal group of members who wished to increase funding for "open" recruiting, the majority of the voting representatives steadfastly rejected this concept. One observation seems legitimate in retrospect: Even the new recruitment regulations led AIAW dangerously close to abandonment of its cardinal principle. The focus on the *student* in her primary role as a *student* moved inexorably toward emphasis on her role as an *athlete*.

In 1981–82, each institution had to declare its commitment to AIAW or NCAA championships. The AIAW's restrictive recruitment rules prompted many large institutions to align their basketball programs with NCAA instead of AIAW's national championship. The basketball coaches especially believed they could not afford to recruit using AIAW regulations, if their peer institutions were recruiting by NCAA regulations. NCAA regulations permitted campus visits paid by the school and active recruiting off campus. Thus in the year of parallel tournaments, most of the top twenty basketball schools selected NCAA competition. This released them from the AIAW regulations and freed them to use the broader regulations for recruitment.[34]

The use of the "letter of intent" was a controversial issue after its initial use during the 1975–76 academic year. The letter bound the prospective student-athlete to the institution with which she had signed a financial aid agreement. In addition, signing the letter of intent protected the student-athlete from the active recruitment of other institutions. The 1979 Assembly made the letter of intent optional for member schools. This was a most liberalizing action which freed both the institution and the student-athlete from AIAW's jurisdiction.[35]

Restructure of AIAW'S Membership

In 1973–74 AIAW sponsored a National Junior College Invitational Basketball Championship. The success of the tournament encouraged an Executive Board vote to maintain a national championship for junior colleges. While these championships were never really financially successful, they offered an opportunity for junior college athletes to have a national championship experience in several sports. AIAW dissolved this division when a majority of the junior/community colleges joined the new Women's Division of the National Junior College Athletic Association. This would be the first men's governance body to conduct a women's national championship and to incorporate women in their structure, foreshadowing the world to come.[36]

A small college national invitational basketball championship occurred in 1975, but the category of "small college" really didn't come into existence until the 1975–76 academic year. The small college division, composed of schools with fewer than 3,000 full-time female undergraduates, sponsored separate championships in ten sports from 1976 until the three division structure of 1978, in which the amount of financial aid provided determined a school's division. In 1980–81 the three divisional structure yielded the largest numbers of participants in state, regional, and national championships that would occur in AIAW.[37]

The question of restructuring both the governance and competitive programs of AIAW was a constant issue within the association. Delegates spent a disproportionate amount of time at the 1976 Delegate Assembly thoroughly considering a restructuring proposal called "Women's Athletics—A Search for Sanity." Following much discussion and many votes, the Assembly declared the following major decisions: (1) AIAW would continue to adopt and endorse regulations rather than guidelines for the control of women's intercollegiate athletics at the national level. (2) There should *not* be a competitive division of the institutions determined by "high intensity" and "low intensity" program commitment (i.e., no three division structure based on financial aid). (3) The criteria essential for any change in regulations should guarantee (a) fair competition for all, (b) protection of the health and safety of all participants, and (c) equal opportunity for women students. (4) AIAW should maintain its relationship with NAGWS/AAHPER.[38]

The decisions made in 1976 did not resolve the critical issue of restructuring and the struggles continued. The 1977 and 1978 Assemblies voted for a plan designed to expand competition and hopefully meet the needs of the diversified membership. The basis of the plan was an institutional "by sport" commitment to one of three divisions. The rationale given for this plan was twofold. It offered (1) institutional autonomy in development of its program and (2) each team the opportunity for high level competition with teams from other institutions funded at a comparable level in that sport.[39]

In reality the plan was much the same as NCAA's divisional (competitive) structure. However, a major difference was the sport by sport commitment. One institution could have teams in different divisions as it developed its program. For the growth process occurring in women's athletics this would permit emerging teams the opportunity to compete at their competitive level. A second important difference was AIAW's commitment to all programs in development of budgets, use of TV funds, and reimbursements. These would occur in all divisions.

Financial aid limits determined classification in the new system. Division I sports allowed up to 100 percent of AIAW's maximum permissible aid, Division II sports allowed up to 50 percent, and Division III sports allowed up to 10 percent. The school's declared division was the one in which it had the most teams. Not surprisingly the largest numbers of scholarships provided in all three divisions did occur in basketball. Basketball also had the largest numbers of institutions competing in any one sport. The new structure ended the large college, small college division after the 1978–79 academic year.[40]

Liaisons and Relationships

AIAW's most significant relationship was with NAGWS/AAHPER. This relationship continued even as AIAW became a separate legal entity, on July 1, 1979. With this new legal structure, AIAW became financially independent, was responsible for its own actions and contractual agreements, and determined all of its own structures, policies, and programs. A major point of agreement in the separation was to continue the liaison relationship with NAGWS and "continue its educational focus in programs, policies and structure whether it is a substructure, a structure or a separate legal entity."[41] AIAW used NAGWS Guides and officials.

AIAW had close liaison relationships with amateur sport governing bodies as well as with the United States Olympic Committee and the United States Collegiate Sport Council (USCSC). It was a member of the USOC and had membership in USCSC. This cooperative stance was most advantageous for expanding programs and cooperative development of high caliber competition for collegiate athletes.[42]

The AIAW, USOC, and the national sport governing bodies (NGBs) had a mutually dependent relationship. Both the USOC and the NGBs were dependent on the educational system for training top level athletes. AIAW depended on USOC and the NGBs for competitive and coaching opportunities. The AIAW and NAGWS accepted active partnership with NGBs. They encouraged women coaches to assist in training programs for Olympic hopefuls and encouraged institutions to provide facilities for elite athletes. NAGWS/AIAW offered their own resources for tryouts, training camps, coaching, and officiating.

The collegiate basketball players and coaches shared a close affiliation with basketball's sport governing body, the American Basketball Association of the USA (ABAUSA). This afforded opportunity for international competition in Pan American Games, World University Games, Olympics, FIBA World Championships, world tours, and Summer Festival competition. The success the United States experienced in women's sports in the last three Olympics (1976, 1984, 1988) was a direct result of having intercollegiate competition and this mutual cooperation. Since 1976, all Olympic women basketball players have been collegiate athletes, as have all of the coaches for international teams.

The NAGWS and AIAW expended major attention, energy, and funding to lobby for enactment of the Amateur Sports Act of 1978. They led the pursuit for the betterment of sports and the financial support female athletes have enjoyed as a result of the ASA.[43]

AIAW sponsored and/or encouraged several international tours by Australia and two Chinese teams. This opened the door for AIAW schools to play exhibition games with both countries. Subsequently, several other countries came to America to compete in exhibition games. They were not officially sponsored by AIAW but they were welcomed to compete against collegiate teams. In addition individual AIAW schools traveled to foreign countries for competition, and individual athletes were selected for touring with American teams abroad.

Another AIAW cooperative relationship, this one with a commercial organization, was important to women's basketball. The April 8, 1978 Underalls All American Classic, in Greensboro, North Carolina, was sponsored by Hanes Hosiery Inc. and Medalist Sports Education. They paid for the country's most talented collegiate female basketball players to compete in an East/West basketball game. This was the first of two such all-star events sponsored by Hanes and Medalist in cooperation with AIAW.[44]

Budget, Finances, Contracts

AIAW's annual budget was initially quite small and dependent on membership dues and NAGWS funding. As AIAW grew in membership and prestige and acquired TV and other corporate sponsorship contracts, its budget neared $1 million. This enabled partial travel reimbursement to national championships. Again basketball was at the forefront in receiving partial travel reimbursements. It was also basketball that first received funds from TV coverage of a championship.[45]

In budgetary matters AIAW conducted and controlled its own business, but AAHPER had final authority over contracts and budget approval until the separation. Originally DGWS/NAGWS financed most of the AIAW program, but by the end of the 1970s AIAW was paying all of its own way in the Association. In fact, it paid overhead and a percentage of its profits to AAHPERD.[46]

AIAW's early monies came primarily from membership dues that ranged from $100 upward to $750 per year, using a sliding scale based on the size of the institution and then divisional structure. The other major source of funding was tournament fees. In the championships AIAW received 75 percent of the profits in the early years, a 50-50 split in the middle years, and 25 percent during the last years. It took an additional 4 percent from the total net income of the larger championships.[47]

Television was, of course, an important aspect of AIAW's intercollegiate sport program. In recognition of TV's potential hazards, yet knowing its potential for needed revenue, the 1976 Assembly passed legislation that designated AIAW the exclusive agency for nonlocal TV on both the regional and national levels. The 1978 and 1979 Assemblies followed with legislation that provided for sharing with member institutions, AIAW, regions, and national championship schools the revenue from TV events and championship profits. This revenue sharing across large and small schools and all three divisional structures was a unique feature of AIAW.[48]

AIAW signed several agreements with commercial firms that benefited both collegiate athletics and AIAW. Examples of such agreements were: Broderick Award for outstanding athlete, the Kodak All-America Basketball Teams, and the Wilson Scholarship Program. There were also several co-sponsorships such as the high school brochure paid for by Coca Cola and the Tea Council for small college tennis. A variety of smaller TV contracts and corporate sponsorship supported banquets and awards or furnished equipment for national championships. The income from all these sources by 1980 was about $50,000 from corporate sponsorship and another $350,000 from TV contracts. In 1981 the sponsorship and TV contracts rose to over $650,000.[49]

The early TV contracts were with TVN in 1978 for at least eight hours of cable national championships. The lucrative NBC and ESPN contracts followed the earlier smaller contracts. The first nationally televised event was the 1978 basketball championship, which appeared on NBC's Sportsworld. The 1979 basketball finals were moved to Sunday afternoon to accommodate NBC. This accommodation added another $10,000 to the AIAW contract. Then in 1980 the entire basketball final was covered live and NBC signed a four-year contract with AIAW, which increased the yearly sum to over $200,000.[50]

The success of negotiations with ESPN and NBC for national TV coverage for several national championships enabled AIAW to reimburse teams' travel and lodging for championships beginning in 1978. The AIAW limited the first year reimbursements to 50 percent of the total expense of the four final teams. In 1980 all teams in the three divisional 24 team basketball championships received reimbursements up to 40 percent. By the 1980–81 academic year the reimbursements for all basketball teams in all divisions was 51 percent.[51]

AIAW wished to maintain its educational focus. However, TV exposure was necessary to continue offering high calibre championships. There was pressure for the membership to increase offerings, services, and the expansion of sports. Championships demanded that commercialization and using the proceeds be a part of the scheme of things. Expansion of the organization, addition of a full-time public relations director, and more national championships, as well as its increased annual budget, are evidence of AIAW's financial responsibilities and new capability to offer services. The separation of AIAW from NAGWS was partly a direct result of AIAW's desire for autonomy to permit commercial contractual agreements and to limit its payment of profits to the Association.[52]

By its final year of operation, AIAW had stretched to the limit its budget, operation, and contributions to member schools. Yet it was able to provide services well beyond the expectations of the organization based on its limited, less than $1 million budget. Its services rendered were significant, particularly if one compares the budgets of the NCAA with budget and services rendered by AIAW. Fiscal prudence was one of the reasons AIAW could offer ever increasing programs and visibility.[53]

AIAW Critical Issues and Struggles

The survival of any voluntary organization is based on its capacity to interact with environmental dynamics internal and external to the organization. For its entire life span AIAW endured a series of threats to its existence and its educational athletic model. There were four major external conflicts: (1) The first event was the lawsuit to permit collegiate female athletes on scholarship to compete in the AIAW championship. (2) The second, Title IX, was of even greater magnitude (it is discussed in Hult's chapter on "The Saga of Competition"). (3) The third was a strong feminist movement to include women's athletics as part of its cause of *exact* equality. Some feminists within AIAW, and to a greater extent those outside the sport traditions, were willing to accept the male norm for determining parity. (4) The fourth, and most significant to AIAW's very existence, was a life threatening struggle with NCAA.

Each of these complex and interrelated conflicts might singly have been of lesser consequence to AIAW and its membership. Perhaps without the first two events, NCAA would have continued to exhibit no interest in women's athletics. After all, an alternative model was no real threat to NCAA's commercial athletic industry.

With new conditions, decision making positions changed, lines of communication became more significant, and the legitimization (commitment to the ideology) was in question. AIAW's basic organizational characteristics changed, as did its influence.

Title IX of the Education Amendments demanded full compliance for secondary schools and colleges by July 21, 1978. The guidelines and implementation regulations had been published in June 1975. This was the single most significant federal legislation to affect the growth and expansion of girls and women's sport. It was also the major roadblock to the women's model of athletics.[54]

Title IX was an external threat to AIAW and NCAA. It mobilized the NCAA for the first time in the area of women's athletics and led both organizations to conflicting positions. NCAA feared that some form of equality for women's athletics would drain resources away from the men's program. It fought the application of the law, at institutional levels, in the courts, in Congress, and in the Office of Civil Rights. AIAW moved as a unified spirit with a network and coalition without precedent within the sporting tradition, to support Title IX. AIAW won this battle.[55]

To the extent that AIAW won on Title IX, the outcome could be interpreted as a *Pyrrhic victory*. Women's athletics were here to stay and were apt to be significantly funded, thereby attracting the interest of NCAA. This precipitated the debate on offering women's programs within the NCAA organization. The final battle for control of women's athletics was still several years away. Yet the constant threatening influences loomed enormous and significant in all the future operations and actions of AIAW and NCAA.

Title IX was also critical to the internal power configuration of AIAW. It was the catalyst in the rift between the traditionalists and the modernists in charting new directions and remodeling the student-centered education-oriented model. Some feminists within AIAW, as well as external feminists, pressured for first class treatment, legislative mandates for greater visibility, larger portions of the money, and a new image of the importance of women's athletics. All of these contributed to AIAW's loss of focus. Feminist consciousness impacted on the younger athletic personnel who rose to power. As they did so, many "Old Guard" retired from the struggle. They saw their dream of the new athletic model pale in the face of the "New Guard" wanting to monopolize

By the 1980s, women's basketball had expanded greatly in number of participants, and the level of skills exhibited had increased. Title IX was a primary factor in this growth, but it led ultimately to the demise of the women's separate model of athletics. Women's athletics was here to stay, but it was not to be governed by a women's organization.

existing resources and tap resources available as a result of the Title IX victory. The "Old Guard" saw the ardent amateurism positions being replaced by acceptance of quasi-professionalism in women's athletics. The AIAW moved to a major/minor (revenue and nonrevenue) concept like the male model. They combined this with a whole series of innovative noneducational approaches to conducting athletic programs.[56]

However, enforcement of Title IX meant that money, facilities, personnel, and authority over amateur athletics must be shared equitably with women's programs. Financial aid must be in proportion to the total number of male and female athletes at each institution. Women in athletics saw the advantage of such parity. But equality could not be reconciled with the women's commitment to remain different and to preserve an educational emphasis when the male model was the norm. Furthermore, feminists and some women coaches wished to have exact equality, right or wrong. In the final analysis, although AIAW recognized the potential problems of being forced to duplicate the male norm, they took that risk and made the total commitment to Title IX.[57]

NCAA also spent enormous amounts of money as it continually sought exemption for so-called "revenue producing" sports through the legislative and regulatory process. NCAA lost the battle for reducing the authority of Title IX, and revenue producing sports were not exempt. Therefore, women's programs required funds. NCAA began to consider and debate the possible inclusion of women's programs in its own organization. This launched the battle for control of women's intercollegiate athletics. In the midst of turmoil, in 1979, AIAW had dissolved its affiliation with NAGWS/AAHPERD. Some armchair historians believe that AIAW lost status and became more vulnerable to attack without the support of AAHPERD.[58]

An indirect result of Title IX was the merging of men's and women's departments of physical education and departments of athletics, although there was no Title IX mandate for mergers. With each new merger, institutional leaders demoted women administrators and directors of physical education and women's athletics to secondary positions. Men athletic directors and men chairs of physical education departments were almost automatically given control of the merged departments. This provided additional power over women's athletic fate and permitted NCAA clear sailing to offering championships. It was the mergers that placed NCAA in a position to dictate to its members the need to join one organization. The actions on financial aid, divisional structure, and recruitment were the major regulations affected by Title IX and would move the AIAW's alternative model of student-centered athletics toward the NCAA model.[59]

NCAA/AIAW

A majority of the women in AIAW wanted to maintain their own organization. But there was a group of women from large institutions and basketball powers who wished to join NCAA. A combination of this dissident voice within AIAW and the all-out campaign by NCAA led to the final demise of AIAW. AIAW's first major conflict then was because of Title IX. The second event, and the "watershed," was the life threatening struggle with the NCAA.[60]

Throughout the 1970s representatives of the AIAW and NCAA discussed possible merger, but neither organization had any real incentive. The NCAA did not really consider the AIAW an equal, and the AIAW would not deal with NCAA on any other terms. The following factors are among the many influences that encouraged NCAA to offer championships for women: (1) enforcement of Title IX, (2) growth of women's sport, increased women's budgets, and women's TV contracts, and (3) the growing representation of AIAW on USOC committees and NGBs. In 1980 Divisions II and III voted for championships for women and in 1981 Division I followed suit. The powerful NCAA Council strongly endorsed the "take over." There was considerable legislative maneuvering both within the ranks of the NCAA and on college campuses resulting in a hotly contested vote and narrow victory for Division I championships, with Divisions II and III already having championships. Days earlier, the AIAW delegates had voted to remain a separate organization (by an overwhelming majority).[61]

For one year both AIAW and NCAA offered women's championships, forcing colleges to choose between them for each sport. The rate of defection from AIAW by larger institutions and the loss of TV contracts made it clear which organization would prevail. The NCAA had far greater resources. They promised to subsidize travel costs to national championships and to not charge additional membership dues for its women's program. Their more liberal recruitment regulations were appealing to most institution's athletic directors (male) and NCAA's voting delegates (94 percent men). AIAW immediately filed an injunction against NCAA to prevent the championships, but this failed. Seeing the inevitable, AIAW suspended operations and concentrated its remaining resources in a lawsuit against NCAA for violation of the Antitrust Act prohibiting monopolies. The suit failed, leading to the demise of AIAW.[62]

As part of the total package for women's national championships, the NCAA had presented to the membership a plan of action to include women in leadership roles. The NCAA agreed to a five-year plan that assured women a maximum of 16 percent representation on the NCAA council and from 18–24 percent membership on other important committees. NCAA selected women chairs in situations where only women competed in a sport, yet even in women's sports a committee of all women was rare.[63]

NAIA

AIAW's relationship with NAIA was most cordial until efforts by NAIA to begin championships for women. While AIAW and NAIA were much closer in philosophical commitment to the student-athlete, the NAIA plan for a single organization and the sponsorship of women's championships was not acceptable to AIAW. There was a definite cooling of relations between the two groups. Nonetheless, representatives of each group met and agreed to determine the will of their membership on the issue. AIAW's Delegate Assembly passed a resolution asking NAIA not to conduct women's championships. NAIA delegates nonetheless in 1979 voted to conduct women's national championships. NAIA started championships in the 1980–81 academic year, but developed a separate Women's Division plan for its national championships.[64] (See also Phyllis Holmes' section on NAIA in this volume.)

AIAW's Legacy

AIAW's legacy to the sports world is monumental. The association was successful for a decade at offering an alternative model of intercollegiate athletics for female athletes. The women created a highly effective governance structure and won the Title IX "war." But AIAW's very success led to its demise as, beyond the wildest dreams of its creators, it fulfilled its mission of providing opportunity for female athletes.

AIAW leaders accepted NCAA leadership roles and provided the role model and mentor system for the present generation of young coaches who came out of the AIAW collegiate team ranks and an entire generation of Olympic female athletes. Chris Cathy Anruzzi, who played for Queens and now coaches at East Carolina, noted: "It freaks me out to think of all those players who were in that tournament and now we're the coaches of today making the decisions for the future of women's basketball."[65]

The struggle for survival of a women's athletic model of intercollegiate athletics failed. The opportunity for the female collegiate athletes, however, succeeded. Women moved into the hierarchy of the NCAA in a planned program that assured women access to some leadership roles. Nowhere was that more apparent than in the sport committees of basketball under NCAA in all three divisions. While the makeup of the committee membership took the power away from the women coaches, there was still a great deal of autonomy by women members of the committee from the ranks of administration. While their autonomy was far less than under AIAW it is greater than some had anticipated.

Thanks to AIAW and an army of volunteer physical educators, a generation of basketball players (and all players in the other 18 championships) had opportunity to reach for the stars. The athletes pursued their championship and Olympic dreams and also became the present generation of basketball coaches. As women's basketball celebrates its 100 years, the basketball athletes can salute those who were their role models, mentors, and leaders with their commitment to "the good of those who play."

Notes

In conducting the research on the AIAW, extensive use was made of the AIAW papers housed in Special Collections, University of Maryland, College Park Libraries. Unless otherwise noted, AIAW endnotes cited are from AIAW "Preliminary Inventory" materials. When specific topics are identified in the Preliminary Inventory, the citation notes the specific topic, followed by P.I. The AIAW National Championships portion of the collection is processed, and any materials from this portion are designated as "National Championships." Thanks to Lauren Brown and his staff in Special Collections for their patience and assistance in uncovering the Preliminary Inventory materials and providing the National Championships papers.

The National Association for Girls and Women in Sport (NAGWS) research completed at the American Alliance for Health, Physical Education, Recreation and Dance (AAHPERD) Archives is cited as AAHPERD Archives. Information contained herein is from the NAGWS collection of the AAHPERD Archives.

1. Eleanor Metheny, "Women in Action: The Story of DGWS, 1892–1958," in *Connotations of Movement in Sport and Dance* (Dubuque, Iowa: Wm. C. Brown Co., 1965), 147.

2. "DGWS Minutes of the Executive Council," Division for Girls and Women's Sports, April 1–6, 1971, Detroit, Michigan, 47, AAHPERD Archives.

3. Joan S. Hult, "Different AIAW/NCAA Eligibility Rules: Tip of the Iceberg?" *Athletic Purchasing & Facilities* (April 1979), 12.

4. National Joint Committee on Extramural Sports for College Women, "Joint Committee Report," June 22, 1958, AAHPERD Archives; DGWS, "Operating Code for the National Joint Committee on Extramural Sports for College Women" (Revised, ND), 1–2, AAHPERD Archives.

5. "Minutes of the Executive Council, Division for Girls and Women's Sports," March 18–22, 1966, Chicago, Illinois (AAHPER), 5–6; DGWS, "Minutes of the Executive Council, DGWS," November 4–6, 1966, Washington, D.C. 24–25, AAHPERD Archives; DGWS, *Procedures for Women's Intercollegiate Athletic Events* (Washington, D.C.: AAHPER, 1967), 2, AAHPERD Archives.

6. DGWS, *Procedures for Women's Intercollegiate Athletic Events*, 4, 22. See also DGWS, *Procedures for Intercollegiate Athletic Events* (Washington, D.C.: AAHPER, 1969), 11, AAHPERD Archives.

7. American Association for Health, Physical Education, and Recreation, "Official Minutes (2) Board of Directors," December 11–13, 1970, Washington, D.C., 62, AAHPERD Archives; "DGWS Minutes of Executive Council," April 1971, 47–51. See also a discussion of the rationale for AIAW in DGWS "Minutes of the Executive Council, DGWS," October 22–25, 1970, Chicago, Illinois, 38–43, AAHPERD Archives.

8. DGWS, "Minutes of the Executive Council, Division for Girls and Women's Sports," October 21–24, 1971, Washington, D.C., 25–26, AAHPERD Archives.

9. Association for Intercollegiate Athletics for Women, *AIAW Hand-Book of Policies and Interim Operating Procedures 1971–72* (Washington, D.C.: AAHPER, 1971), 6, AAHPERD Archives.

10. "AIAW Constitution and Bylaws," in AIAW Minutes of the Executive Board of the AIAW, Harrisonburg, Virginia, May 31–June 4, 1973 (Addendum No. 1 and 2), 8.

11. AIAW, "Minutes of the First Association for Intercollegiate Athletics for Women Delegate Assembly," Overland Park, Kansas, November 4–6, 1973, 5.

12. DGWS, "Minutes of Vice Presidents' and Consultant's Meeting," Kent, Ohio, June 22–25, 1972, 2; AIAW Executive Board Meeting, Betty Hartman, "Summary of Actions taken by DGWS Executive Council During Fall 1972," 3; "Addendum, Open Discussion–Friday Night," in AIAW "Minutes of AIAW Executive Board," St. Louis, December 15–17, 1972, 21.

13. *AIAW Handbook of Policies and Operating Procedures 1973–74* (Washington, D.C.: AAHPER, 1973), 24, 26.

14. AIAW Delegate Assembly Minutes, 1973, 7–8.

15. Ann Uhlir, "Personal Executive Files" Executive Director's File, P.I.; "AIAW, Official Minutes of the Executive Board and Delegate Assembly Meetings," Scottsdale, Arizona, January 11–15, 1976, 27–31.

16. AIAW Delegate Assembly Minutes, 1973, 1–3. The gender of the voting delegate appears on the Membership Application. Microcard of Membership Applications 1973–74 and 1981–82, AIAW Microcard File, P.I.; Donna Lopiano, Report to Executive Board, "NCAA Convention," January 1981. Executive Files, P.I.

17. AIAW, *Directory Charter Member Institutions, 1971–1972*, Division for Girls and Women's Sports (Washington, D.C.: AAHPER, 1972); *Association for Intercollegiate Athletics for Women, Directory 1981–1982* (Washington, D.C.: AAHPER, 1981), 10–55. See also Ann Uhlir, "Athletics and the University: The Post-Women's ERA," *Academe* 4 (1987): 17–36.

18. AIAW, *Student Leadership Manual* (Washington, D.C.: AAHPER, 1978).

19. Mel Greenberg, "Ten Years of AIAW Basketball," in AIAW Basketball Program 1981–82. (Basketball, 1981–82 Files), National Championships.

20. See Jill Hutchison's article for examples of how the sports committees functioned.

21. Joan Hult, "Newsletter" 1977 and "Newsletter" 1978. Ethics and Eligibility files, P.I.

22. AIAW Ethics and Eligibility—*Sanctions*. The Sanctions folders are not in order, but the data about changes are plentiful. E&E Files, P.I.

23. AIAW, Ethics and Eligibility—*Individual Student-Athlete Waivers*, E&E Files, P.I.

24. AIAW, Ethics and Eligibility—*Appeals*. E&E Files, P.I.

25. AIAW, "Rules Standards Committee Reports," 1978–79, 1979–80, 1980–81, and 1981–82. E&E Files, P.I.

26. AIAW, "Minutes of the Winter Executive Board Meeting, Detroit, Mich., Jan. 5, 1980," 20; AIAW, "Official Minutes of the Delegate Assembly, Detroit, Mich., Jan. 6–9, 1980," 20; AIAW, "Official Minutes of the Executive Board, May 5–7, 1981, Washington, D.C.," 16–18; AIAW, "Official Minutes of the Executive Board, Oct., 1981," 12.

27. AIAW Delegate Assembly Minutes, 1973, 6.

28. AIAW Delegate Assembly Minutes, 1973, 5–7; "AIAW Interim Regulations for Financial Aid to Student-Athletes" (May, 1974). See also "Proposed AIAW Regulations for the Awarding of Financial Aid to Student-Athletes," Addendum Executive Board, January, 1974; AIAW, "Mail Vote of the Financial Aid and Recruitment Regulations" in the ByLaws Voting Package for Institutions, 1974.

29. Ibid.

30. "Financial Aid Resolution" in AIAW Delegate Assembly Minutes, 1976, 54; "Financial Aid Regulations and Motions" in AIAW Official Minutes of the Delegate Assembly, January 2–6, 1977, Memphis, Tennessee, 45–60. The vote was 275 for, 145 opposed; AIAW Official Minutes of the Delegate Assembly, Atlanta, Georgia, January 8–11, 1978, 66–70.

31. "Report on Financial Aid and Participation of Schools (By Sport)," The Executive Files, 1981–82, P.I. See also Ann Uhlir, "For Whom the Dollars Toll," *Journal of the National Association for Women Deans, Administrators and Counselors* (Winter, 1984), 13–22.

32. AIAW Delegate Assembly Minutes, Jan., 1978, 60–63; "AIAW Executive and Delegate Assembly Minutes," Los Angeles, California, January 6–11, 1979, 46–47.

33. AIAW Delegate Assembly Minutes, 1979, 47–49.

34. AIAW, "Official Executive Board and Delegate Assembly Meetings," Spokane, Washington, January 5–10, 1982, 40–42; "Motion Booklet for the 1982 AIAW Delegate Assembly," January 6–9, 42–44.

35. AIAW, "Official Minutes of the First Executive Board Meeting, January 4–5 and January 7, 1975, Houston, Texas," 7–8; "Official Minutes of the AIAW Delegate Assembly," January 5–8, 1975, Houston, Texas, 18–19; AIAW Delegate Assembly Minutes, 1979, 45.

36. "Minutes of the Executive Board of AIAW," May–June, 1973, 12, 18.

37. "AIAW Executive Board Meeting," May 22–25, 1974, Dallas, Texas, (Summary of Actions), 2–3; Delegate Assembly, 1979; Ann Uhlir, "The Wolf Is Our Shepherd: Shall We Not Fear?" *Phi Delta Kappan* (November 1982): 172–176; "Affidavit of Donna A. Lopiano, AIAW vs. NCAA," United States District Court for the District of Columbia, Legal File, P.I.

38. AIAW Delegate Assembly Minutes (Part II), January 1976, 23–24, 34–36.

39. AIAW Delegate Assembly Minutes, January 2–6, 1977, 25–29; Delegate Assembly Minutes, January 1978, 77–83; Delegate Assembly Minutes, 1979, 15–33.

40. Delegate Assembly Minutes, 1979, 15–22.

41. Judy Holland, "AIAW/NAGWS Memorandum of Understanding," Delegate Assembly, 1979, Legal Files, P.I. See also AIAW, "Official Minutes of the Fall Executive Board Meeting, Los Angeles, California, October 10–13, 1978"; "AAHPER/NAGWS/AIAW Relationship" (Kansas City, April 3–5, 1978), AAHPERD Archives.

42. DGWS/NAGWS, "Report of the United States Collegiate Sport Council," 1969, 1973, and 1978, *International Competition Files*, P.I. See also NAGWS, "International Competition File," AAHPERD Archives; Fran Koenig to AIAW

Executive Board, "Report on AIAW International Competition, September 30, 1975," International Competition Folder, AAHPERD Archives.

43. Amateur Sports Act of 1978, "Report of the Senate Committee on Commerce, Science, and Transportation" (Washington, D.C.: U.S. Government Printing Office). See also Joan S. Hult, "Women's Struggle for Governance in U.S. Amateur Athletics," *International Review for Sociology of Sport* 24 (November, 1989): 249–261.

44. AIAW, "Underalls All American Classic in Greensboro," (Report from Public Relations), Hanes Hosiery Folder, National Championships.

45. AIAW, "Official Minutes of Spring Executive Board Meeting, Washington, D.C., May 6–9, 1980, (1980–81 Budget)" 27; "1980 Basketball Financial Plan," in AIAW Executive Board Minutes, May, 1980, 19; "1981 Basketball Financial Plan," in AIAW Executive Board Minutes, May, 1980, 19; AIAW "Official Minutes of Spring Executive Board Meeting, Washington, D.C., May 5–7, 1981, (Budget Approval)" 23.

46. DGWS Executive Board Minutes, 1972; "AIAW Working Budget," The Executive Files, 1978–79, P.I.

47. Ann Uhlir, AIAW Executive Director, "1980–81 Working Budget," The Executive Files, PI; *AIAW Handbook, 1972* (Washington, D.C.: AAHPER, 1971); *AIAW Handbook, 1981–82* (Washington, D.C.: AAHPER, 1981), 70. See also Hutchison's article in this book.

48. Delegate Assembly Minutes, 1976, 40–41; Delegate Assembly Minutes, 1978, 84–86; Delegate Assembly Minutes, 1979, 52–56.

49. "AIAW, Broderick Award Contract," Broderick Folders, National Championships; "Kodak All America Basketball Contracts," Kodak All America Folders, National Championships; "Tea Council Contract," Tea Council Folder, National Championships; "List of Contracts and Amounts," Contract Folder, The Executive Director's Files, P.I.; "AIAW 1980–81 Budget Summary," The Executive Files, P.I., 49.

50. "Contract for Sugarman Agreement, 1975–77," "TVN Contract, 1978," "NBC Contract, 1978," "Agreement of Understanding NBC, 1979–1981," all Contracts are together in a Contract Folder, P.I.

51. "Contract, NBC" (Agreement), Contract Folders, National Championships, "Agreement ESPN, 1980–83," Contract Folder, PI; "Reimbursements for Basketball Championships, 1980–81," National Championships-Basketball, 1981; "1980–81 Distribution Plan: Distribution of Receipts for First Three Rounds," Basketball, 1980–81 National Championships.

52. "AIAW Budget, 1979–80"; "AIAW Budget 1980–81"; "AIAW Approved Budget 1981–82"; Letter from Margot Polivy to Peg Burke on AIAW organizational relationships, April 30, 1976, Executive Director's Correspondence File, P.I.

53. Delegate Assembly Minutes, 1980, "Budget"; Delegate Assembly Minutes, 1981, "Budget."

54. "Final Title IX Regulation Implementing Education Amendments of 1972, Prohibiting Sex Discrimination in Education" (Washington, D.C.: U.S. Department of Health, Education, and Welfare/Office for Civil Rights, 1975); *Federal Register*, Department of Health, Education, and Welfare, Office of the Secretary, Wednesday, June 4, 1975, Washington, D.C., Vol. 40, No. 108, Part II. See also AIAW Title IX Files, Legal, P.I. This file contains all actions,

correspondence, and work of AIAW in the struggle for Title IX passage and compliancy. See also Ann M. Seha, "The Administrative Enforcement of Title IX in Intercollegiate Athletics," in *Law and Inequality: A Journal of Theory and Practice* 2(1): 121–325.

55. Joan S. Hult, "The Philosophical Conflicts in Men's and Women's Collegiate Athletics," *Quest* 32(1), 1980: 77–94; Hult, "Women's Struggle for Governance," 254–256; Donna A. Lopiano, "Affidavit of Donna A. Lopiano: AIAW v. NCAA," U.S. District Court for the District of Columbia, 1981; Donna A. Lopiano, "A Political Analysis of the Possibility of Impact Alternatives for the Accomplishment of Feminist Objectives within American Intercollegiate Sport," in Richard E. Lapchick, ed., *Fractured Focus* (Lexington, Mass.: Lexington Books, 1986), 163–176.

56. Hult, "Women's Governance"; Lopiano, "Affidavit of AIAW v. NCAA". See also Joan S. Hult, "Women's Athletics: Power and Politics," North American Society for Sport History, Louisville, Ky., May 1984, unpublished paper.

57. Elizabeth Anne Alden, "Feminism and Women's Sports: The Influence of Four Women's Organizations, 1960–78" (MA Thesis, University of Maryland, 1983); Hult, "Philosophical Conflicts"; Hult, "Women's Struggle for Governance"; Delegate Assembly Minutes, 1979; Delegate Assembly Minutes, 1980; Delegate Assembly Minutes, 1981.

58. Donna A. Lopiano, "AIAW v. NCAA"; Association for Intercollegiate Athletics for Women, Plaintiff v. National Collegiate Athletic Association, Defendant, "Pretrial Brief for the Plaintiff" (Karina Renouf, Margaret Polivy, Alan Bergstein) Civil No. 81-2473 Jackson, J. in the U.S. District Court for the District of Columbia (August 23, 1982). Legal, P.I.

59. Delegate Assembly Minutes, 1980; Delegate Assembly Minutes, 1981; R. Vivian Acosta and Linda Jean Carpenter, "Women in Sport," in Donald Chu, Jeffrey Segrave, and Beverly Becker (eds.), *Sport and Higher Education* (Champaign, Ill.: Human Kinetics, 1985), 313–326; Idem, "The Status of Women in Intercollegiate Athletics—A Five-year National Study," in *Sport and Higher Education*, 327–334.

60. Delegate Assembly Minutes, 1982; Lopiano, "Affidavit."

61. Delegate Assembly, 1982; Lopiano, "Affidavit"; Donna Lopiano to Executive Board, NCAA Convention, January 1981, The Executive Files, P.I.

62. AIAW v. NCAA Civil Action 81-2473, U.S. District Court for the District of Columbia, "Decision and Order," Legal, P.I.

63. "NCAA 5-Year Plan," Women's Athletic Committee NCAA, The Executive Files, P.I.

64. Delegate Assembly Minutes, 1980; Minutes of Executive Board, May 1980.

65. Mel Greenberg, "Hoops World Upheaval" in *NCAA Basketball Preview* (Lexington, Ky.: Host Communications, 1990), 98–102.

Coach Carol Eckman and the West Chester State (Pa.) Ramettes, winners of the first National Invitational Collegiate Basketball Tournament.

17

Women's Intercollegiate Basketball: AIAW/NCAA

Jill Hutchison

The First National Invitational Tournament at West Chester State College, Pennsylvania, in 1969 ushered in the modern era of women's intercollegiate basketball. After three invitational championships (1969, 1970, 1971), the Association for Intercollegiate Athletics for Women (AIAW) sponsored eleven national championships between 1972 and 1982. The National Collegiate Athletic Association (NCAA) began competition in women's basketball in the 1981–82 season and continues to govern national championships. This article focuses on the competitive structures, personalities, rules, and international involvement of collegiate coaches and players from 1969 to the present.

I have relied essentially on my own experience as a basketball coach, my association as member and chair of the AIAW Basketball Committee throughout its history, and my personal papers. I also used selected materials from the AIAW archives housed at the University of Maryland and received assistance from the NCAA headquarters[1] and USA Basketball.

Invitational Tournaments

Carol Eckman, who could appropriately be recognized as the "Mother of National Championships," initiated the National Invitational Collegiate Tournaments. As the coach from West Chester State College, with a national calibre team, she could see the need for higher levels of competition. In spite of the criticism of her peers, her own mentors, and some in her institution, Carol took on the task of providing collegiate women with national championship experience. With assistance from her physical education friends and students, she planned and conducted the event with minimal financial support.

Sixteen teams from around the country gathered at West Chester State for the single elimination tournament with a consolation bracket. Carol Eckman coached her squad to victory over Western Carolina in the championship game. It was a sweet victory for Carol and would prove to be her only National Championship in several attempts over the next few years. Iowa Wesleyan defeated the University of Iowa for third place, while Towson State of Maryland captured the consolation championship. Women's collegiate basketball was truly on its way.

Jeanne Rowlands, a successful coach and pioneer of competitive athletics for women, directed the second invitational tournament in 1970 at Northeastern University in Boston. Jeanne not only was a successful coach but became very active in the international scene. Sixteen teams again filled the bracket (draw) that year with even better national representation. Cal State-Fullerton, coached by Billie Jean Moore, claimed the national title over runner-up West Chester. If Carol Eckman was the "Mother of National Championships," Billie Moore was soon to be tabbed the "Mother of Collegiate Basketball." Her knowledge of the game, coaching expertise, and service to collegiate basketball were models for coaches for years to come. Ursinus College (Pennsylvania) defeated Western Carolina for third place and Southern Illinois University (coached by Charlotte West) was the consolation winner. This was the last season that collegiate basketball utilized the six player roving rules. Research in 1970 supported the fact that female athletes could endure the stresses of competitive basketball using the full court without detrimental effects. This realization and the rule change revolutionized women's collegiate basketball.

The final invitational tournament, using the five player game, was in 1971 at Western Carolina University in Cullowhee, North Carolina. Athletic Director Betty Peele and Coach Betty Westmoreland co-directed the sixteen team tournament. Coach Jill Upton led her team from Mississippi College for Women to the championship title over, once again, Carol Eckman's West Chester State team. Southern Connecticut State College, coached by Louise O'Neal, a member of the women's basketball committee for the next decade, defeated Western Carolina for third place, and Cal State-Fullerton won the consolation bracket.

The period governed by the Association for Intercollegiate Athletics for Women (AIAW) was characterized by rapid growth in the national scope of the game and leadership by the coaches of women's basketball. The Commission on Intercollegiate Athletics for Women (CIAW) actually conducted the first official National Championship. The CIAW was a commission of the Division for Girls and Women's Sports (DGWS) of the American Association for Health, Physical Education and Recreation (AAHPER). Basketball was the last sport to achieve national championship status within the CIAW. Historically, collegiate physical educators had feared that "competitive evils" were inherent in basketball; therefore the 1972 championship reflected a major breakthrough in the attitudes toward intercollegiate basketball for women.

AIAW National Basketball Championships

Illinois State University hosted the first official championship. I directed the tournament while Carol Oglesby (president of AIAW) and Lou Jean Moyer (CIAW chair) supervised the event. The three of us comprised the tournament committee. The major focus of the 1972 Championship was to achieve national representation. For this tournament the basketball committee developed a regional qualifying structure. The new CIAW geographic regions were identified and the winner automatically qualified for the sixteen team national bracket. The selection criteria for the remaining seven teams included: an additional representative from the regions with large numbers of teams competing, the host school's team, and two at-large teams selected on season records and their strength of schedule. In the absence of previous national or even interregional competition, the committee based the seeding for the 1972 championship on the results of the previous two invitational tournaments. Eight teams were seeded: Region 3 seeded first, Region 1B second seed, Region 8 the third seed, etc. In order to avoid teams meeting opponents they had met during the season, the committee placed the remaining eight teams in the bracket. Approximately half the teams were clad in hockey tunics while others wore double knit polyester shorts—culture shock!

The result of the three-day tournament (single-elimination, consolation) was a championship for the small, unrenowned, all girls school Immaculata College (Pennsylvania), a team coached by pregnant Cathy Rush. West Chester was again the bridesmaid as Coach Eckman's troops lost in the finals 52–48. The "Mighty Macs" had arrived piecemeal as funds had been donated for their trip and players were unable to travel together. The school nuns were their most ardent fans and accompanied them even to Normal, Illinois. The third place winner was Cal State-Fullerton. The fourth place went to Mississippi State College for Women, and fifth was Queens College coached by Lucille Kyvallos.

The 1972–73 Championship moved to Queens College in Flushing, New York, under the direction of Coach Kyvallos. The new AIAW was now fully in charge of all national championships. This led to the creation of a basketball committee whose chair the Executive Board of AIAW appointed for a three-year term. Each year basketball coaches present at the Championship elected their own representatives to the committee. All members of the AIAW Basketball Committee were coaches. The sports committee established policies and procedures governing the championships and had an unusual amount of autonomy. The first year's committee included Lou Jean Moyer, Carol Eckman, Jill Hutchison, and Lucille Kyvallos.

During the tournament an AIAW national representative had the final decision-making power over issues beyond the reach of the officials or the authority of the sports committee. For the first time crowd control became one of the off court issues. Coach Kyvallos had to urge her fans to show positive support for the Queens' team, but not rudeness to their guests. It was a nice problem to have in 1973.

The 1973 tournament became a four-day occasion requiring only four of the sixteen teams to play twice in one day. The Championship committee seeded teams from the previous year's championship records, which resulted in the same seeding as in 1972 except for the exchange of seventh and eighth seeds. Immaculata College repeated as the National Champion with a 59–52 victory over host Queens College in front of a packed house of 3,000 cheering fans. Many fans had been turned away at the gate an hour before tip-off. Center Theresa Shank contributed a momentous 104 points during the championship. Theresa would find herself 20 years later as head coach for the 1992 Olympic Team. Southern Connecticut State College (who lost to Immaculata College in the semifinals on a last second shot by Shank) claimed third place with a victory over Indiana University (73–53). Kansas State won the consolation bracket.

The budget was $11,199, with expenses of $6,568. The profit was 25 percent for Queens ($1,157) and 75 percent for AIAW ($3,473). This was a slow start by many folks' standards, but nevertheless a start on financial independence for basketball.

The 1973 season also marked the first AIAW Invitational Junior/ Community College Championship. Amidst a Michigan blizzard Mississippi Gulf Coast Junior College (Perkinston Campus) won a close low scoring game (38–37) against Anderson College of South Carolina. Vincennes, Indiana disappointed the hometown fans by defeating Delta College for third place honors. The blizzard helped contribute to a $236 deficit.

In 1974 both Hawaii and Alaska asked to be considered for selection in the AIAW Tournament. The Basketball Committee decided the schools could apply and submit a video tape for evaluation in addition to their records. Neither team played within the contiguous United States and neither would be selected for several years. The 1974 season also represented the first AIAW sponsored international touring team from Australia, which had been encouraged by Coach Billie Moore.

Perhaps most significant in 1974 was the first inclusion of schools and athletes receiving scholarships. Title IX had mandated that female athletes receive scholarships to play comparable to their male counterparts competing in educational institutions. Several AAU collegiate teams who offered athletic scholarships had dominated the AAU National Championships in the last two decades. Wayland Baptist was the dominant collegiate team in AAU championships while William Penn College (Iowa) and John F. Kennedy University each had won AAU Championships. The 1974 season brought the "showdown" to test whether the collegiate or AAU route had developed the best quality programs. The first year the AIAW declared J.F. Kennedy ineligible for membership because they were not an accredited university. So Wayland Baptist, coached by Dean Weese, and William Penn, coached by Bob Spencer, represented the "AAU scholarship schools." They were also two of the first teams to have male coaches, along with Ed Nixon's team from Ole Miss.

Immaculata captured its third consecutive National Championship defeating Mississippi College 68–53 in the finals in front of 2,500 fans at Kansas State University in Manhattan, Kansas, in 1974. William Penn College placed fourth behind Southern Connecticut State College, and Wayland Baptist College beat Tennessee Tech University (coached by Mary Nell Hutsell) in the consolation finals. It appears the AIAW teams could hold their own against the more experienced AAU collegiate teams. The tournament produced a profit of approximately $2,100 split 50–50 this year between Kansas State and the AIAW.

The first official Junior College Tournament was held in Michigan Center at Delta College with a field of 12 teams. The defending champs, Mississippi Gulf Coast (Perkinston campus), lost a close encounter to Anderson College, who revenged its 1 point loss in 1973 to take the championship by one point, 59–58. Bergen Community College of New Jersey captured third, winning over Grand Rapids Junior College (Iowa). Delta College fans watched their team win the consolations.

The 1974 season also welcomed the National Women's Intercollegiate Tournament (NWIT) in Amarillo, Texas, sponsored by the Chamber of Commerce. Amarillo had expressed an interest in serving as a permanent site for the AIAW Championship; however, the offer never materialized. The AIAW (president, Charlotte West) questioned if teams should be allowed to compete in both the AIAW championships and the NWIT. The AIAW ultimately concluded it should be an institutional choice so several teams entered both competitions. Wayland Baptist won the NWIT defeating defending AAU champion J.F. Kennedy.

Madison College in Harrisonburg, Virginia, under the able leadership of Coach Betty Jaynes (member of the basketball sports committee for many years and currently executive director of the WBCA), hosted the 1975 Championship. The Basketball Committee adopted the leather, narrow-seamed ball for championship competition. Both selection and seeding had been refined for this tournament. Selection now included the nine regional champs, the second place team from the region of the past year's champion, the host school, and five at-large selections to complete the sixteen team bracket. Strength of region, participation opportunities in past national tournaments, and finishing among the top three teams in a given region determined the at-large selection. This was an obvious attempt to allow all areas of the country to develop and to encourage the growth of the game rather than allowing a few areas to totally dominate. For the first time the previous year's results determined team seeds. There was enough interregional competition by now that the Basketball Committee could subjectively compare strengths of regions for national seeding.

Crowd control was the issue of the day in Harrisonburg, Virginia at the 1975 AIAW Tournament. Immaculata fans had developed their own band by beating on metal buckets with drum sticks. Not to be outdone, fans from Delta State University of Mississippi purchased wooden blocks and banged them together for their own noise making section. Unfortunately, tempers, blocks, and sticks began to fly, prompting the prohibition of artificial noise makers. The father of Rene Muth of Immaculata threatened an injunction on the tournament and the AIAW lawyer, Margot Polivy, charged the tournament $650 for consulting fees! Rene later saw those same buckets as they orchestrated her wedding day! Teams paid a $75 entry fee and the first all black team, Federal City College, Washington, D.C., coached by stylish Bessie Stockard, competed in the tournament.

Delta State University, coached by Margaret Wade (later to become a member of the Basketball Hall of Fame), upset Immaculata College 90–81 in the finals—Immaculata's first AIAW tournament loss in four years. Petite guard Debbie Brock led the Delta team to victory in spite of getting sick on the sideline during the championship game. The stress of the moment contributed immeasurably to her illness, but the dominating play of 6'3" post Lusia Harris eased the pain! Immaculata defeated Cal State-Fullerton in the semifinals and Southern Connecticut State College fell to Delta State. Cal State waltzed past Southern Connecticut for third place, and Wayland Baptist captured the consolations. The spectators left no standing room as 2,000 fans cheered their teams. The gate receipts yielded $12,000 profit. Harrisonburg's Channel 53 aired the final game at 9:00 PM the following Wednesday.

Dynamic action at the AIAW National Championship, with college women demonstrating outstanding athletic abilities. Immaculata won its third consecutive championship in 1974 but was finally upset in the 1975 finals by Delta State University, coached by Margaret Wade.

The 1975 season marked at least three other firsts. Queens College and Immaculata played the first women's basketball game in Madison Square Garden in front of over 11,000 fans on February 22, 1975. The AIAW sponsored the first small college invitational tournament, a preliminary effort by AIAW to encourage institutions to vote for a large-small college division based on school size. Jessie Banks directed the 12 team National Invitational Tournament held at Southern Colorado. Phillips University (Oklahoma) routed Talladega College (Alabama) 60–49 for the championship. Ashland College (Ohio) defeated Emporia State (Kansas) for third place honors. California Pomona College buried Midland Lutheran (Nebraska) in the consolations. The tournament lost $658.

Vincennes College in Indiana was the host for the Junior College Tournament. Once again it was Anderson College who won the event by defeating Temple (Texas) for its second championship. Vincennes's fans assisted their favorites to a third place win over Southwest Miss. The tournament showed a $218 profit.

First Kodak All-America Team

Perhaps most exciting in 1975 was the first All-America team sponsored by Kodak in conjunction with Cathy Rush and Pat Kennedy. Coaches nominated players from the regions and selected the winners from video tapes. The top players from each region were considered as All-Americans. William Hunter Lowe was the driving force behind the Kodak All-American program as well as women's basketball's most ardent supporter. He has been affectionately labeled the "Father of Women's Basketball." The original committee included nine basketball coaches from around the country.[2]

Another significant change was on the horizon in 1975. The United States had sent women's basketball teams to the Pan American Games since 1955. This year would be the sixth women's team. However, for the first time, the Amateur Basketball Association of the United States of America (ABAUSA) selected players and coaches primarily from the college ranks rather than AAU. The ABAUSA replaced the AAU who had lost their status as the national governing body for basketball. The ABAUSA included representation from all organizations involved in amateur basketball and collegiate members controlled the voting. Cathy Rush coached the 1975 team, assisted by Billie Moore; manager was Mildred Barnes of Central Missouri State.

The visibility of women's basketball had been greatly enhanced during the 1974–75 season, with a January 27 nationally televised game between the University of Maryland and Immaculata, and the delayed airing of the 1975 AIAW finals. The 1975–76 season marked the first season of television interest by a major network. CBS investigated rights to the championship game. However, most significant was the first official appearance of women's basketball in the Olympic Games. The United States team, coached by Billie Moore assisted by Sue Gunter, and managed by Jeanne Rowlands, won a silver medal after losing to USSR 112–77 in the finals at Montreal. Members of the 1976 Olympic Team were all college players.[3]

Penn State University, under the directorship of Patty Meiser and Della Durant, was the site for the 1976 large college AIAW championship. The tournament showed a profit of $11,160 from receipts of $35,225, shared equally by AIAW and Penn State. Delta State repeated the 1975 victory over Immaculata College (69–64), with a crowd of 7,000 watching the semifinals and final games. Other top finishers among the 16 teams included Wayland Baptist (third), William Penn (fourth), Tennessee Tech (fifth), and Montclair State (sixth). Kodak was now the sole sponsor of the 1976 All-America team. Betty Jaynes chaired the All-American selection committee. Kodak paid AIAW a $3,000 rights fee to sponsor the program. In return Tel-Ra Productions filmed the championship highlights for the Kodak All-America film. Kodak also awarded a huge, prestigious trophy to the National Champions, placing another on display at the Hall of Fame in Springfield, Massachusetts. The corporate world was becoming financially involved in women's basketball for the first time.

The first official small college (fewer than 3,000 female students) national tournament was in 1976 at Ashland College in Ohio. In the finals of a sixteen team single elimination-consolation tournament Berry College (coached by Kay James) defeated cross-state rival West Georgia 68–62. Phillips University was third, with Ashland coming out a fourth place winner. Southeastern Louisiana University beat Francis Marion College (South Carolina) for fifth place. Proceeds amounted to $56.85.

Anderson College won a third straight National Junior College Championship by again defeating Temple, this time on Temple's home court. Peace College (South Carolina) managed a third place finish by overcoming Bergen Community College (New Jersey).

As media interest grew, AIAW expanded opportunities for recognition in 1977 by allowing the media to select an all-tournament team. AIAW also sponsored the Broderick Cup, identifying the best athlete in each sport and the athlete of the year encompassing all sports. The recipient the first year was Lusia Harris of Delta State, and for an unprecedented third time, the Kodak Committee also selected her for the Kodak All-America team. In addition to the $3,000 rights fee, Kodak paid $1,000 to film the championship game. Madison Square Garden again hosted women's basketball when Queens played Montclair State in front of 12,000 fans. In March both ABC and NBC investigated possible coverage of the championship game.

The 1977 season was the last for the sixteen team national format. The tourney was held in the rustic "Barn" at the University of Minnesota in Minneapolis. Coach Linda Wells directed this most successful event. Ticket prices for the finals had gone from free admission in 1972 to $5 in 1977. As the small and large college tournaments began to compete for the top officials, the available pool was diminished critically. For the first time, the Basketball Academy of NAGWS requested sponsorship of a coaches clinic at the championship. This was the first feeble attempt at a coaches association.

Delta State won their third consecutive championship to tie the record set by Immaculata College. Louisiana State University (coached by J. Coleman) was runner-up in a 68–55 battle in front of a crowd of 4,491. Tennessee (coached by Pat Head-Summitt) finished third, Immaculata hung in for a fourth place finish, and Baylor University (Texas) placed fifth in the 1977 championship. It was the first time in five years that the Mighty Macs of Immaculata were not in the final game. The pressure of increased budgets with more scholarships at state-funded schools was having an impact. Although the tournament's income was $52,264, heavy expenses left only $8,330 profit divided equally between the University of Minnesota and AIAW. There was a good deal of negotiation with NBC for national TV coverage, but AIAW's agent, Sugarman, was unable to deliver a contract for the finals. AIAW had to be satisfied with local TV coverage of major games. Radio broadcasts expanded to include the tournament teams' hometown fans.

The small colleges named their first ten member All-America team, sponsored by U-Brand. Southeastern Louisiana University (coached by Linda Puckett) won their first tournament and Phillips was runner-up. The third place finisher was Berry College (Georgia) who beat Biola College (California). The host school, California State Poly-Pomona, managed a fifth place finish by posting a 81–57 victory over Tarkio College (Missouri).

The 1977 Junior College Tournament was the last sponsored by AIAW. Anderson College (coached by Annie Tribble) captured an unprecedented fourth championship. By tenacious defense and cool patience they outlasted Peace College of North Carolina (57–55). Peace's coach was Nora Lynn Finch, member of the AIAW basketball committee and future NCAA women's basketball committee chair. The third place finisher was North Greenville College and fourth place went to Flathead Valley College. The flow of the junior and community colleges into the National Junior College Athletic Association (NJCAA) left too few schools in AIAW to justify a championship. NJCAA was the first male collegiate governance structure to offer a women's national collegiate basketball championship.

After seven years of the sixteen team format for the national championship, the 1978 tournament introduced a "new look." There was grave concern that some teams played two games in one day in the sixteen team structure. There was also an emphasis on increasing crowds, beginning at the state and regional levels and building into the national championship. Crowds were necessary to attract television, and media exposure was critical to the growth of the sport. Therefore, the sixteen-team extravaganza gave way to a whole new approach.

The First "Final Four"

In 1978, there were four "satellite tournaments" and the four winners advanced to UCLA for the first "Final Four" in women's basketball. Judith Holland, athletic director (and future chair of the NCAA Basketball Committee), directed the event, which attracted the first national television network coverage from NBC, as well as 9,531 spectators at Pauley Pavilion. Income rose dramatically under the new tournament structure showing $37,113 profit. Reimbursement for a portion of team expense occurred for the first time. It was a "class event" run with precision. The host team, coached by Billie Moore, first took on Montclair State College to reach the finals. Maryland, coached by Chris Weller, played Wayland in the semifinals to earn a berth in the new format final. In UCLA's first appearance in the national championship Moore's team defeated a scrappy Maryland troop 90–74 to the delight of thousands of UCLA fans. Montclair State, led by Carol Blazejowki, captured third place by defeating Wayland Baptist (90–88) in an exciting preliminary game.

The victory by UCLA marked the end of "small college" dominance of women's basketball in the early 1970s (Immaculata and Delta State) and the advent of large universities with greater financial resources for their programs. Scholarships were now firmly rooted and recruiting wars for top athletes were being won by prestigious institutions with the "big bucks"!

Francis Marion College was the site of the sixteen team small college tournament. The 1978 National Championship went to a newcomer, High Point College (North Carolina), coached by Wanda Briley, with second place honors going to a black college, South Carolina State College. Once again Berry defeated Biola College for the third place trophy. This year Southeastern could do no better than emerge winner of the consolations. Francis Marion's own 5'8" Pearl Moore stole the show, however, by scoring 60 points in a consolation game win over

Eastern Washington State College (114–71)—an AIAW record. She joined the U-Brand All-America small college team and was named the most valuable player.

Another award to recognize the top player in women's collegiate basketball became a part of the basketball tradition in 1978. Carol Blazejowski, the sharp-shooter from Montclair State, received the first Margaret Wade trophy, named after the renowned coach from Delta State. Another first was an All Star Classic sponsored by Hanes Hosiery. Called the Underall All American Classic, it took place on April 8, 1978 in the Greensboro Coliseum. It was a match-up between the best Eastern athletes and best Western athletes. The Eastern team coaches were Pat Head-Summitt and Chris Weller while the Western teams were coached by Sonja Hogg. The event was repeated in 1979. Participants enjoyed an all expense trip for players and coaches and an honorarium went to the coaches and chaperon. The coaches conducted an afternoon workshop for local teams.

Modern women's pro basketball also emerged in 1978 as the Women's Basketball League (WBL) opened their schedule at Milwaukee Arena. The Chicago Hustle defeated the Milwaukee Does 92–87 in front of 7,000 fans. Although the plan was for a twelve team league, only eight teams actually competed in the league, which lasted only two seasons. It folded for lack of funds and poor leadership at the franchise level; horror stories were told of abuses to the female athletes in the pro league.

The 1979 AIAW championship was the first to be held at a neutral site, the Greensboro Coliseum in Greensboro, North Carolina. Nora Lynn Finch of North Carolina State served as the director for the championship. Old Dominion University (Virginia) won its first national championship under the tutelage of Marianne (Crawford) Stanley of Immaculata fame. Stanley became the youngest coach to win a national championship, as well as the first woman to play on and to coach a national championship team. Women's basketball was entering the player-now-coach era. Louisiana Tech entered the scene in 1979 as the national runner-up, coached by flashy Sonja Hogg. The final game was a showdown between 6'5" giant killers Inge Nissen of ODU and Louisiana Tech post Elinore Griffin. Tennessee also was a contender for the title under 1976 Olympian-now-coach Pat Head-Summitt. Tennessee earned third place over Summitt's Olympic mentor Billie Moore of UCLA. Although the NBC live national TV coverage was exciting, the crowd was less so. The total expense was greater than the previous year and the profits less, a $25,920 split between AIAW and North Carolina State.

Probably most significant for the future of women's basketball in 1979 was a request by the Southern coaches to develop a coaches association.

Coaches were seeking input into the governing process. There was concern about the recruiting edge gained by coaches involved in the ABAUSA international program over those not receiving the nod for the prestigious teams. The Basketball Committee supported the proposal and recommended the coaches organization be separate from the one being developed through NAGWS. Unfortunately, nothing materialized for four more years!

There were a few more "firsts" in 1979. The AIAW adopted the Rawlings RLO as the official ball. The Fellowship of Christian Athletes sponsored their first brunch at the Final Four which continues today. The Stay-Free Corporation sponsored the Wade Trophy and selected Nancy Lieberman of Old Dominion as the recipient. Finally, the first female signed an NBA contract. Ann Meyers, UCLA standout, signed with the Indiana Pacers but did not make the cut.

In the small college sixteen team tournament there were rumblings of discontent with the present structure, and the coaches recommended changes for 1980 similar to the large college format. For 1979, Player of the Year Award went to Pearl Moore of Francis Marion College, but South Carolina State College (coached by Willie Simon) was the national champion with an unblemished 25–0 record. South Carolina State was the first black institution to win a National Championship in AIAW competition. The third place award went to Niagara University (New York) who defeated Tuskegee Institute (fourth place trophy), also a black team and a team that had often been among the top in the AAU championships. This would be the last small college tournament. In the academic year 1979–80 AIAW sponsored three divisional basketball championships. The institutions made a sport-by-sport division decision based on scholarships, not the size of the institution.

Major Changes in the 1980s

The decade of the 1980s was to bring major changes to women's collegiate athletics in general and basketball in particular. The NCAA was beginning to express interest in sponsoring women's championships. Some institutions were expressing a desire to have both their men's and women's programs under the same governing structure within the NCAA. Other factions were supporting women's control over women's athletics within the AIAW. As AIAW became more financially secure, the battle lines were drawn.

As the dialogue about AIAW/NCAA governance raged, the 1980 AIAW championship moved to Central Michigan University. Fran Koenig, longtime enthusiast in women's sports, directed the gala event. For the first time AIAW reimbursed a portion of expenses for *all* teams competing in the 24 team championship, instead of only the large college final four. The NBC TV audience watched Old Dominion defeat Tennessee in the finals 68–53. The University of South Carolina upset Louisiana Tech for third place. Nancy Lieberman received the Wade trophy for the second consecutive year. As sponsorships became more usual, the Wilson 2000 jet ball became the official ball for three championships (1980–82). In addition, Wilson sponsored a Most Valuable Player Award, starting the second year of their sponsorship of balls. Each institution represented by a MVP received $500 to be used for the school's scholarship fund.

The AIAW national championship format had been refined even more in 1980. Three divisions now staged final events rather than large college-small college divisions. The Division I bracket expanded from 16 to 24 teams. The committee selected teams from regional winners (ten), the regions of the top finishers in 1979 (six), and eight at-large bids. The top eight seeds received a first round bye. The record from the previous year's finish served as the basis for nationally ranking the top four seeded teams. The selection committee placed the remaining four top seeds in the bracket geographically. Strength of season and geographical proximity were the criteria used for the final sixteen team seeds. All three divisions used the same format, that is, three rounds (a 24 team bracket with the first eight seeded teams having a bye the first round) before the semifinals and finals.

The First National Division II championship was held at the University of Dayton. Playing before its own fans, Dayton (coached by Mary Alice Jeremiah) captured the Division II Championship by defeating College of Charleston 83–53. William Penn (Iowa) and Louisiana College played for third and fourth place, respectively. Thanks to the host team's being in the finals, the University of Dayton tournament showed a $22,336 profit and a history-making number of spectators.

Whitworth College (Washington) was the site of the new Division III Championship. Worcester State College (Massachusetts) travelled to the West Coast to win the first Division III championship by defeating University of Wisconsin at LaCrosse. University of Scranton (Pennsylvania) placed third by soundly defeating Mt. Mercy College (Iowa). Unlike the Division I and Division II tournaments, this one was not financially successful, as the Western spectators were few.

All 72 national championship teams received partial reimbursement for travel and lodging expenses. The AIAW distributed over $141,000 to the teams. In addition, AIAW paid $40,000 in officiating services for 60 games. AIAW took 4 percent of the $171,000 income from entry fees and gate receipts in the first three rounds to partially offset costs.[4]

Perhaps the most distressing issue facing the AIAW Basketball Committee during the 1980 campaign was discrimination. Vivian Stringer, coach at black Cheyney State, had raised objections regarding television coverage that omitted any black programs, representation by black teams at the Hanes All America Classic, and representation on ABAUSA teams. Unfortunately, control of these areas was beyond the realm of AIAW influence, so no specific action could be taken.

The 1980 Olympics brought more disappointments than it did exhilaration. President Jimmy Carter decided the United States would boycott the 1980 Moscow Olympics to protest the Russian invasion of Afghanistan. The Olympic Games had become a political chessboard and athletes and coaches were the pawns! Coach Sue Gunter (LSU) was assisted by Pat Summitt (Tennessee) with manager Lea Plarski from St. Louis Community College. The United States was able to send a team to the qualifying round for the Olympics, the 1979 World Championships, in which the United States finished second to the strong Soviets. In the 1979 Pan American Games the women's team brought home the gold. Pat Summitt, Olympic assistant, coached both teams in 1979. The 1980 Olympic team again showcased the nation's best collegiate players. The college athletes also gained international experience in Japan (FIBA), Korea, World University Games, and, in this country, the USOC festival at Colorado Springs.[5]

The "Big Time" in 1981

The last gala affair sponsored by AIAW was the 1981 Division I National Basketball Championship conducted at the University of Oregon under the watchful eye of the tournament director and assistant athletic director, Chris Voelz. The tournament drawing had again been expanded for the second consecutive year to reflect a complete 32 team single elimination tournament. The higher seeded teams of rounds one, two, and three had the home court advantage before the Final Four at Eugene. The good news was no real "blow-outs" indicating good depth of competition spread from coast to coast. After "paying their dues" with smaller brackets and seeds based on previous year's performance, the 1981 tournament was a statement of progress for women's basketball. Not only was the tournament expanded, but the committee seeded teams only on their current year's performance for the first time! Women's basketball had truly made the big time, and in a short ten year span.

The semi-finalists in 1981 included old Dominion vs. Tennessee with a 68–65 victory for Tennessee. University of Southern California battled Louisiana Tech with a convincing 66–50 victory for LA Tech. The finals pitted rivals Louisiana Tech against Tennessee. LA Tech emerged the winner for its first national championship 79–59. Old Dominion defeated Southern California for the third place trophy. NBC again gave live Sunday coverage to the final game.

Because of high travel costs for individual teams, the sports committee decided to reduce the Division II championship to sixteen teams with two instead of three preliminary rounds before the semi final and finals. The finals again were at the University of Dayton, but Dayton could not muster another championship. This year it was Bob Spencer's William Penn team that emerged National Champs after several years of "almost" stories in the open championships. The College of Charleston finished in second place. The third place trophy went to Cal Poly for defeating a newcomer, Lenoir Rhyne College (North Carolina) in the preliminary game to the final game. The first two rounds had an income of $14,331 but lost $2,354 at the championships with Dayton out of the running. ESPN was on hand to tape the finals for delayed viewing.

At the Division III championships held at the University of Wisconsin, Lacrosse, hometown favorites UW Lacrosse played in the final against little Mt. Mercy of Iowa. A large crowd was on hand to cheer UW on to victory for the National Championship. Such a large crowd to watch a small college championship and the ESPN taping were both exciting features. Worcester State College took third place with fourth place going to newcomer University of Pittsburgh-Johnstown.

The $174,000 proceeds from the three national championships were divided among all the teams in the three division setup. In addition, TV coverage yielded a four-year contract worth nearly $1 million. AIAW reimbursed expenses up to 51 percent for all teams in the three championships. The amount of reimbursement was even greater for the 12 teams in the "final four" of each division. The 1980–81 season was indeed a glorious growth time for the AIAW institutions in all three divisions. While Division III lost some basketball schools to the initiation of women's national championships in the National Association of Intercollegiate Athletics (NAIA), most of the traditionally strong smaller schools stayed with AIAW. The scholarship totals for basketball rose to an all-time high of $4.8 million financial aid with over 6,000 women athletes receiving full or partial aid for competing in basketball. A new record, 880 AIAW collegiate institutions competed in basketball this year with 529 offering financial aid.

The 1981 tournament structure was a response to the improved quality and visibility of women's basketball. However, the NCAA was showing increased interest in women's sports and would begin offering championships in 1982. The AIAW however was not quite ready to fold as the 1982 tournament rotated to Region 1 and the final Division I Championship was held at the historic Palestra in Philadelphia. What a fitting end to AIAW Division I basketball.

Neither the NCAA nor the AIAW national tournament was "much to write home about" in 1982. The strength and depth of the 1981 teams were now split between the AIAW and the NCAA as schools declared their allegiance. The potential for greater financial rewards through the NCAA lured a majority of the better funded teams and left a diminished pool for the AIAW championship.

The AIAW final National Championship tournaments were not the same calibre as prior years. The best teams divided between the two tournaments, with most of the 20 top teams selecting the NCAA Tournament. The Palestra event was sponsored by the University of Pennsylvania. Although it was planned with great enthusiasm and efficiency, the crowds and the proceeds were disappointing. The semifinals pitted giant killer Texas against always tournament-tough Wayland Baptist with Texas coming away the winner. Rutgers (New Jersey) and newcomer Villanova (Pennsylvania) squared off for the other semifinals with Rutgers emerging victorious. The finals went to Immaculata player-coach Theresa Shank and her Rutgers Knights, while Jody Conradt's Texas Longhorns had to settle for second place. Because NBC broke its AIAW National Championship contract there was no national TV coverage of the tournament. It also was a financial disaster, with an

In the 1982 National Championships, the last sponsored by AIAW, the Division III winner was Concordia College of Moorhead, Minn. Always a power in their region, the Concordia team (above) defeated the host team, Mt. Mercy (Iowa). (Photo by John Borge, courtesy Concordia College)

$8,800 debt—a clearly devastating effect of the NCAA championships. The most historic gym in basketball, however, was a fitting end for what would be the last AIAW hurrah. There would not be another year.

Division II and III ranks were considerably reduced as many institutions elected to compete in the NCAA championships or Division III schools in the NAIA championships. Several of the consistent winners, particularly in Division III, chose to align with NCAA or NAIA championships. This brought several new schools to the winner's circle in both divisions. The Division II championship went to a perpetual power in Division II and in the former small college championships, Frances Marion College. They defeated host school College of Charleston, another power among small colleges. A newcomer, North Dakota State University, lost a heartbreaker (77–76) to William Penn, another traditional basketball power.

Division III, with the choice of three championships to attend, welcomed a newcomer to the winner's circle. Always a power in their own region, Concordia College of Moorhead, Minnesota took the crown from host team, Mt. Mercy of Iowa in a thriller 73–72. Another University of Wisconsin school, Whitewater, captured third, defeating newcomer Millerville (Pennsylvania).

Only AIAW participants could be considered for the Kodak All-America Team, because of Kodak's contracted obligation to AIAW. However, the newly formed Women's Basketball Coaches Association (WBCA) would also name an All-American Team from among all players in the collegiate game, not just AIAW. The WBCA would soon become the new home for the Kodak All-Americans!

If there were a lesson to be learned in the transition between AIAW and NCAA, it was to maintain the unity of women's basketball at all levels. Divided, the coaches and schools represented individual opinions but united they had political clout and influence. Unity was imperative for prosperous growth. Bring on the next challenge!

NCAA National Championships

In 1982 the NCAA[6] sponsored its first national basketball tournament for women at the Scope in Norfolk, Virginia. Old Dominion was the host institution. The women's basketball committee from AIAW immediately realized two major governing differences between the AIAW and the NCAA. First, the AIAW basketball committee had mostly coaches, while the NCAA basketball committee included primarily administrators at either the institutional or conference levels. Coaches no longer had direct control over conducting the championship. Nora Lynn

Finch (North Carolina State, past member of the AIAW basketball committee) played a significant role in developing the NCAA championship. She served as chair of the basketball committee for its first seven years.

The second difference was the geographical qualifying structure in AIAW compared to the conference qualifying pattern in NCAA. In retrospect, the AIAW state and regional structures provided more "equal playing field" for all institutions. The conference organization promotes the "haves and have nots" concept and stratifies programs more, even within divisions. In general, women's programs followed the lines of their institutional men's programs in conference affiliation. A select few women's programs deviated and formed conferences for women's sports only (e.g., Gateway, High Country conferences).

The 1982 NCAA basketball championship was a 32 team bracket with all first round games at home sites of the higher seeds followed by four regionals of four teams each. The winners of each regional advanced to the Final Four at the Scope. Thirteen conferences received automatic bids in the inaugural tournament. Team seeding occurred within the four regions, not nationally. In the semifinals, Louisiana Tech overpowered Tennessee 69–46 and Cheyney State (coached by Vivian Stringer) defeated Maryland (coached by Chris Weller) 76–66 in front of 6,000 fans. A national CBS television audience and 9,531 fans watched the championship game between Louisiana Tech and Cheyney State. The 1982 championship earned the top TV rating of 7.3. This rating would be the highest of any subsequent ratings during the first ten years of NCAA sponsorship. The CBS has televised every women's NCAA championship game. Louisiana Tech defeated Cheyney 76–62 for their first national championship. The media selected an all tournament team and Kodak completed the final season of their AIAW contract.

The Women's Basketball Coaches Association (WBCA) held their first national convention at Virginia Beach, associated with the NCAA tournament. Approximately 100 coaches attended the inaugural affair, which focused on developing a set of bylaws for operation. Kodak continued their All-America team, but it was now to be selected by the WBCA. Champion joined Kodak as the second charter corporation affiliated with the WBCA. The WBCA would become the most significant influence on the growth of women's basketball in the decade of the 1980s.

The 1983 NCAA championship greatly resembled the 1982 version with one major exception. For a one-year trial, eight conferences played opening round games to earn one of the four at-large positions in the 32 team bracket. The basketball committee awarded 14 automatics to conferences. For the first time ESPN televised games prior to the championship. The CBS rating for the final was 7.0, down slightly from 1982, but played on Easter Sunday.

The 1983 championship at the Scope introduced Cheryl Miller, a freshman, to the national audience, and the selection committee easily declared her MVP. She had led her USC Trojans, coached by Linda Sharp, to a 69–67 victory over Louisiana Tech before 7,387 screaming fans. The USC team reached the finals by defeating Georgia 81–57 in the semis, and Louisiana Tech defeated hometown favorite Old Dominion 71–55 in front of 8,866 fans.

The 1984 championship added three conferences to bring the list of automatics to 17 in the 32 team field. The tournament structure reverted to that of the 1982 championship without the opening round playoffs. UCLA became the first institution to host both an AIAW championship and an NCAA championship. USC won its second championship playing in front of a hometown crowd of 5,365 at UCLA. USC again beat Louisiana Tech 62–57 and Tennessee beat Cheyney 82–73 in the semis with 7,000 attending. USC then defeated Tennessee in the finals 72–61. The CBS rating dipped to 6.4 for the 4:00 PM game. Cheryl Miller was again named MVP.

Olympic Gold in 1984

The United States hosted the Summer Olympic Games in Los Angeles in 1984. The powerful Russian team did not enter the '84 Olympics, in response to the U.S. boycott of the 1980 Olympic Games, but the two dominant world powers met in the World Championship in 1983 when the Russians defeated the Americans. Coach Pat Head-Summitt and her assistants Kay Yow and Nancy Darsch were determined to bring home the first gold in women's Olympic basketball, and that they did.[7] The all-collegiate U.S. team dominated pool play and emerged as gold medalists for the first time in history. The entire U.S. women's basketball community proudly waved the red, white, and blue. In 15 years, women's basketball had grown from sports days to an Olympic gold medal!

Time marches on, and the Olympic gold proved a boost to women's collegiate basketball as well. The Women's Basketball Committee achieved a milestone in 1985 when the NCAA Executive Committee allowed the Women's Basketball Committee to seed the top eight teams nationally instead of just regionally. The committee again placed the remaining 24 teams in the brackets based on geographic location, except when it was necessary to move a lower team to balance a bracket. There were again 17 automatics in the 1985 championship. In an effort to ensure a viable profit, a guarantee of $5,000 in ticket sales for first round hosts was a requirement in the bids. In the selection of first round sites, the nod went to the higher seed if bids were comparable.

In 1985 the Final Four was held in The Drum at the University of Texas in Austin. Old Dominion defeated Northeast Louisiana and Georgia beat Western Kentucky in the semis with 7,648 in attendance. Old Dominion, coached by Marianne Stanley, proceeded to win their second national championship, overcoming powerful Georgia 70–65. Tracey Claxton of Old Dominion was the tournament MVP. The ESPN televised all four regional finals and the national semifinals with a 1.5 average rating. The CBS rating on the final game again dipped to 5.6.

The numbers of teams participating in Division I basketball, the quality of competition, and the income generated in all rounds of the national championship increased steadily in the first four years of NCAA sponsorship. Basketball had become the flagship for women's sports and it was showing healthy growth. As a result, in 1986 the committee increased the championship bracket to 40 teams with 18 automatics. Seeding followed the pattern set in the 1985 championship. The top 16 teams had a bye in the first round. First round guarantees rose to $6,000.

Rupp Arena in Lexington, Kentucky was the site of the 1986 Final Four directed by the University of Kentucky. The crowd swelled to 8,000 for the semifinals and dwindled to 5,662 for the finals. The semis saw Texas 90–Western Kentucky 65, and USC 83–Tennessee 59. Texas, coached by Jody Conradt, went on to win a first championship 97–81

Jill Hutchison, head women's basketball coach at Illinois State University, Normal, and author of these recollections of national championships, here shows off the new official ball for girls and women's basketball.

over USC and the famous Cheryl Miller. Clarissa Davis of Texas was the MVP selection. ESPN's average rating dropped to 1.2 and CBS final coverage rose to 6.5 on this Easter Sunday.

The Texas victory in 1986 was a year premature as they hosted the 1987 Final Four once again. The Lady Longhorns had stars in their eyes as they approached the 1985–86 season. The bracket remained at 40 with the addition of one automatic bid. However, Texas almost doubled the previous attendance marks attracting ticket sales of 15,615. Unfortunately, after Texas's old nemesis Louisiana Tech eliminated Texas 79–75 in the semi, many fans did not return to the final game. Tennessee also beat Long Beach State 74–64 in a battle between Pat Summitt's aggressive defense and Joan Bonvicini's transition offense. Tennessee dominated Louisiana Tech in the finals 66–44 holding Coach Leon Barmore's Lady Techsters to 33 percent field goal shooting with tenacious defense. The ESPN's average ratings rose to 1.7 and CBS fell slightly to 6.1. Tonya Edwards from Tennessee won the MVP of the 1987 All Tournament team.

In 1988 the NCAA Women's Basketball Committee began an unprecedented two-year stint at the Tacoma Dome in Tacoma, Washington. Unfortunately, attendance dropped to 1986 levels of 8,719 in the semis and 8,448 in the finals. The coasts were not proving as lucrative or as accessible for attendance as the heartland.

The basketball committee initiated a new concept in seeding on the 1988 bracket, by seeding two tiers of four teams each. The first tier was the number one seed in each region; the second tier was placed in the regional brackets to ensure good competition and preserve some geographical identity for spectators. The remaining 32 teams' placement in the brackets depended primarily on geographic location.

The crowd was somewhat removed from the game physically in the spacious Tacoma Dome but the fans were still able to appreciate the battles in the semifinals: Louisiana Tech 68–Tennessee 59, and Auburn 68–Long Beach 55. The final between Louisiana Tech and Auburn was the first time two male coaches, Leon Barmore of Louisiana Tech and Joe Ciampi of Auburn, met in a national final. This guaranteed that for the first time a male coach would win a women's basketball championship. Leon Barmore and the Lady Techsters prevailed in a barnburner as Auburn fell 56–54. Erica Westbrook of Louisiana Tech led the 1988 All Tournament team and was MVP. The ESPN average rating of 1.4 was comparable to previous years, but the 4.3 rating by CBS was a drop of 1.8 from 1987.

The year 1988 was critical in international basketball. For the first time in 12 years the USSR and United States would both participate in the Olympic Games in Seoul, Korea. Coach Kay Yow of North Carolina

State led the U.S. squad. Her assistants were Sylvia Hatchell of rival North Carolina and Yow's younger sister Susan Yow of Drake University. The 1988 Olympic team again included only collegiate stars.[8]

Yow, her staff, and team had successfully met the first challenge by winning the World Championship for the first time in 1986. This competition is an automatic qualifier for the Olympic Games and brings with it the top seed. They were equally successful in "bringing home the gold" by defeating Yugoslavia in the finals in Seoul. The Soviet Union had been eliminated. Not only had the United States won the gold, but this time the Soviets were there and we were on foreign soil. The supremacy of U.S. women's basketball had finally been established.

NCAA Championship Bracket Expanded

Following the 1984 and 1988 Olympiads, the NCAA championship bracket expanded. In 1989 48 teams with 19 automatics made up the bracket. It would be fun to project what 1993 has in store! The 48 team bracket eliminated first round byes, and 16 first and second round games had to be held on college campuses before four regionals led to the Final Four.

A new experiment was on the horizon. The men's Final Four was held in Seattle the same weekend as the women's championship in nearby Tacoma in 1989. The intent was obvious: make the women's championship more accessible to the media servicing the men's event and provide more national visibility for women's basketball. Although media coverage increased somewhat, the fear of many materialized; the women's championship played second fiddle to the men's gala affair. A noble effort, but a lesson well learned.

The crowds for 1989 did increase about 1,000 over the 1988 figures in the Tacoma Dome with 9,030 at the Friday night semifinals and 9,575 at the Sunday afternoon final. In the semis Auburn had a rematch of the 1988 final with Louisiana Tech and this time emerged victorious 76–71. Tennessee beat a scrappy Maryland team 77–65. This set up a rematch of the Southeast Conference championship between Auburn and Tennessee, which had been won by Auburn and their aggressive match-up zone defense. However, the Lady Vols were not to be denied as Tennessee pumped in 76 points to Auburn's 60 for the 1989 title. The MVP was Bridget Gordon. The ESPN's ratings averaged 1.6 while CBS climbed back to 5.4.

Just as Texas had won in 1985 and was unable to repeat when they hosted the tournament in Austin in 1986, Tennessee also was unable to win when they hosted the championship in their 24,000 seat arena in Knoxville in 1990. However, the basketball fans had set a new attendance mark even without Tennessee participating in the Final Four. An actual head count crowd of 19,467 watched the semifinals on Friday night, which surpassed the capacity of the Denver Coliseum, site of the 1990 men's Final Four. For the first time the women outdrew the men. Then 20,023 spectators came back for the finals on Sunday. Women's basketball had established its own appreciative audience. The only change in the 1990 tournament structure was the addition of two more automatics, bringing the total to 21.

The semifinals matched Virginia, who had upset Tennessee in the Mideast Regional, against Stanford. It was the first appearance for either school in the Final Four. Debbie Ryan coached Virginia and Tara Vanderveer coached Stanford. Stanford won easily before the Sunday afternoon audience, a full house. Two old nemeses, Louisiana Tech and Auburn, met in the other semifinal game. It was Auburn's turn once again as Tech fell to the Alabama team. This set up a showdown between rookie Stanford and veteran Auburn playing in its third consecutive final game. Experience did not prove the deciding factor as Auburn was bridesmaid for the third time. Unfortunately, the CBS rating was its lowest in history at 3.7, a consistent decrease since 1982, and the ESPN averaged 1.35. Without any doubt in the minds of the voters, Jennifer Azzi of Stanford was the MVP.

The noteworthy issue at the 1990 championship was the announcement that Oklahoma had dropped its women's basketball program just prior to the Final Four. Immediate action by the Women's Basketball Coaches Association (WBCA) brought national media attention to the issue and threatened legal action against the University of Oklahoma. The administration reinstated the program within one week. Another battle had been won and the threat of Division I programs dropping their women's basketball had been squelched, at least for the moment. The war for continued development of women's basketball may never end.

Summary

The evolution of women's collegiate basketball has been a fascinating reflection of the more encompassing role of women in society in the twentieth century. It began with players in bloomers behind closed doors using few, but significant, modifications of Naismith's rules in the 1890s. It developed into AAU national championships by the 1920s, with players in satin outfits and using women's rules with a court divided into thirds. The physical education classes, intramurals, and play days replaced the highly competitive games, in the larger colleges and universities, in the 1920s and 1930s. The 1940s, 1950s, and early 1960s saw a move from play days to sports days toward varsity programs while the AAU tournaments continued to flourish outside the educational setting. However, as women began to emerge from their social cocoons, they also began to break through previously male-dominated sports barriers. Only the strong survived the frontier-like challenges of changing the social image of the female athlete, and basketball was one of the last frontiers. It responded like a trooper.

Basketball has consistently been the highest participation sport in women's collegiate activities. In 1990 a total of 764 NCAA institutions offered intercollegiate basketball. Participants rose by 198 in just one year from 1988–89 under NCAA.

The increase in women's collegiate basketball participation is also paralleled by an increase in those wanting to watch the ever-improving performances. Attendance has grown significantly every year of NCAA participation to a 1990 total of nearly four million spectators. In Division I alone attendance has risen from 1.2 million in 1982 to 2.3 million in 1990, an increase of more than 90 percent. The 1990 average attendance for regular season games was 775 in Division I, led for the fifth consecutive year by the University of Texas, averaging 7,525 per game. Tennessee was second for the fourth year, averaging 5,682. For the first time in history, a major network (CBS) will cover both the national semifinals and finals as well as at least three regular season games in 1991.

As participation and attendance have grown, the game has also been refined. The skills of female athletes are well developed even beyond many of their male counterparts. The finesse game of women's basketball requires refined skills, as opposed to the power game of men played above the net. The sophisticated strategies of the 1990s are a far cry from the zones and patterned offenses of the late 1960s and early 1970s. Women's collegiate basketball has progressed from an embryo to adolescence, but it has barely scratched the surface of adulthood as it celebrates its centennial anniversary!

Notes

1. The facts about the AIAW basketball championships have been verified by the editors. The primary source for verification was the AIAW Archives, housed in the Maryland Room (Special Collections), University of Maryland, College Park Libraries. For additional information or specific references contact, in writing, Joan S. Hult, Department of Kinesiology, University of Maryland, College Park, MD 20742. If interested in general AIAW topics, researchers may write to Lauren Brown, Special Collections, College Park Libraries, University of Maryland. All remaining endnotes are explanations or clarifications of Hutchison's reflections or provide additional information by the editors.

2. The chair of the first Kodak committee was Louise O'Neal (Southern Connecticut). Members of the First All America team were: Carolyn Bush (Wayland Baptist), Marianne Crawford (Immaculata), Nancy Dunkle (California State-Fullerton), Luisa Harris (Delta State), Charlotte Lewis (Illinois State), Ann Meyers (UCLA), Patricia Roberts (Tennessee), and Mary Scharff (Immaculata).

3. The 1976 women's Olympic basketball team members were: Cindy Brogdon (Mercer University), Nancy Dunkle (California State at Fullerton), Lusia Harris (Delta State University), Pat Head (University of Tennessee), Charlotte Lewis (Illinois State University), Nancy Lieberman (Far Rockaway High School), Gail Marquis (Queens College), Ann Meyers (UCLA), Mary Ann O'Connor (Southern Connecticut State), Pat Roberts (Emporia State University), Sue Rojcewicz (Southern Connecticut State), and Juliene Simpson (J. F. Kennedy College).

4. In Ann Uhlir's executive director of AIAW announcement of the distribution of basketball monies she noted: "The distribution was just for basketball; it is indicative of what other women's sports with the potential for public interest and support may soon enjoy," June 6, 1980, p. 4.

5. Members of the 1980 Olympic team included: Carol Blazejowski (Montclair State College), Denise Curry (UCLA), Anne Donovan (Old Dominion University), Tara Heiss and Kris Kirchner (University of Maryland), Debra Miller (Boston University), Cindy Noble and Holly Warlick (University of Tennessee), Lataunya Pollard (Long Beach State), Jill Rankin (Wayland Baptist College), Rosie Walker (Stephen F. Austin University), and Lynette Woodard (University of Kansas).

6. Information concerning the NCAA championships has not been verified by the editors. A majority of the information, however, has been researched by Hutchison and additional information obtained from the NCAA office. The author would like to thank Tricia Bork for her assistance in providing the essential material for the NCAA Division I Championships, and Lynn Norenburg, USA Basketball, for information on international competition. This portion of the article reports the results and actions of ONLY the Division I championships. The NCAA, however, conducts Women's Basketball Championships in Divisions II and III.

7. The 1984 women's Olympic basketball team included: Cathy Boswell (Illinois State University), Denise Curry (UCLA), Anne Donovan (Old Dominion University), Teresa Edwards (University of Georgia), Lea Henry and Cindy Noble (University of Tennessee), Janice Lawrence and Kim Mulkey (Louisiana Tech University), Pam McGee (University of Southern California), Carol Menken-Schaudt (Oregon State University), Cheryl Miller (University of Southern California), and Lynette Woodard, who later signed with the Globetrotters (University of Kansas).

8. Members of the 1988 Olympic basketball team included: Cindy Brown (Long Beach State University), Vicki Bullett (University of Maryland), Cynthia Cooper (University of Southern California), Anne Donovan (Old Dominion University—a third unprecedented appearance), Teresa Edwards and Katrina McClain (University of Georgia), Kamie Ethridge and Andrea Lloyd (University of Texas at Austin), Jennifer Gillom (University of Mississippi), Bridgette Gordon (University of Tennessee), Suzie McConnell (Pennsylvania State University), and Teresa Weatherspoon (Louisiana Tech University).

18

Coaching and Game Reflections, 1940s to 1980s

Mildred Barnes

The evolution from playing a six player, three court game with empty stands to a five player, full court game with thousands of spectators lends credence to the saying "We've come a long way, baby!"

The three court game was still in evidence as late as the end of the 1930s. The game was played by teams consisting of from six to ten players. If played with six players, the two forwards, two centers, and two guards each were limited to one-third of the court. The guards "guarded" the forwards and passed the ball to one of the centers whose sole purpose was to pass the ball to the forwards, who were the only players permitted to shoot. It was a game that had little player movement due to the confined court space and was a dull game by today's standards! Often the attire for the game was bloomers and a white middy blouse with a red tie.

Six Player Two Court Game

The three court game transpired to a two court game in which there were three guards and three forwards with a center line dividing the court in half. In many states interscholastic play was not permitted for girls in public schools, although parochial schools and rural schools often engaged in interscholastic games under a man coach on a limited basis. In most instances rural schools competed earlier than did large city systems. In areas where interscholastic sports were disallowed, play days and sport days became popular. The play day was an occasion on which a number of schools met at one location and players from each school were divided onto teams so that each team was a combination of players from several schools. Teams would then compete against each other, generally in a round robin tournament with games consisting of one 10–15 minute playing period. Players coached themselves. Usually when the tournament was over, players socialized over soft drinks and cookies.

Progressing from this early extracurricular activity, sport days were introduced. Once again schools would meet at one locale, but would compete as a unit against other schools. Competition would be in the form of a round robin tournament with limited time periods. The means for selecting players for these contests varied. Early, the teams were often a winning intramural team or a combination of the best players participating in intramurals. These teams were usually not preselected for extensive practice sessions before a sport day occasion. However, the early semblance of interscholastic games appeared as teachers began to "coach" during the progress of play. The sport day became the forerunner of interscholastic sports, which were finally approved by state governing associations by the 1970s.

Early, the typical uniform in public schools and colleges was a tunic and blouse, with one team wearing colored "pinnies." Later, shorts became popular, but pinnies persisted. At the same time, players competing in AAU games often wore matching satin blouses and shorts. The conclusion of contests was marked by teams, coaches, and sometimes parents gathering to socialize.

The game was started by an official with a "throw-in" to a player positioned in the center circle. This procedure followed every "basket" and free throw. As a result, a team realized it would acquire possession of the ball without interference whenever the opponents scored.

As interscholastic athletics for girls and women developed there were no organized conferences, although schools in the boys conference generally were scheduled. There were few championships in colleges, but some states maintained state high school tournaments. Coaches secured game officials, and the same officials were often scheduled to officiate all games for that school during the entire season. This occasionally was a significant factor in a closely contested game. Since the official recovered the ball after a field goal, teams were at the mercy of the speed with which the official put the ball in play at the center circle. As a visiting coach with my team ahead by just a few points, it always pleased me when the opposing coach's official strolled slowly toward center court before putting the ball in play!

The basic offensive maneuver was a "give-and-go" play or a "pick" on or off the ball. Having only three players on a half court, there was ample space to move, and offensive players were less encumbered than now by weakside defense. Because of the vast area that the defense had to cover, they generally played between the opponent and the basket as opposed to overplaying passing lanes as is commonly done today. This made it considerably easier to move the ball into scoring position.

Played with one dribble only, driving to the basket was limited. Lay-ups, one and two. hand set shots, hook shots, and running one hand shots were the common means of scoring. The dribble was often used to take a player into scoring position for a running one hander, if a lay-up could not be realized. Since the advent of the jump shot, the running one hand shot has all but disappeared from modern play.

Subsequently, two and three dribbles were introduced. Each additional dribble allowed greater court coverage and change of direction. Not only useful to offensive players, it was used by defensive players who, following an outlet pass, could dribble to the center line for a short pass to a teammate.

To alter strategy, defensive players often changed from player-to-player (as it was called) to a one-two, triangle zone. Depending on the strength of the opponents, the triangle was inverted sometimes. It is from the utilization of this zone that the triangle and two defense has developed as an unorthodox means to stop two outstanding shooters in modern play.

During this period a "press" was introduced. After an unsuccessful field goal attempt, the forwards would hustle back to the center line and establish a formidable barrier to passing the ball across the center line. As a result, lob passes were used extensively to a forward positioned close to the center line. It was not unusual to see two or three forwards standing at the center line asking for the ball with an outstretched hand. Forwards became very adept at keeping a defender at their backs and reaching toward the open sideline for the pass. When a change in the rules provided that the ball would be inbounded behind the end line following a successful field goal and free throw, the press was used even more extensively.

High school seasons at this time were often limited to eight to ten games although scheduling was often more extensive in the Midwest and East. Regional, district, and state championships were almost non-existent, except in states such as Iowa, Texas, Oklahoma, and North Dakota.

Roving Player Game

Increasingly, there was an outcry for a game that permitted greater movement by players. Conservatives believed any change from a six player, two court game would lead to the demise of the game. Liberals suggested that eventually girls and women would play the "boys" game, so why not now? The rules committee struggled with this dilemma and reached a compromise by continuing with a six player team but allowing one player on each team to run full court. Since this was the game played in AAU, it permitted more cooperation between schools and AAU rules. It provided for four players from each team to be at the offensive end of the court.

Generally, the same player "roved." The rover was a player who was considered to have greater stamina and better defensive and offensive skills. Conditioning for roving players was a problem due to their unique full court play. Most of their cardiovascular improvement developed from running in scrimmage-type situations. Preseason conditioning was nonexistent! Running outdoors in parks or on local streets often elicited questions from local police. Training rooms were off limits to girls and women. How times have changed!

During a game, a roving player would occasionally change "on the fly" to confuse the opponents, particularly while playing player-to-player defense. Instead of the usual rover crossing the center line, a signal to a teammate would initiate a different player to rove.

Two notable tactics developed at this time. Playing a two-two (box) and/or a one-two-one (diamond) zone became popular. These zones continue to be played today as special defenses with the fifth player guarding a shooter player-to-player. With a dearth of good outside shooters, four player zones became very popular. Coaches realized that players could effectively "jam" the lane and prevent much inside scoring. What developed was a defense labeled "streets and alleys" (from the elementary school game). After a pass was made, the defense players would abduct their arms to a 90 degree angle so that two players would almost have fingers touching. This eliminated any cutting through the lane as the forward would be called for charging when contact occurred. This action led to a rule change that prevented defense players from guarding with "arms extended horizontally." If contact arose as a result of an offensive player's cut through the lane, blocking was called on the defensive player.

A second strategy that became effective was trapping an offensive player at the juncture of the center line and the side line. Utilizing the side line and three defensive players, the trap was more effective then than it is today! A team would trap the ball-handler with a defensive player, a rover, *and* an offensive player who had to remain in the back court. This effectively provided a three player trap without greater defensive sacrifice than the two player trap currently provides. A rule change later disallowed this practice. It is clear that one of the reasons rules are added or changed is to prevent circumvention of the philosophy or intent of the rules.

Another strategy that developed was the use of the "stall." At this time the stall was even more effective because there was no 30 second clock and no "back court" rule. As a result, teams developed a passing game in which they could maintain possession of the ball for minutes at a time. To alleviate a closely guarded situation, the ball would be passed into the back court. Often in the last few seconds of the game the ball would be passed to a guard who dribbled around the back court with others chasing. "Keep away" on a full court was very successful!

Five Player Game

The debate continued on the merit of playing the boys game. Many coaches believed that the change to a five player game was inevitable. Some were still concerned about adopting the boys game! Others questioned the ability of girls to run full court. This view came at a time when girls and women were playing field hockey and lacrosse, games which were played in 30–35 minute halves (modified for high school) with no substitutions and no time outs!

Without evidence to repudiate the physiological capability of girls and women to compete full court, the rules committee suggested that two years be devoted to experimental rules in which the five player, full court game would be tested. High schools and colleges alike engaged in the experiment. At the end of the experiment, there was overwhelming support for the change to the five player game. Thus, in February 1971, the DGWS-AAU rules committee voted unanimously to adopt rules for the five player game. Subsequently, the National Federation of State High School Associations also approved the five player game.

This major rule change prompted numerous workshops and conferences to help coaches learn techniques and strategies. Probably the leading contributor was the Olympic Development Committee. Through the efforts of Sara Staff Jernigan and others, money was budgeted for a series of week-long conferences in a variety of sports. Basketball was given particular attention. Foremost coaches in the country served as consultants and session leaders throughout the conferences. These developmental conferences continued for several years and helped many women coaches to develop expertise.

Statewide High School Programs

A few states demonstrated leadership in developing statewide programs for high school girls. Among the front-runners were Iowa, Oklahoma, Texas, and Tennessee. The Iowa Girls High School Activities

Union, responsible for girls athletics (and forensics and music), focused on addressing the needs for girls athletics in the state. Consequently, it developed district, sectional, and state tournaments in a wide variety of sports. It is, however, the gate receipts from girls basketball that fund other programs. To this day, Iowa has sellout crowds for their six player state championship. The "Sweet Sixteen" tournament runs an entire week and is recognized as a model for other state championships. It continues to outdraw the boys high school championship.

Having moved from the East Coast where victorious teams were presented an eight inch trophy, imagine my surprise when I saw the Iowa state championship trophy standing five feet tall! Seeing one of the teams playing in a uniform with a midriff caused a second look. I wondered whether anyone would try a hook shot. (No one did!)

Development of College/University Programs

In the early 1960s there were scattered intercollegiate basketball programs for women. Many colleges, however, were using sport days to avoid the ban on intercollegiate play. Highly competitive play could be found primarily in AAU competition and tournaments. Basically, the outstanding teams of that era were small colleges which competed in AAU leagues, and they were already in the process of recruiting top players in the country. The Wayland Baptist Flying Queens, Tennessee Business College, and Iowa Wesleyan College were synonymous with high calibre play.

At that time the AAU was the governing body in the United States for a variety of sports, including basketball. The AAU selected basketball teams to participate in international events, including the Pan American games. Foreign travel by a U.S. team often was an intact AAU team with the trip funded by team sponsors (as Neal describes in Chapter 19).

In the mid to late 1960s, more and more colleges and universities began to implement an intercollegiate program. Title IX hastened the expansion in the 1970s. Competition was generally of a local nature with teams playing other institutions in close proximity. Games were still followed by a social hour. Programs were underfunded. Bake sales and car washes were common techniques employed by players and coaches to supplement meager budgets. Local businesses were solicited for financial support. While traveling, proper nutritional habits suffered as fast food was commonly all that was affordable. And fast food restaurants in that era did not provide salad bars!

To offset the sociological stigma against women's athletics, coaches often reminded their team about the importance of "ladylike" behavior.

Before jeans became acceptable apparel, the dress code demanded that skirts be worn by players and coaches to games. Slowly, acceptable apparel moved toward pants in the 1970s and ultimately to the jeans of the 1980s. It is interesting to note that there seems to be a preference among many female coaches toward wearing dresses or skirts again. Only the 1990s will determine whether that is a trend. The number of teams traveling in warmup suits has increased. This gives evidence that coaches are concerned with the choice of apparel chosen by players and are exercising a means to control their appearance.

While competition was developing, colleges and universities of varying sizes competed against each other. Generally teams in close geographic proximity were scheduled. Institutions with an enrollment of 5,000 or less might be competing against the "giants" with over 25,000 enrolled. At this time, play was still competitive among these unlikely rivals, and teams such as Westchester and Immaculata won the invitational national tournaments of 1969–71 and early AIAW championships.

Until off-campus recruitment and scholarships were allowed by AIAW regulations, this competitive structure was maintained. At that point, those institutions with better budgets gained the immediate advantage. Recruitment strategies developed significantly and the larger institutions (higher budgeted programs) had advantages unknown to smaller institutions (lower budgeted programs). Although some smaller institutions continued to recruit highly skilled athletes for a period of time, the writing was on the wall. Scheduling contests in warm climates over Christmas vacation, scheduling a contest in a community close to the hometown of a recruit from another area of the country, better travel arrangements (including better transportation, motel, and meal allowances), and the lure of a "big" school being better than a "small" school were some of the recruiting ploys used successfully by recruiters from large institutions.

The off-campus recruitment and provision for scholarships changed the attitude of many of the more skilled players. When all programs were extremely underbudgeted, athletes truly played for the "fun of it." They provided their own shoes, traveled long distances by bus, ate almost exclusively on fast foods, engaged in money-making efforts, were subjected to scorn rendered by much of society, played in almost empty arenas, and received little or no media attention. They had to love the game in order to endure these conditions!

The attitude of players today has changed. There is much more attention given to "What is in it for me?" How many pairs of shoes do I get? Where do we get to play? What kind of facility do we play in? Will it be full? What kind of media attention is provided? Often a recruit selects an institution based substantially on responses to these kinds of questions.

Once institutions demonstrated different financial commitments to the program, the development of division play was a natural transition. Rather than having all institutions competing at one level, small and large colleges and then Divisions I, II, and III were implemented by NCAA and AIAW member institutions. Ultimately, the three divisions were taken over by NCAA and small colleges moved to NAIA competition.

Early, teams continued to play institutions higher or lower than the division to which they belonged. But now NCAA institutions are penalized if they play an institution from a lower division (by not gaining the same credit for the contest for regional tournament competition). At this point in time, it is very difficult for NCAA Division II and III teams to upgrade their schedule by competing against higher division institutions. Junior colleges and institutions in the NAIA continue to compete on one level.

Changes Over the Years

Several important changes that have transpired in the last 20 years are worthy of note. The advent of the 30 second clock eliminated for all practical purposes the "stall" at the end of the game. Teams still utilize the concept to some degree, but tactics often employ running all of the options on the offense before a shot is attempted as opposed to running a "true" stall, like the four corner offense.

The advent of the three point shot has altered recruiting practices. Coaches are looking for players who will add that dimension to their team. The addition of this rule has significantly changed the complexion of close games. A two point lead in the final seconds of the game no longer automatically provides at least a tie game. Basic offensive tactics changed as teams acquired outside shooters. Traditionally, the common practice offensively was to pass the ball around the perimeter until a passing lane to a post player was established for an inside shot. Teams now are passing inside to get defenses to collapse so that the ball can be passed outside for unhindered three point attempts. The smaller ball provides greater skill development in ball handling and shooting.

The Women's Basketball Coaches Association was founded in 1981 for the purpose of unification of coaches of girls and women's basketball teams involved with youth groups from the public sector and at the high school and college levels. It also promotes women's basketball nationally and internationally. In just less than a decade membership has increased to over 3,000 coaches. A conference for coaches is held annually at the site of the NCAA Division I Championship.

Coaching clinics sponsored by commercial agencies originally were geared only toward male coaches. Jokes were crude and females who dared to attend caused many an eyebrow to be raised! Now these same agencies are hiring women as speakers and coaches to address both male and female audiences.

Head coaches no longer volunteer their services nor must they recruit volunteer assistant coaches. At the college level, coaches are often hired exclusively by the Athletic Department and command legitimate salaries. Camps, shoe contracts, radio and television shows, and other "perks" increase the financial reward.

Coaches now have support staffs that include assistant coaches, graduate assistants, secretarial assistance, and the full support of the sports information director. The head coach is no longer solely responsible for all of the travel arrangements, scouting of opponents, recruitment of players, coaching and teaching during practice sessions, and community involvement; such responsibilities may be delegated. At the high school level the demand for coaches sometimes exceeds the number of qualified teachers employed by the system and additional coaches must be recruited from the local community. Coaches sponsor summer camps that augment their incomes.

Games that were once played in an auxiliary facility now commonly are played on the primary basketball floor. Women's games, formerly relegated to afternoon settings, now are scheduled in prime time or precede men's games. Media attention has increased significantly. Still, newspaper coverage from other areas of the country is limited and the coverage on television news programs remains appallingly absent!

Concerns

One of the most alarming trends is the significant increase in the number of men coaching girls and women's teams and the lack of women athletic directors. This lack of role models for girls and women will have a cumulative effect in the future unless strong efforts are made immediately to increase the number of women coaches at all levels of competition. The same concerns are registered about the dearth of women officials. Whereas significant gains have been made in the number of women in many professions, such is not the case in coaching and officiating.

The advent of more male coaches has led to increased references and comparisons with male players and with coaches of men's teams. How often reference is made to players like Michael Jordon and Larry Bird! The tactics and teaching techniques of Bobby Knight, Dean Smith, etc. are often extolled. Why are the references not to players such as Theresa

Edwards, Katrina McClaine, and Lynette Woodard and to such distinguished coaches as Pat Head Summitt, Billie Jean Moore, Jody Conradt, Cathy Rush, Virginia Wade, and Kay Yow, among others. Interestingly, for the first time ever the Basketball Hall of Fame Committee named Pat Head Summitt as the recipient of the John Bunn award in 1990, emblematic of the outstanding basketball coach in the country. During the presentation, Billy Packer commented that Pat Summitt is recognized as one of the greatest coaches of all time, including men's and women's coaches! Such a declaration attests to Pat Summitt's capabilities and to the progress made by women who are coaching today.

Conclusion

Girls and women's basketball has reached a level of play that was barely envisioned just twenty years ago. The calibre of play will continue to improve significantly. Another professional league will begin to operate successfully in the twenty-first century. Dunking will become a vital part of the appeal for spectators.

Players, coaches, and commercial agencies which will profit from the increased appeal of the game should remember those pioneers who helped develop the game and competitive opportunities: Katherine Ley, Phebe Scott, and Maria Sexton, members of the original Commission on Intercollegiate Athletics for Women; Carol Eckman, who initiated the first national intercollegiate tournament; Mimi Murray, who helped structure the first television contract for women's athletics; Cathy Rush of Immaculata and Margaret Wade of Delta State, whose teams were so successful; early outstanding players such as Nera White, Charlotte Lewis, Lusia Harris, Ann Meyers, and Nancy Lieberman; and the first AIAW Basketball Committee, under the leadership of Lucille Kyvallos.

As greater success is attained by players and coaches, their contributions should be well documented. Continued efforts should be provided by the Women's Basketball Coaches Association to assure that pioneers and notable players, coaches, officials, and contributors are recognized for their contributions. Effort must be made to endorse qualified individuals to be elected into the Basketball Hall of Fame to have their exploits recognized along with those of Senda Berenson, Margaret Wade, and Bertha Teague.

19

Basketballs, Goldfish, and World Championships

Patsy Neal

My dad put up a basketball goal for me when I was very young. Unfortunately, he hung it right next to our fish pond. I was the only kid in the neighborhood who had a perpetual mildewed basketball, water lilies hanging out of my sneakers, and psychotic goldfish swimming around in my shirt.

As if that wasn't bad enough, I became known as the "basketball player who had the calf." Lest this seem like a real quirk of nature, let me explain that while I was in high school my motivations were quite different from those experienced by today's players. While athletes today mainly work hard for money, scholarships, status, publicity, pro contracts, and commercial opportunities, *my* goal was a small, bow-legged Hereford calf which my dad had promised me when I hit 30 points in a ballgame.

However, when I managed to bounce in, kick in, and throw in 29 points one night, the ante suddenly jumped to 35 points. Not easily discouraged, I "hung tough" and managed 33 points the next night. I realized I really had my old man running scared when he emphasized at the dinner table the next night that he wished I would hurry up and hit 40 points so he could be true to his word and give me the calf.

I had a strong feeling that the calf was going to be old and grey and struggling to gasp its last breath before she would be mine. But not so, for when I plunked in 44 points, my dad opened the door to the barn, and I walked proudly through the manure to claim my calf.

I don't think I have ever been as strongly motivated since that experience. Perhaps coaches don't really know how to psyche up players.

It was in the spring of my senior year in high school that I saw a three-line paragraph in the bottom corner of the sports page about Wayland

College having won the National AAU Basketball Championship. I had never heard of Wayland College, much less the National AAU Tournament, but thinking that I would prefer playing basketball in college over farming and raising cows, I wrote to Wayland asking if there was any way I could play for them. I mentioned the fact that I had averaged over 40 points a game my senior year, had made All-State, and had a growing herd of eight cows.

The Wayland coach invited me to Plainview, Texas for a tryout, but added he thought it would be nice if I left the cows home. Since I had never been out of the state of Georgia, my parents thought it would be best if they drove me to Plainview. I should add that *they* had never been out of state either!

At the time, it did not seem strange to me that I was the one who contacted the coach, or that I paid my own expenses to Texas to try out for the team. The thing that *did* seem strange was the way everyone out there talked. I couldn't believe anyone could drawl like that. Being from Georgia, I wasn't used to such abuse of the English language!

I found out that Wayland was unique in many ways. First, they gave basketball scholarships to women. And second, their women's team flew to games in four Beechcraft Bonanzas while the men's team went by car and bus (quite a switch, huh?). The sponsor of the women's team was Claude Hutcherson, a businessman who owned the local airport, and so they called the women's basketball team the Hutcherson "Flying Queens."

Fortunately, they didn't tell me until after the try-out that Mr. Hutcherson wanted to take me up in one of his planes for a flight around the city. It's hard enough to come off the farm, drive 1,300 miles to a foreign land, and work out with a couple of All-Americans in an effort to get a college scholarship. But to ask someone to go up in a small four-seated passenger plane that looked like someone had thrown it together from one of those do-it-yourself kits was asking just a little too much.

I was not a coward however. Dumb, maybe . . . but coward, no.

I wiped off my sweaty hands on my blue jeans and hugged my parents for what I thought was my last farewell. I had my eyes closed as they squeezed my helpless body into the plane. All I can say about that first trip in the air is that basketball *must* have meant more to me than life or death. I flew only because they told me that in order to play for the Queens, you had to be able to fly. I personally would rather have played for the Hutcherson Trucking Queens.

When the weekend was finally over, I went home tired and sore, but with a four-year full scholarship to play with the Flying Queens. I was both elated and scared about my good fortune. I was excited that I had the chance to get a college education while playing basketball—and afraid that there would not be enough sick sacks in the whole wide world to last me those four years.

My college years at Wayland (1956 to 1960) were priceless for me. My freshman year, I sat on the bench a lot, building character. When someone mentioned the National AAU Free-Throw Tournament, I decided that anything that was free, I was entering. I practiced until my toenails turned blue and won the championship with 48–50. Afterwards, my coach told me I needed more practice, that I shouldn't have missed those two shots. That was the year our team won the National AAU Tournament for the third straight year.

The fact that stands out most in my mind from my sophomore year is that our team had a winning streak of 131 games going into the 1958 National AAU Tournament. Then Nashville Business College broke this string—and our hearts—with a four-point victory for the championship.

My junior year, I ran so many laps the floor began to feel like it had grooves in it. Our coach was still suffering from our loss in the AAU national finals and conditioning seemed to be a real hangup with him.

This was also the year when vitamins and salt tablets started appearing on the table in the dressing room. After a week's supply of pills lasted over a month, the manager carefully made a chart with each of our names on it. Daily she placed the pills in the block with our name so she could tell who was taking the pills and who wasn't. It was easy enough to move one's pills to someone else's block. One player took eight doses of vitamins one afternoon before realizing the pills on her block were not all hers.

Over the years, our team had some real "characters." We were playing a highly competitive sport at a time when sports for women were not readily accepted by our society. Consequently, it seemed that the few teams which did exist attracted independent, self-determined individuals. Each had her own ways of doing things.

"Wash" especially remains in my memory. We were playing the "roving player" game at that time, with two stationary guards, two stationary forwards, and two players who could move around the whole court. "Wash," who was a real speed demon, stole the ball from one of the opponents and went flying down the court at a pace that would have made a gazelle envious. One of the opposing stationary guards managed to steal the ball back and passed it up court to a teammate. "Wash," who was traveling fast enough to break the sound barrier, made a semicircle to reverse her direction and started back up court, letting out a loud "Beep, beep! Whooooooom!" From that day on, "Wash" was better known as "The Roadrunner."

Four significant happenings stand out in my mind about my junior year. Wayland won the National AAU Tournament again, I made the All-American team, and I was selected to play with the United States team in the 1959 Pan-American Games. The fourth memory involves a 6'2", hypochondriac teammate weighing about 225 pounds. She staged one of her fainting spells at halftime and gently rolled over between the seats on the bleachers. Our coach and the manager tried for several minutes to get her out, then realized she was firmly stuck. We left her there as play continued (and for all I know, she may be there still).

Being selected to play in the Pan-Am Games during the summer of 1959 was one of the highlights of my life. A lot of people deserve credit for my participating in those games, but perhaps the most credit goes to Delta Airlines, not my coaches. When I went from home to Atlanta to board the flight to Chicago, I discovered my ticket had been sent to Asheville, N.C. by the AAU. I cried a lot, polished up the Pam-Am emblem on my travel bag, and in general threw a temper tantrum. I *wanted* to get on the plane to fly to Chicago, and *I wanted to get on in Atlanta.* (I had given up my cows and the farm for the moment.) Delta personnel recognized that a screaming, yelling college student in front of their desk was bad for business. They let me board in Atlanta.

The Pan-Am Games were something special. I can still remember marching into Soldier's Field and standing in awe at the opening ceremonies. I can also vividly remember the thousands of pigeons being set free in the stadium to rove the air space in soaring, majestic flight. (It seemed that most flew right over my head and their scoring percentage was better than mine.)

Even though the AAU did send my plane ticket to the wrong place, the rest of their organization was good and they housed us in a first-class hotel. It was right across the expressway from the Chicago lakefront. For days, we looked yearningly at the beach just a few hundred yards away, and finally several of us weighed the odds and shot across eight lanes of traffic to get to the water. We repeated this process for three days. Finally, a youngster, who had stood on the side of the road and watched us each day as we made the mad sprint across the lanes, pointed out the pedestrian crossing going *under* the expressway.

To save face, we told him our coach made us cross the highway to increase our speed and reflexes for the games. Where I came from, tunnels under roads were only used for cattle crossings.

My senior year, I really became educated and had opportunities beyond my dreams. Not only did we play an extensive schedule of basketball across the United States, but we also had a series of games in Mexico. It was my first trip out of the country. I was praying we would drive to Mexico, but of course we flew south of the border in our four little Beechcraft Bonanzas.

I don't remember if we won or lost our games. I *do* remember playing in a converted bullring in 30 degree weather, while watching my breath float about me like cotton candy. I also remember our coach standing on the sideline fussing at us for complaining so much about having to play in the cold. I can still hear him telling us that the cold was all in our mind. It was easy enough for him to say—he had on a heavy coat and gloves. Our motto that year, regardless of the circumstances, became "It's all in your mind!"

After our games were over in Mexico, we flew back to the states in a snowstorm (we told coach it was all in his mind). The weather was so bad that we got off course, so we flew low along a railroad to find our

Patsy Neal, who played for the Wayland Baptist College Flying Queens and for an independent AAU team called the Utah Lakers, was selected for the All American team three times. (Photo courtesy Wayland Baptist University)

way out of the mountains. The pilots assumed that the railroad went *around the mountains*. I wasn't so sure. I do know that we scared a lot of goats that day! Between concentrating on sick sacks, I could see them scattering in all directions.

My senior year at Wayland was indeed a good one. I had learned to take Dramamine before our flights and I was selected to play against the Russian All-Star team in a series of games across the country, including Madison Square Garden.

I *think* Madison Square Garden was impressive, but I'm not sure. The Russians had a 6'8" player, and I was so awed by her size that I didn't really see anything else. I remember her well because I looked straight into her belt buckle all night—it just happened to be at eye level.

That was the first time that I was elbowed on the top of my head. In all fairness, I must say it was purely accidental. I just happened to be jogging too close to her as we went down court and the natural swinging action of her arms brought her elbow over the top of my head.

Playing against the Russians taught me a new tolerance for people from other countries with different cultural backgrounds. Among my favorite possessions are souvenirs given to me by players from foreign countries, but the one that stands out most in my memory has to be the lump on my head given to me by the 6'8" Russian.

I made the All-American team again in my senior year, but Wayland lost the AAU Tournament. Even though my college career ended on a losing note *score-wise* I felt that I had come out way ahead *knowledge-wise*. After all, I knew how to use sick sacks; I knew how to cross busy expressways; and I knew how to avoid head elbowing.

When I graduated from Wayland, I knew I was leaving many friends. I even felt a certain loss toward Bernard Beechcraft, III. I also felt that my best basketball days were still ahead of me. However, I found there were few opportunities open for women to continue playing basketball beyond college.

Eventually I decided to play with an independent AAU team called the Utah Lakers. After playing four years at Wayland, the years with the Lakers were like going from riches to rags. Trying to find a sponsor for our team was a constant struggle and most of the time, we paid our own expenses. The AAU should have been proud of us, for if there were ever a team that played without financial gain, and purely for the fun of it, it had to be ours. I wouldn't even accept free gum from my coach for fear I would lose my amateur status. I always brought my own gum and stuck it down in my sock during the game.

While with the Utah Lakers, I made the AAU All-American team a third year and was selected to play with the United States team in the World Basketball Tournament in Peru. I guess the selection committee decided that anyone who loved basketball enough to play in Utah and drive as much as 500 miles to play a game deserved some kind of a reward. Since women's basketball was not included in the Olympics until 1976, the World Basketball Tournament took its place in my era. My greatest thrill—and a special reward—was for me to carry my country's flag as captain of the United States team. (Fortunately, there were no pigeons.)

After getting used to playing before six or seven friends in Utah, it was an unbelievable experience to play before 30,000 spectators each night in Peru. It took us a long time to adjust to the sounds of so many people at the games. When something displeased the Peruvian spectators, they would send out loud, shrill whistles. One of our girls was very disappointed when she found out they were not reacting to her shapely legs.

Each team had to work its way up through an elimination tournament held in several locations in Peru in order to reach the finals in Lima. We played in some cities where the water was impure, so we drank cokes to cut down the possibility of getting stomach bugs. All games were played on outdoor courts (most of which had been converted from soccer stadiums), and the heat and humidity were terrible. I found myself drinking 20–30 cokes a day just to replenish my fluids. We even brushed our teeth with coke. The first thing my mom said when I returned home was "Why are your teeth so brown?"

The people from Peru treated us royally. They had a great respect for athletes, and they could not do enough for us. Everywhere we went, there were crowds following us. I signed autographs on everything from shoestrings to coke bottles.

One day, our team was walking in a public park, and as always a crowd was milling around us. It wasn't long before we heard a voice shouting "Wait! Wait!" When we turned around, in the far distance we could see the head of one of our players stranded in the middle of hundreds of Peruvians. We kidded her later about how white her face looked in comparison to the faces of the Peruvians, and how lucky she was that most Americans are much taller than South Americans so that she stood out above the crowd.

Remembering this player's head protruding above the sea of people in the park reminds me of a big difference in the seating arrangements for the players and coaches in the Peruvian stadiums. Unlike our courts, where benches are placed on the sidelines for the team, some of the Peruvian stadiums had dugouts below the level of the court for the players and coaches. It was a strange sight to be running up and down the court and to see bodiless heads on the sidelines turning back and forth with the action of the game.

We also had to get used to playing on outdoor courts. Morning and afternoon games were the worst, since we had to look into the sun on high passes and rebounds. We also had to cope with the wind (and with one player who kept spitting into it to test its direction). Night games were the best. There was no sun, the winds were gentle breezes, there was little moisture being sent up into the air by my teammate, and the outskirts of the playing court were in enough shadows that I didn't have to watch disjointed heads moving back and forth in the dugout.

The year after the trip to Peru, I was selected to play with the United States team on a tour of France, Germany, and Russia. The first stop was in Paris, and being in training as we were, we were surprised to see that wine was served with our meals. France had a water problem, so it was their custom to drink wine, even at a young age. We were older, but enjoyed the custom. During one game, one of our players said "Pass the wine," as she reached out for a towel in the huddle. From that night on, our coach saw to it that cokes accompanied our meals.

I have more memories stored away about Russia than any other country I visited. Most are very personal thoughts dealing with their different way of life, but there were some humorous moments.

The last stop on our Russian tour was Tbilisi. I thought we had goofed up in directions during our flight and had landed in Mexico on a railroad. There were no lights on the airstrip as we got out of the plane. In the dark, our assistant coach fell in a ditch while walking from the plane to the hangar and cracked several ribs. We told him that if he had been taped up properly, he wouldn't have gotten hurt.

We were more excited about watching the Tbilisi May Day parade than about our game. My roommates and I had never seen anything like it and, watching from our hotel window, were totally engrossed in the colorful scope of the parade. All at once we heard the angry voices of Russian soldiers bursting into our teammates' room next door. We quickly decided it was our coach's job to help out, since he had told us before the trip that it was our job to play the game and his job to make decisions and call the plays. For once, we agreed with him.

When things finally settled down, we found out that some of our players had been sitting in the window watching the parade in their shorts. Having played basketball in our shorts all our lives (bloomers had already gone out of style, thank you), we did not realize that wearing shorts in public would offend the Russians. Only the calmness and clout of our interpreter prevented anything more than a severe scolding. Interestingly, the Russian basketball uniforms made our American shorts look like long johns in comparison. I never understood why it was okay to wear shorts during sporting events but not in our hotel rooms.

But at the next game, everyone kept their warm-ups on as long as possible. Better to be hot than dead, or is it warm than red?

After our series of games in Russia, we flew to Germany. When we arrived, I felt like kissing the ground because the three weeks in Russia had been depressing. We all gained a new appreciation of democracy and personal freedom.

I had stomach problems while at the World Basketball Tournament in Peru, so all during the European trip I was extra careful about what I ate. It was all in vain—two days before leaving Germany for home, I woke up seeing five shades of green and feeling like elephants had set up housekeeping in my stomach. We had a game that night, and I decided that the only honorable way to get out of the game was to die on the bench during the national anthems. Fortunately, the other team didn't show up to play, and I refused to go without fanfare.

I have heard other people comment on the beautiful sights to see in Germany. But even today, all I can remember about Germany are green rooms and endless commodes.

I would like to be able to say that I played happily ever after following that European trip. However, I had not been home long when I did a "no-no" and lost my amateur status, eliminating any further chance for international competition.

Please don't laugh when I tell you what I did to bring the wrath of the AAU down upon my head. I wrote a basketball textbook.

Being a teacher, I thought it only logical that I should teach others what I knew the most about. However, the AAU decreed that it was all right if I wrote about something I knew nothing about, but I couldn't write on the subject in which I was best qualified. Discounting Beechcraft Bonanzas, taping, and stomach bugs, that only left basketball.

I decided a challenge is a challenge is a challenge. The AAU decided a pro is a pro is a pro.

I cried for a long time after I lost my amateur status. Little did the AAU know that I was probably one of the purest amateurs around, in spite of the textbook.

I still shoot around in gyms just for the fun of it, and I still love running up and down basketball courts and feeling tired and drained at the end of a pick-up game. And I still keep my gum in my sock.

A basketball is a basketball is a basketball.

At the 1973 AIAW National Championship held at Queens College, Immaculata defeated Queens in the finals. Above, Immaculata's Marianne Crawford (Stanley), #23, drives for a lay-up as Maggie Hilgenberg of Queens, #10, defends. (Photograph by Richard Lee)

20

Queens College: Success with No Frills

Lucille Kyvallos

Because I was a part of a whole population of women athletes who never got a chance to show their talents, I coached with commitment and did whatever I could to propel women's competitive opportunities. My experience at Queens College reflects the growth and changes in women's basketball in the years 1968 through 1980.

The Drawstring Case

Since my parents worked, I spent many afternoons in 1946 at the age of 14 in a school recreation program where I learned to shoot and play basketball with the boys. I loved the game right away and spent many summer hours playing "3 on 3" and perfecting my shooting and passing. I bought my own basketball and sewed a drawstring case for it so I wouldn't have to deal with the awkwardness of walking through the streets of New York with a basketball under my arm.

In high school, competitive athletic programs were closed to girls so my friends and I formed a girls basketball team, the Rustics, that played in the Police Athletic League and Mirror Park Department League and won the City Championship in each league. Later on I played for Our Lady of Perpetual Help, a collection of top New York City players in the Metropolitan Life Insurance Basketball League that played by men's rules. While competing in leagues and tournaments I often won Most Valuable Player and high scorer awards. In fact, spectators would bet on my shots. (One man said he won $350 on my shooting in the Newburgh, New York tournament.) My creative passes faked out the defense

355

and found their destination in the hands of a cutting teammate. Sometimes opponents triple teamed me.

It was common knowledge that I had the ability to play on the collegiate men's team, but there was no structure through which women like myself could compete on a national and international level before and after I graduated from Springfield College in 1955. I played semi-pro ball under an alias. The New York Cover Girls, later the Arthur Murray Girls, traveled to small Northeastern towns to play the local men's teams for entertainment or as a fund-raiser. Our routines were somewhat like the Globetrotters'.

Queens College—1968–72

After teaching physical education and coaching the women's basketball team at West Chester State College (Pa.) from 1962 to 1966 (and losing only two games in four years), I started coaching women's basketball at Queens College in 1968. Because New York public high schools did not have competitive athletic programs for girls the quality of the college play in the area was poor. Competition was very laid back and social. In an attempt to deemphasize competition, after the game punch and cookies were served to both teams.

The keys to improvement that first year were developing the talents of inexperienced players and emphasizing defense. I recruited women from the campus who were interested and had native physical ability—quickness, speed, jumping, strength. My two-hour practices were purposeful.

Other colleges were playing zone defense—inept, stationary, and immobile—all of which reinforced the feminine ideal of the epoch. Our team was taught to play man-to-man. They learned to locomote, position themselves in relationship to the ball and to their opponent, space themselves, intercept passes, and block shots. "Defense first" was my goal and tactics. That first season we won 10 out of 12 games. But more importantly, the women were learning the discipline necessary to become committed athletes.

A Lesson in the Smoky Mountains

Our second year, 1969–70, was also successful (10-3). The third year, 1970–71, saw a new emphasis on women's intercollegiate athletics. Our team advanced through a state tournament and new regional structure culminating in the national intercollegiate tournament at Western Carolina University at Cullowhee, North Carolina.

When we arrived on the Smoky Mountain campus our players were excited and filled with awe. We were there to play basketball but we were distracted by the differences in the geography and in the way people spoke and behaved. It was a new experience for us. We lost our first game to Kansas State because we could not maintain a focus. We then won a double overtime game against Illinois State in the consolation round, but were knocked out in the next game by Cal State-Fullerton. This momentous experience became an energizer in the future, reminding us of all the wonderful things that were within our grasp. When our 23–4 team landed at the airport a huge crowd awaited us—friends, school chums, colleagues, parents, brothers and sisters, all waiting for us, cheering and congratulating us like heroes.

Trouble with the Men

A postscript to the 1970–71 season had to do with the men's basketball coach. Basketball coaches are very competitive, but it was always my contention that we didn't want to compete with the men's program and we didn't want to "prove" anything to them—we just wanted a chance to compete.

Inadvertently things got mixed up in the New York *Times* listing of basketball scores on February 7. Readers were amazed to discover that Queens College had upset Central Connecticut State College 66–44. The men's basketball coach reluctantly admitted to admirers that the win was posted by the women's team, which sported an 11–0 record, in contrast to the men's 6–10.

This kind of incident along with our playing in Madison Square Garden and receiving continuous coverage in the New York *Times* and New York *Post* created a great deal of tension between the men's basketball coach and the women's program. Sexist men in the department continued to needle the men's coach.

Defense—Because It's Mental

With the start of the 1971–72 season additional goals had to be identified. Again we emphasized tough defense and second effort shots on offense. The second goal was to pull down defensive rebounds which would lead directly to fast breaks. Defense has a direct relationship to the team's offense and to a large degree is mental. Defense involves assessing your opponent's strengths and weaknesses and exploiting the weaknesses. That year we averaged 72 points per game to our opponents' 37 and pulled down 54 rebounds a game to our opponents' 27. Federal City College from Washington, D.C. was the first team that made an effort to defense our fast break, but they did not succeed. Federal City was just one of several tougher teams from outside the New York metropolitan area that I sought to strengthen our schedule.

We were lucky to have as a starting guard Debbie (the Pearl) Mason, who dazzled and astounded spectators, opponents, and teammates alike with behind-the-back dribbling, double pumps on lay-ups, and long swishing jump shots. She was an outstanding defensive player as well, stealing passes with her quickness and endurance.

Undefeated during the regular season, we moved past the New York State championship and our first three games in the regionals. We had a 24-game undefeated win streak going, the longest winning streak of any intercollegiate basketball team in New York State in over 30 years. But we lost to our perennial rival, Southern Connecticut State College, in the regionals.

Because of our regional strength, we were one of the two teams who went to the national intercollegiate tournament. After an initial loss to Phillips University of Oklahoma we played tough and beat Cal State-Long Beach in the consolation final. As a result we came out fifth in the country. Now we were really launched.

1973 AIAW National Tournament at Queens

Although other teams within the area only played each other, Queens College was now reaching out to the strongest teams it could possibly attract to the area. We knew that these games would strengthen our own team's performance and serve as a model for the metro area. Certainly local high school and college coaches and players were always coming to watch our games.

We were awarded the AIAW national championship and after advancing through the state and regionals we would be in it! The public relations office with Ed Jaworski really did a great job in contacting the media and getting us on radio shows and sending out releases. The best 16 teams in the United States were coming to compete in the New York area, teams from Texas, Utah, California, South Carolina, and Indiana.

It was an interesting mix and the media were very curious about us. Some of the headlines included words like "hairpulling," "hot pants," "bloomers and blushes," and they "can't wait for locker room interviews." The women athletes who made it into print would have to endure the sexism of the male sportswriter but these reporters were turned around and totally impressed with the calibre and intensity of play. The New York *Times, Daily News,* Long Island *Press, Newsday,* and later even *Sports Illustrated* featured the AIAW tournament. After we defeated UC-Riverside (the tallest team in the tournament with a 6'2" and a 6'1" player), Stephen F. Austin in overtime, and Indiana University through our better conditioning (we played two games in one day, for example), the spectators were on the edge of their seats through the final victory by Immaculata.

At the end of the season, Queens College recognized our program and me as adding to the life of the college. We really did perk it up, I must say!

1973–74—International Competition

In 1973–74 we added a tournament in Canada and two games with Montclair and Immaculata College—the toughest schedule in our area and probably the country. We had a refined fast break, strong rebounding, the speed and quickness of Debbie Mason, and team unity. I always viewed team unity as a synergy with the whole being greater than the sum of its parts; thus five players on the court could have a greater effect if they maximized playing together.

On February 24, 1974 we played Immaculata at home, a major event, and news of it spread all over the country. Immaculata had a two-and-a-half-year win streak, had been National Champions for two successive years, and featured Theresa Shank, a center who had spent the previous summer playing in the World University Games in Moscow. Immaculata came down with three busloads of fans including nuns from their hometown, and the gym was packed with 2,000 spectators. When the buzzer sounded Queens had won.

Gail Marquis, a 5'11" sophomore, was pitted against Shank. The other matchup was between Debbie Mason and Mary Ann Crawford, an excellent ball handler. The game seasawed back and forth. With 40 seconds to go and Immaculata up by 1, I called a time-out and set up a pick-and-roll play between Mason and Marquis. Debbie was to dribble to the right side of the basket, expecting 5'5" Stanley to play her tight, and Marquis would then set a pick on Stanley and roll to the basket. As Debbie drove by Gail, Mary Ann lost her defensive position and Theresa had to pick her up, creating a mismatch. Debbie passed the ball to Gail and she went in for an uncontested jumper which put us one point up, 57 to 56 with 25 seconds left on the clock. Pandemonium broke loose. You couldn't hear yourself think. With 25 seconds to go, Immaculata had the ball. Our defensive plan was to trick them by showing a man-to-man press, except that Debbie would press Stanley loosely. We knew Mary Ann did not have a good outside shot so we could sluff off on her a little while showing her a man-to-man press. Immaculata had trouble getting their passing lanes open. Mary Ann saw Debbie in front of her, but couldn't drive and was too far out to take an outside shot, so she tried to lob a pass in to Theresa on the free throw line, but the defense jumped and batted the ball away. With 8 seconds to go Debbie grabbed the ball and held on for the win. We had beaten a team that was invincible in the eyes of the nation.

But February 24 does not a season make. Southern Connecticut was going for its third successive Northeast regional championship and they were ranked number three nationally, while we were number two. I prepared our team very carefully for the Southern Connecticut game, since they had a full-court press and two All Americans. The last thing I did before we took the court was conduct a team meeting. I made them believe that they were giants and that they not only *could* win, but they *would* win if each player executed her task. They came out of that meeting with a focused resolve while the Southern Connecticut crowd was yelling and screaming for blood. Everyone played magnificently; we won the Northeast crown and advanced to the AIAW nationals at Kansas State University.

It was difficult for our women to maintain the intensity of a lengthy game and postseason schedule. We didn't know how to take continued pressure, especially after miraculous wins over Immaculata and Southern. We ended up number seven in the country.

1974–75—Madison Square Garden

The highlights of our 1974–75 schedule included playing three nationally-ranked teams, including Immaculata in Madison Square Garden. The Immaculata-Queens matchup was to be a test of ability and drawing power. Our public relations representative Ed Jaworski said the NCAA was going crazy: "You ought to read their newsletter," he said. The NCAA was not happy about a women's game in the Garden and all the media attention it was getting.

I think what really captured the public's imagination was the fresh spirit of competitiveness that girls and women were bringing to basketball—perseverance, rising to the occasion, performing heroic feats, never letting down, coming back from 20-point deficits, scoring free throws under great pressure, and just the raw enthusiasm that players and teams brought to the game. It wasn't as if we were 6'8" forwards, blasé about shooting free throws or dunking the ball. The public could identify with us. We were the underdog who turned everything around. This climb to the top was an exciting period in the history of women's basketball.

The high percentage shot in the men's game was always considered to be the lay-up because it is taken close to the basket. This was not really based on the reality of the game. Young girls, especially those playing Catholic Youth Organization ball, were taking long outside shots and scoring consistently. Some were taking them with two hands, some with one hand in the style of Bob Cousy. They were so skillful and accurate in their long-distance shooting that these really had to be considered high percentage shots. The U.S. men always thought the outside shot was a lower percentage shot, but when I coached in the World University Games in '77 it was clear to me that the European teams featured the outside shot, but then the long shot had always been an integral part of the girls and women's game. Its importance was never recognized until the men changed their rules by rewarding themselves with 3 points for scoring from outside. The effect this had on their game was to challenge their defenses, encourage some very interesting tactics, and improve the men's game.

So women's basketball at the Garden was the hottest game in town. A prominent basketball magazine included a women's section that year and also had articles about Title IX. Title IX said basically that a school could not spend $3,000,000 for men's athletics and $39.95 on women's. This was the prologue to scholarships for women.

Game day arrived. Twelve thousand people were filing into Madison Square Garden to the strains of Helen Reddy's "I am Woman." It was a breathtaking game. Immaculata would set up and score and Queens would answer, then Immaculata would run a pattern and Queens would steal the ball and score, and so it went, nip and tuck. In the final five

Queens was Northeast Regional Champion in 1973–74. (Photograph by Richard Lee)

minutes Immaculata led by 1. A Queens player was called for a personal foul. She was also called for a technical and the wrong Immaculata player went to the line and shot both the personal and the technical, increasing the score to 55–51. Confusion reigned and the momentum changed in favor of Immaculata. Queens fought back but was unable to overtake them and ended on the losing end of a 65–61 score. Even though Queens lost, we knew we would be part of the history of women's basketball and that we had made a major contribution to pushing this women's sport forward.

Queens wound up ninth in the country that year, but the success of our performance in the Garden led to the question of women playing in other major arenas throughout the United States. And if the women did play regularly in big arenas, would they fall prey to high pressure recruiting? Until women's scholarships entered the picture, the recruitment of players was conducted more on a local level and it was totally contingent upon the reputation of the college. The top programs were in state or private colleges with small athletic programs like Southern Connecticut State College, Queens College, and Immaculata. The large universities like Michigan, UCLA, Tennessee, Stanford, and Georgia did not have highly developed programs during this period.

1975–76—China and Changes in the Wind

The 1975–76 season opened with the People's Republic of China National Women's Basketball Team, which was touring the United States. Because of the Nixon era and the opening of China to the United States, the public relations dished out by the Chinese team was "friendship first, competition second." They beat us 85–58, or as one pundit said, "Murder on the Orient Express." They were a national team in phenomenal shape. The cultural experience for our women was immeasurable.

One thing that was becoming apparent was the inconsistency in rules interpretation on many levels; teams that went out of state suffered and the home team advantage, ours and our opponents, was exaggerated. Queens, Delta State (a powerhouse and number one in the country), Southern Connecticut, and Immaculata played in Madison Square Garden again. Most of our team that season was made up of sophomores who lacked competitive maturity in light of the high-powered competition. We ended the season 20–5, and about ninth in the country. *Popular Sports* selected a 1976 Women's All American team, with Gail Marquis on the first team.

But the whole quality of women's competition was changing. I felt more pressure to deliver because of our previous achievements but it was getting more difficult because of the advent of scholarships. Large institutions jumped on the bandwagon and started recruiting top talent away from the established programs by giving full scholarships. Nancy Lieberman, for example, a local product from Queens, was highly recruited across the United States in 1976 and wound up going to Old Dominion in Virginia. Debbie Miller from the Bronx, New York ended up at Boston University. Other highly talented young players nourished in the New York metropolitan area were going to Long Island University, St. John's, and C.W. Post. Colleges like Queens not only had to compete against nationally ranked programs but had to worry about the local schools that were nipping at our heels.

Recruiting became difficult for institutions like Queens. Young high school athletes were awed by the scholarships that seemed to reflect their self-worth. We had to go for "sleepers." We looked for youngsters at the high school level who had not peaked and had been averaging 20 to 25 points a game, not the ones generating a lot of publicity. I had to go for the solid player who had not yet arrived. In the midst of this, Queens College as part of the City of New York was hit with the devastating budget cuts of the summer of 1976—budgets, services, and personnel were diminished. Morale was terrible.

But there were some great moments for some of our best women. In the summer of '76 Gail Marquis made the U.S. Olympic Team and during the 1976–77 season our 6'2" star center, Althea Gwen, turned her career around after having had to turn in her uniform for not showing up for practices. I lectured her about commitment and responsibility and motivated her, pointing out what she could be and how she almost threw it away and would throw it away unless she really shaped up. Later she would become an All American and hold national rebounding records.

It was that season the Manufacturers Hanover Trust Bank sponsored a New York State tournament with prize money, which we won and used for a women's basketball grant-in-aid fund. In addition Queens played Old Dominion, losing by one point. Olympian Nancy Lieberman "didn't let her admirers down," according to *Newsworld* on January 24, 1977, "scoring 31 points and drawing gasps with her variety of schoolyard moves that are now starting to creep into the women's game." That year Carol Blazjowski, "the Blaze," a scoring sensation from Montclair State set a Garden record of 52 points—a record for both men and women. Lusia Harris and Delta State played before 12,000 at the Garden.

By the end of that season Queens under my coaching had won over 150 games and, more importantly, set a model for other schools to improve their program quality. I was named Coach of the Year by the second annual Coaches Clinic selection committee and went to California to receive my award and to lecture.

I was also selected women's basketball coach for the U.S. team that would go to the World University Games in Bulgaria. We were a team having nine players who had never played international rules. We had two women who were 6'2" with everyone else 6' or under. We may not have been the 12 best players in the country, but we worked hard. We used the right moves at the right moments, implemented strategy with tricks, and our coachable personnel executed well and with perseverance. We beat Bulgaria twice, Romania, Canada, Czechoslovakia— teams that could have beaten us easily. We lost to the Russians, who had players 6'8", 6'6", and 6'4"—and only two women under 6'—but came up with the silver medal.

1978—No Garden for Us

Although Queens had helped get the Madison Square Garden games off the ground, setting attendance records of 12,000 the first year we played, 7,000 and 10,000 in the second year, and over 12,000 in the third year, we were not invited to play in the Garden in 1978. They said they wanted to go further and didn't feel they owed us anything. Our ten-year 171–53 record and customary national ranking and nationwide publicity were disregarded. They matched up Montclair State against Rutgers and UCLA against Delta State. The tournament did not draw particularly well—5,100 in the first round and 6,700 in the second.

In order to bolster our playing schedule and showcase women's basketball, Queens College had initiated the Queens College Holiday Tournament the previous year. In 1977–78 we expanded it to eight teams, inviting Old Dominion University, Providence College, Fordham, Oral Roberts University, Michigan State, Concordia from Canada, and Southern Cal. We won it, squeaking past ODU and Nancy Lieberman, 70–67. We also won the Manufacturers Hanover Tournament again. The previous season, if we were behind by a few points we wouldn't work together to come back. This year if a concentration lapse occurred, the team would hold together on the court, discuss its strategy, and go back out strong, ready for the next play. This year they believed in each other. It was really fantastic; this squad would go a long way with that attitude.

An editorial in the New York *Daily News* congratulated us for our winning program as did the New York State Legislature. We were perceived as winners in our hometown, an exhilarating feeling in troubled times. After winning the regionals, we went to the national tournament at Rutgers. After being down by as many as 17 points to the University of Mississippi, we came back and beat them 74–71. We lost to our nemesis, Montclair State, 75–60, but ended up the 1977–1978 season 30–3, one of the best records in the history of Queens College women's basketball.

Men's Model of Athletics

By the 1978–79 season, large institutions like Tennessee, Penn State, Texas, North Carolina State, UCLA, Maryland, and Missouri were pushing their way to the top of the women's basketball world, and teams like Delta State and Immaculata were in demise. Money was making a big impact and women's basketball was shifting into a higher gear from the previous level of play. Institutions that were pouring money into their programs were beginning to get dividends and do very innovative things with their programs, with competition keener than ever.

I never had a losing season at Queens College, primarily because I'd been able to develop talent. We developed into a competitive program on the national level even without the benefit of a large budget or athletic scholarships. We received $5,000 for the team's operation; that was the budget for the season. The program really was a no-frills affair. There were no towels, no extra uniforms, no laundry service, no meal money, no warm-ups for practices, no money for scouting opponents or for making trips outside the metropolitan area for high-power recruiting. In 1978 we were able to provide two grants-in-aid for two out of four players recruited.

Sexist Sabotage

Many years of my coaching were marred by a small minority of men in the Department of Physical Education who were unhappy with the attention the women's basketball program was receiving. The department chairman tried to curtail our progress and strip us of the money necessary to keep our program viable. I became aware that a hidden agenda to undermine our program was to be brought up at the next Student Activities meeting—scheduled to take place during our practice! The team marched en masse to the meeting. We pleaded our case and the department chairman's proposal to limit our use of student activity funds was reversed. While the College administration (with no funds) supported us, the department chairman did not. He even refused to accept a generous grant from the Alumni Association earmarked for our program.

Under these disheartening conditions, I found that the joy and satisfaction that coaching had given me had eroded. At the end of the 1979–80 season I submitted my resignation. The president of the College asked me to reconsider but I was too burned out to continue. Queens College students, faculty, and alumni were thrilled, proud, and supportive of the excellence and recognition that the women's basketball program had achieved throughout the years. But now it would come to an end.

Despite the demise of this pioneer program we proved that it could be done. Against the odds, we showed that at Queens College women athletes could perform at an elite athlete level. Excitement was infectious as women athletes across the country brought to the game their own fresh spirit energizing collegiate basketball. A model had been created for a new generation of coaches who could rise to new heights with their basketball programs.

In March 1990 I was invited to the Final Four of the NCAA Division I Women's Basketball Championship where I received the Founders Award from Kodak and the U.S. Basketball Writers Association. I was touched and honored to be recognized for my achievements. At the same time, I was delighted to see that Tara Van Derveer, winning coach of the 1990 National Championship, Stanford University, had played for Indiana University in the 1973 AIAW National Basketball Championship at Queens College. It became clear to me that the work of those early years had come to fruition and the baton had been passed.

My thanks to Rosalie Gershon for her work as editorial consultant.

Section 6
Basketball for a Special Population

21

Women's Wheelchair Basketball

Brad Hedrick and Sharon Hedrick

Women's wheelchair basketball was formally introduced during the 1968 Paralympics (the wheelchair counterpart to the Olympic Games) in Tel Aviv, Israel. That year, the Israelis used their home-court advantage to defeat teams from Argentina, Austria, Great Britain, and the United States to take the sport's inaugural gold medal. Twenty-two years later, in July 1990, at the World Cup Wheelchair Basketball Championship for women held in St. Entienne, France, a young but very skillful USA team advanced decisively to the final and defeated the perennially powerful West Germans 58–55, thus winning the second world championship in the history of USA women's wheelchair basketball. Between these two events lies the brief chronology of women's wheelchair basketball, and within this chapter the development, status, and future of this relatively new sport will be explored.

Origin of Wheelchair Sport

Wheelchair basketball is the oldest organized sport in the world for individuals with locomotor disabilities. Popular opinion holds that the sport originated in Veterans Administration (VA) hospitals in the United States during the mid-1940s.[1] The March 22, 1948 edition of *Newsweek* heralded the sport's introduction with a cover picture of a wheelchair athlete and a story about a game between teams from Halloran VA Hospital and Cushing VA Hospital, which was played in Madison Square Garden before a crowd of more than 15,500.

The sport's first national championship was contested by five VA hospital teams in 1948 under the aegis of the Paralyzed Veterans of America. The PVA Championship, as it came to be known, was subsequently awarded in 1949 and 1951. However, because the distances separating the various hospital teams limited head-to-head competition for the PVA Championship, the title was determined by having a third party compare the teams' records in a manner similar to that used by the NCAA to determine its national champion in collegiate football. In addition, only VA teams comprised exclusively of veterans with spinal paralysis were allowed to vie for the coveted PVA title; community or "civilian" teams and individuals with disabilities other than spinal cord paralysis could not participate. Not surprisingly, this structure alienated the latter two groups and prompted the development of the world's first nationally organized sport program for individuals with locomotor disabilities, the National Wheelchair Basketball Association (NWBA).

In 1949, five community-based teams and a rogue VA hospital team agreed to participate in the first National Wheelchair Basketball Tournament (NWBT). The NWBT was held at the University of Illinois at Galesburg. During this historic event the participating athletes organized the sport's first national governing body, the National Wheelchair Basketball Association (NWBA). Today, the NWBA has grown to include an intercollegiate division, a junior division, and a women's division, encompassing 27 conferences, 186 teams, and nearly 2,000 athletes.

The first international play in wheelchair basketball is believed to have occurred in 1954 when the Montreal Wheelchair Wonders of the Canadian Paraplegic Association participated in the sixth NWBT.[2] The next year, the NWBA Eastern Conference champions, the Pan American Jets, traveled to Stoke Mandeville in England and won the first wheelchair basketball competition sanctioned by the International Stoke Mandeville Games Federation. Since then, wheelchair basketball has spread to every continent, and over 60 countries. To date, it remains the only wheelchair team sport played worldwide.

The Impetus for Women

Although wheelchair basketball was conceived and initially organized in the United States, American women were not immediate beneficiaries of this developmental leadership. Indeed, the NWBA constitution prohibited women from participating on member teams for the first 25 years of the organization's existence. It was not until 1974 that the NWBA delegate body voted to amend the constitution and end this discriminatory practice. During the interim between 1949 and 1974, a few local programs allowed women to practice and play "unofficial" games with their teams; however, for the most part, women's wheelchair basketball in the United States was dormant. A similar trend was evident on the international front.

Men participated in international wheelchair basketball during both the first Paralympic Games in Rome in 1960 and the 1964 Paralympics in Tokyo. However, women were not afforded this opportunity until the 1968 Paralympics in Tel Aviv, Israel. For the USA women, this tournament represented their first opportunity ever to play other women's teams. The 1968 Paralympics sparked interest in the development of women's wheelchair basketball programs in the United States. For the first time, women were starting to get involved.

Two years after the Tel Aviv Paralympics, on the campus of the University of Illinois at Urbana-Champaign, the nation's first women's team was born. Known as the Illinois Ms. Kids (the team name was changed in 1986 to the "Fighting Illini"), the team filled its schedule for the first three years by playing wheelchair teams comprised of non-disabled individuals. However, in 1974 the Ms. Kids achieved a milestone in the chronology of USA women's wheelchair basketball; they hosted a game with another American women's team. This historic game occurred on February 24, 1974 in Champaign, Illinois. The Ms. Kids played host to the Southern Illinois University Squidettes and defeated the visitors by the score of 34 to 14.[3] From that moment, women's wheelchair basketball in the United States began to acquire momentum. In 1975 the first National Women's Wheelchair Basketball Tournament was held in Dearborn, Michigan. Since that time, 16 NWWBTs have been held with the national championship being won by six teams. Table 1 shows the teams competing in each of the 16 championship games of the NWWBT, the tournament site, the championship game scores, and the champion team's coach.

Concurrent with this growth, the women's wheelchair basketball game was also growing and improving internationally. As reflected in Table 2, the sport has been dominated internationally by the West Germans. Since 1974 the West Germans have won 7 of 14 international tournaments (the European Championships and Pan American Games are not included in this total due to their restricted competitive fields). However, the USA program steadily improved during the 1980s, and the decade culminated with the United States displacing the West Germans as the world's best during both the 1988 Paralympics in Seoul, South Korea and the 1990 World Cup in France.

Organizational Structure

Since its inception, wheelchair basketball, like all other sports pursued exclusively by individuals with disabilities, has been organized outside the existing national and international governing bodies of sport for nondisabled competitors. Internationally, wheelchair basketball is ad-

Table 1
National Women's Wheelchair Basketball Tournament Results

Year	Location	Championship Games	Coach
1975	Detroit, MI	Motor City Wheelers ....26 Southern Illinois U 9	Tim VanderMeiden
1976	Detroit, MI	Canada.................................23 Motor City Wheelers 16	Don Royer
1977	Champaign, IL	Canada................................. * Illinois Ms. Kids..................... *	Don Royer
1978	Lexington, KY	Illinois Ms. Kids....................41 Twin Cities Rolling Gophers 24	Bob Szyman
1979	Carson, CA	Twin Cities Rolling Gophers ....32 Southern California Sunrise......23	Terry Hanson
1980	Golden Valley, MN	Southern California Sunrise......39 Twin Cities Rolling Gophers 37	Clarre Adler
1981	Colo. Springs, CO	Southern California Sunrise......28 Illinois Ms. Kids....................21	Clarre Adler
1982	Sacramento, CA	Twin Cities Rolling Gophers ....21 Illinois Ms. Kids....................14	Terry Hanson
1983	Champaign, IL	Illinois Ms. Kids....................35 Twin Cities Rolling Gophers 21	Brad Hedrick
1984	Las Vegas, NV	Southern California Sunrise......29 TC Wheels of Fortune.............24	Les Hayes
1985	San Diego, CA	Southern California Sunrise......39 Illinois Ms. Kids....................34	Les Hayes
1986	Chicago, IL	Illinois Ms. Kids....................49 Southern California Sunrise......26	Brad Hedrick
1987	Dallas, TX	Courage Rolling Gophers ....48 Univ. of Illinois Fighting Illini ..31	Bob Szyman
1988	Kansas City, MO	Courage Rolling Gophers ....46 Univ. of Illinois Fighting Illini ..35	Bob Szyman
1989	Hartford, CT	Courage Rolling Gophers ....55 Univ. of Illinois Fighting Illini ..51	Bob Szyman
1990	St. Louis Park, MN	Univ. of Illinois Fighting Illini ..47 Courage Rolling Timberwolves .37	Brad Hedrick

*No score presented. Tournament was round robin. Canada & Illinois both had 3–1 records. Canada was awarded the championship based upon point differential.

Table 2
International Women's Wheelchair Basketball Results

PARALYMPIC GAMES

1968 Tel Aviv, Israel
1. Israel
2. Argentina
3. USA
4. Austria
5. Great Britain

1972 Heidelberg, Germany
1. Argentina
2. Jamaica
3. Israel
4. Germany
5. Canada
6. Great Britain
7. Yugoslavia

1980 Arnhein, Netherlands
1. Germany
2. Israel
3. USA
4. Argentina

1984 Aylesbury, England
1. Germany
2. Israel
3. Japan
4. Canada
5. USA
6. Netherlands

1986 Toronto, Canada
1. Israel
2. Germany
3. Argentina
4. Canada
5. USA

1988 Seoul, Korea
1. USA
2. Germany
3. Netherlands
4. Canada
5. Japan
6. Israel

INTERNATIONAL STOKE MANDEVILLE GAMES—
Aylesbury, England

1970
1. Argentina
2. Great Britain
3. Jamaica

1973
1. France
2. Germany
3. Great Britain

1975
1. Germany
2. Israel
3. Argentina

1977
1. Germany
2. Canada
3. USA

1978
1. Germany
2. Israel
3. USA

1982
1. Germany
2. Israel
3. Sweden

1986
1. Germany
2. USA
3. Japan

WORLD CUP CHAMPIONSHIPS

1990 St. Entienne, France
1. USA
2. West Germany
3. Canada
4. Holland
5. Australia

EUROPEAN CHAMPIONSHIPS

1974 Kerpape, France
1. Germany
2. France
3. Yugoslavia

1987 Lorient, France
1. Germany
2. Israel
3. Netherlands

1989 Charleville-Meziere, France
1. Holland
2. West Germany
3. Israel

PAN AMERICAN WHEELCHAIR GAMES

1971 Jamaica
1. Canada
2. Argentina
3. USA

1973 Argentina
1. Argentina
2. Canada
3. USA

1975 Mexico
1. Argentina
2. Mexico
3. Canada

1978 Brazil
1. Canada
2. Argentina
3. USA

1982 Halifax, Canada
1. USA
2. Canada
3. Mexico

1986 Puerto Rico
1. Argentina
2. Canada
3. Mexico

ministered under the aegis of the International Stoke Mandeville Games Federation (ISMGF). The ISMGF was organized in 1948 in England by British neurosurgeon Sir Ludwig Guttman, whose interest in promoting the rehabilitation of spinally injured WWII veterans was the impetus for this action.

Within the United States, women's wheelchair basketball had no organizational affiliation before 1974. However, during its 1974 delegates assembly the NWBA assimilated women's wheelchair basketball by amending the constitution to allow women to play on member teams and creating a Women's Division. The purpose of the division was to promote the development of women's teams and to oversee the administration of the annual NWWBT. Unfortunately, the Women's Division was not empowered to amend NWBA playing rules for women's play until 1986, although challenges to the carte blanche acceptance of men's rules were voiced as early as 1977.[4]

From 1974 till 1986, women's teams in the United States either participated in conferences comprised predominantly of men's teams or remained independent and scheduled games with appropriate and available men's and/or women's teams. In 1986, Midwestern women's teams

Wheelchair basketball generates skill and intensity as Mary Ann O'Neil of the Courage Rolling Timberwolves prepares to reverse dribble against the tight defensive pressure being applied by Jean Driscoll of the University of Illinois Fighting Illini. (Photo by Curt Beamer, *Sports 'n Spokes*/Paralyzed Veterans of America, 1990)

started to congregate during the season to play round-robin tournaments in such cities as Minneapolis, Chicago, Champaign, Illinois, and Whitewater, Wisconsin. These tournaments later evolved into the first women's wheelchair basketball conference.

The North Central Conference of the NWBA was comprised of the Courage Center Rolling Gophers-A of Minneapolis, the RIC Express of Chicago, the University of Illinois Fighting Illini from Champaign-Urbana, and Wright State University Lady Raiders from Dayton, Ohio. Concurrently, a similar round-robin tournament was taking place in California among the West Coast teams. Formal West Coast conference play, however, has not yet materialized.

Since 1975, 24 women's teams have been formed in the United States and have competed in the National Women's Wheelchair Basketball Tournament.

Eligibility Criteria and Player Classification

Eligibility for the PVA Championship and all ISMGF sanctioned international competitions prior to 1984 was limited to individuals with spinal cord injuries. However, since its inception, the National Wheelchair Basketball Association has utilized a functional rather than etiology-based approach to eligibility. The NWBA allows any individual with a "permanent, severe leg disability or paralysis of the lower portion of the body who would be denied the opportunity to play basketball were it not for the wheelchair adaptation" to participate. Obviously, this means that individuals need not require a wheelchair for mobility to be eligible. Indeed, individuals who are functionally ambulatory but cannot run, jump, or move laterally due to a permanent physical disability are eligible.

Unfortunately, because of this inequity in eligibility criteria many NWBA players could not play internationally in the ISMGF sanctioned international competitions due to its restriction to spinal injured athletes. However, in 1982 the Basketball Subcommittee of the ISMGF lobbied and won the right to open competition to individuals with disabilities other than spinal cord paralysis. As a result, all wheelchair basketball competitions sanctioned by the ISMGF since the 1983 World Wheelchair Games in England have allowed "other" lower-extremity impaired individuals to participate.

Although the early NWBA teams played without restriction as to the level of disability of the members, inequity between the spinal injured players and their lesser disabled amputees and/or orthopedically disabled counterparts was apparent. More and more, lesser disabled players were usurping the positions of their spinal injured teammates, much to the chagrin of the latter. To address this problem a physical classification system was introduced in 1964 wherein players were categorized according to their level of disablement.

The NWBA system incorporated three classes which represented varying degrees of lower extremity motor loss corresponding to specific levels of spinal cord paralysis. Within the system, a class I player, the most severely disabled, has complete motor loss at or above the seventh thoracic vertebra. A class II player has complete motor loss originating at the eighth thoracic vertebra and descending through the second lumbar vertebra. Finally, a class III player is an individual with a lower extremity motor deficit consistent with loss of innervation at or below the third lumbar vertebra. The composition of teams on the floor is controlled using a points system wherein no team is allowed to put more than 12 points on the floor at a time. Thus, if three class III players are played, a class II and a class I or two class Is would have to be played to assure that the 12-point maximum is not exceeded.

The physical classification system was perceived as a means of controlling inequity resulting from the participants' varying levels of disability and as a means of assuring the vitality of the roles of individuals with more severe disabilities. Today, the physical classification system remains an integral facet of wheelchair sports. However, the criteria of physical classification in international wheelchair basketball has undergone significant change.

Internationally, the medically-oriented physical classification system based on the spinal paralysis model was used until 1984. However, due to the growing interest in accommodating individuals with disabilities other than spinal cord injuries and the prevalence of incomplete spinal lesions among those with spinal cord injuries, the medical classification system was perceived as generally inadequate.

Due to dissatisfaction with the medical classification system, interest began to accrue for the development of a functional classification system. In 1984 a functional classification system for wheelchair basketball was introduced for use in the World Wheelchair Games held in England.[5] In contrast to the medical classification system, which relied almost exclusively upon diagnosis-oriented classes, the functional classification system relied upon the assessment of the athlete's functional potential using three basketball-specific tests that emphasized trunk stability and were so rudimentary as to eliminate error due to skill variation. Based on these data and information regarding the individuals' medical status a classification was derived. One major advantage to the functional classification over medical classification was that the individual could be observed while playing games to validate the credibility of the functional assessment. In the current ISMGF wheelchair basketball classification system a point system regulating team composition was developed wherein athletes may be classed in half-point increments between 1 and 4.5 points (i.e., 1.5, 2.5, and 3.5 classes are possible). The point total for the players on the floor may not exceed 14.0 points.

Rules of Play

Wheelchair basketball is played internationally by the rules of the International Amateur Basketball Federation (FIBA) with exceptions to accommodate the use of the wheelchair. The most notable exceptions are: players are allowed five seconds in the free throw lane instead of the customary three seconds, players are allowed to double dribble, and the traveling violation is amended to accommodate wheelchair use with players not being allowed to push more than twice on the rear wheels with one or both hands without passing, shooting, or dribbling the ball. Taking the third push constitutes a traveling violation. Players are also not allowed to lift off the wheelchair seat or to use their lower extremities to gain an unfair playing advantage.

Rules also exist which regulate the design of the wheelchair. For instance, the footrests may not exceed a standardized height from the floor. The diameter of the rear wheels and the height of the seat are also restricted. To assure that playing surfaces are not damaged by contact with the wheelchairs, protective coverings must be attached to the forward-most part of the wheelchair which would come into contact with the floor if the wheelchair was to tip forward. Finally, only gray or white rubber, nonmarking tires are allowed for use. In the United States, the game is played by NCAA rules with similar modifications to accommodate the use of the wheelchair. Current NWBA basketball rules may be obtained from the Office of the Commissioner, 110 Seaton Building, University of Kentucky, Lexington, KY 40511.

With regard to rules which are specific to the women's game, few have been introduced. Unlike their nondisabled counterparts, women wheelchair basketball players have not gone to the smaller diameter basketball. In 1977 a *Sports 'n Spokes* editorial by Soulek[6] strongly advised women's teams to introduce the use of a smaller basketball. However, it was not until 1986 that the Women's Division was empowered to amend NWBA playing rules for women's play. To date, the smaller ball has not been introduced. There are two major reasons for this. First, USA women's teams wish to maintain consistency with the ISMGF women's rules which still require the larger diameter ball. Second, the sparse distribution of women's teams requires that women's teams play a number of games against men's teams to fill their schedules. To maintain consistency throughout the season they have opted to stay with the larger ball. The NWBA Women's Division did introduce the

FIBA "right of option" rule for shooting free throws. This rule allows a team whose player is fouled to take the ball out of bounds rather than shoot the one and one free throws when the latter is an option.

Trends

The number of women's wheelchair basketball teams active during any given year has remained relatively static since the late 1970s. Additionally, most teams have had relatively short periods of activity. Only five teams have been around for 10 or more years and the modal value for years played of the 24 teams which have been formed is only two years. The demographics of disability and the socialization of women with disabilities are probably significant contributors to this lack of growth and the limited lifespan of teams.

The majority of the participants in wheelchair basketball are individuals with spinal cord injuries and according to most estimates, 70–75 percent of the spinal cord injured population is male. Thus, only 25–30 percent of the disabled population most likely to pursue wheelchair basketball are women. Add to that the traditional deterrents to the sport socialization of women, exacerbated by the presence of a locomotor disability, and it is easy to understand the limited growth of women's wheelchair basketball. Of course, counterbalancing these negative trends are some rather positive ones which bode well for the future of the sport. The introduction of increasingly more sophisticated sports wheelchairs, the proliferation of instructional camps, programs for disabled youth, and the influx of the more skilled novices will likely have a significant, positive effect upon women's wheelchair basketball both qualitatively and quantitatively in the future.

Since the first NWWBT, improved play has characterized women's wheelchair basketball. The total points scored in the first eight NWWBT championship games was less than 51 points on the average compared to over 75 during the last eight championship games. The factors contributing to this improvement have been multiple.

First, the technology of the sport has been improved. The Henry Ford philosophy of "they can have any color they want so long as it's black" was typically applied to wheelchair manufacturing prior to the late 1970s. For the most part the wheelchair was perceived as a medical appliance and not a piece of sports equipment. This changed, however, as athletes who were dissatisfied with the limited performance potential of medical appliance quality equipment began to introduce innovations that transformed the industry and the nature of wheelchair basketball. Aircraft quality alloys were introduced to improve the strength to weight ratio

Women's wheelchair basketball is a fledgling sports movement with great potential, aided by improvement of sports wheelchair technology, increased availability of instruction, changes in the sport socialization of women, and federal mandates that provide equal access to sport programs for individuals with disabilities. Above, the Fighting Illini's Sharon Hedrick, #51, puts up a shot between two Timberwolves, Karne Casper-Robeson, #12, and Susan Hagel during the 1990 championship game. (Photo by Curt Beamer)

of wheelchairs used for sports and critical features affecting propulsion and the handling of the wheelchair were made adjustable for individual adaptation. The lighter, stronger, and more maneuverable wheelchair that resulted dramatically improved the speed and quickness with which the game was played.

A second factor that has contributed to the improvement of play in women's wheelchair basketball has been the creation of instructional wheelchair basketball camps hosted by the NWBA and the Paralyzed Veterans of America. Many of the best women players in the United States today owe their success to the instruction and training they received at these camps. Along a similar vein, in 1987 developmental instructional camps were introduced in numerous cities around the country to give potential USA team members the opportunity to receive instruction from our nation's best coaches in an effort to improve their performance internationally. The success of this program is evidenced by the United States' back to back world championships in 1988 and 1990.

The proliferation of local wheelchair sports programming for young people with locomotor disabilities has also aided women's wheelchair basketball by identifying talent and providing instruction earlier. Finally, as the effects of Title IX become more pervasive and increasing numbers of young women become interested in sports it is likely that a ripple effect will be observed in women's wheelchair basketball with a greater number of women with disabilities being predisposed to pursue sports after disability onset.

Notes

1. S. Labanowich, "Wheelchair Basketball: A History of the National Wheelchair Basketball Association and an Analysis of the Structure and Organization of Teams" (Doctoral diss., University of Illinois at Urbana-Champaign, 1975).

2. Ibid.

3. R. Szyman, "Ladies of the Court: Women Cagers Want Competition, and Not Just on the Men's Teams," Sport 'n Spokes 1(4)(1975): 7–8. (This periodical is published by Paralyzed Veterans of America, Washington, D.C.)

4. M. Soulek, "Women & Basketballs," Sport 'n Spokes 2(5)(1977): 11.

5. H. Strohkendl, "The New Classification System for Wheelchair Basketball," in Claudine Sherrill, ed., Sport and Disabled Athletes: 1984 Olympic Scientific Congress Proceedings (Vol. 9) (Champaign, Ill.: Human Kinetics, 1986), 101–112.

6. Soulek, "Women & Basketballs."

7. L. Howell, in R. M. Goldensen, J. R. Dunham, and C. S. Dunham, eds. Disability and Rehabilitation Handbook (New York: McGraw-Hill, 1978), 565–572.

Section 7
The Past, Present, and Future

22

The Future Is the Present in Organizations for Basketball

National Federation of State High School Associations

The National Federation of State High School Associations is an affiliation of over 51 state high school associations, with 18,000 member high schools representing over a half million athletic personnel. In 1920 a group of men interested in high school athletics formed the Federation. While in the 1950s they discussed high school athletics for girls (particularly in basketball), they were discouraged by the women involved with physical education and sports days for girls. It was not, therefore, until the 1960s that they encouraged state high school associations to include girls athletics in their jurisdictions. The Federation is not a governing body; it is a federation of state associations that offers services to its state associations, including girls sports rules, and serves as an advocate for secondary school programs. It holds membership in the USOC and has voting rights on many NGBs. It also has a close liaison with NCAA, NAIA, and NJCAA.[1]

Six professional organizations that belong to the Federation "promote growth, development and prestige among the professions which compose interscholastic activities."[2] These include approximately 160,000 athletic administrators, coaches, officials, and interscholastic "spirit coaches." The nonathletic organizations include approximately 900 music and speech and debate professionals. The Federation publishes more than eight million publications annually, including rulebooks for 13 sports. Its periodicals include *News*, *Target*, *Interscholastic Athletic Administrator*, and *High School Sports*. Since the early 1970s, the Federation's

379

publications have included articles about female athletes and coaching. The most popular topic has been basketball.

Brice Durbin, executive director of the Federation, describes its objectives. The Federation oversees activities that encompass more than one state high school association or which can best be operated on a nationwide scale, for example, national meetings, publications, and interscholastic events. It maintains records, suggests programs, and provides services, materials, and any other assistance needed by state associations. Its constituency consists of administrators of all interscholastic activities, coaches, officials, and judges, as well as the students it protects. The Federation attempts to identify critical issues and provide solutions, and to promote the educational values of interscholastic activities to the nation's public.

Since 1980 the Federation offers accident insurance for the athletes and a million dollars worth of liability insurance for its professional members. It offers a program, TARGET, to assist youth with alcohol and drug abuse problems. At its yearly convention, the Federation offers workshops, coaching clinics, and discussion groups on critical issues.

The state high school athletic associations are solely responsible for conducting programs and administering state sanctioned programs, with the Federation acting primarily in an advisory capacity. The Federation suggests eligibility rules for sports, codes of conduct, minimum facilities, medical attention, and scheduling.

Since the mid-60s the Federation has pledged itself to encouraging state high school athletic associations to develop varsity programs for

The Illinois State Championship game in 1985. (Photo by John C. Dixon, for the *Champaign News-Gazette*)

girls. In line with that goal, the Federation published its own girls basketball rules in 1971. Because of each state's autonomy in developing its own girls sport activities, the structures differ widely. Within the state associations there are 26 women assistant executive directors, two women associate executive directors, and a number of state boards that have women on them—and at least three have had women presidents. Nevertheless, competitive opportunities for girls abound in every state.

Through the Amateur Sports Act, more girls are being given opportunity to compete in grass-roots level developmental programs and in Olympic sports and to develop into world class athletes through the junior NGB teams. For example, in basketball, there are developmental programs throughout the country, and four teams are formed to compete in the Sports Festival. The Federation not only encourages this new opportunity, but contributes its expertise and guidance to individual athletes. It also encourages its basketball coaches to become involved in the Olympic movement programs.

A 1988–89 "Sports Participation Survey" conducted by the Federation indicated that the most popular girls sport was basketball. That year 16,173 schools and 379,337 girls were involved in basketball. Basketball has, since the 1970s, been the most popular competitive sport for high school girls.[3]

In 1989, the National High School Sports Hall of Fame was initiated. To date, seven women athletes and/or coaches have been inducted into this Hall of Fame: Bertha Teague (also in the Naismith Basketball Hall of Fame), Denise Long Andre, Kim Mulkey, Cindy Noble, Janet Karvonen, and the more familiar collegiate athletes, Lynette Woodard and Cheryl Miller. These athletes had to be nominated by their state high school associations and have been an outstanding high school athlete as well as post-high school.

The Federation's motto is "School Activities: The Other Half of Education." Because of its educational commitment to developing strong girls programs, especially in basketball, the future is promising for high school girls interested in high level basketball competition.

Notes

1. Thanks to Susan S. True, assistant director, NFSHSA, for information vital to this work; "National Federation of State High School Associations," in the Final Report of the President's Commission on Olympic Sports 1975–1977, Volume II, *Findings of Fact and Supporting Material* (Washington, D.C.: U.S. Government Printing Office, 1977), 359–382.

2. Brice Durbin, "NFSHSA Fact Sheet," National Office, FSHSA, 1990.

3. Susan S. True to Joan S. Hult, Correspondence, November 20, 1990.

National Junior College
Athletic Association

The National Junior College Athletic Association (NJCAA) is a sports governance organization that provides competitive opportunity in basketball to over 6,000 female junior college student-athletes. The NJCAA was conceived in 1937 in California to promote and supervise a national men's program of two-year junior college sports and activities consistent with the educational objectives of junior colleges. It became the National Junior College Athletic Association in May 1938. An invitational basketball tournament at Compton, California led to the nationwide basketball program for men sponsored by the NJCAA. In 1975 the NJCAA accepted the responsibility for providing national competition for their institutional members' women's programs. It is from this structure that the present regional and national tourney grew. The organization functions as a national governing body for over 515 junior and community colleges. It offers a full program of sports for men and women.

The Women's Division of the NJCAA developed out of a desire to make women's athletics an integral part of the total educational process. It fosters sound educational goals consistent with those of the member institutions. It started, as had the men's program, with an invitational basketball championship. The AIAW was already offering championships for female junior college athletes in basketball, volleyball, and golf. However, the NJCAA perceived its role to include providing championships for women.[1]

The pioneer efforts of Orville Gregory led to the first national championships for junior college women. The following excerpts are from the *1990–91 NJCAA Women's Basketball Guide* and describe clearly the primary motivation for initiating national championships for women.

> Hanging tough when the competition gets rough. . . . That's what the NJCAA Women's Basketball National Championship Tournament is all about—24 of the nation's best women's basketball teams vying for the coveted championship in a 35-game match-up. Orville Gregory, athletic director at Johnson County Community College, Kansas, first saw the need for a women's tournament, ironically, after seeing the disappointment of the JCCC men's team when they lost their bid for a berth in the men's nationals. If they felt such disappointment at missing their tourney, Gregory thought, then what must the women feel when they didn't even have a national event?"[2]

Only seven teams had shown any enthusiasm by December 1973, but Gregory persisted. Finally the idea caught fire—too late for a 1974 tournament—but plans were put into motion for a 1975 competition. (There was, however, a national invitational in 1974.) Sixteen of the nation's 22 regions were represented the first year. The Temple Junior College (Texas) team won the top honors. They beat North Iowa Area Community College, Northern Oklahoma, and Seminole, Oklahoma.[3]

By the next year's tournament 19 teams from 18 regions competed and 22 by 1978. All 24 regions were participating by 1984. For Gregory, the greatest satisfaction in watching the tournament grow has been "the response of the crowds as they have come to discover what fine athletes women basketball players really are."[4] Thanks to the persistence of Orville Gregory, who saw his dream grow from a minor invitational meet into a nationally prominent event.

There is equal representation for institutions in the Women's Division through 24 elected regional directors for each division. The programs are available to all community colleges. The men's and women's divisions are separate, as are their tournament sites, but they work together to develop and maintain eligibility rules, which are applied equally to all athletes. The organization offers national and regional championships.

The first year, the Women's Division had three national championships: basketball, volleyball, and tennis. Invitational championships were slated in six other sports. The Women's Division had 296 members by 1976. In 1976–77 there were four women's championships and eight invitational championships, while membership grew to 345. By 1990 the Women's Division membership reached 453 schools, and there were 12 championships. The expansion of members and sports led to the 1982–83 authorization for a new administrative assistant with primary responsibilities in the Women's Division. One of her tasks was to return more women to leadership positions.[5]

Lea Plarski had headed the Women's Division since its inception in 1975 until elected in 1989 as the first woman president of NJCAA. A published NJCAA Position Paper on "Leadership Roles of Women in Two-Year College Athletics" strongly urged women to advance within their *regional structures* to positions of leadership.[6]

The NJCAA Women's Basketball Committee is responsible for setting policies and procedures for approval by the Board of Directors of the NJCAA. This committee is made up of regional directors, assistant regional directors, and the coaches association president; it thus represents all areas of the country. The chair is B. J. Graber from Weatherford College (Texas). All the coaches of women's basketball teams are eligible for membership in the Basketball Coaches Association. They conduct their championship in a separate location from the men's basketball championships.[7]

Each of the 24 regions determines regional policies and procedures for qualification to its championship. Each has a regional play-off for a berth in the national championship. All athletes must be certified and eligible athletes. Temple Junior College of Texas won the first National Junior College Championship.

The handbook for the Women's Division reminds the members that as an organization they meet the individual needs of all students by providing national competition for all eligible member schools through regional affiliation. The Women's Division emphasizes that it is dedicated to meeting the needs of all women athletes, providing them with the highest caliber of national competition in a wide range of sports. As is true of the other governing organizations in higher education, basketball is the most popular sport for women, and more institutions field basketball teams than any sport.

Two-time national championship coach Evelyn Blalock sums up the excitement and thrill of being a champion in basketball: "This one feels just as great as the first . . . This one was at our back door. Our fans had a chance to share the joy with us. That means something."[9] That means a lot to the female athletes in the National Junior College Athletic Association Basketball Championship.

Notes

1. George E. Killian, ed., "History of the National Junior College Athletic Association" in *Official Handbook and Casebook of the National Junior College Athletic Association* (Colorado Springs: NJCAA, 1990).

2. NJCAA, "Tournament Celebrates 16th Year with Rich History," in *1990–91 NJCAA Women's Basketball Guide* (Colorado Springs: NJCAA, 1990).

3. Ibid.

4. Ibid.

5. Killian, "History of the NJCAA."

6. NJCAA, "NJCAA Position Paper: Leadership Roles of Women in Two-Year College Athletics," *Official Handbook, NJCAA,* 1990.

7. *Women's Basketball Guide,* 13.

8. *Women's Basketball Guide.*

9. Pat Turner, "KC: National Champions," in *Women's Basketball Guide,* 26.

National Association of Intercollegiate Athletics

Phyllis Holmes

The National Association of Intercollegiate Athletics (NAIA) is the governing body for small to medium sized institutions who do not embrace the philosophy of "big-time" athletics. The National Association of Intercollegiate Basketball (NAIB) was founded in 1940 as an outgrowth of a basketball tournament initiated in Kansas City's Municipal Auditorium in 1937. This tournament of 32 teams still remains the world's oldest and largest intercollegiate basketball championship. In 1952 when the organization expanded to include other sports, the NAIB became the NAIA as it is known today. The NAIA led in allowing representation and participation to predominately black institutions. As an organization that has adhered to a strong philosophy of educationally-based athletics, the NAIA was a model for the AIAW in establishing policies for student-athletes. The NAIA has maintained its membership at approximately 500 institutions throughout its 50-year history and has been headquartered in Kansas City, Missouri.

At the annual meeting in March 1980, the NAIA approved the establishment of a women's division and a championship events program, which was initiated in the 1980–81 academic year. The NAIA Women's National Basketball Championship evolved from the original eight-team tournament begun in 1981 to a 16-team tournament in 1984, and finally expanded to a 32-team tournament for the 1991 championship.

In 1991, the NAIA will have two divisions of competition for both men's and women's basketball. Institutions will declare Division I or II based on a set of criteria that indicates "emphasis" of program and centers predominately on financial aid and enrollment. The number of teams participating in each of the championships will be determined by a formula reflecting the number of institutions per division, as well as per district.

The NAIA held its first Women's National Basketball Championship March 12–14, 1981, at Kemper Arena in Kansas City, Missouri in conjunction with the 44th annual Men's Basketball Championship. In the first year 100 teams participated in district competition. A total of 26 teams competed in area play-offs with eight teams advancing to the finals. These eight teams included Azusa Pacific University (California), Texas Southern, Northern State College (South Dakota), Missouri Western State University, Berry College (Georgia), Saginaw Valley

State University (Michigan), Virginia State University, and Kentucky State University.

In the three-day championship series over 12,000 fans were exposed to good basketball as the women's teams shared the arena and the spotlight with the men's teams in Kansas City. In the championship double-header, 9,000 fans saw seventh-seeded Kentucky State upset top-seeded Texas Southern 73–67, to capture the first NAIA women's national title. Kentucky State's Carolyn Walker was the tournament MVP, and head coach Ron Mitchell was the NAIA Coach of the Year.

The second women's championship followed the same format. That year the number of teams participating in district play increased to 203 teams, and 27 of 32 districts held district play-offs. With this increase in participation, in 1981, Mary Ann Wiedenmann of Southern Methodist University was hired as an assistant executive director on the NAIA national staff. One of her responsibilities, as the first woman to hold such a key staff position, was staff liaison to women's basketball. That year saw the formation of the NAIA Women's Basketball Coaches Association. The women's basketball championship event coordinator, Phyllis Holmes of Greenville College (Illinois), became the first coaches association president.

Also in the second year of competition, a rating system and All-District and All-American team selections were initiated for women's basketball. The top-rated team, Southwestern Oklahoma State, completed a 33–0 season and dominated the championship series, rolling over Missouri Southern 80–45 in the finals. Southwestern Oklahoma's freshman Kelli Litsch was tournament MVP and was selected as first team All-American. Head Coach John Loftin was Coach of the Year.

In 1982–83, the demise of AIAW led to the expansion of the NAIA women's basketball program from 203 to 377 participating teams. Thirty of the 32 NAIA districts conducted championship play-offs. Southwestern Oklahoma State repeated as champion with a win over sixth seeded University of Alabama at Huntsville. The leading scorer of the tournament, Kelli Litsch, was once again MVP and her coach, John Loftin, was again Coach of the Year.

El Kahim Shrine Temple for the benefit of hospitals for crippled children sponsored the 1983–84 National Championship at the Five Seasons Center in Cedar Rapids, Iowa. The tournament expanded to 16 teams chosen from 15 bi/tri district competitions with the at-large team being the highest-ranked team not surviving the bi/tri district play-offs. That was the first of two years that the women's tournament did not share the limelight with the men. Over 5,000 spectators attended the four-day event, with a crowd of fewer than 1,000 attending the final game.

The team from the University of North Carolina at Asheville won the tournament, that institution's first team in any sport to win a national championship. The UNC-Asheville Lady Bulldogs, playing for their coach Helen Carroll, who had earlier announced that she would resign for health reasons at the end of the season, pulled a stunning 72–70 overtime upset over the University of Portland (Oregon). Sheila Ford of UNC-Asheville was the MVP, setting a single-game scoring record of 41 points and a single-game rebounding record of 21. Carroll was the Coach of the Year.

Two undefeated teams, Saginaw Valley State University with a record of 32–0 and Southwestern Oklahoma State with a record of 33–0, met in the championship game of the 1985 tournament in Cedar Rapids. Saginaw Valley State University, coached by Marsha Reall, was the only team to have appeared in all five NAIA Women's Basketball Championships. It was fitting that NAIA's first female four-time All-American, Kelli Litsch, hit an 18-foot baseline jumper with 18 seconds left to give Southwestern Oklahoma a 55–54 victory and a perfect season. In Litsch's four years, the Lady Bulldogs won three national titles and compiled an outstanding 129–5 record. Litsch received her third MVP award and Coach Loftin his third Coach of the Year Award in 1985.

Because of the poor attendance at the tournaments in Cedar Rapids, the 1986 championship was returned to Kansas City. The expansion to 16 teams made it necessary to play the early rounds downtown in Bartle Hall. The women's teams played their remaining rounds in conjunction with the men's tournament at Kemper Arena. The NAIA was still the only athletic association to have a men's and women's double header championship.

In the 1986 championship, Francis Marion College (South Carolina), the number one seed and best offensive team in the nation, had little difficulty winning. Francis Marion beat its four opponents by a combined total of 110 points. The Lady Patriots in their first three games defeated Dominican College (New York) 109–41, Wingate University (North Carolina) 89–71, and Georgia Southwestern 85–78. Their final victim, falling by a 72–65 score, was Wayland Baptist, a perpetual power in the early days of collegiate basketball. Francis Marion's head coach, Sylvia Rhyne Hatchell, was Coach of the Year and Tracy Tillman was MVP.

In 1987, before a near record breaking crowd of 8,137, NAIA's winningest team, Southwestern Oklahoma, captured its fourth championship in five years with a 60–58 win over North Georgia College. The only time Southwestern Oklahoma appeared in a national tournament and did not win the title was in 1984 when they lost in the quarter finals to champions UNC-Asheville. North Georgia's Brenda Hill, with 22

At the 1989 NAIA National Championships, at the Kemper Arena in Kansas City, Southern Nazarene University met Western Washington University in the semifinals, defeating them and going on to win the championship. (AP LaserPhoto, Steve Wolgast)

points in the championship game, giving her 115 points for the week, broke the previous record of 110 points set by Sheila Ford of UNC-Asheville. Hill set a single-game scoring mark of 42 points and was named the MVP. The Coach of the Year for the fourth time was Southwestern's John Loftin.

Those who thought the absence of four-time national champion Southwestern Oklahoma meant the end of District 9 dominance got a rude awakening in the 1988 championship. The Lady Chiefs of Oklahoma

City University kept the title in the Sooner State for the fifth time in NAIA's eight-year history. In the title game, Oklahoma City, with four members of the Colombian National Team playing on its team, defeated Claflin College (South Carolina) 113–95, setting a new record of total points scored in one game. Also, the combined total of 208 points was a new tournament record. The Lady Chiefs delighted the fans with long-distance shooting, as Patricia Ordonez hit 8 of 13 field goals from the three-point range. On her way to capturing the tournament's MVP, Claflin freshman guard Mariam Walker set nine tournament records, including scoring 62 points in one game. Although Saginaw Valley bowed to Dillard University (Louisiana) in the first round, this was their eighth consecutive appearance in the NAIA tournament.

Perhaps the saddest saga in the championship was that of top-seeded Wingate University (North Carolina), who came into the tournament with a 31–0 record. Wingate had dedicated its season to the memory of Debbie Powers and Julie Hamilton from Converse College (South Carolina), who had died in a traffic accident in October as their team returned home from a scrimmage at Wingate. Their dream of an undefeated season and a national championship ended in a semifinal loss to Oklahoma City.

In 1989, Claflin College entered the championship for the second straight season favored to win the title. However, once again the Pantherettes lost in the finals—to a team from Oklahoma that was making its first appearance. For Claflin, who had averaged more than 100 points per game during an unbeaten season, it was another bitter taste of frustration.

The 8,529 fans, the third largest championship crowd since the move to Kemper Arena in 1975, enjoyed a fast-paced high-scoring game with 17 lead changes in the second half. With 19 seconds to play, on a jump shot by Jenese Glover, Southern Nazarene University pulled off a 98–96 upset over Claflin. The bright spot for Claflin was All-American Miriam Walker-Samuels, who scored 326 points in eight games, surpassing the 257 points amassed by Kelli Litsch in 12 games. Sophomore Walker-Samuels, who averaged 40.5 points a game, was the MVP.

Before 1989, the NAIA National Convention had been held in Kansas City in conjunction with the Men's Basketball Championship. At the 1988 Convention, the membership approved separating the convention from the tournament. This historic decision gave impetus to separating the women's championship from the men's, thus allowing women's basketball to develop its own identity.

The 1990 NAIA Women's Basketball Tournament found a new site and possibly a new home in Jackson, Tennessee. Located between Memphis and Nashville, in a strong basketball community, Jackson provided enthusiasm and tremendous local support. During the week of the NAIA women's championship, excellent basketball was show-cased before over 26,000 fans in Oman Arena.

The tournament was moved to a new place, but the result was the fifth verse of a familiar tune. For Southwestern Oklahoma's coach, John Loftin, it was the "thumb-game." The Lady Bulldogs gave him his fifth NAIA championship ring. An enthusiastic crowd of over 4,000 fans saw the Lady Bulldogs defeat the University of Arkansas-Monticello 82–75 for the title. It was the seventh time in the tournament's history and the fourth consecutive year that an Oklahoma team won the National Championship. The Lady Bulldog's tournament experience paid off despite having only nine players and no All-Americans on its roster.

Tina Webb of the Arkansas-Monticello Cotton Blossoms was the MVP, the fourth time that the MVP had been selected from the losing team. She joined Kelli Litsch in being selected a first team All-American for four consecutive years. For the first time in any NAIA championship, two national anthems were played, because Simon Fraser University (British Columbia, Canada) was one of the 16 qualifying teams.

Because of the enthusiastic support and the overwhelming success of the championship in Jackson, the NAIA National Executive Committee approved a 32-team women's tournament for 1991. For the first time, each of the NAIA districts will advance a men's and a women's team to the national championship.

In 1990, the tenth anniversary of the Women's Championship, 396 teams and approximately 6,000 female athletes participated in NAIA women's basketball; 191 teams competed in district play-offs, the first round of the national championship. For these student-athletes, basketball becomes a memorable educational experience. In the future, with the new divisions and an increase in the number of teams participating, even more student-athletes will be able to benefit from this experience.

Kelli Litsch, a four-time NAIA All-American at Southwestern Oklahoma State University, led SWOSU to three national titles as a player. She was also assistant head coach for two other champion teams, in 1987 and 1990. (Photo courtesy Southwestern Oklahoma State University)

National Collegiate Athletic Association

The National Collegiate Athletic Association (NCAA) is an amateur sport organization of 828 institutional members.[1] Organized in 1906 as a football reform movement, the Association's major goal is to serve as an overall national intercollegiate governance, legislative, and administrative body for the conduct of national championships. The purposes of the Association are: (a) to initiate, stimulate and improve intercollegiate athletic programs for student-athletes and (b) to promote and develop educational leadership, physical fitness, sports participation as a recreational pursuit and athletic excellence.

The underlying position of NCAA is that competitive athletic programs should be a vital and integral part of the educational community and that the athlete should be an integral part of the student body. The NCAA sponsors 23 sports, 11 for women and 13 for men. It conducts 76 separate national championships in a three division structure. More than 18,000 men and women student-athletes annually compete in these events for national titles. Division I has 23 national collegiate championships (10 women's and 13 men's). There are 20 national collegiate Division II championships (9 women's and 11 men's) and 24 national collegiate Division III championships (11 women's and 13 men's). Women's basketball championships are offered in all divisions. Riflery and skiing championships are combined for men and women.

In celebrating the tenth year of women's athletics in the NCAA, David S. Smale, NCAA publications editor, reviews the ten years: "Beginning with cross country in the fall of 1981 . . . the NCAA has crowned 290 national champions in 14 different sports and three divisions. And since that date 698,405 female student athletes [actually fewer, since some compete in more than one sport] have participated for 42,784 teams through the 1988–89 academic year."[2] In 1981–82, 74,248 female athletes competed in NCAA championships. In 1982–83, when AIAW had no championships, over 80,000 women participated. During the 1988–89 academic year, 91,406 student-athletes competed on 5,700 teams.[3]

The NCAA voted in 1980 to offer women's championships for Division II and Division III institutions the following year. In 1981, the voting delegates elected to include national championships for Division I institutions as well. The negotiations between NCAA and AIAW are discussed elsewhere in this collection. By the 1981–82 academic year, individual institutions had to decide where their women's programs would compete that year. In the sport of basketball 17 of the top 20 teams in Division I competed with the NCAA. In the meantime, the NCAA Women's Committee had negotiated a five-year governance plan to assure women a percentage of leadership roles in the organization. Those percentages have been maintained, with approximately the same percentages stated in the original agreement.

An institution's division selection is based on its commitment to athletic scholarships. Each collegiate institution must declare membership in one of the three divisions. Each may compete outside of its primary division in one sport for men and one for women. In Division III, no financial aid based on athletic ability may be offered. In Division II, financial aid may be offered up to 50 percent of maximum scholarships permitted in each Division I sport. Football is further subdivided based on strength of the program.

The NCAA conducts the most comprehensive amateur sport program under one governance organization in the country. While high school programs are more extensive, they are not covered by a single organization, but rather through affiliation with the National Federation of State High School Associations. The institutions affiliated with the NCAA have the largest and best financially endowed sports programs. The NCAA member institutions command vast resources to operate their sports programs. More than 275,000 student-athletes (men and women) competed in intercollegiate programs last year. In basketball, men and women competed on 1,584 teams.

Besides conducting championships, the NCAA negotiates TV contracts for sport coverage and publishes and disseminates rule books, films, books, periodicals, and manuals. The Association awards postgraduate scholarships, enforces its policies and regulations, and administers medical insurance programs. It conducts the National Youth Sports program with support from the federal government. Thousands of economically disadvantaged youth have been taught sport skills and received instruction in educational and personal development with the support of the federal government, NCAA, and sponsoring member institutions. Recently the NCAA has sponsored special clinics on drug education, academic preparation, and skill development programs before each national championship through Youth Education through Sports (YES) sponsored by corporate partners. It also partially reimburses member institutions for team travel and lodging for national championships.

The NCAA is a powerful force in international competition. It was an important agent in the revoking of AAU's franchise from FIBA and awarding the NCAA-backed ABAUSA the franchise for governance of USA international basketball NGBs in 1973–74. It gained additional power and prestige when the women joined the NCAA. In fact, it became the largest controlling interest in USA Basketball (formerly ABAUSA), providing most of the coaches, personnel, and players for both national and international basketball competition. Without the cooperation of the NCAA, the international teams would be less than effective in winning championships, and the cost would be prohibitive. The NCAA colleges and universities also provide the facilities, players, and coaches for the Olympic-sponsored programs.

The organization's voting representatives govern the NCAA's policies and regulations. Some decisions are made within each division, and other important changes come before the entire assembly. A very strong NCAA Council oversees governance and formulation of policies, along with offering strong recommendations to the membership regarding important legislative issues. A great deal of power and authority is vested in the NCAA Council. An equally powerful Executive Committee is empowered to administer the Association's finances and championships.

Allegations of rules violations are referred to the Association's enforcement department and Committee on Infractions. An appeal process is available after the Committee on Infractions renders its decision and any resultant penalties are reported to the institution. The NCAA Council or Executive Committee makes the final decision on appeals. A compliance service department offers special convention workshops and seminars to educate the membership and help to further the integrity of intercollegiate athletic programs.

Unlike other collegiate governance organizations, the NCAA sport committees are governed by administrators, not by coaches. Each of the three divisions, for example, selects its own basketball sports committee to govern its championship. Committee members are elected at the annual convention and serve three-year terms. Separate men's and women's basketball committees are independent from each other in policy-making. Selecting only administrators for the committee does impede some actions that women coaches would like to take. However, the committee membership is comprised primarily of women who have coached basketball.

Changes in rules, format of the basketball championship, the site for the preliminary rounds, and the final championship are decisions of the basketball committees. The seeding of teams is also the responsibility of each basketball committee. In Division I there are automatic bids for 22 conferences, and the rest of the field of 48 teams are at-large teams selected by the committee. Judith R. Holland, associate athletic director at the University of California, Los Angeles, is currently chair of the Division I committee.

The Kodak All-America is under the auspices of Kodak and the Women's Coaches Association of the NCAA in each division. The all-tournament teams are selected by a special tournament committee. The NCAA basketball coaches association convenes at the Final Four.

The television windfall for 1990–91 will substantially augment monies available for reimbursement. Funds will be proportionately contributed to Division II and Division III championships to engender reimbursements closer to parity with the Division I championship. The additional money will also enable Division I to derive a profit from its championship for the first time.

In a discussion about the future of women's intercollegiate athletics in the NCAA, Judith Holland said to the Women's Basketball Committee: "During the '90s we would like to see us progress so that when the current TV contracts expire, we would be able to have a contract solely for the women's basketball tournament. Now there is something you can measure. There is something that tells you that you have gone to the next level."

Richard Schultz, executive director of NCAA, thinks it is a realistic goal. "I've long been an advocate of women's basketball developing on its own merits," he said. "Don't piggyback on the men's program. Do what's right for women's basketball and focus on what will cause women's basketball to grow on its own. It's an achievable goal."[4]

And so the women's basketball program has set its sights for the future. If the past is any indication of the future for coaches of women's basketball, they'll get the new contract, and they'll continue to provide opportunity for more and more women to experience the excitement of intercollegiate athletics.

Notes

1. Thanks to Merrily Dean Baker, assistant executive director of the NCAA, for information and assistance.
2. David S. Smale, "Championships Reach Many," *NCAA Review* 9:11.
3. Ibid.
4. NCAA Women's Basketball Committee Report, 1990.

Marianne Crawford Stanley, outstanding Immaculata College player, was women's basketball coach at Old Dominion University (Va.) and led her team to two AIAW national championships. She was the first woman to earn an AIAW national title as both player and coach. Old Dominion was the host institution for the first NCAA women's championship in 1982.

Women's Basketball Coaches Association

Betty F. Jaynes

During the Olympic Festival in Syracuse, New York in July 1981, a group of outstanding collegiate women coaches met to discuss forming a women's basketball coaches association. Pat Summitt called me about the formation, and I was enthusiastic about the meeting. I immediately promised my support and willingness to help develop a long overdue coaches organization, although I was unable to attend the historic first meeting.

The combined coaching experiences and winning records of coaches present was impressive enough for a Basketball Hall of Fame gathering. Among those spearheading the project were Jill Hutchison, Theresa Grentz, Vivian Stringer, Kay Yow, Nora Lynn Finch, Marianne Stanley, Colleen Matsuhara, Pat Summitt, Fran Garmon, and Mary DiStanislao. These women were a few of the early AIAW leaders in basketball. Hunter Low of Eastman Kodak joined the women for this meeting, which was a benchmark for girls and women's basketball.

The early 1980s were turbulent years. The NCAA/AIAW controversy had dramatically affected the women basketball coaches. Institutions with NCAA and AIAW basketball programs were the most visible. This demanded that institutions make a difficult decision. Should they continue their allegiance to AIAW, who had assisted them in fulfilling their dreams as players and coaches, or move to a program that would permit recruitment regulations and financial support more in keeping with the coaches desires? The dispute disrupted a fellowship of women who had stood shoulder to shoulder in the development of the best possible basketball programs for female athletes and against the male establishment. Most of these women had been charter members of AIAW with its dream of an athletic model designed for and with the coaches and athletes. The decision to compete in AIAW or NCAA national championships in basketball in 1982, therefore, was a painful decision. Most of the large universities with strong basketball programs selected the NCAA national championship.

Athletic talent and coaches were thus split into separate championships, and coaches felt the alienation from one another. They also believed that two different championships would dilute the field. Basketball coaches were accustomed to the AIAW women's 16-team marathon and its opportunity for coaches to see one another socially and professionally. As the format changed, the women coaches then all gathered at the final four championships. They expressed warm feelings as well as loyalty and commitment to one another and to the game of basketball. The new alliance with NCAA brought an altogether different experience, with administrators rather than coaches running the national championships.

Most of the women's basketball coaches were aware of the existence of the National Association of Basketball Coaches, which was and still is the professional association for men's basketball coaches. It was evident that the NABC did not want to allow membership to women's coaches. They had their own issues as well as their own identity. It was understandable that to take on such a large group of women's basketball coaches would be to their disadvantage; indeed, they were incapable of servicing such an addition. The question then became—where do the women hang their hats? The NAGWS offered its coaches association as a forum for coaches, but many of the new breed of women coaches did not come out of the physical education tradition.

The formation of the coaches association, therefore, would unify women's basketball programs and provide a network and support group for the task of building a program from within the men's governance of NJCAA, NAIA, NCAA, and the high school National Federation. At the festival meeting, although the association did not have a name, the coaches selected Jill Hutchison of Illinois State University to be an interim president. Hutchison's charge was to develop what would become the Women's Basketball Coaches Association. The coaches also decided to set a fall organizational meeting, hoping to have a larger representative group to work out the details of organization. Hunter Low, longtime representative from the All America project, promised that Kodak would underwrite the cost of that meeting. Low and Bill Orr, president of Tel-Ra Products, hosted the group in Wayne, Pennsylvania on September 1, 1981. The same women who were present at the initial meeting also attended this meeting with the addition of several women like myself who had been active coaches and leaders of basketball for many years. The Board of Directors came from among the coaches present. The coaches appointed Betty Jaynes interim executive director and Tim Stoner legal counsel.

I have fond memories of the electric meeting. The excitement was contagious. Here was a group of professionals preparing to embark on what would quickly become a strong voice and force for women's basketball. We each had our own critical local issues, but we also had a common goal. We wished to unify all those who coached any level of female basketball in the United States. We hoped to provide them with the personnel and resources to develop individual coaches in order to collectively offer excellent coaching experiences for young athletes. The new Executive Board envisioned its goals to serve, inform, organize for unity, represent coaches, and educate the public about basketball. The initial thrust would be to publish the *Backboard Bulletin*, increase membership, develop sponsorships, and conduct an inaugural convention.

The Board determined it should be the driving force of the newly named Women's Basketball Coaches Association (WBCA). The membership on the Board should be representative of nine geographical districts, plus each division of women's basketball, NCAA Divisions I, II, and III, NAIA, NJCAA, and assistant coaches. In addition, secondary school coaches ought to be a part of the governance structure. The membership should include equal representation of head coaches and assistant coaches. We also envisioned that a select group of outstanding college coaches should provide leadership by serving as the Executive Committee. The Executive Committee would include the officers of the Association. The design of the organization would have the experienced coaches serve as role models and mentors to the assistant coaches and young head coaches.

As interim executive director I would have to work out of Wayne, Pennsylvania, which required a move from James Madison University where I had been basketball coach for 12 years. It was a difficult but extraordinarily exciting move, even though Virginia had been my home for most of my professional life. To give birth to an association that would support and direct the explosion of women's basketball was enough motivation to give me the courage to redirect my career. I felt humbled by the trust placed in me and excited about the future of women's basketball. I also felt, however, an awesome responsibility to coaches of women's basketball, just as I had felt excited and responsible for the growth and development of basketball in the formative years of collegiate women's basketball.

We worked out of Wayne for the first five years through the generosity of Bill Orr of Tel-Ra Productions. They contributed a rent free office for the organization until we became financially stable. During the five years our membership increased and sponsorships, convention attendance, and publications increased dramatically. Our program was taking off and the coaches' leadership was superb. We grew from 200 members in 1981 to 1,500 members in 1985. The convention attendance similarly grew from 99 people in 1982 to 700 participants. Our budget reached $200,000 with five official corporate sponsors.

In the summer of 1986, the WBCA moved to Atlanta, Georgia. The Executive Board felt the move would enhance the Association's growth and help it to become financially independent and to achieve a new level of growth and advancement. The Atlanta Chamber of Commerce welcomed us with many contributions of furniture and support. In addition, the Tip Off Club and Athlete Sports Council quickly assisted in making the WBCA a strong force in the sporting community.

The WBCA's second five years brought additional members, bigger and better conventions, and greater recognition of coaches and athletes. More attention focused on the educational opportunities for coaching skills and strategies, providing nurturing advice and training techniques essential for elite female athletes.

The organization has used publications as the key to education and the flow of information to and between coaches. The publication of *Coaching Women's Basketball, At the Buzzer,* and *Backboard Bulletin* contributed to better understanding of preparing female athletes and informing coaches of essential strategies and information.

The late 1980s found us as the "different voice" in higher education athletics. The WBCA realized that with the onslaught of legislative changes that college presidents demanded from athletic programs, it needed to play a more effective role in the enactment of legislation affecting women's basketball. The Board of Directors created a Women's Basketball Issues Committee to facilitate legislative action in the various governing bodies. As committee chair, the Board selected Charlotte West, associate athletic director of Southern Illinois University. Her charge was to present legislative matters at NCAA conventions and to act as a sounding board on critical issues in other basketball governances. The WBCA, for example, was the prime mover in reinstating the basketball program for the women at the University of Oklahoma during the women's final four in March 1990.

By the tenth anniversary year, there were 3,000 members, six outstanding publications, ten award programs, 1,600 convention participants, and six official sponsors. The WBCA continues to have excellent elected leadership. Fiscally all is improved as the organization has a $500,000 balanced budget.

With all of these accomplishments, the WBCA remains a force for the unification and professionalization of coaches of basketball. As a former president, Gooch Foster of the University of California, stated: "The WBCA represents your connection with the rest of the basketball world. . . . In a very real sense the WBCA is your voice to the powers that be, and to effectively represent the concerns and needs of the women's basketball coaches of America, we must maintain a strong, unified effort. . . . Our mission is clear. We must remain a strong, viable organization working together toward the continued growth of our game."[1] At this writing, the Women's Basketball Coaches Association remains the only association in the world that is the undisputed advocate of quality basketball programs for girls and women.

Notes

1. Gooch Foster, *Scholastic Coach* 58 (February 1989): A.

The 1976 USA Women's Basketball Team, the first to participate in the Olympic Games, winning a silver medal. 1st row (L-R): Nancy Lieberman, Ann Meyers, Juliene Simpson, Sue Rojcewicz; 2nd row: Gail Weldon, trainer, Cindy Brogdon, Mary Anne O'Connor, Pat Head, Billie Jean Moore, head coach, Sue Gunter, assistant; 3rd row: Jeanne Rowlands, manager, Pat Roberts, Gail Marquis, Nancy Dunkle, Lusia Harris, Charlotte Lewis. (Photo credit, USA Basketball)

23

Title IX, AIAW, and Beyond
A Time for Celebration!

Marianna Trekell and Rosalie M. Gershon

The era of the Association for Intercollegiate Athletics for Women (1971–1982), including enactment of Title IX (1972), was an exhilarating one for women's basketball. It was a time of firsts!

The first AIAW National Championships were followed within a decade by the first NAIA and NCAA championships, the latter two without effort on their part since the fruits of AIAW's successful three divisional structure came to them already ripened. The AIAW, poorly funded and supported by vast numbers of dedicated volunteer professionals and a small national office staff, bequeathed ready-made championships to the very governing body which had fought Title IX, the NCAA. The AIAW had garnered a million dollar TV contract that would soon permit full reimbursement to schools for travel and lodging for championships. After much discussion and some consternation because of the elitism implied, AIAW had permitted Kodak All-America selections and then individual achievement awards. The most prestigious in the AIAW era were the Wade Trophy, the Broderick Award (and Broderick Cup), and women's induction into the Naismith Basketball Hall of Fame in Springfield, Massachusetts. Less prestigious, but equally important to the players was membership on an all-tournament team and the Most Valuable Player award at the basketball national championship each year.

The first large infusion of institutional funding for athletic scholarships and programs occurred in the mid-1970s and changed the complexion of the college rankings. Nonscholarship and low budget schools like Wayland Baptist, Immaculata, Delta State, Montclair State, and Queens fell by the wayside as other better funded programs like those of Old

Dominion, Tennessee, UCLA, Texas, Louisiana Tech, and others got exposure. Publicity was enhanced by availability of information through the AIAW sportsline and better reporting of women's sports scores. The "king of hype," Mel Greenberg, initiated weekly polls. More and more people were exposed to women's basketball as the top teams traveled nationwide and other teams played at home in double-headers with the men's teams. At the University of Iowa came the first crowd to number over 20,000 spectators.

The first female sports commentators like Donna DeVarona and Cathy Rush as well as female sport celebrities were captured by the TV cameras. The first nationally televised women's basketball game came in 1975 when Immaculata rolled over Maryland before a Sunday afternoon nationwide audience.

Even a women's professional basketball league resulted from the pool of college-prepared athletes. Previously there were several pro teams such as the Red Head All Americans and a number of semiprofessional and professional teams who played in local or regional contests. However, none was as celebrated as the new eight-team league established in 1978, after a false start in 1976–77.

Basketball was included in the Olympic program for the first time in 1976, although the Pan American games had been a part of the women's basketball heritage since 1955, the FIBA-World Championships since the 1950s, and the World University games since 1967. Significant federal legislation, the Amateur Sports Act, was enacted in 1978. This led to the National Sport Festivals and the development of junior and senior elite athlete competitions in basketball and more highly structured and better financed developmental camps.

For the first time, the names of the more successful coaches became better known through their national championship and international coaching activities. Grass-roots efforts in the 1970s included mushrooming of basketball camps for secondary school and collegiate athletes, AAU age group competitions, and Olympic developmental camps.

All of these firsts were fueled by the spirit of the times, a kind of messianic feminism determined to get equal rights for previously denied female athletes. *WomenSports* magazine became the counterpart of *Sports Illustrated* to carry the message and bring visibility of the female athlete to the public. The physical education establishment had worked for decades to develop a vast democratic pool of sport participants. By the late 1970s the cream would rise to the top; the elite players would also have their chance. The physical educators' "pyramid theory" of sport participation had succeeded.

The AIAW era had its roots in cookie sales for team funding, financial hardship, and cultural gender stereotyping. The women leaders at each institution had to fight for new sports and coaches, each new piece of equipment, each new uniform, each expanded schedule and better facilities. The new liberal proponents of interscholastic and intercollegiate competition stepped forward with a new boldness to demand parity. The male-dominated athletic scene was unduly alarmed, assuming all this activity would tap their resources and thus impoverish men's football and basketball teams. When the AIAW era ended in 1982 it was enjoying the limelight of national television, money, crowds, better conditions at institutions with more equal access to facilities, and scholarships proportionate to men's.

The first basketball stars fought lonely individual battles to play basketball when there was meager cultural support to do so. Four of the best from the AIAW era are profiled in this chapter: Delta State's Lusia Harris, Montclair State's Carol Blazejowski, UCLA's Ann Meyers, and Old Dominion's Nancy Lieberman (photos on pp. 416–17). The new awards, national and international opportunities, mentoring, the professional leagues, and basketball camps are also discussed. In preparation for this article, Marianna Trekell wrote to Harris, Blazejowski, Meyers, and Lieberman as well as other of the past's top name women's collegiate basketball players from the AIAW years. She asked what they had accomplished, what they believed to be their greatest hopes and disappointments, and what they are doing now.

While these four athletes typified the AIAW era, other greats such as Ann Donovan, Lynette Woodard, Cheryl Miller, and Clarissa Davis bestrode the NCAA era. The post-AIAW athletes who answered included Teresa Edwards, Katrina McClain, and Janet Harris, University of Georgia stars (photos on p. 420). Their responses to the questionnaire are surprisingly similar to those of the earlier stars. One glaring exception is that many of the post-AIAW competitors have gone to Europe or Japan to play in the lucrative foreign leagues.

At first the term "AIAW stars" appears logically inconsistent; nowhere was the term "student-athlete" and the concept of treating athletes as much as possible like the other students more heralded than in that bastion of the "women's model of athletics," the AIAW. Moreover, the AIAW tried to treat all sports equally rather than emphasizing only the top revenue producers such as basketball. It championed a Robin Hood theory of tournament winnings, so that the rich would not necessarily become richer, and the top ten would not eternally replicate themselves through TV exposure. The proceeds from TV were to be placed in a contingency fund for use by all three divisions and all schools appearing in a national championship. This dream, however, did not become fully realized because only basketball had succeeded in making a large sum of money before the AIAW demise.

Most of the leaders and physical educators turned athletic director/ coach and supported a nonscholarship form of athletics until deterred or emboldened by the Title IX legislation. Yet under this "yoke" collegiate sports thrived. Record numbers of state, regional, and national championships were held. Through hard-won TV contracts and public exposure, women's gymnastics, swimming, volleyball, track and field, and softball—in addition to basketball—began to take off commercially. And then suddenly there was basketball and the first great stars, all of whom appeared on television in the championships.

The superb athletes of the AIAW era loved the sport and rose to the top levels of competition, including the defunct women's pro league. They remain active in the sport today as coaches, teachers, commentators, and other role models.

The future looks bright. As one of America's greatest performers, Cheryl Miller of USC, said when the United States triumphed in the 1984 Los Angeles Olympics, "There will be a player who raises our game to the next level."[1]

Awards

AIAW's philosophy favored participation and a team concept over winning and individual achievement. Recognition awards were initially avoided. Accordingly, female college athletes were relative latecomers in receiving national acclaim through major awards. First was the national award for basketball achievement, the Kodak All-America Award for the top players in the country in 1976. All of the athletes mentioned in this article have been Kodak All-America Award recipients as well as all-tournament players. In the later years, many also received the Most Valuable Player Award at national championships. Within the AIAW structure the Kodak All-America Award, the Wade Trophy, and the Broderick Award were all prestige awards. The four athletes studied all received Broderick Awards and/or the Wade Trophy.

In 1977 the Broderick Award was established by AIAW, given in each sport. A Broderick Cup was also given to the best athlete in AIAW sports. Basketball winners of the Broderick Awards included: 1977, Lusia Harris (also Broderick Cup); 1978, Ann Meyers (also Broderick Cup); and 1979 and 1980, Nancy Lieberman. The Broderick Awards continued for many years under NCAA, as has the Kodak All-America Award.

The most prestigious award of the 1970s and still important is the Margaret Wade Trophy, established in 1978 and given to the top female college basketball player. The recipient must first be a Kodak All-Amer-

Margaret Wade (right) presents the award named after her to Shelly Pennefather in 1987. Established in 1978, during the AIAW period, the Wade Trophy remains a prestigious honor for the top female college basketball player.

ican. Attention is also given to the student's academics and service to the sport. Best known of the Wade Trophy winners are Carol Blazejowski, Montclair State (1978), Nancy Lieberman, Old Dominion University (1979, 1980), and Lynette Woodard, Kansas (1981), and in the NCAA era Cheryl Miller, USC, is the best known athlete.

The award's namesake was a pioneer in the establishment and advancement of women's collegiate basketball. A sense of having been "present at the creation" permeates the AIAW era and is conveyed by an incident which occurred when the Wade Award's sponsor, Stayfree, went to Cleveland, Mississippi to get Wade's permission for the use of her name. She remembers, "I guess I read 15 or 16 pages of the information he gave me before it really dawned on me that the Margaret Wade Trophy meant me."[2] She was 19 in 1932 when basketball was dropped at her school, Delta State University, because "the sport was too strenuous for young ladies." "We cried and burned our uniforms but there was nothing else we could do," she stated.[3]

After 41 years, Delta State in 1973 revived women's basketball, asking Wade to be the coach. They enjoyed three "glory years" as undisputed national champion. In 1975 they were undefeated, in 1976 had one loss, and in 1977 had three losses. Led by Lusia Harris, the first "superstar," Delta State established the longest win streak in women's collegiate basketball (51 games) until Louisiana Tech won 54 in 1982.

Wade is beloved for her triumph over adversity. Before she took the reins at age 60 at Delta State (1973) she had survived two major cancer operations, arthritis of the knees, and an auto accident for which she was hospitalized. She was well known for her down-home sense of humor and attachment to her girls and their families, her career commitment to the sport, and her outstanding record (610 wins, 112 losses for combined high school and college teams). She retired in 1979.[4]

The player awards discussed above culminated in the induction of women into the Hall of Fame. The first three women were inducted into the Naismith Basketball Hall of Fame in Springfield, Massachusetts, in April 1985. The trio included Margaret Wade and Bertha F. Teague for their coaching and contributions to the game and Senda Berenson Abbott for her instrumental role in developing women's basketball. Teague, "Mrs. Basketball of Oklahoma," spent her entire 42-year career coaching her hometown Byng High School in Ada. She won 1,275 games and was respected as a teacher, author of an early women's basketball book, and clinician par excellence. A large Wade Trophy with the pictures of all the winners stands in the Hall of Fame, and Ann Meyers' UCLA uniform is among the memorabilia there.[5]

International Play

Even before World War II women's Amateur Athletic Union (AAU) teams were traveling to Europe to compete in international competition, as were several teams from the secondary and collegiate ranks. Before the Amateur Basketball Association of the United States of America (ABAUSA) was formed in 1973, the AAU held the franchise for international competition and governed USA men's and women's basketball within the country. It fielded hundreds of women's teams through industrial leagues, school teams, and recreational leagues. The AAU sponsored national tournaments for women starting in 1926. From 1929 forward they sponsored a 32-team tournament, celebrating 50 years of championships in 1977. After ABAUSA took over basketball and the collegiate programs grew strong, the AAU lost its franchise from the USOC and its basketball championships lost many players and teams. In the last decade, therefore, the AAU has emphasized its Youth Sport Programs for girls, sponsoring age group teams.

USA Basketball, formerly ABAUSA, is the National Sports Governing Body (NGB) for Basketball within the U.S. Olympic Committee. It recently included the pro organizations, now eligible to participate in the Olympics. It has on its governing board representation from the NBA, NCAA, NJCAA, AAU, NFSHSA, the U.S. Armed Forces, the National Association of Basketball Coaches, and the Women's Basketball Coaches Association for the purpose of controlling international competition. This is the organization that selects the coaches and handles the eligibility of players and developmental programs for basketball.

The various international competitions in which the United States now participates are the Olympic Games, the Pan American Games, the World University Games, the Williams Jones Cup, and the Federale Internationale Basketball Association (FIBA) World Championship. In basketball circles, the World Championship title is considered as prestigious as the Olympic title. The United States women captured their second consecutive gold medal at the World Championship in 1990 in Malaysia. The first year of the championships in 1953 a strong American team, mostly from an AAU National Championship college (Nashville Business College), won the first gold medal, repeating their performance in 1957. It was a long dry spell until the AIAW athletes and coaches entered the picture, to win the FIBA gold in 1979.

Next to the Olympics, perhaps the next most prestigious international competition patterned after the Olympics is the Pan American Games. The United States competed in the first Pan American games in 1951, but a USA women's basketball team did not compete until 1955. The World University Games for university and college student-athletes in the United States was originally under the control of the National Collegiate Sports Council. The American Alliance through its associations controlled the program, but the USOC provided much of the funding.

Alberta Cox instructing at an NAGWS basketball skills clinic in the 1960s. Cox, who coached the USA national team for several years, was a proponent of intensified training for international play.

These games came under the jurisdiction of the USOC by the end of the 1970s.

The U.S. Olympic Committee developmental training camps were a major part of the international competitive story that began in 1966. The USOC, in a Washington, D.C. meeting, accepted the developmental proposal for women's basketball set forth by Clifford H. Buck, Laurine M. Mickelsen, and Alberta Cox. Cox reported that "from this moment on, our sport grew with leaps and bounds, and became limitless in its international future."[6] But the progress toward world class achievement took time. Following are some highlights that capture the temper of the CIAW and AIAW times.

In 1967, according to Cox, the national team coach, "never has the U.S.A. ranked so low as the 11th position which they earned. Our experienced players were old and did not have the necessary stamina— our young players were simply awed by it all." A further problem was collegiate use of the six player roving player game instead of the five player game, so adjustments were essential and difficult. But by the following summer, in 1968, another developmental training camp was held in Sulphur, Oklahoma. Cox said, "some fifty-odd young players made the trip to a very hot and sultry locale to simply 'put theirs on the line' and most of all to 'learn'. . . . Young USA was being molded. . . ."[7]

Then in the summer of 1969 a training camp in Arkadelphia, Arkansas prepared a national team for a South American tour of ten games following the selection of the U.S. team. Cox wrote after that tour:

> I have seen this group win basketball games as well as win friends for our country. They entered the throngs of people and gave away thousands of American flags with not a single incident of demerit shown to the Stars and Stripes. They won over crowds with ability and a smile, and in many of the identical cities where several of our politicians received much criticism and ill treatment.[8]

The team came away from the tour with many new friends and experiences and a 9–1 record.

A 1971 international tour ended with an eighth place finish in the World Championship in Brazil. Alberta Cox was head coach with Carolyn Moffatt as assistant coach for the tour; Moffatt's report captures the disillusionment of the time:

> How can you express a feeling of success when you finish 8th in the World Tournament? On the other hand, how can you be disappointed in an 8th place finish when the U.S. finished 11th in the last World Tournament? . . . How would you like the responsibility of coaching the U.S. Team in a tournament against the 12 best teams in the world, knowing these teams have been practicing for months and some even for years together, and you, as the U.S. Coach, finally meet all twelve of your players on the floor together

for one practice before you play the defending World Champion team? [Problems] . . . the girls not in condition at all; what kind of offense can you teach them; what defenses should they use against the speed of the Asian and South American teams as opposed to the strength and size of the European teams . . . and what to do to keep morale and teamwork high.[9]

In the 1976 Olympics in Montreal there was a breakthrough for the women's basketball team. This was the first time women's basketball appeared as an Olympic sport, and Lusia Harris scored the first two points in Olympic women's basketball history. The Soviet team, undefeated in international competition since 1958, easily won the gold medal with Iuliana Semenova, $6'10\frac{1}{2}''$ and Olga Sukharnova, $6'8''$. "Not all of the foreign teams have a $7'2''$ center," says Lusia Harris, referring to one of the Soviet Union's star players, "just most of them."[10] According to Assistant Coach Phyllis Holmes, the U.S. national team "did the impossible in Montreal. . . . Winning the silver was a brilliant victory. Montreal Olympic Coach Billie Moore of UCLA and her staff are to be commended for their work in leading the team, not only to a qualifying berth, but to the second-place finish."[11]

Amateur Sports Act

The President's Commission on Olympic Sports in 1975–77 brought about an overhauling of the entire Olympic structure, which culminated in the Amateur Sports Act of 1978. Significant features of the Act for female athletes were: development of national headquarters for NGBs and a training center for all Olympic sport teams in Colorado Springs, an annual National Summer Sport Festival, and transfer of leadership in Olympic sports from AAU to independent NGBs. Most sports for women were identified as undeveloped sports, thus requiring that more funds be provided for grass-roots programs, training of elite athletes, and research. The Act is responsible for revitalizing the Olympic program, bringing it on a par with those in the Eastern Bloc countries, while attempting to maintain the United States idea of nonprofessionalism and assisting with private funding for the Olympic movement. Another feature of the Act was the initiation of the Summer Olympic Festival that features junior and senior women's basketball teams and a host of developmental camps for future world class athletes.[12]

In 1979 the national team included Lieberman, Blazejowski, and Meyers, with Pat Head Summitt as coach. They finally brought the gold back from the FIBA World Championship to add to the Olympic silver, after the long drought. Throughout this period AIAW coaches came to the forefront and AIAW athletes became the mainstays of our international basketball teams. By the end of the AIAW era, AAU coaches and athletes were fewer and fewer in number in comparison with those developed on the college scene. In 1977, for example, the women's team included Ellen Mosher and Marian Washington. Both were future AIAW and NCAA women basketball coaches with highly regarded teams to their credit.

Sue Gunter and Pat Head Summitt were set to coach the 1980 Olympic team, when President Jimmy Carter decided to boycott the Moscow Olympics. The boycott was a tremendous lost opportunity for the female athletes, but also for the sport itself. The exposure would have given basketball much needed media coverage. Instead, the athletes stayed home and competed in the Sport Festival.

The junior national teams, resulting from the Amateur Sports Act, accept athletes 20 years old or younger. They compete in the Junior World Championships every four years and in all of the summer National Olympic Sports Festivals, as well as international tournaments. Younger talent is thus developed and they gain valuable foreign experience and cultural exposure. This is the future generation.

The U.S. Olympic Festivals, also a result of the Amateur Sports Act, are sponsored by USOC and USA Basketball. They are annual events with the exception of the Olympic year. Four regional basketball teams consisting of the best collegiate athletes compete against each other in a festival tournament. Players 20 years old or younger compete on the junior teams at the Sports Festival.

With 1982 came the end of the AIAW era, the dawn of the NCAA and NAIA, and a U.S. national team who finally beat the Russians. The new era brought outstanding coaching and collegiate athletes to the national team, which won the gold medal in the 1984 Los Angeles Olympics. Pat Head Summitt coached, and outstanding participants included Cheryl Miller, Anne Donovan, Kathy McLaine, and Teresa Edwards.

The post-1984 Olympic years were exciting. The national team went 18–0 in international play in 1986 through the talents of Cheryl Miller, Ann Donovan, and Clarissa Davis and the excellent coaching of Kay Yow with Marianne Stanley and Sylvia Hatchell assisting. The 1988 gold medal in the Seoul Olympics was a sweet victory over the Russians and a full complement of other international teams. Kay Yow brought her well-prepared team to a victory over Yugoslavia for the gold. It's on to Barcelona in 1992 and Atlanta in 1996.

Amateur Athletic Union Youth Sport Program

The AAU girls youth sport basketball program was started in 1972 and is now entitled the "AAU/Carrier Girls Basketball Program." The

Carrier Heating and Cooling Company along with the AAU sponsors the program. Two of the objectives cited are:

> AAU/Carrier Girls Basketball should provide programs for the maximum number of young athletes to compete while encouraging the participation of each youth. . . . Opportunity should be available for self-improvement and advancement to senior programs for those participants without undue pressure and over-expectations.[13]

Participants must be AAU members. Age divisions for basketball tournament competitions for 1991 will be 12 and under, 13 and under, 14 and under, 15 and 16 and under, and a team for those 18 and under.[14]

The summer AAU tournaments draw many college and university women's basketball coaches, who assess the participants for recruiting purposes. The AAU generally sponsors six tournaments a summer. The rules used for these AAU games are those of NCAA women's basketball.

Summer Camps

Another first during the AIAW era was the girls basketball camps. As far back as the 1960s the Red Heads sponsored a girls basketball camp at Camp Courage, Mississippi to teach youngsters the sport of basketball—and of course to recruit potential greats for the Red Head basketball teams. Among the earliest camps were those of Pat Kennedy in cooperation with Cathy Rush. Very soon, however, Rush formed her own camp, as did many of the successful coaches of the 1970s. Also among the early basketball camps were those held in New Jersey for players in the Catholic Youth Organization and in private Catholic high school leagues.

By the early 1980s girls basketball camps could be found on the campuses of most successful basketball schools in the country. The coaches designed their camps much like boys and men's basketball and football camps. Thousands of girls attend these camps, which are sometimes sponsored for entire teams as well as for individual players. College athletes work as camp counselors, forming a new mentoring system for younger athletes and permitting role modeling to occur even as the student-athletes are still in school. In order to keep control, most state high school associations have established regulations regarding camps and/or coaching schools, and the NFSHSA offers guidelines for conducting girls basketball camps and for policies acceptable for camps.

Most basketball coaches are aware of two of the most popular basketball camp programs: the "B/C All-Stars" and the "Blue Stars." These programs are geared to increase the skill level of high school girls and college and university women who have demonstrated basketball talent. In addition to ability, the vast majority of campers must be able to pay $300–$400 per week for the experience, although there are some scholarships based on need. It is very difficult to contact basketball coaches during the summer—they are either doing summer camps or out observing "blue chip" basketball players. It is common knowledge that, according to one college coach, "the skill level of high school girls has really improved. With more opportunities they start earlier to build their skills."[15] They build these skills in summer camps, in the NCAA camps for underprivileged youth, and in the USOC sponsored A,B,C developmental camp programs. The basketball camp is in reality a recruitment center for athletes, and it is also used by institutions to recruit their coaches, by promising they can run a basketball camp on college campuses.

Women's Professional League

At Milwaukee Arena a crowd of 7,824 turned out for the official opening of the Women's Professional Basketball League on December 9, 1978. The Chicago Hustle team beat the Milwaukee Does 92–87.[16] The original professional league was formed in 1976 under the leadership of Jason Frankfurt, a former stockbroker, who envisioned a 12-team nationwide women's basketball league. His league collapsed before the first game, but it set in motion Bill Byrne, who had taken part in the formation of the World Football League for a brief moment in history. He decided to become the self-appointed president of the Women's Basketball League (WBL) in 1978. Byrne convinced enough investors to form an eight-team league the first year and expanded it to fourteen teams the second. Several outstanding players, such as Karen Logan, who had played for the Red Heads, were drafted, but many others were not outstanding. Besides the Chicago and Milwaukee teams the others included Houston Angels, Iowa Cornets, Dayton (Ohio), New Jersey Gems, and New York Stars. The teams finished the season with the Chicago team having ten of its games televised by WGN-TV. The average attendance per game was about 1,200 throughout the league.

The players were signed for $6,000 to $10,000 until the second year when Ann Meyers signed a $50,000 contract. The Gems were the only team willing to pay such a high salary, but this disrupted the harmony and brought tension to the league coaches and players. The second season (1979–80), however, proved even more problematic. Several new teams folded, and other teams lost money and fans. Stable support from loyal fans did not materialize in nearly all of the sites. One by one the teams could not meet their expenses and the league folded. The teams in San Francisco, St. Louis, New Jersey, and Chicago continued to function efficiently, but the New York Stars, for example, lost money nightly. Nonetheless, the New York Stars, coached by Dean Meninger, beat the Iowa Cornets for a second straight championship.

The third season brought only one new team to the league as the price for a new franchise was $500,000. Even with a reorganization the structure was still in constant trouble and the athletes' lives were constantly disrupted. They were shuttled around from team to team, sometimes not even getting their paychecks. The league survived its third season, but with only a few teams. A notice was sent to the press that there would be no fourth season.

The WBL folded because it faced obstacles not foreseen by the early owners. A central issue was the treatment of the athletes, the lack of spending on public relations, and a different attitude by the fans and owners toward women professional basketball players from that afforded men. There was an "image issue" related to sexist attitudes and fears about the femininity of the players. Perhaps too the pool of players wasn't large enough for all team members to have outstanding talent. Men were mostly the supporters of the teams and as men they still somewhat watched *women* play as opposed to watching *athletes* compete. As individuals and corporations looked to start another league in the post-AIAW era, in 1984–85 the Women's American Basketball Association marketing personnel attempted to determine the real cause of the collapse of the pro league. Whatever the causes, the WABA also folded soon after the Dallas Diamonds won the championship.

The collegiate and AAU athletes were disappointed in the failure of the first women's pro league; they had done more than their share to keep the league alive and to provide the environment for loyal fans. In fact, many felt they compromised their self-esteem by submitting themselves to the "beauty" ideals of the owners and some of the fans instead of their own sporting ideals. And some players thought the owners had contributed less than their fair share in advertising and financial support and had provided second-class travel and lodging arrangements. Athletes and observers of the WPBL tend to place the blame partly on the franchise owners, partly on the lack of a large enough pool of talent when they initiated the pro teams, and partly on the lack of historical tradition for large numbers of spectators. There wasn't a natural audience available to the athletes.

After the professional leagues died, the outstanding women athletes were still looking for an opportunity to compete on the same high level as college and yet to make a living. Although players would prefer to play professionally right here in the USA, Lynn Nornberg, former coach at the University of Kentucky and presently assistant executive director of USA Basketball, estimates "about 500 U.S. women are playing basketball overseas."[17] Professional leagues outside the United States exist in Spain, Italy, Germany, Scandinavia, and Japan.

Teresa Edwards and Katrina McClain participate on foreign teams and it is estimated they each earn up to $200,000 for a six-month season. Lynette Woodward played in Europe before joining the Globetrotters. All of the women playing overseas are not making six figure salaries, but are able to make a decent living—something they simply could not do in the Women's Professional Basketball League.

The First Superstars

Lusia Harris (Stewart)   was the first dominant center in the women's game. Immaculata's Cathy Rush has said of her, "She's incredibly strong. The strength in her arms and hands is exceptional for a girl."[18] Lusia grew up the seventh of nine children on a vegetable farm in Minter City, Mississippi (population 200). Just as she was about to enter Alcorn A&M, a black college with no women's basketball team, Delta State University recruited her.[19] At 6'3" she was a great all around player for Delta State, a high scorer (47 points against Immaculata in Madison Square Garden, February 21, 1976) who excelled at the inside game, notably her 8-foot jumper. In her junior year, for example, she scored 58 points in one game and averaged over 31 points with a 62 percent field goal record and 15 rebounds per game.

According to Barbara Damrosch in *WomenSports*, Harris had several scholarships at Delta State, one federally funded and all academic (DSU had no athletic scholarships for women and has since dropped to Division II in the NCAA). An avid reader, especially of the novel and black history, Harris maintained a B+ average. She later worked in Admissions and earned her bachelor's and master's degree. In the at-the-time 88 percent white school in the heart of the Mississippi Delta, Harris was voted Homecoming Queen.

Along with Coach Margaret Wade, Harris had transformed the small southern school into a hotbed of basketball, with legions of Lady Statesmen fans including, according to a November 1976 *WomenSports* article by Barbara Damrosch, "600 groupies following the team to away-games, passing out glittery T-shirts that read 'Lady Statesmen are Dyn-O-Mite' and sticking little gummed cotton bolls on everyone in sight." When the team came home, "a caravan of 50 to 60 cars joins them in cities along the way and they ride into Cleveland [Mississippi] with a police escort."[20]

Harris now considers as her greatest achievements "winning the National Championship three years in a row and playing in the Olympics—

the most exciting times of my life." She adds, "I really thank God for giving me the talent and the ability to think successfully. . . . We all must realize of course that time is of the essence for those things worth accomplishing. One must be willing to sacrifice. One must be willing to understand and to appreciate those things for which she is capable. We then too must be understanding toward our peers and others and work extra hard for the goals we desire and try hard to overcome various obstacles."[21]

Harris was high scorer on the 1976 national team that included the young Nancy Lieberman and Ann Meyers. The three-time Kodak All-American participated in the World University Games in Bogota in 1975 and the Pan American Games in Mexico City the same year. For a brief time Harris played for the Houston Angels in the Women's Pro Basketball League in 1980 but soon learned that the support for a professional team was not there. Having been an assistant basketball coach at Delta State, she would like to return to coaching at the college level when her two children are older. She is currently teaching physical education and coaching high school basketball in Greenwood, Mississippi.

Carol Blazejowski, "The Blaze," was a hotshot scorer for nonscholarship school Montclair State, the only such school to make it to the final four in 1978. After an exceptional final four tournament (40 points in the semi and 41 in the consolation), she beat out Ann Meyers for the Wade Trophy in 1978. She was a three-time Kodak All-American, leading the nation in scoring in her junior and senior years with 35 and 38 points per game. Over her four years at Montclair she shot close to 60 percent—and not on close range shots. Carol, according to her coach, Maureen Wendelken, "was a pleasure to coach and a model for the other members of the team in her dedication and her success as an honor student."[22] She grew up on the New Jersey playgrounds and modeled her game after the men's pros she saw on television. "I can't think about what I should have, which I could have if I was a guy," she has thought from time to time.[23]

Blazejowski participated in the World University Games in Bulgaria in 1977 when the U.S. national team got a silver medal. In the U.S.-Soviet game in 1980 she scored 38 points and was top U.S. scorer in the tournament. She played in the World University Games again in 1979 in Mexico City when the United States got the gold and in the 1979 Pan American Games in Puerto Rico. It was a keen disappointment when the national team coach, Billie Moore, cut her from the Olympic team hopefuls in 1976. In 1980 she decided against signing with the pros in order to play in the 1980 Olympics, which were then boycotted by

STARS OF THE AIAW ERA

Lusia Harris,
Delta State, Miss. (Photo
courtesy Delta State
University Office of Public
Information)

Nancy Lieberman, Old Dominion
University, Va. (Photo courtesy
Old Dominion)

Ann Meyers (right),
University of
California-Los Angeles
(ASUCLA photo by
Terry O'Donnell)

Carol Blazejowski,
Montclair State
College, N.J.
(Photo courtesy NBA
Properties, Inc.)

the United States. She played during the 1980–81 year with the New Jersey Gems of the women's pro basketball league.

Today she remains active in the sport by holding "Blaze's Eastern Basketball Camp" annually, working as a clinician at summer camps, and playing in summer leagues. She recently changed from working in sales and marketing for a sporting goods company to working in the front office of the National Basketball Association.[24]

Ann Meyers (Drysdale) was UCLA's first female scholarship athlete. The 5'9" Meyers competed in track and field and volleyball in addition to basketball, where she played guard, forward, and center. At Sonora High School she had competed in basketball, volleyball, field hockey, track and field, softball, badminton, and tennis. She was the first four-time Kodak All-American and in 1978 she won the Broderick Award for the top basketball player and the Broderick Cup for the outstanding female U.S. athlete. Her B.S. from UCLA was in sociology.

The middle child in a family of 11 children, Ann is the younger sister of Dave Meyers, a UCLA All-American, who has commented, "Ann was trained in a boy's world. She never wanted to be termed 'just a girl' and that's why she's had so much success in women's sports."[25] Her sister Patty was a successful volleyball coach at Pepperdine College. Ann remembers her teen years clearly: "I was very, very introverted. I was a loner. I never had any close friends. The boys would accept me to a certain extent because I could play sports, but I wasn't totally accepted because I wasn't a boy. And with the girls, I was never totally accepted because I was always playing with the boys."[26]

Meyers was an outstanding international competitor. She was the first high school player to ever make a national team (1974). She participated in the 1975 World Championship Games in Colombia and the Pan American Games in Mexico City, in the 1976 Montreal Olympics, in the 1977 World University Games in Bulgaria, on a 1979 All-Star Team against China in Madison Square Garden, and in the 1979 World Championship Games in Korea and Pan American Games in Puerto Rico.

Married to famous Los Angeles Dodgers pitcher Don Drysdale, she has two sons, Don, Jr. and Darren. She is known as the only woman drafted by an NBA team, the Indiana Pacers, but was then given a front office job. Later, she played (receiving the highest salary in the league) with the New Jersey Gems and was Most Valuable Player in the league before the money ran out. "Sports is a business," she has said. "They don't care. If they can use you, fine, and once they can't that's it."[27] But like Nancy Lieberman, she has successfully moved into the larger sports world (as opposed to the physical education or women's domain) and has worked as a broadcaster since 1979.

Nancy Lieberman (Cline) has continuously distinguished herself as a spokeswoman for women's basketball and astute student of the game. She wrote a book, *Basketball My Way*, and taught the natural tennis star Martina Navratilova the value of training and discipline. Lieberman was the only one of the four AIAW stars featured here to attend school out-of-state. Her coach at Old Dominion University, Marianne Stanley, said of her after ODU won its second national championship in 1980, "You don't find many guards that'll rebound the way she does. You don't find many players who can completely control the tempo and complexion of the ball game as Nancy does. I don't think I've seen many people who have her confidence. You can't teach that. Nancy probably had that when she was born. She probably came out of the womb swinging."[28]

Lieberman was awarded the Wade Trophy in 1979 and 1980. At 16 she was the youngest member of the 1976 Olympic team in Montreal. She also remembers joining the women's basketball team in her sophomore year at Far Rockaway (New York) High: "I never knew that other girls were playing basketball. I had always thought of myself as one-of-a-kind. My family and friends had tried to discourage me from playing. They said I had no future and that I would never go to college and grow up to be a nice young lady. It was hard. I took a lot of garbage because women's athletics were not acceptable."[29]

Because Lieberman was a streetball player who later became a point guard she changed the nature of women's college basketball. Her first-year coach at ODU, Pam Parsons, explained: "Players who are taught to play by the book are so worried about doing it right and pleasing the coach that they don't free-lance, improvise plays. Maybe the influence of the streetball players will teach the others that basketball is more than x's and o's on a blackboard."[30] In "Artists on Asphalt" Lynn Glatzer points out that "Streetball is not for the frail or the faint-hearted. . . . One of the first techniques you learn in streetball is how to throw an elbow, knee or hip. It's the only way to get close enough to the basket to shoot." When Lieberman started playing streetball she was the only girl around. Now, she says, "there are hundreds of girls on the schoolyards." "Streetball is also an ego-trip," Lieberman said. "In the schoolyards if you wanted the ball, you had to steal it." Former Queens Coach Lucille Kyvallos commented, "To many streetball players, the concept of team play is totally alien. It's tough for these kids to learn techniques and strategies because they never had to think about it before."[31]

Lieberman got her degree in marketing from ODU and has been doing a cable talk show called "Women Talk Sports." "We're having fun with it," she said in *Women & Sport*. "Most of all we want to see women talking sports with each other. We want people to see that we are knowledgeable in sports. I want little kids to watch the show and say, 'Wow, I don't have to quit. I can still be a girl and be hard-nosed and athletic.' Most girls stop playing sports in high school because they think that they're not going to continue to be feminine."[32] She also broadcasts for ESPN and other cable and network TV shows.

Lieberman played for the Dallas Diamonds in the last season of the women's pro league, and again for the Diamonds when they won the championship in the brief renewal of pro basketball. She played for a men's professional team in Springfield, Massachusetts and for the Long Island Knights (1987) in a men's pro basketball league, the first female to ever play in such. In 1988 she went on a Harlem Globetrotter tour, and in 1989 was a member of the U.S. national basketball team. She intends to make the 1992 U.S. Olympic team.[33]

STARS OF THE 1980S

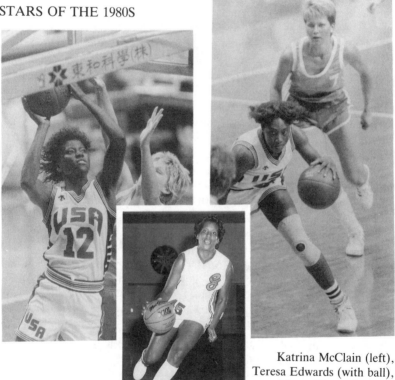

Katrina McClain (left),
Teresa Edwards (with ball),
and Janet Harris (below),
all of the University of
Georgia. (Photo courtesy
University of Georgia)

Mentoring/Coaching

Before the 1970s women lacked elite and international basketball experience, which is why the players in the early AIAW championships and the first U.S. national teams had such an immediate impact on the growing number of collegiate programs. Great coaches make great teams and great teams make coaches more visible. Thus were dynasties established.

It is one of the purposes of the new Women's Basketball Coaches Association to encourage and perpetuate mentoring. It is, however, no longer so easy for women to coach on the college level. Men are coaching approximately 50 percent of collegiate women's basketball teams. Winning is bought at the expense of fewer female role models and the old problem continues of "nowhere to go" after a woman's collegiate playing days are over. Even a previous All-American like Tara Heiss of the University of Maryland had to "pay her dues" at her home school. Many will have to come up through the ranks of high school, junior college, small, and then large college coaching. It will be harder to find television exposure and immediate glory a la Marianne Crawford Stanley.

One of the earliest basketball dynasties was Wayland Baptist with Patsy Neal and Jody Conradt. Patsy Neal became an AAU All-American in 1959, 1960, and 1965. She starred in international competition and served on numerous U.S. teams. She has stayed in the mainstream of basketball by writing books, conducting clinics, inspiring young basketball players, and coaching in small colleges. Jody Conradt's achievements after her years as a Flying Queen are full of role model activity.

Several coaches came out of AAU and early AIAW competition. Marian Washington and Ellen Mosher Hanson turned to coaching after their years of national AAU and international play. Cathy Rush developed Marianne Crawford Stanley, formerly of Old Dominion and now of USC, as well as Rene Muth Portland of St. Joseph College and then Penn State, and Theresa Shank Grentz of Rutgers. The coach of the first great dynasty, the Immaculata Mighty Macs, Cathy Rush holds grass-roots level training camps and workshops and sometimes appears as a television commentator. Marianne Crawford Stanley was the first woman to capture an AIAW title as both player, in 1973 and 1974, and as coach of ODU, being the youngest AIAW or NCAA coach in the top winners circle. Theresa Grentz coached the U.S. team in the 1990 Goodwill Games where the United States won the gold by defeating the Soviet Union. She will coach the U.S. Olympic team in 1992.

The second generation of players is now moving into the top 20 teams in the rankings. Joan Bonvicini of Long Beach State had Louis O'Neil as her coaching mentor at Southern Connecticut. Pat Head Summitt was a protegee of Billie Moore (UCLA), who coached the first American team to participate in Olympic basketball in Montreal in 1976. Moore then coached Ann Meyers, as well as Linda Sharp of USC, who in turn coached the great Cheryl Miller. Moore got her B.A. from Washburn University in Topeka and an M.S. from Southern Illinois. While assistant athletic director and varsity basketball coach at Cal-State Fullerton, she compiled a 148–17 record. "Coaching," she has said "is the ideal teaching situation. You have a small number of students during a long period of time."[34]

Two prominent minority coaches are Vivian Stringer and Marian Washington. Stringer, formerly of the black powerhouse Cheyney State, is now coaching nationally ranked teams at the University of Iowa and has coached in major international competition such as the World University Games in 1985. Marian Washington, who was on the 1971 national team with Pat Head Summitt, developed the all-time great Lynette Woodard at the University of Kansas.

Representative of "second generation" coaches is Pat Head Summitt, who played for the University of Tennessee-Martin and was a member of the 1976 national team at the Olympics, and now coaches at the University of Tennessee-Knoxville. Her team won the 1991 NCAA Women's Basketball Championship.

Pat Head Summitt of the University of Tennessee gained early experience as both a top college and international team participant. She moved on to coach numerous elite players at the University of Tennessee and on U.S. national teams. Billie Moore of UCLA coached her on the national team. After Summitt's junior year of college she began playing at the international level. She holds the Olympic silver as a player and gold as a coach (1984 Los Angeles Olympics) and has produced 6 Olympians, 11 All-Americans, and 21 international players.

Summitt's competitive career began at age nine. Three years later she "suffered a minor setback when, in an attempt to touch the basketball net, she leapt off the school gymnasium/auditorium stage and broke her arm. Terribly disappointed over not being able to play, 12-year-old Pat soaked the cast in water and chipped away at the plaster so she could bend her elbow enough to practice shooting. Apparently this did not interfere with the healing process, and by the next season she led her team in scoring."[35]

In 1966 the Head family moved from Montgomery, Alabama, to Cheatham County so she could attend Cheatham County High School in Ashland City, which had a basketball team. As a senior "Bone" Head scored 28 points and 14 rebounds per game and was a great leader. Fifteen years after being named Most Popular Girl by the student body she returned to see the high school gym renamed for her. She entered the University of Tennessee at Martin in 1970 because it had a competitive basketball program. In 1972 UTM with 5'10" Head at forward competed in the AIAW national basketball championship at Illinois State, won by Immaculata. The national exposure led to an invitation to try out for the World University Games and she competed in Moscow in 1973. After suffering a nearly career-ending knee injury in her senior year, she went on to play on the 1976 U.S. women's Olympic squad. In 1974 she began her coaching career at UT-Knoxville.[36]

Texas boasts several international coaches. Jody Conradt, University of Texas, developed Clarissa Davis, the 6'1" forward who led Texas to the NCAA title in 1986 and was the 1989 Wade Trophy winner. Other coaches from Texas colleges are Sue Gunter, former coach at Stephen F. Austin, and Fran Garmon, of Texas Christian University, who coached the U.S. national team in the 1984 Olympics.

The East boasts of early and present outstanding coaches the calibre of Lucille Kyvallos (Queens), Louise O'Neil (Southern Connecticut), and Chris Weller (Maryland). These coaches are also a volunteer army who work behind the scenes promoting, organizing, and providing leadership in collegiate basketball.

A family success is that of the Yows, Debbie, Susan, and Kay. Kay was assistant Olympic coach in 1984, head coach of the Goodwill Games in Moscow in 1986, and Olympic coach in Seoul in 1988. Coach Theresa Shank Grentz of Rutgers, who won the AIAW championship in 1982, has been nominated to coach the 1992 USA women's team. Coach Grentz talks of balancing her life as wife, mother, and coach. She says: "My husband (Karl) is a very special man. Male or female, a coach's spouse has to be very special."[37] Grentz, along with the coaches named above, has "made it" in the "big leagues."

Some distinguished male coaches include Andy Landers of Georgia, Joe Ciampi of Auburn, and Leon Barmore of Louisiana Tech. They have been in the midst of the top ten polls the last few years and frequent visitors to the final four, with Barmore and Sonja Hogg coaching the AIAW national championship winners.

Jill Hutchison has been a different kind of mentor, active on committees and bringing women into organizational structures, as well as coaching winning teams at Illinois State University. One of the first basketball sports committee members in AIAW and an officer of the new Women's Basketball Coaches Association, she and Betty Jaynes, while "invisible" compared to the famous coaches above, have edited NAGWS *Guides* for basketball and worked diligently in the service of the sport year in, year out.

The future for coaches is actually not as bright today as it was a decade ago. Not only are there more female athletes as potential coaches, but there are more and more men moving into the coaching ranks as the salaries become more equal to men's. Salaries for coaches have improved rapidly for the top women's teams. Some of the top coaches are making $50,000 along with special contracts for summer camps and talk shows. Before the emergence of AIAW the majority of coaches and administrators for girls and women's sports were female. Since then there has been a decrease in the number of women who hold such positions. Carpenter and Acosta indicate that "the proportion of women coaching women's teams has dropped from 90 percent to 47.3 percent in 1990."[38] Recently an assistant women's basketball coach at the University of Georgia was selected to be an assistant coach of the University of Kentucky men's basketball program. Bernadette Locke, a former basketball player, is the first woman to coach in a Division I men's basketball program. She "hopes her hiring will make the future a bit brighter for other women coaches."[39]

Conclusion

As Merrily Baker, the last AIAW president, past women's athletic director at the University of Minnesota, and now executive member of the NCAA staff, has said, speaking of the AIAW era: "It was the happiest ten year explosion ever felt in girls and women's sports." In a similar vein, Debbie Becker in the NCAA Basketball Preview comments: ". . . no decade has had such a profound impact as the 1980s. Better coaches, stronger players and vastly increased media exposure marked the most explosive period of growth in the sport's history."[40]

Thus it is that the last two decades have built on each other and the happy result is a program of women's basketball that is alive and well on every front. The girls secondary basketball programs are expanding.

The college programs are building a spectator following. The Olympic movement is ever increasing in the calibre of the athletes and the opportunities being offered to more and more female athletes. It would seem, therefore, that the two critical issues not receiving high marks as we move through the decade of the 1990s are the limited opportunity for girls and women to have role models and mentors in the coaching ranks and the dearth of opportunity for employment of players as coaches and as professional basketball players.

But the foundation for women's basketball is secure. As Agnes Wayman reported in the 1908–09 *Basketball Guide*, "The athletic girl has come to stay."[41] Her culture approves, the sports world welcomes her, and the basketball courts are calling her to come play.

Notes

1. Paul Attner, "Never an American Team Like This One," *Sporting News* (August 20, 1984): 15.

2. Jacqui Salmon, "Margaret Wade, a Prize Coach," *WomenSports* (May 1982): 42.

3. Pat Tashima, "Delta State Rebounds for Glory," *WomenSports* (December 1975): 36.

4. Jacqui Salmon, "Wades Delta Team," *Women's Sports* (December 1975): 40.

5. "Seven Elected to Basketball Hall of Fame," Basketball Release, Naismith Memorial Basketball Hall of Fame (Basketball Hall of Fame: Springfield, Mass., April 7).

6. Alberta Cox, "The Completion of a Trial Period Brazil II. World Championships for Women." June 18, 1971 Unpublished Report to DGWS: 1. (DGWS International Competition File, AAHPERD Archives).

7. Ibid.

8. Ibid.

9. Carolyn Moffatt, "1971 Women's World Tournament Report," June 15, 1971: 1–2. Unpublished Report (DGWS International Competition File, AAHPERD Archives).

10. Barbara Damrosch, "First Woman in History to Sink an Olympic Basket," *WomenSports* (November 1976): 68.

11. Phyllis Holmes, "Preview of Women's 1980 Basketball," *Coaching: Women's Athletics* (Jan./Feb., 1980): 6–7.

12. *The Final Report of the President's Commission on Olympic Sports 1975–77*, Vol. I, Executive Summary and Major Conclusions and Recommendations (Washington, D.C.: U.S. Government Printing Office, 1977); Amateur Sports Act of 1978: "Report of the Senate Committee on Commerce, Science, and Transportation" (Washington, D.C.: U.S. Government Printing Office, 1978).

13. "Girls Basketball," *AAU Brochure 1990* (Indianapolis, Indiana: AAU, 1990), 7.

14. AAU Brochure.

15. Kathy Lindsay, women's basketball coach, University of Illinois, interview by Marianna Trekell, June 27, 1990.

16. Al Harvin, "Women's Pro Basketball League Passes Its First Test," *New York Times* (April 29, 1979): Sec. 5, 4.

17. Debbie Becker, "More Career Possibilities for the Elite," *USA Today* (September 14, 1990): Sec. C, 2.

18. Damrosch, "First Woman in History," 68.

19. Damrosch, "First Woman in History," 67.

20. Ibid.

21. Marianna Trekell, "Reflections of a Women's Basketball Player," Results of a Questionnaire Answered by the Athletes, Dept. of Kinesiology, University of Illinois (August, 1990).

22. Maureen Wendelken, "Profile—Carol Blazejowski," *Coaching: Women's Athletics* (Jan./Feb., 1979): 22.

23. Tony Kornheiser, "Carol Blazejowski, Pro in an Amateur World," *WomenSports* (January 1979): 30.

24. Trekell Questionnaire.

25. Hugh J. Delehanty, "Lady in Waiting," *WomenSports* (November 1981): 41.

26. Ibid.

27. Delehanty, "Lady in Waiting," 40; Trekell Questionnaire.

28. Joe Jares, "Monarchs of All They Survey, Part II," *Sports Illustrated* (March 31, 1980): 14.

29. Donna Foote, "Palm Prints on the Ceiling," *WomenSports* (March 1979): 31.

30. Lynn Glatzer, "Artists on Asphalt," *WomenSports* (March 1977): 34–36.

31. Ibid.

32. *Women & Sport Newsletter* (March 1989): 6.

33. Trekell Questionnaire.

34. Marty Delman, "Billie Moore in Bruin Blue," *Coaching: Women's Athletics* (Sept./Oct., 1977): 18.

35. Nancy E. Lay, *The Summitt Season* (New York: Leisure Press, 1989), 37.

36. Lay, *The Summitt Season*, 37–43.

37. "Olympic Coach Carries Torch for Parenthood," *USA Today* (September 13, 1990): Sec. C 2.

38. Linda J. Carpenter and R. Vivian Acosta, "Women's Positions," Report to Women's Groups, 1990 (Unpublished Report).

39. "William Reed, "Scorecard: Here's How It's Done, Guys," *Sports Illustrated* (June 15, 1990): 12.

40. Debbie Becker, "Women for All Seasons," *On the Road to the Final Four*, NCAA Basketball Preview (Lexington, Ky.: Host Communications, 1990), 114.

41. Agnes Wayman "Hints Along General Lines," in *Basket Ball Guide 1908–09*, Senda Berenson, ed. (New York: American Sports Publishing Co., 1908), 59.

Appendix

Women's Basketball
Time Line

1885   Founding of the Association for the Advancement of Physical Education

1891   Basketball invented by James Naismith

1892   Senda Berenson Abbott introduced basket ball to Smith College students

First inter-institutional contest (University of California and Miss Head's School)

1893   Clara Gregory Baer introduced basket ball to girls at Sophie Newcomb College, New Orleans

1895   Baer published first basket ball rules for women— "Basquette"

First publicly played basketball game in the South (demonstration game at the Southern Athletic Club in New Orleans by Sophie Newcomb College Students)

1896   First women's intercollegiate basketball games on the West Coast (University of California-Berkeley vs. Stanford University; University of Washington vs. Ellensburg State, second game)

1899   First Women's Basketball Rules Committee Meeting, Springfield College

1901   First "official" publication of *Basket Ball for Women* (three court game) by the Spalding Athletic Library with Senda Berenson as editor

1903   * Halves shortened from 20 minutes to 15 minutes

1905   * Six to nine players on a team, 11 officials

Executive Committee on Basket Ball Rules (National Women's Basketball Committee) formed under auspices of the American Physical Education Association

1910   * Eliminated the single dribble

* Rule changes

1913	Officiating first appeared in *Guides*
	* Return of single dribble
	* May use two court division instead of three, if small court
1916	* No coaching during game (except half-time)
1917	National Council of APEA appointed a Committee on Women's Athletics, of nine women, to oversee athletics for women; basketball became a subcommittee
1918	* Rewriting of rules to conform to men's wording and sequence
	* Basket with open bottom instead of closed basket with pull chain became official
1919	Play Day including basketball in California high schools
1921	* Two hand overhead, and shotput and back to basket goals (1925) 1 point
1922	AAU Women's (Track and Field) team to Women's Olympics in Paris
	Women's Athletic Committee protested AAU action
1923	First *Official Handbook of the National Committee on Women's Athletics* published
	Formation of the Women's Division of the National Amateur Athletic Federation (NAAF)
	Women athletes were to register with AAU: women's physical education organizations protested the AAU action
1924	Publication of *The Sportswoman* (Magazine)—1924–1936
1925	37 states had high school varsity basketball and/or state tournaments
1926	First AAU National Women's Basketball Championship, using men's rules
1928	Women's physical education organizations formally protested women's entry in the Olympic track and field events (also all events 1932 and 1936)
	Formation of first national officiating boards—Women's National Officials Rating Committee (WNORC)
1931	Techniques of officiating included in the *Guides*
1932	* Guarding on all planes permitted
	* All goals count two points
1935	AAU published its own women's basketball rules
1936	Formation of an All American Red Heads Team; used men's rules and competed against men's teams.
1937	*Standards in Athletics for Girls and Women* published
1938	* Three court game changed to two court game, 6 players
1941	First National Intercollegiate Championship for women (golf)
1949	* Two bounce dribble (limited dribble) introduced
1952	Nine states published girls high school rules.
1953	World Championships USA-Gold Medal

1953	* Rules and wording modifications to be more like the boys game
1955	National Leadership Conference on Girls and Women's Sport
	USA Women's Basketball Team to the Pan American Games
1956	* Three seconds limit in the lane
	* Ball can be tied with two hands
1956	Tripartite committee to study golf and intercollegiate championships
1957	National Joint Committee for Extramural Sports for College Women
1958	National Conference on Social Changes in Sports and Implications for Physical Education and Sports Programs
1960	* Tie ball with one hand allowed
1961	* Two court roving player game
	* Three bounce dribble
1962	* Player can "snatch" the ball from another player
1963	*Policies and Standards* encouraged varsity and elite competition
	First National Sport Institute with USOC
	WNORC became Officiating Services Area (OSA)
1964	DGWS officials officiated at AAU championships
1965	*Guidelines* developed for conducting interscholastic and intercollegiate events
	Joint Committee AAU/DGWS Rules established
1966	* Unlimited dribble introduced
1966	Commission on Intercollegiate Athletics for Women (CIAW) approved sanctioned tournaments for 1967
1967	DGWS/CIAW National Championships
	CIAW published *Procedures for Women's Intercollegiate Athletic Events*
	U.S. collegiate players in World University Games
1969	First National Invitational Basketball Tournament, West Chester, Pa.
1971	* Five player-full court game (DGWS and AAU)
	* 30-second clock
	Association for Intercollegiate Athletics for Women founded
	National Federation of State High School Associations wrote own set of girls basketball rules
1972	Title IX of the Education Amendments of 1972
	First Official AIAW/CIAW Basketball National Championship
1973	Amateur Basketball Association of USA formed and replaced AAU as basketball national sport governing body

1973	First year of scholarships for women in AIAW
	First junior college AIAW Invitational National Championship
1974	OSA becomes Affiliated Boards of Officials (ABO)
1975	* Twenty-minute halves
	* Bonus rule for free throws
1975	First National Women's Wheelchair Basketball Tournament
	First women's basketball game in Madison Square Garden (Queens vs. Immaculata)
	Small College AIAW Basketball Invitational
	Title IX Guidelines published
	First nationally televised regular season game (Immaculata vs. University of Maryland)
	First Kodak All-America Team
1976	Women's basketball included in the Montreal Olympics
1977	First Broderick Cup for most outstanding athlete in AIAW (Lusia Harris, Delta State)
1978	First AIAW national televised basketball championship game (NBC)
	AIAW Large College Final Four at UCLA
	Title IX final compliance date, July 21
	Formation of the Professional Women's Basketball League (eight teams)
	First Wade Trophy (Carol Blazejowski, Montclair State)
	Amateur Sports Act (ASA)
1979	AIAW became a separate legal entity from NAGWS/ AAHPERD
	USA won gold medal at the World Championships (first since 1957)
1980	Three Divisions Final Four Championships (AIAW)
1981	Last year AIAW National Championships
	First year NAIA Women's National Championships
	First NCAA Women's National Championships
1981	Women's Basketball Coaches Association (WBCA) formed
1982	USA National Team beat USSR team
1983	New Agenda Conference on the Future of Women's Sports
1984	Women won a gold medal in the Los Angeles Olympics
1984	* Smaller ball for women's basketball introduced
1985	Three women inducted into the Basketball Hall of Fame
	Last year for officiating ratings in basketball from NAGWS
	Last year NAGWS basketball *Guides* published
1987	* Three point field goals
1988	Gold medal in basketball in the Seoul Olympics